CHARLEMAGNE'S SURVEY OF THE HOLY LAND

Dumbarton Oaks Medieval Humanities

Series Editor
Jan M. Ziolkowski

CHARLEMAGNE'S SURVEY OF THE HOLY LAND

*Wealth, Personnel, and Buildings of a
Mediterranean Church between Antiquity and the Middle Ages*

■　■　■　■　■

with a critical edition and translation of the original text

MICHAEL McCORMICK

DUMBARTON OAKS RESEARCH LIBRARY AND COLLECTION
WASHINGTON, D.C.

19 18 17 16 15 14 13 12 11   1 2 3 4 5

Library of Congress Cataloging-in-Publication Data

McCormick, Michael, 1951–
    Charlemagne's survey of the Holy Land : wealth, personnel, and buildings of a
Mediterranean church between antiquity and the Middle Ages : with a critical edition
and translation of the original text / Michael McCormick.
        p. cm. — (Dumbarton Oaks medieval humanities)
    Includes bibliographical references and indexes.
    ISBN 978-0-88402-363-0 (alk. paper)
1. Palestine—Antiquities. 2. Jerusalem—Antiquities. 3. Historic buildings—Palestine.
4. Church buildings—Palestine. 5. Palestine—Description and travel—Sources.
6. Palestine—Church history—Sources. 7. Christians—Palestine—History—To 1500—Sources.
8. Palestine—History—638–1917—Sources. 9. Charlemagne, Emperor, 742–814.
10. Carolingians—History—Sources.   I. Title.
    DS111.1.M38   2010
    956.94'02—dc22

                                2009022797

www.doaks.org/publications

Designed and typeset by Barbara Haines

Cover image: The Madaba Map, detail: the Nea Church. Madaba, Jordan (photo courtesy of the
                Archive of the Studium Biblicum Franciscanum—Jerusalem)

To Giles Constable
Mentor, friend, and teacher

▪ ▪ ▪ ▪ ▪ ▪ ▪ ▪ ▪ ▪ ▪ ▪ ▪

CONTENTS

ILLUSTRATIONS

TABLES

ACKNOWLEDGMENTS

The present study grew out of a larger inquiry into the contacts between Eastern and Western Christendoms in the eighth and ninth centuries originally sponsored by a John Simon Guggenheim Memorial Fellowship; I am thankful for its support, which allowed a firsthand examination of the Basel roll, and for the cooperation of Martin Steinmann, then director of the Universitätsbibliothek, Basel. To Dr. Steinmann and Dr. Ueli Dill I am thankful also for permission to publish the photographs of the roll. Among other scholars who lent a hand at various stages, I am grateful to the late Bernhard Bischoff, Oren Gutfeld, Adam Kosto, Jodi Magness, Paul Meyvaert, Deborah Tor, and Yoram Tsafrir. Paul Edward Dutton gave the manuscript meticulous scrutiny and improved the final text in innumerable ways. Kelly Lyn Gibson carefully refined the maps that I designed for this book. Jesse R. Halvorsen kindly helped with the final preparation of the book manuscript. The text published here was the subject of two graduate seminars at Harvard University, and this study and its author enjoyed much the stimulus that came from those meetings with the wonderful young scholars who participated in the seminars. Finally, I am grateful to my admired friend and colleague Jan Ziolkowski for encouraging me to publish this work at the remarkable institution that he now directs. Dumbarton Oaks has played a considerable and even decisive role in my life, and it is there that the research leading to this study began.

Three factors prompted the decision to publish the text. My research required a proper edition of texts which have usually been cited in an extremely mediocre version; the textual problems were in fact so difficult and complex that merely citing from the manuscript would have required impractically lengthy commentary (see chapter 11). The long-promised critical edition from Germany has yet to appear. And, now some years ago, the birth of Thomas Kennedy McCormick III deprived his father of sufficient sleep to interrupt work on another, more complex monograph. The whiling away of long nights in the company of this fine young fellow seemed more enjoyable still if it was interspersed with useful textual study—study that continued when the birth of Elena Sylvie enriched our little family. But it is only now that, thanks to the incomparable largess of the Andrew W. Mellon Foundation, I have enjoyed the leisure to develop the historical study required for a fuller exploitation of that earlier textual work and to experiment in the genre of microhistory. The fact that this unique document opens a path to the comparative study of early medieval religious institutions, and particularly of monasteries East and West, combines with the profound influence on my research, career, and life of the foremost exponent of monastic history in our time and former director of Dumbarton Oaks, to make the dedication of this little work to a very big man, utterly natural.

15 August 2008
Cambridge, Mass.

A FORGOTTEN
VOYAGE TO THE EAST

A FEW YEARS AFTER CHARLEMAGNE'S imperial coronation rocked the Mediterranean world at its spiritual and political core, a small group of his men assembled for a now forgotten voyage across the early medieval sea. We do not know where or exactly when they took ship, but others just like them had embarked from the booming little slave-trading port emerging out of the Po River delta, Venice. Among their number were surely some Franks and likely someone who had lived in Italy. Their mission? As his advisor remembered a decade or two later, the aging emperor was used to spreading his wealth around the great shrines of the Mediterranean.

> He was very dedicated to maintaining the poor, and to the disinterested generosity that the Greeks call "alms" [*eleimosina*], as is natural for someone who was attentive to do so not only in his homeland and in his own kingdom, but also across the sea in Syria and Egypt and Africa, where he had learned that Christians were living in poverty. He took pity on their indigence, and was accustomed to send money to Jerusalem, Alexandria, and Carthage. This was the main reason he sought the friendship of overseas kings, so that some measure of relief and mitigation might reach the Christians who reside under their domination.[1]

Perhaps in response to a specific request from the patriarch of Jerusalem, the king had decided to include the shrines of the Holy Land among the beneficiaries of his largess. But the canny old ruler was not writing any blank checks. Just as he deployed the *missi dominici*, the king's personal envoys, to discover what was really

---

1   Einhard, *Vita Karoli magni* 27, 31.18–32.2. For the sources and implications of Einhard's phrase "disinterested generosity" (*gratuitam liberalitatem*), see chapter 1, note 6. For more on this passage, see also chapter 9.

going on in the far-flung provinces of his empire, so he dispatched personal representatives to determine firsthand the real needs of the Palestinian church.

In these final, imperial years of his reign, Lord Charles and his entourage were more than ever interested in counting, enumerating, and inventorying his farms, churches, and other resources. So too for the Holy Land. How many monks, how many nuns, how many hermits were there? In what language did they pray? And, of course, how many were the king's own subjects? How big was the patriarch's staff? Ever practical, the king and his advisors worried about the roofs of the great shrines: if they were bad, the buildings were lost. So how big were they? And just how much did the patriarch at the far end of the sea spend each year, and on what? The *missi dominici* Lord Charles was dispatching across the spaces of sea were charged with getting answers to these questions, preferably firsthand, even if that meant finding Greek and Arabic interpreters who could put their questions to people in the know. In the excitement of their preparations, the envoys forgot to take a measuring rod.

No single source tells this story in these terms. But the details emerge from a close analysis of documents whose neglect by historians of Charlemagne's reign is as remarkable as the documents' content and implications. To make these inert witnesses speak is the purpose of this book. To recover and hear the voices buried on a ninth-century parchment roll and distorted by modern "critical" editions require no little analysis, much of it highly technical in nature and involving careful philology, paleography, and archaeology. That is the price of hearing, accurately, a voice too long silenced.

The result will be a picture of a Carolingian king in action, of his envoys at work surveying the people, buildings, and finances of the Christian church of the Holy Land. Just as the great king's reign rode and even affected developments across the Mediterranean world and beyond, so this unusual set of documents forces us to cross many boundaries too long entrenched in the study of the first millennium of our era. For we will need to look into the Arab and Byzantine worlds, obviously, to elucidate a Carolingian mission into their part of the globe. But it was a Carolingian mission, and we will have to return frequently to the Frankish Empire in western Europe. Beyond comparing religious establishments there and in the Levant, we will hear echoes—with implications for our understanding—of the great king, his closest collaborators, and how in the last decade of a glorious reign, they approached the imposing challenge of governing an early medieval empire in accordance with God's will as they understood it.

Charlemagne's reign is rich in remarkable documents. They have elicited considerable attention from historians: Einhard's biography among historical literature, the models for estate management *Capitulare de villis* and *Brevium exempla* among economic records, the *Opus Karoli regis* (alias *Libri Carolini*) among political and theological tracts, and the list goes on. Relatively scant attention has been accorded the *Breue commemoratorii de illis casis Dei* and the documents preserved with it on an ancient scroll in Basel (Öffentliche Bibliothek der Universität Basel, N I 2, Bll. 12 u. 13; figures 1 and 2). That owes much to the way in which scholarly inquiry has become compartmentalized since the early nineteenth century. Unceasing specialization has produced remarkable triumphs in historical understanding. Yet it also creates blinders. Only the fact that the document studied here is "Western" can explain its passing almost unknown among Byzantinists; only the fact that it concerns the Middle East can explain medievalists' never mentioning it in the same breath with the *Brevium exempla* or the Carolingian polyptychs. Perhaps too the ill-founded impression that the early medieval Mediterranean was some stagnant sea discouraged attention to a witness that flies in the face of that conventional wisdom. As that impression fades in the light of new research on the lively world of early medieval communications in the Mediterranean, it is time to reconsider this near-forgotten record. [2]

Though first published over a century ago, the group of documents preserved in Basel and commonly called the *Breue commemoratorium* has endured remarkable neglect outside a small circle of specialists of Holy Land pilgrimage and archaeology. It has never merited the honor of an edition in the Monumenta Germaniae Historica. The text itself is known chiefly in a mediocre edition, although a sometimes-misleading English translation of its tricky Latin exists; standard guides to medieval or Byzantine sources or histories of Charlemagne rarely mention it.[3]

2   On communications and "connectivity" in the early medieval Mediterranean, see especially P. Horden and N. Purcell, *The Corrupting Sea: A Study of Mediterranean History* (Oxford, 2000); and M. McCormick, *Origins of the European Economy: Communications and Commerce, A.D. 300–900* (Cambridge, 2001).

3   The documents that are the subject of this study are most frequently cited from the edition of Titus Tobler and Auguste Molinier, *Itinera hierosolymitana et descriptiones Terrae Sanctae bellis sacris anteriora* (Geneva, 1880), 1.2:301–5. This is arguably the worst of all the editions produced to date. The Basel roll does not appear in, for example, W. Wattenbach, W. Levison, and H. Löwe, *Deutschlands Geschichtsquellen im Mittelalter: Vorzeit und Karolinger*, 6 fasc. (Weimar, 1952–73); L. Halphen, *Charlemagne et l'empire carolingien* (Paris, 1947); I. E. Karagiannopoulos and G. Weiss, *Quellenkunde zur Geschichte von Byzanz (324–1453)*, 2 vols., Schriften zur Geistesgeschichte des östlichen Europa 14 (Wiesbaden, 1982); H. G. Beck, *Kirche und theologische Literatur im byzantinischen Reich*, Handbuch der Altertumswissenschaft 12.2.1 (Munich, 1959); and L. Brubaker, J. F. Haldon, and R. G. Ousterhout, *Byzantium in the Iconoclast Era (ca. 680–850): The Sources, an Annotated Survey*, Birmingham Byzantine and Ottoman Monographs 7 (Aldershot, 2001). Mine is the only mention in the relevant volume of *The New Cambridge Medieval History*. See M. McCormick, "Byzantium and the West A.D. 700–900," in *New Cambridge Medieval History*, ed. R. McKitterick (Cambridge, 1995), 2:349–80, at 376. Beginning with an important article by Karl Schmid, however, the *Breve* has garnered increasing attention from Western medievalists concerned with Carolingian relations with the Holy Land and Mediterranean communications more generally. See K. Schmid, "Aachen und Jerusalem. Ein Beitrag zur historischen Personenforschung der Karolingerzeit," in *Das Einhardkreuz. Vorträge und Studien der Münsteraner Diskussion zum arcus Einhardi*, ed. K. Hauck, Abhandlungen der Akademie der Wissenschaften in Göttingen, Philologisch-historische

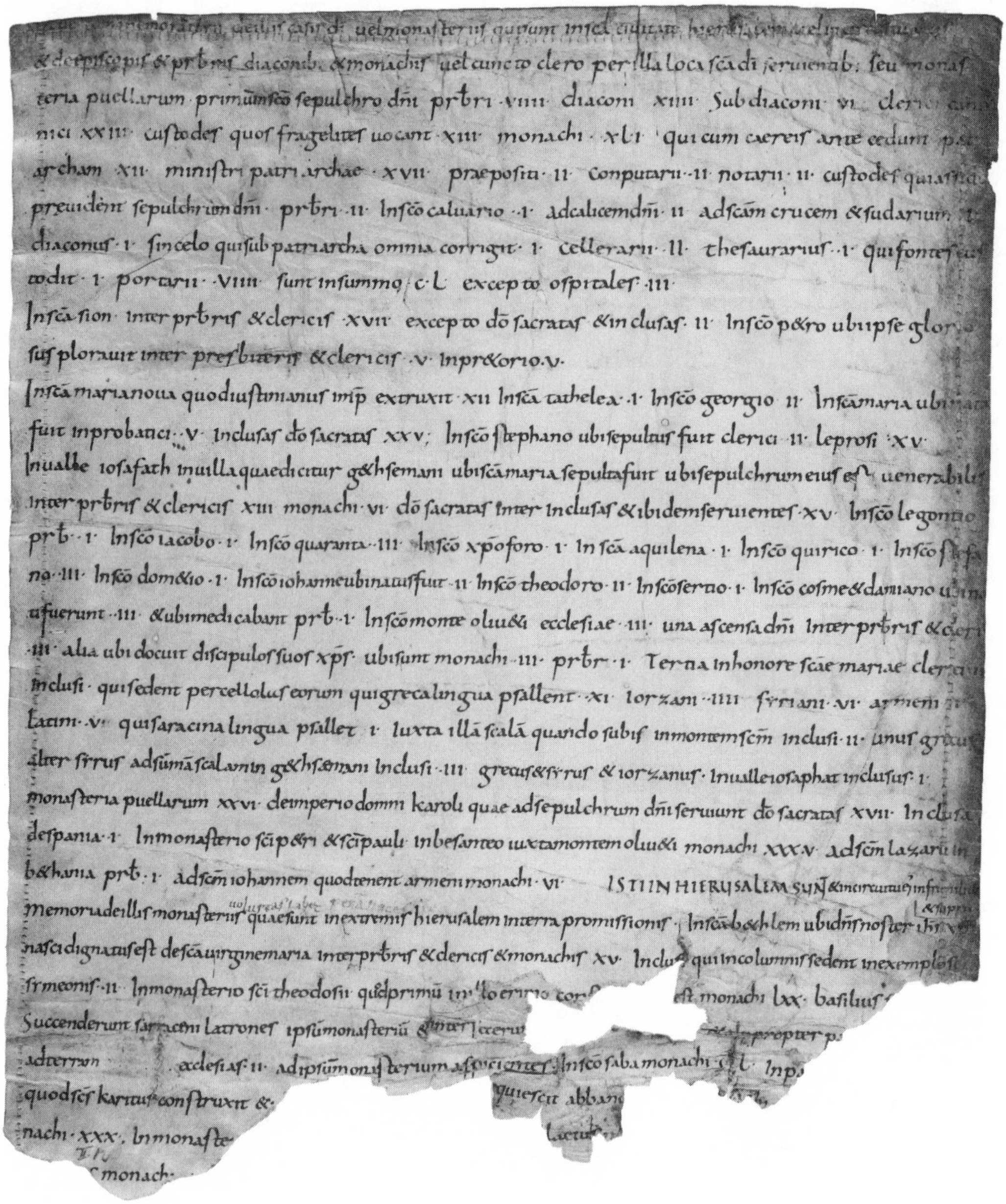

FIGURE 1
The Basel roll, part 1. Basel, Öffentliche Bibliothek der Universität, N I 2, Bl. 12
(photo courtesy of the Library)

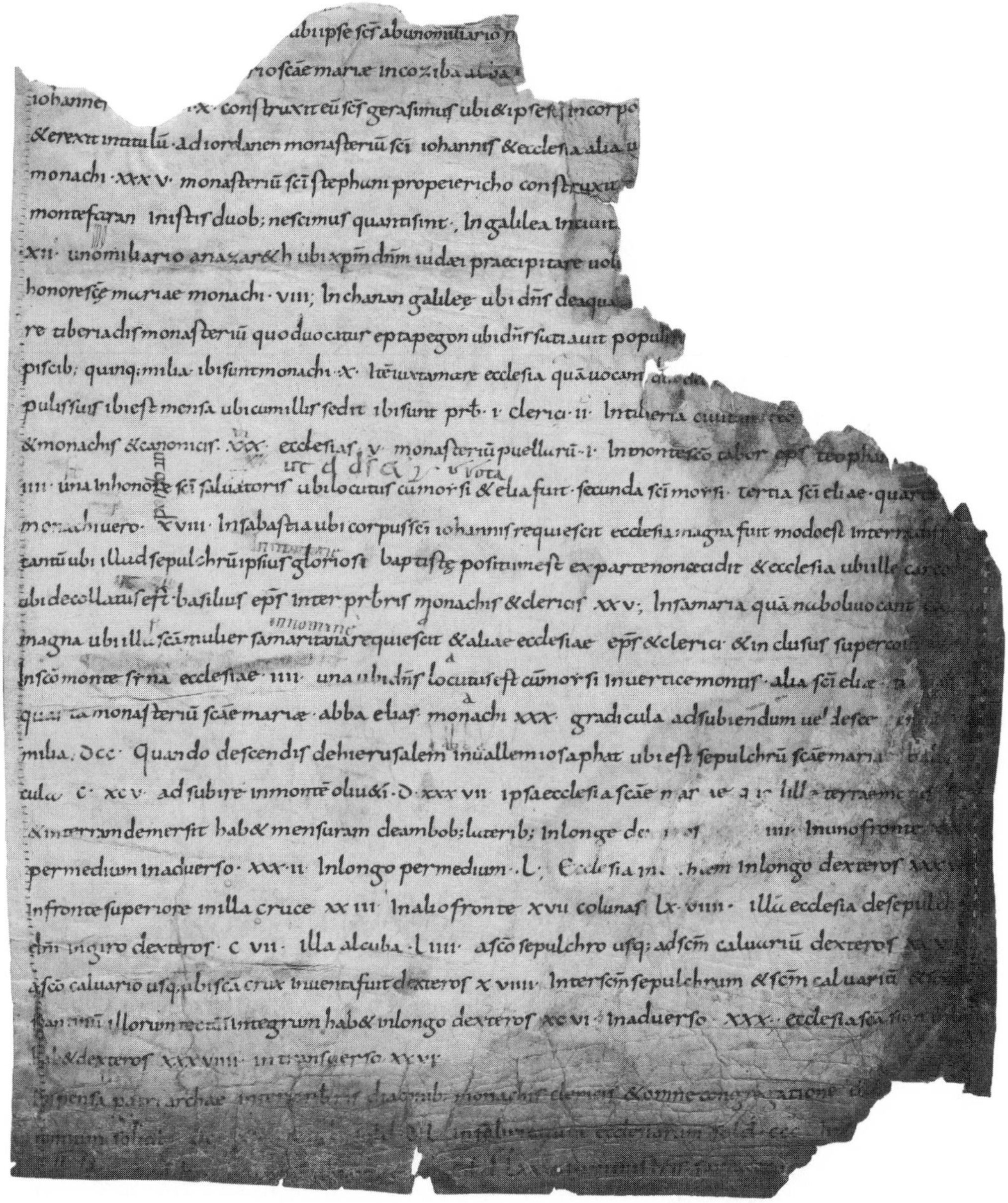

FIGURE 2

The Basel roll, part 2. Basel, Öffentliche Bibliothek der Universität, N I 2, Bl. 13 (photo courtesy of the Library)

Yet this document has much to teach us about an early medieval government in action, about comparative religious sociology, and about the passage from antiquity to the Middle Ages.

The absence of a thorough study and critical edition of so extraordinary a document naturally inclined some modern scholars who have encountered it to prudent reserve.[4] Is this document really what it seems to be? At first blush it strains credulity: a church-by-church survey of the orthodox Christian religious establishments in the Holy Land that supplies details and statistics on their personnel—names of superiors, numbers, sex, religious dignity, and, for certain among them, ethnicity; indicates the Palestinian church's most pressing architectural problems, complete with detailed measurements of the greatest, now lost, Christian monuments of the Holy Land; and records the annual expenditures of the patriarchate of Jerusalem. If these documents are what they seem, what are the implications for our understanding of the social and economic situation of the patriarchate of Jerusalem and for monasticism and the Christian church in the Holy Land in the harrowing passage from late antiquity to the Middle Ages? Can we derive from these extraordinary records comparative insights into Christian religious institutions of the late antique past as well as those of the early medieval present? And was the *Breue commemoratorium*'s first and greatest editor wrong in immediately recognizing behind it the hand of Charles the Great? This, if any, is a case that warrants a microhistorical approach.

The second part of this investigation clarifies the essential features of the group of documents. When, why, and how was the roll written? Determining the date and purpose of the documents allows us to place them in the proper historical context. It is possible to propose the names of the men Charlemagne sent on this mission, one of whom will emerge from the shadows to appear as an important collaborator of the king and his cousin Adalhard in these years. At the very least, his mission prepared the way for the inquest consigned in the roll. The mission returned to Europe in the spring or summer of 808 and perhaps carried home the original of the administrative roll with its precious data. To judge from a surviving record, that roll was used in a meeting of the king and his advisors in 810. In all

Klasse, 3rd ser., 87 (Göttingen, 1974), 122–42; M. Borgolte, *Der Gesandtenaustausch der Karolinger mit den Abbasiden und mit den Patriarchen von Jerusalem*, Münchner Beiträge zur Mediävistik und Renaissance-Forschung 25 (Munich, 1976); K. Bieberstein, "Der Gesandtenaustausch zwischen Karl dem Grossen und Hārūn ar-Rašīd und seine Bedeutung für die Kirchen Jerusalems," *ZDPV* 109 (1993): 152–73; and McCormick, *Origins*, 152.

4 Schmid, "Aachen und Jerusalem," 139: "Ob die Aufzeichnung . . . von einem Gesandten Karls des Grossen gemacht wurde, womöglich zum Zwecke der Verteilung von Almosen im Heiligen Land . . . muss . . . neu geprüft werden." With obvious disapproval, A. Kleinclausz, "La légende du protectorat de Charlemagne sur la Terre Sainte," *Syria: Revue d'art oriental et d'archéologie* 7 (1926): 211–33, here 224 n. 3, similarly considered "bien audacieux" Tobler's opinion that the document was produced by some envoy of Charlemagne.

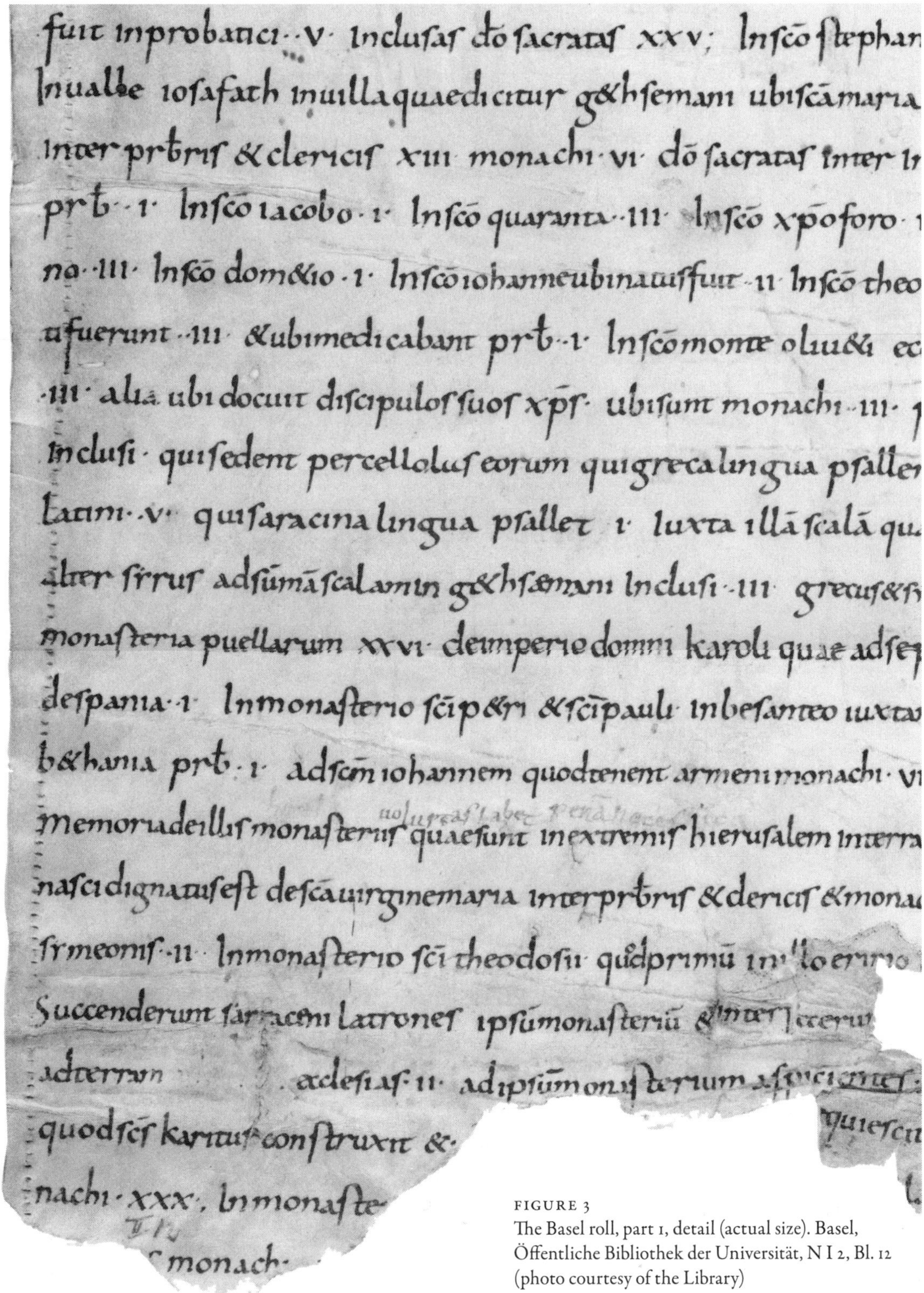

fuit inprobaticı̃·v· Inclusas dõ sacratas xxv; Inscõ stephan[

Inualle iosafath inuilla quaedicitur g&hsemani ubiscãmaria

inter prbris & clericis xiii monachi·vi· dõ sacratas inter ı[

prb·ı· Inscõ iacobo·ı· Inscõ quaranta·iiii· Inscõ xpoforo·

na·iiii· Inscõ dom&io·ı· Inscõ iohanne ubinatusfuit·ii· Inscõ theo[

afuerunt·iiii· &ubimedicabant prb·ı· Inscõmonte oliu&i ec[

·iiii· alia ubidocuit discipulos suos xps· ubisunt monachi·iiii·

Inclusi· quisedent percellolus eorum quigrecalingua psalle[r]

latini·v· quisaracina lingua psallet·ı· Iuxta illã scalã qu[

alter srrus adsũmã scalam in g&hsemani Inclusi·iii· grecas&f[

monasteria puellarum xxvi· deimperio domni karoli quae adse[q]

despania·ı· Inmonasterio scĩ p&ri &scĩ pauli inbesanteo iuxta[

b&hania prb·ı· adscõ iohannem quodtenent armeni monachi·vi

memoria deillis monasteris quae sunt inextremis hierusalem inter[ra]

nascidignatus est descã uirginemaria inter prbris &clericis &mona[

srmeonis·ii· Inmonasterio scĩ theodosii quodprimũ in illo erimo

Succenderunt saraceni latrones ipsumonasteriũ &[...]ecerun[

adterram ... ecclesias·ii· adipsũmonasterium as[...]

quodscs karitus construxit &·

nachi·xxx· Inmonaste[

monach·

FIGURE 3
The Basel roll, part 1, detail (actual size). Basel,
Öffentliche Bibliothek der Universität, N I 2, Bl. 12
(photo courtesy of the Library)

likelihood, Charlemagne acted on the materials he had caused to be collected, and sent wealth to the patriarch of Jerusalem to address some of the Christians' greatest needs in those troubled years in the Middle East. We will consider the enigma of why a purely administrative copy of such a file should have been made a few decades after the meeting and decision-making process for which it had originally been compiled. In the end there can be no doubt that this dossier was drawn up early in the ninth century by one or more westerners who had been charged with a mission to survey Christian houses in the Holy Land for the benefit of a very powerful person in Frankland.

Understanding how the roll was composed—its sources and the delicate features of the languages involved in its composition, not least the late Popular Latin so typical of Carolingian administrative writing that underlies the surviving copy—is essential to correctly assessing its content. The three documents preserved on one roll in Basel are "An Inventory Memorandum of God's Houses or Monasteries in and around the Holy City of Jerusalem" (*Breue commemoratorii de illis casis Dei uel monasteriis qui sunt in sancta ciuitate Hierusalem uel in circuitu eius*; hereafter Breve, to reflect the common English pronunciation of the Latin word), a "Memorial of the Monasteries that are in the Promised Land outside of Jerusalem" (*Memoria de illis monasteriis quae sunt in extremis Hierusalem in terra promissionis;* hereafter Memorial or Memorial of Monasteries), and a truncated "Yearly Expenditures of the Patriarch" (*Dispensa patriarchae inter presbiteris, diaconibus, monachis, clericis et omne congregatione eccle<siae per unum> annum;* hereafter *Dispensa* or Expenditures). This part of the investigation will demonstrate that these authentically Carolingian documents were established in the Holy Land by Franks, including someone whose Latin usage points to some connection with Italy. They collected their data orally and mostly firsthand, with the aid of Greek and Arabic interpreters, rather than by means of Greek administrative documents. We will see reasons for thinking that the work of these most unusual royal envoys, or *missi dominici*, was accomplished to a high level of professionalism and quality.

The third part of this study provides a new critical text of these three documents. The new text corrects a number of errors and inaccuracies in previous editions, including especially the one usually cited today. It also attempts to restore the numerous damaged portions of the text. A detailed textual commentary justifies these restorations. Along with the photographs, that commentary will allow future scholars, in the manner of epigraphers, to judge my work and suggest new readings without obliging them to journey to Basel to see the original. A new translation clarifies how I have understood the late Vulgar Latin of the text, and will make this improved text available to a wider audience. By establishing the facts and value of this unique witness to an exceptional moment of Mediterranean history, the considerable investment of parts 2 and 3 will make possible the full and assured exploitation of its testimony.

Part 1 begins with that testimony. Anyone who wishes to begin with the critical study of the records that part 1 presumes need only skip ahead to parts 2 and 3. What the Basel roll tells us about the wealth of the patriarchate of Jerusalem invites comparison with the data we have on other Mediterranean churches. Such a comparison lets us situate the Jerusalem church among contemporary institutions and over a broad timescale—from late antiquity to 800. The comparative approach clarifies the church's relative wealth and helps us assess whether the Christian church in the Holy Land flourished, as some have thought. That assessment continues in the next chapter, which investigates the extraordinarily detailed report on the ecclesiastical personnel of the Christian church. Those details afford a unique opportunity to investigate what we might call religious sociology. The information on sizes of monastic and cathedral communities and convents of women and the unique data on hermits and their languages of prayer allow us to ask questions about the proportions of monks and nuns, of males and females, and even of different ethnic groups among Holy Land religious. Enlightening as these data are on their own, they gain in significance when viewed comparatively.

Over time, the changing size of the Christian church in Palestine emerges clearly; over space, the contrasts and similarities with Byzantine and contemporary Frankish houses appear no less distinctly. That comparison invites us to look back to early medieval France. Two documents have analogies with the Basel roll that are not entirely coincidental, for they too were prepared for Charlemagne's eyes. They allow us to examine more closely the details of the personnel structure and development of the episcopal churches of Lyons in exactly the same years and provide a valuable backdrop for the data from the Holy Land. All this allows a clearer assessment of the trajectory of the Christian establishment of the Holy Land since late antiquity—a trajectory that appears less rosy in this light.

The final chapter of part 1 takes us into early Christian archaeology for, in addition to gathering new elements for the prosopography of the Palestinian church, it lays out the testimony of the Memorial on the architectural dimensions of the shrine of the Resurrection, the Nea Church of Justinian, the Zion (Sion) Church in Jerusalem, and the Nativity Church in Bethlehem. Once we have uncovered the source of the misunderstanding concerning the units of measurement that the Memorial furnishes for these buildings, it becomes possible to interpret correctly the dimensions reported by the *missi dominici*. The implications for a correct reconstruction of the lost monuments of the Nea and Zion shrines both fit and modify our understanding of the archaeological evidence presently available about these great churches of the later Roman Empire. The investigation may thus foster further study of the document, which should interest historians of Carolingian administration no less than Byzantinists, specialists of medieval religious sociology no less than archaeologists, and historians of the Holy Land. And, it is hoped, the reader will come to share the author's conviction that, although this administrative dossier does not name the person who ordered its creation, there can little doubt that that person was the only living ruler mentioned by the Basel roll—and indeed, mentioned in a manner redolent of intimacy—Lord Charles.

Part One

A MEDITERRANEAN CHURCH IN THE EARLY MIDDLE AGES

COMPOSED A CENTURY AND A HALF AFTER the Muslim conquest, the Basel roll paints an extraordinary statistical portrait of what had been one of late antiquity's most thriving and influential churches. The three documents preserved on that roll were compiled in the Holy Land around 808 by envoys sent by Charles the Great (see part two). They were largely eyewitnesses who sought information from Greek and Arabic speakers. They consigned their findings in plain administrative records written originally in the late Popular ("Vulgar") Latin that typifies earlier Carolingian administrative documents. The picture that they draw has moved at least one distinguished specialist of the Holy Land to consider the Christian church as "flourishing."[1] Another finds the number of buildings they attest "very impressive," but he underscores the waves of persecution Christians experienced at the hands of the Muslim authorities and others.[2]

The documents copied on the roll allow us to verify and deepen these views. The opportunity is all the more exciting in light of the recent growth of archaeological investigation. Archaeologists are shedding much new light on the economic and social development of Palestine and Syria in the final Roman (or "Byzantine" as local nomenclature has it) and early Islamic phases. On the basis of the new edition and translation, we start with the wealth of the church, the economic data, which throws light on the soil in which religious institutions must grow and flourish or dwindle. We move on to consider the roll's truly remarkable data about the institutions and personnel of the patriarchate of Jerusalem and its religious establishments. We do so in two ways: by comparing them with what is known of the same or similar situations in late antiquity, and by viewing the data in contemporary context, whether in terms of the purchasing power of the money mentioned or the numbers and sizes of similar Christian religious institutions in the Byzantine and Frankish empires. One of the most interesting points of contemporary comparison, as we shall see, turns out to be another document prepared for Charlemagne in the same years. This one describes the state of the religious houses in Lyons, France. Transported by reviving communication infrastructures, the religious and institutional ferment of the Carolingian empire reached Jerusalem itself, and we shall trace the dim shape of that ninth-century impact in the presence of western religious women, the monks and hermits on the Mount of Olives, and Charlemagne's hostel for pilgrims. Last but by no means least, renewed study of the Basel roll will shed new light on the archaeology of the late antique Christian monuments of Jerusalem.

---

1 J. Wilkinson, *Jerusalem Pilgrims before the Crusades*, 2nd ed. (Warminster, 2002), 24.
2 M. Gil, *A History of Palestine, 634–1099*, trans. E. Broido, 2nd ed. (Cambridge, 1997), 442 and 469–78.

Chapter One

■ ■ ■ ■ ■ ■ ■ ■ ■ ■ ■

THE RELATIVE WEALTH
OF A MEDITERRANEAN CHURCH

HISTORIANS AND ARCHAEOLOGISTS have long recognized that we must understand the wealth of societies, communities, and individuals to mark the overall trend of late antique and early medieval civilization. Literary sources dominate the surviving written record of the period from Justinian's successors to Charlemagne and Harun al Rashid. These sources are not as abundant and, above all, not as interested in economic questions as we would like. This has obliged historians to imagine ways of coaxing indirect economic information from witnesses who never meant to supply it. The new economic archaeology has begun producing unexpected data on exchange, settlement, agricultural production, and much else, supplying unforeseen information and insight into the economies that fostered the post-Roman world. The new information naturally complicates and sometimes compromises older understandings. The view that the early Arab centuries destroyed a vibrant economic world of late antiquity in Syria and Palestine has now been largely abandoned. More recently a kind of consensus has held that these centuries prolonged the economic stagnation (or worse) that others believe prevailed at the end of the sixth century. Most recently, some scholars have argued for renewed economic dynamism beginning around 700 and accelerating in the later eighth century but one that in much of the region may have continued a gentle upswing that had started at the end of the Roman era.[1]

---

[1]   Alexander Kazhdan (1925–1997) first argued from archaeological evidence for urban decline in the seventh and eighth century in the areas Byzantium was able to hold against the Arabs. See "Vizantijskie goroda v VII–IX vv.," *Sovetskaja arkheologija* 21 (1954): 164–88. These insights were developed by C. Foss in "The Persians in Asia Minor and the End of Antiquity," *EHR* 90 (1975): 721–47, and "Archaeology and the 'Twenty Cities' of Byzantine Asia," *AJA* 81 (1977): 469–86. Important local work has begun to clarify the complexities of later sixth-century urbanism in the eastern Mediterranean. See, for example, J. Russell, "Anemourion," in *EHB* 1:221–28. Hugh Kennedy connected sixth-century urban decline with the situation under the early Arab caliphs: "From *polis* to *madina*: Urban Change in Late Antique and Early Islamic Syria," *Past and Present* 106 (1985): 3–27; and "The Last Century of Byzantine Syria: A Reinterpretation," *ByzF* 10 (1985): 141–83. For the chronology on which much of the archaeological debate turns, the ceramic is crucial.

In our age of renewed and growing knowledge, it is imperative to return to the rare records whose administrative and economic purposes make them more directly amenable to addressing questions of wealth. Knowing that such early medieval records are anything but immune to imperfection does not lessen their value as a different kind of witness whose figures and conceptualization of costs appear to be—and indeed had to be—accurate to a degree different from the casual numbers bandied about by some literary sources.[2] The last three lines transcribed on the Basel roll offer the mutilated beginning of just such a document: "Expenditures of the patriarch, including for priests, deacons, monks, clerics, and the entire congregation of the church for <one> year." Of course, we must consider these figures with open eyes: how much was lost with the bottom of the roll, what coins were being counted, how does the wealth in question compare with that of similar institutions and individuals, and what of its purchasing power? Finally, given that this list of expenses must have been prepared to generate or solicit funds to cover those expenses, it may have been in the patriarchate's self-interest to make those expenses appear larger than they really were. These caveats do not diminish the value of the economic data that the annual expenditure list offers and that at least one accomplished economic historian has tried to use, albeit with earlier, erroneous readings of almost all the numbers.[3] The Expendi-

---

J. Magness, *The Archaeology of the Early Islamic Settlement in Palestine* (Winona Lake, 2003), has argued that much of the ceramic evidence has been erroneously dated and does not sustain the thesis of dramatic decline in the Levant in the later sixth or early seventh century and, although it is difficult to follow the fate of Christians and Jews in southern Palestine in the seventh and eighth centuries, one can discern there an increasing Muslim presence. A. Walmsley, *Early Islamic Syria: An Archaeological Assessment* (London, 2007), detects in the latest archaeological evidence of the material culture modest but continuous development in town and country in the seventh century. In his view, change accelerated around 700, leading to a period of dramatic change in the late eighth and ninth centuries. Some of this diversity of opinion is of course due to the precise theme (ceramics; urban vs. rural settlements), period, and places that different scholars have investigated, occasionally abetted by the assumption that ancient economic cycles were somehow infinitely slower and longer than, say, later medieval or early modern ones. C. Wickham, *Framing the Early Middle Ages: Europe and the Mediterranean 400–800* (Oxford, 2005), 609–27, admirably synthesizes the evidence for the towns of this region.

2   A. Murray, *Reason and Society in the Middle Ages* (Oxford, 1985), 141–57, launched the debate on early medieval innumeracy, nuanced by R. Sonntag, *Studien zur Bewertung von Zahlenangaben in der Geschichtsschreibung des früheren Mittelalters: Die Decem Libri Historiarum Gregors von Tours und die Chronica Reginos von Prüm*, Münchener historische Studien, Abteilung mittelalterliche Geschichte 4 (Kallmünz, 1987). Although the situation in the commercially vibrant world of the Middle East differed from the early medieval West they investigated, one notes a similar nonchalance, for instance, with respect to military forces in literary sources: see, for example, M. McCormick, *Origins of the European Economy: Communications and Commerce, A.D. 300–900* (Cambridge, 2001), 412–13, on fleet sizes in Arabic sources.

3   E. Ashtor, *Histoire des prix et des salaires dans l'Orient médiéval*, Monnaie, prix, conjoncture 8 (Paris, 1969), 259–60, deserves credit for briefly considering the roll's data; unfortunately the errors of reading of the sums in the edition available to him limit the value of his conclusions.

tures sheds light on the financial posture of the patriarchate of Jerusalem in the opening decade of the ninth century, allowing us to begin to appraise the state of the Christian church in that time and place and explain its trajectory since the balmy days of late antiquity.

1. Annual Expenditures of the Patriarchate of Jerusalem around 808

As noted, modern opinion varies on the economic posture of the Christian church in the Holy Land at the time of Charlemagne's mission, but it tends to reach a rather positive appraisal, precisely on the basis of the evidence from the Basel roll.[4] One astute witness must have known and spoken with the royal envoys who had actually studied the question in the Holy Land. He had a decidedly different opinion. The way Einhard tells the story, Charlemagne "learned" that "across the sea . . . Christians were living in poverty." He speaks of their "indigence" and Charles's desire to bring them "relief and mitigation."[5] Einhard's explicit assertion is underscored by the resonance of the authority he echoes: from the favored Christian apologist Lactantius, the learned royal advisor borrowed the Ciceronian expression "disinterested generosity" to describe Charlemagne's virtue. In the *Divine Institutions*, Lactantius critiques an opinion he attributes to Cicero—manifestly still widespread in the late Roman Empire of his own day—that money should be given only to "suitable" beneficiaries. Wealth given to the miserable and poor was wasted, since they were unable to reciprocate, and the expenditure weakened the person who wished to do good. On the contrary, maintains Lactantius, wealth could and should be given to those too impoverished to offer something in return.[6] Of course, some might be tempted to think that Einhard is merely posturing here, finding an impressive-sounding pretext for presenting his hero as an exemplar of Christian virtue in imperial rulership. Others might suspect that even if the "poverty" and "indigence" of Christian communities in the Muslim lands were historically accurate, they characterized the general run of Christians and not the ecclesiastical institutions. Such a view, however, squares rather poorly with Einhard's naming of two patriarchal sees and the metropolis of Africa as the beneficiaries of Charlemagne's largess.[7]

---

4   Above, p. 3, notes 1 and 2.

5   Einhard, *Vita Karoli magni* 27, 31.23–25: "Ubi Christianos in paupertate vivere conpererat, penuriae illorum conpatiens pecuniam mittere solebat. . . ."

6   Einhard's "disinterested generosity" (*gratuitam liberalitatem*) stems from Cicero, *De legibus* 1.48.9, manifestly through the discussion of Lactantius, *Diuinae institutiones* 6.11.14, 521.17–20. In the surrounding discussion, 6.10.9–6, 11, and 28, 515.12–524.12, Lactantius lays out a philosophical argument against his contemporaries' disdain for the poor and the disabled and critiques generosity calculated to generate useful returns.

7   Einhard, *Vita Karoli magni* 27, 31.22–23: "Hierosolimis, Alexandriae atque Cartagini." On Einhard's depiction of the geography of Charlemagne's largess, see, further, chapter 9. On the

The actual expenditures of the patriarch of Jerusalem, as recorded, partially preserved and correctly transcribed from the third document of the Basel roll, allow us to test Einhard's testimony on the impoverished state of the Christian communities in the Holy Land and, by extension, of Egypt and Africa as well. Table 1.1 summarizes the financial data furnished by the new edition of the roll.

The first question is, which coins were the envoys counting? The sums are either given in the local coinage or they have been translated into Frankish equivalents. If the expenses are listed in the Frankish notional unit of account, the shilling (*solidus*) of silver, then the 1,660*s* total deciphered expenditures appearing in table 1.1 would equal 19,920*d* or 83 pounds in Carolingian money, equivalent in modern terms of weight to 33.86 kg of silver.[8] If solidi refer, on the other hand, to the local coinage of the Holy Land, then we are seeing here expenditures reckoned in what contemporary western Europeans called "solidi mancosi," or "mancusi." They borrowed the last word from the Arabic *manqush*, as in "al dinar al manqush" (engraved dinars) and used the expression to designate the gold dinars from the Arab world that circulated in parts of western Europe, particularly Italy, and that seem to have been familiar everywhere from Anglo-Saxon England to papal Rome.[9] In this case, 1,660*s* would equal 7.1 kg of gold.[10] Since the legal value of the gold-to-silver ratio in the caliphate was 1:10, this means that the 7.1 kg of gold was theoretically worth about 71 kg of silver.[11] Depending on the answer to this question, the wealth of the patriarchate appears very differently.

The second question is, how much of the annual expenditures of the patriarchate have we lost? Damage obscures what proportion of total expenditures survives in the figures still visible on the roll, yet the surviving portion is clearly sizable. In late antiquity the Roman church allocated revenues on a proportional system divided into four quarters. One quarter went to the pope, one to the clergy, one to the repair and lighting of the churches, and one to the poor.[12] If such a formula were applicable in the East and the lighting amount is missing from the Jerusalem figures, we might be looking at a total annual expenditure in the vicinity of 2,500*s*, assuming that the expenditures for the patriarch and the clergy together

---

supreme ecclesiastical status of Carthage within the late Roman diocese of Africa, see C. Briand-Ponsart and C. Hugoniot, *L'Afrique romaine de l'Atlantique à la Tripolitaine, 146 av. J.-C.–533 ap. J. C.* (Paris, 2006), 377.

8   That is, since one shilling had twelve silver pennies, which each weighed 1.7 g, and 240 pennies made one pound (£), 1,660*s* × 12*d* = 19,920*d* / 240 = £83. 19,920*d* × 1.7 g = 33.86 kg of silver.

9   McCormick, *Origins*, 319–84.

10   That is, 1,660 solidi mancosi weighing 4.25 g: 1660 × 4.25= 7.055 kg of gold.

11   P. Spufford, *Money and Its Use in Medieval Europe* (Cambridge, 1988), 51.

12   In the Spanish system, one-third each went to bishop, clergy, and church fabric. For both late Roman systems, see A. H. M. Jones, *The Later Roman Empire, 284–602: A Social, Economic, and Administrative Survey* (1964; reprint, Baltimore, 1986), 902.

TABLE 1.1 Annual expenditures
of the patriarchate of Jerusalem, about 808

Purpose	Amount *in solidi*
For the priests, deacons, monks, clerics, and the whole congregation of the church \<of Jerusalem\>	700*s*
For the \<patriarch\>	550*s*
For the buildings	300*s*
For *ca****	***
\<For ?\>	30*s*
\<For the Saracens\>	80*s*
For the servants of the Saracens	***
Total deciphered expenditures	1,660*s*

Notes: For a detailed justification of the new readings, see below, chapter 11, textual commentary, on lines 58–60. For the date, see chapter 8. At least two items lack figures and are not included in the total; the manuscript is truncated after "For the servants of the Saracens." Restored words are enclosed in angled brackets. Asterisks mark lacunae.

amounted to about one half of the total annual outlays.[13] On the other hand, a system of fixed stipends was widely diffused among eastern Mediterranean churches in late antiquity. The substantial discrepancies among the sums assigned to the clergy, the patriarch, and the building fabric suggest that a system of fixed stipends more likely underlies the expenditure account recorded here. In fact, the patriarch's annual expenditure of 550*s* comes very close to a budget based on 365 days.[14] Whichever system applied in Jerusalem, the evidence on the structure of church budgets in late antiquity makes it unlikely that the missing items of expenditure more than doubled the sum of the figures detected here. The fact that the numbers drop off to smaller ones in the last preserved line of the roll further signals that the biggest budgetary items were already accounted for on the surviving lines. Thus a purely hypothetical total of 3,320*s* (= 1,660 × 2) more likely overstates than understates annual patriarchal expenditures. We can feel fairly confident that in the opening years of the ninth century, the annual expenditures of the patriarchal

13   That is, 700 + 550 = 1,250*s* × 2 = 2,500*s*.

14   Jones, *Later Roman Empire*, 903, cites an example obviously based on the number of days in a year. In our case, 550*s* divided by 365 days equals 1.5068*s* per day. Hence it is tempting to think that the total annual income expended by the patriarch according to the roll was rounded up from an exact 547.5*s* (1.5*s* × 365).

establishment of Jerusalem fell between 1,660s and 3,320s, and more probably toward the lower end.

As we shall see, another unit of measure used in the roll concealed a local reality under a Frankish name.[15] This suggests that here too we are looking at the sums as they were expressed in Jerusalem. Calling the gold coins of the caliphate solidi would occasion no surprise: the Arab dinars that circulated in Italy and even Frankland at this time were also called solidi. There they were often, though not universally, qualified with the Arabic loan word as *mancosi* to distinguish them from the local units of account also reckoned in solidi, of different value.[16] In fact, a counterfeit dinar has turned up in Saxony, only twenty-five kilometers from Charlemagne's palace at Paderborn, and a court poet refers to dinars in a way that assumes familiarity.[17] One of Charlemagne's main advisors, and the head of his court's liturgical life, used the Arab coins to pay his own liturgical performers in his home cathedral of Metz.[18] Another consideration also argues that the *Dispensa*'s figures are in Arab gold dinars. When referring to their own silver coinage, Carolingian documents commonly translate big sums into pounds, the largest local monetary unit of account (£1 equals 20s equals 240d), rather than specifying large numbers of *denarii* or solidi. Thus in northern Italian records of the period we read of sums of 30s but of £8 of minted silver. In a document apparently drawn up near Brescia in 813, Charlemagne's cousin and close advisor, Adalhard of Corbie, referred to small sums of 8d and 5s but large ones of £15 and £3 silver.[19] The same manner of thinking about large quantities of coins prevailed north of the Alps. Thus a capitulary of 805 estimated the wealth of individuals in terms of pounds, and a couple of decades later the Polyptych of St. Germain

15 See chapter 5.2.
16 See McCormick, *Origins*, 323–37, esp. 333, on Fortunatus's will, whose many sums in solidi are only specified in part as solidi mancusi, though others probably also are in the same (Arab) coinage.
17 M. McCormick, "Charlemagne and the Mediterranean World," in *Am Vorabend der Kaiserkrönung: Das Epos "Karolus Magnus et Leo Papa" und der Papstbesuch in Paderborn 799*, ed. P. Godman, J. Jarnut, and P. Johanek (Berlin, 2002), 193–218, here 193–94; Theodulf of Orleans, *Carmen* 28.163–77, 498. Compare McCormick, *Origins*, 336–37 and 346.
18 Bishop Angilramn (768–791) championed the imitating of Roman customs in Frankland. In this respect too he conceivably could have been following papal example by ostentatiously distributing the Arab gold coins to his clergy. We know in any case that solidi mancosi circulated at Rome around 780. See McCormick, *Origins*, 335–36. I did not know of Angilramn's document when I wrote about the penetration of Arab coins into the Carolingian economy; it strengthens the conclusions drawn there. The text has been edited by M. Andrieu, "Règlement d'Angilramne de Metz (768–791) fixant les honoraires de quelques fonctions liturgiques," *Recherches de sciences religieuses* 10 (1930): 349–69, here 351.14–352.2 and 354.39.
19 *Codex diplomaticus Langobardiae*, nos. 83, 84, and 88, pp. 156–59 and 164–65, respectively. For more on Adalhard, see below, p. 83.

regularly converted larger quantities of denarii into pounds and remaining denarii.[20] Arab coinage, on the other hand, seems usually not to have been counted in larger notional units of account such as pounds, even though weighing was a normal part of money payment in the caliphate.[21] In other words, if the Expenditures were offering sums in Frankish shillings rather than in Arab gold dinars, we would expect the first sum of 700s to be written in the usual Frankish notation as £35, the second, 550s, as £27, 10s, and so on. Finally, as comparison will show, even in the local gold currency, the Christian church does not look like an exceedingly rich institution. If the sums were given in Carolingian silver currency, the totals would be so low as to imply a very, perhaps even desperately, impoverished institution.[22] In sum, the evidence indicates that the Expenditures detail the annual outlays of the Holy Land church in the local, gold currency.

2. Assessing the Wealth of the Holy Land Church

Given that the Expenditures' sums probably reflect gold dinars, how much wealth did they represent? Comparison with incomes attested in approximately the same period in the Middle East affords a rough idea of the Palestinian church's level of wealth insofar as we can judge from its disbursements. If it is true that a mason in Iraq at about the same time earned 1.5 dinars a month, then the patriarch spent about thirty-six times such a craftsman's annual earnings.[23] Even allowing for the inflation that seems to have occurred in the ninth century, the patriarch's 550 dinars pale in comparison with the sums of tax revenues, calculated in the hundreds of thousands or even millions of dinars, produced by the richest provinces of the caliphate in the tenth century, if we may rely on data gathered from the Muslim historians.[24] But the patriarch's expenditures seem to compare favorably with the earnings of contemporary officials who headed various administrative services of the caliphate. Their annual emoluments have been estimated at 360 dinars; in

20 MGH Capit 1:125.19–31, no. 44.19; Irmino, *Polyptych* 1.42, p. 3.

21 See the discussion in A. Grohmann, *Einführung und Chrestomathie zur arabischen Papyruskunde* (Prague, 1955), 186–88; specific examples, for dirhams, 208–9. Examples are abundant in the Cairo Geniza. See S. D. Goitein, *A Mediterranean Society: The Jewish Communities of the Arab World as Portrayed in the Documents of the Cairo Geniza*, vol. 1 (Berkeley, 1967), 230–34.

22 Understood in terms of Carolingian silver currency, the patriarch's annual expenditures would have come to £27.5 and the total recoverable expenses of the patriarchate to £58. With the former sum, the patriarch could scarcely have bought two horses in the surely less expensive markets of the Frankish Empire. See, for example, P. Riché, *Daily Life in the World of Charlemagne*, trans. J. A. McNamera, 2nd ed. (n.p., 1988), 119.

23 Ashtor, *Histoire des prix*, 65.

24 Idem, *A Social and Economic History of the Near East in the Middle Ages* (Berkeley, 1976), 138–39. See above, note 2, on inflated numbers of ships in Arab historians.

the early tenth century, officials of higher, ministerial rank earned between 1,200 and 6,000 dinars a year.[25]

It is possible to take this a little further in terms of purchasing power. The Islamic gold dinar was supposed to weigh 4.25 g, which would mean that, in absolute terms, 2.98 kg of gold was expended annually on the clergy of the patriarchal establishment. To translate this into terms that are more meaningful for grasping how much the patriarchal wealth could buy, we can use that information that a mason in Iraq at exactly this time was reported to earn 1.5 dinars a month. The 700 (dinars) allotted to the whole personnel of the patriarchate was therefore enough to pay for the labor and, presumably, support 38.9 masons and their families for a year. If, to be on the very conservative side, those families were reckoned at five persons, we may surmise that the sum could have supported some 194 persons; the number would of course increase with a higher multiplier for the family size. If the price levels of Jerusalem and Iraq were similar, 700s would therefore have sufficed for the maintenance of about 194 persons at the economic level of masons and their families, a total that comes close to the 162 personnel of the patriarchate tabulated by the Breve. We cannot know whether or what proportion of these patriarchal personnel had dependents that would have been supported by the total of 700s, but a substantial share of them did not. The Breve explicitly classifies 41 individuals as monks and another 23 as canons. The former were necessarily celibate, and that also may have been true of the ecclesiastics identified as canons. In addition, the exceptionally monastic character of the Palestinian church as a whole suggests that some significant part of the remaining ecclesiastical officials were also monks and therefore celibate.

We can also consider the sums from the perspective of wheat prices and consumption. In Upper Mesopotamia in the 770s, 0.125 dinars would buy 100 kg of wheat; 700 dinars were therefore the equivalent of 560,000 kg or 560 metric tons (i.e., 5,600 quintals).[26] In Egypt, where grain had been cheap since at least the time of Rome, the price of 100 kg of wheat rose in the first half of the ninth century to more than 0.3 dinar, so that 700 dinars could have purchased some 233.3 metric tons of wheat.[27] If a person requires approximately the (kilo)calories equivalent to the energy of 300 kg[28] of wheat flour per year, 700 dinars might supply the wheat flour equivalent for somewhere between 777 and 1,866 persons for a year, at the more and less expensive wholesale prices of wheat flour.[29] Rough and ready though

25 Idem, *Histoire des prix*, 65–66.

26 Idem, *Social and Economic History*, 93. Compare idem, *Histoire des prix*, 42, where it is clear that this is the price paid to farmers, and that still lower prices occurred in subsequent years.

27 Idem, *Social and Economic History*, 94.

28 F. Braudel, *The Structures of Everyday Life: The Limits of the Possible* (New York, 1981), 134.

29 The reckoning here is based on Ashtor's data and is very approximate. Ashtor is sometimes unclear on whether he is reporting wheat flour or wheat; obviously if the latter is true, the quanti-

these estimates are, they indicate that the patriarchal resources were ample for the 162 persons mentioned on the patriarchal staff, even presuming that a number of servants and the like have gone unmentioned. If, however, as is less likely, this sum was supposed to have been spent on all the Christian religious personnel of Jerusalem and immediate environs, it probably still would have sufficed to feed more than 400 mouths, but such a reckoning would reduce considerably the aggregate level of the patriarchal clergy's disposable wealth.[30]

The nature of the payment of 80s that appears to have gone "for the Saracens" is unspecified, but one is tempted to think of the *jizya*, the annual tribute that the Islamic authorities imposed on protected religious minorities. The *jizya* was supposed to be set on a per capita basis. It may be coincidence, but the calculated total of the 163 personnel of the Holy Sepulcher comes very close to 0.5s each, which in fact approximates the *jizya* rate assessed on poor people in 867.[31] However, this would be a lower rate than the rate of one dinar per head reported for the region.[32]

---

ties of wheat flour and therefore energy equivalents would be lessened, resulting in smaller numbers of people who could be fed for a year with 700 dinars. Nevertheless, he reports that "la différence entre les prix d'une certaine quantité de froment et de farine était dans les pays orientaux minime" (*Histoire des prix*, 48). He seems usually to give (ibid., 12 and 45) the wholesale price, apparently as charged by wholesale merchants but sometimes as paid to farmers, also mentioning the usual profit margin of wholesale grain merchants.

30 The former interpretation seems to me more likely for the words "Dispensa patriarchae inter presbiteris, diaconibus, monachis, clericis, et omne congregatione eccle<siae per unum> annum." In any case, the wording of the Expenditures of the Patriarch makes clear that the outlays concern only the ecclesiastical establishment. In Carolingian capitularies of this period, *congregatio* virtually always refers to a religious house of canons, monks, or nuns, as quick examination of the usage in the capitularies of Charlemagne documented in eMGH5 shows.

31 Bernard the Monk, *Itinerarium* 7, 312–13, reported that in 867 the *jizya* was calibrated to each person's wealth, varying among 3, 2, and 1 gold pieces, or 13 denarii. At that time, according to A. H. Ehrenkreutz, the exchange rate was 25 dirhams to 1 dinar, which would make the lowest *jizya* in his time equivalent to about one-half of a dinar. See "Money," in *Wirtschaftsgeschichte des vorderen Orients in Islamischer Zeit*, Handbuch der Orientalistik 1.6.6.1 (Leyden, 1977), 96. On Bernard, see McCormick, *Origins*, 134–38, with further references.

32 See, in general, C. Cahen, "Djizya," in *EI²* online, according to whom the rate generally imposed, apparently at the conquest, in the towns of Syria and Upper Mesopotamia was one dinar per head. The *jizya* was applicable to able-bodied adult male non-Muslims, although there is evidence for lump-sum fixed payments negotiated at the outset also (ibid.). Notwithstanding the possible fit between the 163 persons and the 80s, it is conceivable that this was a sum negotiated at the outset, when Jerusalem surrendered to the Arab conquerors in 638, and so may reflect the size of the patriarchal establishment—a theoretical 80 persons—in that period of devastation. The erroneous reading—by 500—of the edition of Tobler and Molinier suggested to Gil (*History of Palestine*, 153) that this payment was the *jizya* for the entire Christian population of Jerusalem, and he further hypothesized that the "580" dinars represented the tribute for 580 Christian families and deduced that the Holy City then was populated by 580 Christian families. R. Schick equally suggested that this figure might reflect "a collective poll tax paid through the patriarch as head of the community": *The Christian Communities of Palestine from Byzantine to Islamic Rule: A Historical and Archaeological Study*, Studies in Late Antiquity and Early Islam 2 (Princeton, N.J., 1995), 168.

In sum, a first assessment of the financial data that can be recovered from the Expenditures of the Patriarch suggests that the patriarchate enjoyed wealth of a modest order, and that the patriarch himself had access to a style of life comparable to that of some mid- to higher-level caliphal officials.

The impression of the relative modesty of patriarchal resources—or at least outlays—finds reinforcement from the scattered data available on the financial posture of similar institutions outside the caliphate. Although such calculations can always be criticized in their individual components (e.g., the extrapolations behind the Rome figures or the assumption that the precious metals of gifts were always as pure as those of coins) or in interpretation, table 1.2 gives a good idea of the general order of magnitude of sums involved in different aspects of church life in the Mediterranean basin in this period. It speaks volumes that the patriarch of Grado traveled to the Frankish court with more money in his saddlebags than the patriarch of Jerusalem spent in a year to maintain the most prestigious shrines in Christendom. While the divergences among the types of sums we can detect are real, and the expenditures of the patriarch were not negligible, his outlays pale in comparison to the kinds of sums mentioned as revenues, gifts, and the like of churches in the contemporary Byzantine Empire and western Europe. The discrepancies between Jerusalem's wealth and that of the other churches implied by this table make very clear why the patriarch of Jerusalem turned to western Europe for the financial help that surely lies behind the genesis of these records.

So the Jerusalem patriarchate of the early ninth century appears relatively poorly funded in the light of the wealth associated with contemporary churches in Christian realms. But perhaps it had ever been thus. How had Jerusalem fared under the late Roman Empire? Justinian legislated on the fees that bishops were allowed to pay in connection with their election and, of interest to us, he clearly classified them according to the revenues of the bishop's church.[33] The first group comprised the five patriarchates. There, the customary new bishop's donation was limited henceforth to a maximum of 20 pounds (6.48 kg) of gold: the patriarchates that customarily had lower gratuities attached should keep lower ones, and those with higher customary gratuities should not exceed 20 pounds. The second tier comprised those bishoprics whose *revenues* were apparently considerably lower, at 30 pounds (9.72 kg) or more per annum: their bishops were not allowed to give more than a total of 400s, that is, 5.5 pounds (1.8 kg) at the late Roman and Byzantine denominational rate of 72 gold s. to one pound, and so on. If one works out the ranges of incomes and the commensurate fees Justinian authorized for the lesser bishoprics in cases where both are clearly specified, the fees run between

33 Justinian, *Novellae* 123.2, 597.22–25, of AD 546, which specifies that the second class of bishoprics are those with revenues around 30 pounds of gold per annum; compare the brief but trenchant discussion of Jones, *Later Roman Empire*, 905–6.

about one-eighth and one-half of revenues and tend to cluster around one-fifth or one-sixth.[34] This hints that the revenues of the five patriarchates in 546 might have ranged between 40 and 160 pounds (12.96–51.8 kg) of gold. The lower figure might suggest that, in the crude terms of gold weight, what we would guess could be the maximum of patriarchal expenditures around 808—for the sake of hypothesis, the double of the documented expenditures, or about 14 kg—approximated the low end of patriarchal revenues in late antiquity. If the five patriarchates tended toward the higher end, however, things look very different.

In fact, the higher end is probably the correct interpretation. Ravenna was not one of the five patriarchates. It was nevertheless richly endowed, since its revenues, around 525, appear to have totaled 12,000s, that is, 166.67 pounds (54 kg) of gold.[35] A potentially well-informed hagiographical text reports that in 610 the new patriarch of Alexandria discovered 8,000 pounds of gold in the patriarchal treasury.[36] We have already seen (table 1.2, item 14) that in the early eighth century, Rome apparently still derived annual revenues of 350 pounds of gold from its southern Italian patrimonies, which likely were its main holdings.

More data from very close to home underscores that, compared to late antiquity, the financial posture of the early medieval Christian institutions of Jerusalem had substantially diminished. The ninth-century patriarch's documented expenditures (7.06 kg) look unimpressive compared to the revenue stream of just one of the institutions that had been under his predecessor's care in the sixth century; even our hypothetical doubling of the expenditures does not reach the sixth-century revenue level. When Justinian founded a 100-bed hospital for sick pilgrims in the Holy City, he established for it an annual revenue that, when he

34 The figures are as follows: for the second tier, converting the sums to their metric weight (1 lb = 72s; 1 s. = 4.5 g, i.e. 1 lb = 324 g), the fee works out to approximately 18.5%; 30–10 pounds of revenue warrants 300s, that is, 1.4 kg, or 14.4%–44% of the revenue; 10–5 pounds warrants a fee of 120s, that is, 540 g, or 16.9%–33.8%; 5–3 pounds at 42s (189 g), or 12%–19%; 3–2 pounds: 28s, that is, 126 g, or 13%–19%. *Novella* 123, 3, 597.19–598.10.

35 Agnellus, *Liber pontificalis ecclesiae Ravennatis* 60, 319.28–30, quoting a decision of pope Felix IV: "Quartam patrimonii Ravennensis ecclesia, hoc est tria milia solidorum. . . ." Jones, *Later Roman Empire*, 905, interprets *patrimonium* as referring to the actual revenue rather than the capital goods which produced that revenue. The word can take either meaning: *ThLL* 11.1:751.44–754.12.

36 *Vita Iohannis Eleemosynarii* (BHG 887v) 48, ed. H. Delehaye, "Une vie inédite de saint Jean l'Aumônier," *AB* 45 (1927): 5–73, here 68.36–37, in a passage quoted from John's will. No later than the tenth century (when Metaphrastes revised it), this valuable and underused work epitomized the lost biography written by John's close associates, John Moschus and Sophronius of Jerusalem, as well as the surviving biography by Leontius. It is loaded with authentic details that have not otherwise survived, as Delehaye emphasized. Compare A. Kazhdan and N. P. Ševčenko, "John Eleemon," *ODB* 2:1058–59. Although shorter, the independent abbreviation *Vita Iohannis Eleemosynarii* (BHG 887w), ed. E. Lappa-Zizicas, "Un épitomé inédit de la Vie de S. Jean l'Aumônier par Jean et Sophronios," *AB* 88 (1970): 265–78, supplies further numerical data excised by BHG 887v.

Item	Amount	Approx. weight in kg of gold[a]	Item Number
Jerusalem			
Ca. 808, patriarchal budget			
For clergy	700 dinars	2.98	1
For the \<patriarch\>	550 dinars	2.34	2
For the buildings	300 dinars	1.28	3
Other expenditures	110 dinars	0.47	4
Total recorded annual expenditures	1,660 dinars	7.06	
Byzantine Empire			
795, remission of customs duties from the fair to the church of St. John, Ephesus	7,200 Byz. s.	32.4	5
811, coronation gratuity[b]			
To the patriarch of Constantinople	3,600 Byz. s.	16.2	6
To the clergy (of Hagia Sophia)	1,800 Byz. s.	8.1	7
811, Christmas gratuity[b]			
To the patriarch	1,800 Byz. s.	8.1	8
To the clergy (of Hagia Sophia?)	7,200 Byz. s.	32.4	9
830, empress's coronation and wedding gratuity[b]			
To the patriarch	1,080 Byz. s.	4.86	10
To the clergy (of Hagia Sophia?)	1,080 Byz. s.	4.86	11
Ca. 899, customary largess to "the Great Church" (i.e., the Hagia Sophia)[b]			
From an emperor (basileus) who becomes autokrator	7,200 Byz. s.	32.4	12
From a junior emperor	3,600 Byz. s.	16.2	13

Sources: Nos. 5–9, and 12: Theophanes, *Chronographia*, respectively: AM 6287, 1:469.27–470.1; nos. 6–9: AM 6304, 1:493.32–494.1 and 494.28–33; nos. 10–11: *Vita Theodorae imperatricis* (BHG 1731), 3, 260.58–60; for the date, ibid., 274; nos. 12–13, Philotheus, *Cleterologium*, 99.5–6 and 13; no. 14: Theophanes, *Chronographia* AM 6224, 1:10.11–14; nos. 15–18: P. Delogu, "Oro e argento in Roma tra il VII ed il IX secolo," in *Cultura et società nell'Italia medievale. Studi per Paolo Brezzi* (Rome, 1988), 273–93, here 273–77, Grafico 1 (see also notes d and e); no. 19: *Documenti relativi alla storia di Venezia*, 45, p. 78; no. 20: Justinian doge of Venice, Will, 21.

[a]Data set in italics are converted from silver to gold equivalents. Weight in gold is calculated by multiplying the weight of a dinar (4.25 g) or Byzantine solidus (4.5 g) by the number of coins; in converting silver to gold, I have used the ratio that seems to have applied in each region: that is, for Byzantine and Arab sums, a gold-to-silver ratio of 1:10; for western Europe, I have applied the ratio of 1:12. See, on these ratios, Spufford, *Money*, 51.

[b]Items 6 to 11 are specific gratuities mentioned in the sources. Their amounts may therefore have been irregular, as the frequency of nos. 6–7 and 10–11 certainly was. Items 12 and 13 are explicitly identified as customary sums.

TABLE 1.2 *(continued)*

Item	Amount	Approx. weight in kg of gold[a]	Item Number
Western Europe			
731–32, revenues of the church of Rome, apparently annual, confiscated by emperor Leo III	25,200 Byz. s.	113.4	14
772–95, Pope Hadrian I's estimated average annual gifts to churches of Rome[c]			
In silver	72.9 lb (= 23.9 kg)	*1.99*[a]	15
In gold	70.7 lb	23.15	16
795–816, Pope Leo III's estimated average annual gifts to churches of Rome[d]			
In silver	1,105 lb (= 361 kg)	*30.08*	17
In gold	72.3 lb	23.67	18
Ca. 826, Fortunatus, patriarch of Grado, traveled to the Frankish court with this amount of *argento facto de mesa*	61 lb (= 19.97 kg)[e]	*1.66*	19
829, cash gift to a monastery by the Doge of Venice, presumably in silver	200 lb[f] (= 65.48 kg)	*5.46*	20

[c]As estimated and calculated from the *Liber pontificalis* by Delogu, "Oro e argento," Grafico 1, with discussion and caveats at 273–77. He estimated Hadrian's total gifts in gold as 1626.6 lb, and in silver as 1677 lb, and suggested the metric value of the Roman pound (327.4 g; ibid., 273 n. 2), which I have divided by the 23 years of his pontificate.

[d]Delogu, "Oro e argento," estimates 22,100.11 lbs of silver and 1446.6 of gold, reckoned by the same metric value, and divided by the 20 years of his reign (from 27 December 795 to 11 June 816).

[e]Assuming the same metric conversion factor that Delogu uses for Rome: see above, note c.

[f]Assuming these are Roman pounds of silver. If Doge Justinian was using the Carolingian monetary pound, that would have meant 48,000*d*, which, if to the full weight of contemporary non-Venetian Carolingian issues, should work out to 81.6 kg of good silver. However, an analysis of their chemical composition which I organized shows that nominally Frankish coins struck at Venice typically weighed less and were of lesser fineness than northern issues: G. Sarah, M. Bompaire, M. McCormick, et al., "Analyses élémentaires de monnaies de Charlemagne et Louis le Pieux du Cabinet des Médailles: l'Italie carolingienne et Venise," *Revue numismatique* 164 (2008): 355–406.

expanded the hospital to 200 beds, he doubled to 3,700s.[37] By the crude but telling yardstick of raw weight of the gold coins, that one unit of the patriarchal responsibility had revenues of 16.65 kg of gold in the sixth century—more than twice the total estimated maximal expenditures of the patriarchal establishment three centuries later. Yet another element underscores the difference between late antique and early medieval levels of wealth enjoyed by the patriarchs of Jerusalem. At the end of the sixth century, the bishop of a relatively insignificant see in Galatia enjoyed an annual stipend of 365s (1.64 kg) which, by our crude yardstick, represents more than half the gold equivalent of the annual expenditures (2.338 kg) assigned to the particular account of the early medieval patriarch.[38]

In an ideal world, the next step would be to translate these approximate measures into purchasing power in terms of a standard commodity, such as wheat, and thus to obtain a definitive understanding of the relative strength of patriarchal finances about 808. The reason for this further step is that it would be very surprising if the purchasing power of a gram of gold did not vary across three hundred years of sweeping change in the economic structure of the eastern Mediterranean. Unfortunately, we are a long way from a comprehensive understanding of price structures and movements in the early medieval Middle East, whether under Byzantine or Islamic rule, essential though these data are to understanding any economy. We are further still from even pioneering efforts to compare these prices with those prevalent under the later Roman Empire.[39] Any attempt to refine the crude indication gleaned from raw weights of gold in terms of prices is bound to come with plenty of caveats. Nevertheless, it is worth considering the new data from Jerusalem by this yardstick also, so long as we recognize that such a first attempt to compare the very different economies of the late Roman Empire and the Abbasid caliphate offers only an initial assay and that its accuracy is only as good as that of the work on which it is founded.

Translating these sums of gold into their purchasing power of wheat in the two periods is no easy task. The evidence to hand indicates that wheat prices changed both in the sixth and across the eighth and ninth centuries, complicating efforts to identify suitable comparanda. It is unclear whether the fluctuations observable in the sixth century were just that—temporary movements—or whether they may have been part of the long-term trend toward higher grain prices that the most recent study has found in the Byzantine Empire between the sixth and the ninth centuries.[40] However, the extraordinary and at least partially successful efforts of

37 Cyril of Scythopolis, *Vita Sabae* (BHG 1608) 73, 177.9–14. Cf. Jones, *Later Roman Empire*, 901.
38 George, *Vita Theodori Syceotae* (BHG 1748) 78, 65.1–8.
39 Beyond Ashtor's two monographs for the early caliphate see, for Byzantium, the recent survey of C. Morrisson and J.-C. Cheynet, "Prices and Wages in the Byzantine World," in *EHB* 2:815–78. Wickham seems not to consider the question of prices in *Framing the Early Middle Ages*.
40 Morrisson and Cheynet, "Prices and Wages in the Byzantine World," 830.

the imperial government to stabilize grain prices in the capitals would appear to warrant some confidence in the less extreme prices recorded in some numbers for the sixth century.[41] The annual revenues we have just estimated for the five patriarchs in Justinian's time ranged between 40 and 160 pounds of gold. What we have just seen about the annual revenue of just one institution under the patriarch of Jerusalem suggests that his aggregate late Roman revenues may have tended toward the higher figure. In any case, table 1.3 collects, harmonizes, and compares the evidence on the cost of wheat in the sixth, eighth, and early ninth centuries in terms of documented expenditures and hypothetical revenues.[42]

At first blush, this wheat equivalency seems to offer a much more optimistic impression of the patriarch of Jerusalem's financial posture under the early Abbasids. In absolute terms, the amounts of gold spent by the patriarch pale in comparison to those available to his late antique peers, especially if the late antique patriarch enjoyed revenues toward the higher end of the spectrum we have suggested. Nevertheless, they would seem to have been able to purchase more, even considerably more, wheat in his economy than they could have done in the late Roman one, judging from the cost of wheat in eighth-century and sixth-century Egypt, respectively (table 1.3). One might reasonably object that one cereal is insufficient for gauging definitively the respective costs of living in two economically advanced and complex civilizations. Nevertheless, it is equally fair to imagine that cereals formed the dietary foundation of the overwhelming majority of the population in both cases. This is what the written sources certainly indicate for the later

41 M. McCormick, "Bateaux de vie, bateaux de mort: Maladie, commerce, transports annonaires et le passage économique du Bas-Empire au moyen âge," in *Morfologie sociali e culturali in Europa fra tarda antichità e alto medioevo*, 2 vols., Settimane 45 (1998), 1:35–122; and, in general, J. Durliat, *De la ville antique à la ville byzantine. Le problème des subsistances*, Collection de l'École française de Rome 136 (Rome, 1990).

42 To inoculate the reader against overconfidence in the seeming precision of the figures in this table, let me spell out how I made the calculations beyond the assumptions in the note to table 1.3. Except for the "Equivalent price in grams of gold," items 3–5 are taken directly from the works of Ashtor, as specified. Items 1–2 translate the prices given by Morrisson and Cheynet in terms of 1/40 or 1/33 of a solidus for a *modios thalassios* of wheat into decimal equivalents and multiply by 7.8125, the factor needed to reach 100 kg. The purchasing power of 1s is obviously 40 or 33 *modioi thalassioi*, which gives the basis for the final equivalence of the revenues in metric tons of wheat. Furthermore, Morrisson and Cheynet report at least six different prices of wheat from Egypt dated to the "sixth century." The only two which are more precisely dated are one of Justinian's reign, from 541 (1/40 of a solidus) and one much higher price from the late sixth century which is identified as such at 1/2s or 1/12s (depending on the version of the text) for the same quantity. They also report another "sixth-century" price of 1/46s, one of 1/13s, and an average of 1/33s based on an unspecified number of sixth-century prices ranging from 1/26 to 1/40 of a *nomisma*. I have used the one price from Justinian's reign and the average in table 1.3, presuming that the unspecified sixth-century price of 1/13s would, like the one reported either as 1/2 or 1/12, have been qualified as high. For the purposes of comparison, at that high price of 1/13s, the estimated patriarchal revenue range could have purchased between 479.23 and 1,916.93 metric tons of wheat.

TABLE 1.3 Calculated purchasing power of estimated and documented patriarchal expenditures or revenues: early Abbasid Caliphate versus late Roman Empire

Date	Place	Price of 100kg of wheat	Equivalent price in g of gold	Amount of grain in metric tons a patriarchate could have bought each year based on . . .		Item
				Patriarchates of the late Roman Empire (6th c.)		
				. . . estimated revenues of the least wealthy patriarchate (*2,880s = 12.960 kg*)	. . . estimated revenues of the most wealthy patriarchate (*11,520s = 51.840 kg*)	
541	Egypt	0.195s	0.879	1,475	5,898	1
6th c.	Egypt	0.234s[a]	1.066[a]	1,217	4,866	2
				Patriarchate of Jerusalem (ca. 808)		
				. . . documented annual expenditures (1,660 dinars = 7.055 kg)	. . . hypothetical maximum expenditures (3,320 dinars = 14,110 kg)	
770s	Upper Mesopotamia	0.125 dinar	0.53	1,328	2,656	3
8th c.	Fayyum, Egypt	0.075 dinar[a]	0.32[a]	2,158	4,316	4
1st half 9th c.	Fayyum, Egypt	0.3 dinar[a]	1.275[a]	553	1,106	5

Assumptions and sources: ITEMS 1–2: 72 imperial solidi of 4.5 g to a pound; prices given are based on a *modios thalassios*, which contained 12.8 kg of wheat; Morrisson and Cheynet, "Prices and Wages in the Byzantine World," table 5, p. 822; compare 817. ITEMS 3–5 (and see further note 42): one dinar equals 4.25 g of gold; one *irdabb* of Fayyum contained 109.6875 kg of wheat (equivalence given by Ashtor, *Histoire des prix*, 79; in his article "Mawāzīn," *EI²* online, accessed January 21, 2008, he offers a slightly smaller Fayyum *irdabb* of 103.22 kg for wheat); Ashtor, *Histoire des prix*, 77–79 and Ashtor, *Social and Economic History*, 93. Arab dinars and Byzantine solidi are taken to be of approximately equal fineness. Equivalences in metric tons are rounded off to the nearest unit.
[a] Average price.

Roman Empire, and the bones of the late Romans themselves are now beginning to confirm the picture.[43] The early results point in a similar direction for the Muslim Levant.[44]

However, a closer look at table 1.3 shows that an important shift occurred in the first half of the ninth century: if these figures are indeed reliable, they indicate that the cost of the staff of life and indispensable foundation of the Mediterranean diet nearly tripled in the space of a generation or two. The upward trend would continue until the tenth century or later.[45] In this light, the patriarchate would soon confront a severe constriction of its purchasing power, if it had not already done so. Finally, in a broader perspective, it has been observed that the wheat prices of the seventh-century caliphate, if accurately interpreted to date, indicate a much lower cost of basic foodstuff than under the late Roman Empire at its eastern Mediterranean peak. In the Islamic Levant, only in the ninth century did the price of wheat catch up with and even surpass late Roman levels.[46]Although the data are more scarce there, the Byzantine Empire also seems to have experienced a sharp rise in grain prices over the eighth and ninth century.[47] The soaring grain prices must have constituted a powerful incentive for the diffusion of the new crops and farming techniques from the Indian subcontinent into the caliphate. Perhaps we have here an economic trigger for the Islamic agricultural revolution.[48]

In sum, the decline in the wealth of the church of Jerusalem since late antiquity is not unambiguous. In absolute terms of weights of gold, it looks drastic. If the price of wheat about 808 was closer to what it had been in the 770s in Upper Mesopotamia or Egypt, the patriarch was not doing terribly badly. If, however, the price of wheat had begun to nearly triple, his expenditures may have been reduced to somewhere between a third and three quarters of his late antique revenues, with the less favorable figure stemming from the figures actually preserved on the roll and the more favorable figure reflecting my quite high upper boundary estimate of the ninth-century revenues. In relative terms, the annual expenditures of the patriarch look similar to those of middle-level officials in Iraq, although we may

43 E. Patlagean, *Pauvreté économique et pauvreté sociale à Byzance, 4e–7e siècles* (Paris, 1977), 47. For archaeological confirmation, see M. Salamon, A. Coppa, M. McCormick, et al., "The Consilience of Historical and Isotopic Approaches in Reconstructing the Medieval Mediterranean Diet," *Journal of Archaeological Science* 35 (2008): 1667–72.

44 E. Ashtor, "The Diet of Salaried Classes in the Medieval Near East," *Journal of Asian History* 4 (1970): 1–24, here 2–3. Bread is clearly at the center of the diets of rich and poor alike, as vividly evoked from the Cairo Genizah by Goitein, *Mediterranean Society,* 4:233–44.

45 Ashtor, *Histoire des prix,* 453–59.

46 G. Ostrogorsky, "Löhne und Preise in Byzanz," *BZ* 32 (1932): 293–333, here 319–21; Ashtor, *Histoire des prix,* 454.

47 Morrisson and Cheynet, "Prices and Wages in the Byzantine World," 830.

48 A. M. Watson, *Agricultural Innovation in the Early Islamic World: The Diffusion of Crops and Farming Techniques, 700–1100* (Cambridge, 1983), esp. 126–34.

suspect that price levels were higher in Iraq than in the Holy Land. Even though he had probably experienced a decline in disposable wealth compared to his late antique predecessors, the patriarch of Jerusalem was clearly not close to abject poverty, nor would this have been true of his ecclesiastical subordinates. Also, in comparing the situation to late antiquity, we should not lose sight of the crucial fact that the patriarchal throne seems to have been vacant for at least half a century after the Muslim conquest. The leadership of the patriarchal institution, if not the institution itself, had in some sense been restored only since the vacancy ended around 700.[49] Finally, the Expenditures clarifies one important aspect of patriarchal finances that was probably of major importance for the mission and Charlemagne's subsequent decisions about Jerusalem. In the early eighth century, Egyptian workmen were paid two-thirds of a dinar per month to build the Great Mosque of Jerusalem.[50] Assuming no change in price levels over the intervening century, the building budget of the patriarchate would have sufficed to hire a crew of only thirty-eight unskilled laborers for one year, without considering the cost of materials, architects, and skilled laborers. Given that price rises had occurred by the beginning of the ninth century, the patriarch's effective building budget will have been that much reduced.[51] The cost of construction work combines with the small funds available for building to make this clear: economic reasons would have urged the church of Jerusalem to turn to the distant Christian monarch who was spreading his generosity widely around the churches of his empire and beyond.

If the financing of the patriarchal church of Jerusalem had witnessed some kind of decline since late antiquity and in any case cut a very modest figure next to other contemporary churches of similar or lesser rank, how did its human component fare? Another way of assessing the development of the patriarchate since late antiquity concerns not the finances, but its staffing. It is to that problem, and the opportunities for comparative insights over time and across the early medieval Western world, that we move next.

---

49 V. Grumel, *La chronologie*, Traité d'études byzantines 1 (Paris, 1958), 451; compare A.-M. Eddé, F. Micheau, and C. Picard, *Communautés chrétiennes en pays d'Islam du début du VIIe siècle au milieu du XIe siècle* (Condé-sur-Noireau, 1997), 61.

50 Ashtor, *Histoire des prix*, 90.

51 Ibid., 92, for Egypt, and 453–63, for the general upward trend of the cost of living in Egypt and Iraq. Data are insufficient for direct conclusions about Syria and Palestine, but the general tendency presumably followed that of the neighboring regions.

. . . .

Chapter Two

A BUMPY ROAD
FROM LATE ANTIQUITY

The Holy Land Churches

I T IS REMARKABLE TO BE ABLE to put questions of relative and absolute size to any early medieval church. For the quantitative data they preserve, the Breve and the Memorial of Monasteries have few close parallels from their own or earlier times. If we will need to consider at some length the complicated question of what is missing from the roll, that is a small price to pay for the opportunity to learn the number of the patriarchate's personnel and to estimate how many served in the provincial bishoprics, the numbers of monks and nuns, and indeed the overall sex ratio of religious or the ratio of cenobitic to eremitic monks. It is more complicated, but not impossible to ask how, over time, this situation might have compared to late antiquity and, over space, to other churches.

Naturally these two documents are not without their shortcomings. But the problems turn out to be relatively minor, and do not undermine the generalizations that can be drawn from them. It is an extraordinary piece of good fortune that, at the same time that this report reached him, Charlemagne received a remarkably similar document about a major Frankish church from one of his own archbishops and that this Frankish document survives. Although its scope and contents do not overlap exactly with those of the Jerusalem reports, the similarity is great enough to warrant asking questions about what we might call the comparative religious sociology of the churches of Lyons and Jerusalem in the early ninth century. This chapter will analyze the testimony on the number of the religious personnel of the Holy Land church about 808 in comparison to the halcyon days of late antiquity. Not only will it prove possible to demonstrate the relative decline of the church, it will be feasible to assess the approximate scale of that decline.

No late Roman document survives that enumerates the personnel of the churches of Jerusalem and that would allow us to chart directly how the patriarchate's size changed over time.[1] We can, however, get an indirect comparative

---

1   We do have numbers of individuals whose bodies were found and buried in different parts of the city in the wake of the Persian sack of Jerusalem in 614. Leaving aside the reliability of these

TABLE 2.1 Numbers of ecclesiastical dignitaries of two patriarchal churches compared: Hagia Sophia, Constantinople, 535 and 612, and the Holy Sepulcher complex, Jerusalem, about 808
(percentages rounded to the nearest 0.5)

Personnel	Justinian 535 Quantity	%	Heraclius 612 Qty.	%	Breve ca. 808 Qty.	%
	Constantinople Great Church				Jerusalem Holy Sepulcher	
Priests	60	11.5	80	13.5	16	26.7
Deacons	100	19	150	25	15	25
Deaconesses	40	7.5	40	6.5		
Subdeacons	90	17	70	11.5	6	10
Subtotal	**290**	**55**	**340**	**56.5**	**37**	**61.7**
Lectors	110	21	160	26.5		
Psaltai	25	5	25	4		
Ostiarii	100	19	75	12.5		
Undifferentiated (lower) clergy					23	38.3
Subtotal	**235**	**45**	**260**	**43**		
Total	**525**	**100**	**600**	**99.5**	**60**	**100**

Note: The Holy Sepulcher figures here refer only to the same ecclesiastical dignities documented in Constantinople, not the total personnel. The Breve explicitly excludes from its total the staff of the three hostels (on which, see below, chapter 4.3), but it is uncertain whether the excluded personnel included any clerics not represented in the main entry.

glimmer from sixth- and seventh-century legislation that attempted to limit the bloated staffing of the patriarchal cathedral of the imperial capital, the Hagia Sophia (table 2.1). In 535, even though he recognized that the ecclesiastical personnel was far more numerous, Justinian attempted to set a future cap of 525 persons for the dignitaries attached to the Great Church, as the cathedral was known. The emperor specified the ceilings on various individual ranks within the cathedral clergy.[2] He proposed to reach those numbers by attrition. Notwithstanding the intervening near century of crises, defeats, and epidemics, Justinian's effort had no

---

numbers, there is no way to discern, for example, what part of the 290 individuals reported to have been found dead on the altar of the Nea might have been from the church's personnel as opposed to those who in vain had sought asylum there. *Expugnationis Hierosolymae A.D. 614 recensiones Arabicae*; trans., 23.15, p. 52.

2   Justinian, *Novella* 3.1 (AD 535), 21.12–19; for the numbers, see 21.3–12.

A Mediterranean Church in the Early Middle Ages

TABLE 2.2 Personnel of the Blachernae shrine, Constantinople, 612

(percentages rounded to the nearest 0.5)

Personnel	Quantity	%
Priests	12	16
Deacons	18	24.5
Deaconesses	6	8
Subdeacons	8	11
Subtotal	**44**	**59.5**
Lectors	20	27
Psaltai	4	5.5
Ostiarii	6	8
Subtotal	**30**	**40.5**
Total	**74**	**100**

lasting success, since Heraclius was forced to deal with the same situation. In 612, that emperor fixed the total number of ecclesiastics at 600, 14 percent higher than Justinian's hoped-for maximum.[3] In addition, he specified the maximum number of various church officials, presumably recruited mostly or entirely from the ranks of the 600 personnel of the Hagia Sophia. In fact, just seven years later, perhaps out of political considerations, given his extreme reliance on the patriarch Sergius I, Heraclius was obliged to nullify these provisions, and it is entirely plausible that even these elevated numbers do not represent the high point of the staffing of the Great Church of Constantinople in the seventh century.[4] As tables 2.1–2 lay out, the comparable categories show that the ninth-century clergy of the patriarchate of Jerusalem was an order of magnitude below that of the sixth- and seventh-century patriarchate of Constantinople.

The early medieval ecclesiastical establishment of the patriarchate of Jerusalem was about one-tenth the size of its counterpart in the sixth- and seventh-century capital. The relative proportion of priests was much higher in Jerusalem, whereas that of deacons and lower clergy was comparable. The number of subdeacons in Jerusalem was more in keeping with the targeted size of that contingent at the Hagia Sophia in 612. Although we may well suspect that the patriarchal establishment of Jerusalem was always smaller than that of the mighty imperial capital, it is edifying to observe that, in absolute numbers, the desired maximal size

---

3   Heraclius, *Novella* 1, here 64.43–68.79.
4   J. Konidaris, "Die Novellen des Kaisers Herakleios," *FM* 5 (1982): 33–106, here 94–100.

of the clergy of just the important shrine of the Blachernae in Constantinople in 612 (table 2.2) compares most closely to that of the entire Jerusalem patriarchate two centuries later.[5] Save for the number of priests, the early medieval clergy of the Holy Sepulcher or, as it was known among the Byzantines, the Anastasis ("Resurrection") complex was nevertheless smaller in every respect than even an important but secondary shrine of Constantinople two hundred years earlier. Although this is certainly not a direct and decisive comparison—it is possible, if not likely, that the Jerusalem patriarchate had long been a smaller-scale operation than its Constantinopolitan counterpart—the comparison suggests that the reconstituted early medieval patriarchate of Jerusalem may well have shrunk since late antiquity. We can deepen our understanding by extending the comparison to the rest of the Holy Land church as documented in the roll. But first a glance at some problems.

1. Shortcomings, Ambiguities, and Solutions

The Basel documents are not without shortcomings and ambiguities, especially when they look beyond Jerusalem. Naturally for the Franks, who were so sensitive about their own religious righteousness, the documents are concerned only with orthodox establishments.[6] Other, less obvious shortcomings may affect the picture we deduce from them and must be taken into account: rounding of figures, occasional ambiguity in categorizing groups, and, most importantly, churches Charlemagne's envoys may have missed. For the Holy Sepulcher, the figures the Breve reports smell of exactness—nine, fourteen, six, twenty-three, thirteen, forty-one. But totals divisible by five increase elsewhere in Jerusalem, and they are frequent in the second document. This strongly suggests that the Memorial provides rounded-off estimates rather than actual head counts. A similar explanation may lie behind the rounded numbers of cloistered women in a time and place when sexual segregation was pervasive.[7] The exceptional precision of the count of nuns in the

---

5   Heraclius, *Novellae* 1, 68.80–89.

6   The only possible exception seems to be the mention of Armenians at line 24. However, the phrasing about this church is unique. Most of the entries simply name the church and the number of religious associated with it. In this case alone do we have a verb of possession (*tenent*), hinting that the Armenian presence was viewed as somehow illegitimate ("at St. John, which the Armenians hold, six monks"). Notwithstanding the theological conflicts with Constantinople, many Armenians assimilated smoothly into the highest ranks of the very orthodox society of Constantinople. The classic study is A. P. Kazhdan, *Armiyane v sostave gospodstvuyushchego klassa Vizantijskoi Imperii v xi–xii vv* (Erevan, 1975). Armenian adherents of Chalcedonian orthodoxy may have remained numerous into the eighth century at least. See N. G. Garsoïan, "Armenian Church," *ODB* 1:179. See further, on the Armenian control of this church, J. T. Milik, "Notes d'épigraphie et de topographie palestiniennes: IX. Sanctuaires chrétiens de Jérusalem à l'époque arabe (VIIe–IXe s.)," *RevBibl* 67 (1960): 354–67 and 550–91, here 562–63.

7   For details, see chapter 6.3.

Jerusalem monastery (line 22), whose community of twenty-six women includes seventeen nuns from Charlemagne's empire, is telling of the compilers' priorities.

Another interpretive complication arises from the slightly ambiguous way the Breve's long section (lines 9–12) on the staffing of the churches other than the patriarchate and Anastasis complex records groups. It identifies the numbers it gives as "priests and clerics" for the first two entries but then does not repeat the explicit identification of the category (i.e., "priests and clerics") for the next five entries. It resumes specifying at that point, from the second number at St. Mary at the Sheep Pool, which refers to nuns. Neither the churches referred to nor the nature of the document give any reason to doubt the obvious interpretation that the unspecified entries are also listing in those five unlabeled entries the total number of ecclesiastics attached to each shrine. The tendency to lump together priests and other clergy is nevertheless regrettable, since it precludes a comprehensive analysis of the relative proportion of priests—a valuable element for evaluating the social makeup of a church.[8] Even with these qualifications, however, the figures contained on the roll have few early medieval parallels for the wealth and value of their statistics.

Another question is how exhaustively the roll reports churches. There is no reason to suspect any missing Jerusalem shrines in the Breve. But beyond Jerusalem, is the reporting of churches in the Breve and Memorial really as complete as Charlemagne's informants could make them? A will o' the wisp aside, the only major omission identified to date has been the roll's silence on the famous shrine to St. George at Diospolis, the biblical Lod, or Lydda (mod. Lod).[9] The Anglo-Saxon pilgrim and future Frankish bishop Willibald had visited the site around 725, although his Life says nothing about a religious community; the Frankish pilgrim Bernard does mention a monastery there in 867.[10] It is not impossible that the shrine had suffered a temporary eclipse about 800: certainly one Arab source links difficulties between the Christian shrine and the new rulers with a forced transfer of population from Diospolis to the new city of Ramla.[11] However, a

---

8   See, for example, O. G. Oexle, *Forschungen zu monastischen und geistlichen Gemeinschaften im westfränkischen Bereich*, Münstersche Mittelalter-Schriften 31 (Munich, 1978), 101–2.

9   J. Wilkinson, *Jerusalem Pilgrims before the Crusades*, 2nd ed. (Warminster, 2002), 25. The "Nestorian Hermitage of the ninth century," which occasionally shows up in the literature, seems to be an error. See Y. Hirschfeld, "List of the Byzantine Monasteries in the Judean Desert," in *Christian Archaeology in the Holy Land: New Discoveries*, ed. G. C. Bottini, L. Di Segni, and E. Alliata, Studium biblicum franciscanum, Collectio maior 36 (Jerusalem, 1990), 1–90, at 73.

10   Hugeburc, *Vita Willibaldi* (BHL 8931) 4, 99.17–18; compare Bernard the Monk, *Itinerarium* 10, 314. On Willibald and his niece's account of his pilgrimage, see M. McCormick, *Origins of the European Economy: Communications and Commerce, A.D. 300–900* (Cambridge, 2001), 129–34, with further references.

11   Already in the 680s devotees of St. George in Constantinople were reporting hostility to the shrine, which can only be associated with the Muslim conquerors. See Adomnan, *De locis sanctis*

bishop of Lydda is mentioned in a contemporary Palestinian source, so there may be a gap here in the Memorial's coverage of episcopal sees.[12]

Three further possible omissions concern monasteries. One may involve a monastery near the Jordan River. Writing in approximately the same years as the roll was compiled, Leontius, the Palestinian biographer of St. Stephen the Wonder Worker of Mar Saba, mentions his hero's annual visits to Kalamon, "The Monastery of the Reeds." This fifth-century foundation lay some two kilometers from the neighboring monastery of St. Gerasimus, which the Memorial does mention. Stephen's visits occurred before 794.[13] Although the available space makes it appear unlikely, it is not impossible that Kalamon figured in the roll's lacuna after the monastery of St. Gerasimus.[14] However, there is a better explanation for the omission. Kalamon absorbed its neighbor sometime before the twelfth century; Greek pilgrims usually referred to this monastery simply as "St. Gerasimus," while a thirteenth-century ex libris from the house identifies it as the "monastery of Father Gerasimos, which is called Kalamon."[15] It is possible that what a contemporary Palestinian saint's life refers to as the "monastery of Kalamon" is indeed that house, and that it had already absorbed its neighbor St. Gerasimus by then. Like later Greek pilgrims, the Frankish investigators could have recorded the combined monasteries under the more famous name of St. Gerasimus.[16] One

---

3.4.1–13, 229.1–231.58. Later, in the ninth century, some relics of the Christian martyr Abd al Masih (fl. ca. 810–860) were deposited there in a monastery of St. Cyriacus. See S. H. Griffith, "The Arabic Account of 'Abd al-Masīḥ an-Naǧrānī al-Ghassānī," *Le Muséon* 98 (1985): 331–74, here 374; compare 357. On the decline of Lod-Lydda-Diospolis, the rise of Ramla, and hostility to the shrine of St. George attributed to the early eighth century, see M. Gil, *A History of Palestine, 634–1099*, trans. E. Broido, 2nd ed. (Cambridge, 1997), 104–6, esp. 106 n. 29; and M. Sharon, "Ludd," *EI²* *online*, consulted 5 July 2006.

12   There is no reason to think Lydda figured in the missing line ends of the roll's edge, judging from the substantial parts that remain. The acephalous work of Leontius, *Vita Stephani Thaumaturgi* (BHG 1670) 131, 556B, mentions Eustratius, a former monk of Mar Saba, "now" bishop of Lydda. Compare the complete text as it survives in Arabic translation: Leontius, *The Life of Stephen of Mar Sabas*, ed. and trans. J. C. Lamoreaux, 62.4 and 62.6, trans. 98–99, where his name is given as Eustathius. Leontius wrote the *Life* in the first decade or two after 800. See Lamoreaux's discussion, ibid., x.

13   The date of the saint's death. On Kalamon, see S. Vailhé, "Répertoire alphabétique des monastères de Palestine [1]," *ROC* 4 (1899): 512–42, at 519–20; S. Vailhé, "Les laures de Saint Gérasime et de Calamon," *Échos de l'Orient* 2 (1898–1899): 106–19 at 112–17; and Y. Hirschfeld, *The Judean Desert Monasteries in the Byzantine Period* (New Haven, 1992), 31, table 2, and xviii, map I. Leontius, *Vita Stephani Thaumaturgi* 24–25, 514A–B; 30, 515F; compare the Arabic version, 28.2 and 33.6, trans. 43 and 52. For the date of Stephen's death, 31 March 794, see ibid., x.

14   For details, see below, chapter 11, textual commentary on lines 31–32, here 32.

15   Vailhé, "Les laures de Saint Gérasime et de Calamon," 117–19; gift notice of the manuscript on 118.

16   Epiphanius Hagiopolites, *Descriptio Palaestinae* 11, 79.13, mentions the tomb of Gerasimus as situated in a fortification and refers to a monastery of Sts. Zosimas and Anthimos two "miles" east of it that could roughly fit the location of Kalamon. Unfortunately, the eighth- or ninth-century

A Mediterranean Church in the Early Middle Ages

final consideration powerfully reinforces this conclusion. That voluminous Life of St. Stephen the Wonder Worker, which refers so frequently to Kalamon and the other monasteries of the Judaean desert, never mentions the house of St. Gerasimus.[17] The most obvious explanation is that Kalamon had, by 800, already fused with St. Gerasimus. It is, in other words, much more likely that the Memorial accurately reflects the changing fate of two neighboring monasteries than that it has omitted a religious house here.

Leontius also mentions a monastery called Khoura before 794. It apparently involved one or more caves, and has left no other trace, so that Khoura looks like a minor establishment; in fact it has passed almost unnoticed by modern specialists as well.[18]

Finally, the Memorial does not explicitly record the monastery of Kastellion, three and a half kilometers from Mar Saba. Although it is conceivable that this house could have figured in the lacuna at this point in the roll (line 30), most specialists concur that the lacuna must, rather, have featured the famous monastery of Euthymius. That great house still flourished in this period and might well have boasted the large community of thirty monks the Memorial mentions at this point.[19] Kastellion was still functioning toward the middle of the eighth century, but its status by 800 is unclear. The Sabaite eyewitness of the massacre at his monastery mentions attacks on several other houses but says nothing about nearby Kastellion. His silence suggests that Kastellion may have been practically deserted

dates of Epiphanius's account and its composite parts are unclear. See A. Kazhdan, "Epiphanios Hagiopolites," *ODB* 1:714–15. Wilkinson, *Jerusalem Pilgrims*, 20, dates the core between 638 and 692, and another part after 717. Zosimas is presumably the hermit near the Jordan who converted the ex-prostitute in the legend of St. Mary the Egyptian. See, for example, *Synaxarium Constantinopolis* 578.8–580.4.

17 A search of the Greek text on the full text database of the *Acta Sanctorum* confirms this reader's memory of the absence.

18 Leontius, *Vita Stephani Thaumaturgi* 36, 518C and 40, 520B; compare the Arabic version, 30.4 and 31.2, trans. 46 and 48. It has passed almost unnoticed by modern specialists as well. Lamoreaux, *Life of Stephen*, 46 n. 151, identifies it with the monastery of "Hor" where St. Anthony Ruwah, who was martyred in 799 by Harun al Rashid, went looking for the "bishop of the monastery" according to his Arabic life, 7, ed. and trans. I. Dick, "La passion arabe de S. Antoine Ruwaḥ, néomartyr de Damas (†25 déc. 799)," *Le Muséon* 74 (1961): 109–33, here 131; compare Vailhé, "Répertoire alphabétique [1]," 526. However, the Ethiopian version and the Arabic abbreviation call this same monastery "Coreb" or "Chorib," that is, the monastery of Khorembe, known to have existed in late antiquity near Kalamon. See P. Peeters, "S. Antoine le Néo-martyr," *AB* 31 (1912): 410–50, 432 n. 1.

19 The fathers of the monastery of St. Euthymius alerted their colleagues at Mar Saba of impending violence in 797. See Stephen of Mar Saba, *Martyrium XX Sabaitarum* 18, 15.22–31. On the chronology used by this work, see below, chapter 8, note 18. Leontius, *Vita Stephani Thaumaturgi* 14, 509E, 17, 510B, and 176, 577F, also mentions the monastery of St. Euthymius; compare the Arabic version, 21.6, 22.1, and 77.2, trans. 34, 35, and 125, respectively. See chapter 11, textual commentary on lines 30–31.

because of the attacks of 797. Even were it not temporarily abandoned, Kastellion may simply have come to be considered a kind of dependency of the big neighboring monastery, for St. Sabas had founded Kastellion also; indeed, sometime before 794, a holy man of Mar Saba had been concerned to correct the wayward ways of one of Kastellion's (former?) monks.[20]

In sum, unlike the omission of the episcopal see Diospolis, there is no unequivocal evidence that the Frankish envoys missed a significant community in the main monastic centers of Judaea and the Jordan Valley. Moreover, the fact that the report confesses failure to obtain data concerning the two houses of St. Stephen's near Jericho and Pharan (lines 34–35) strongly suggests that it aimed at a complete accounting. Figures are inexplicably lacking for a convent of women reported in Tiberias and for the clergy attached to the episcopal see of Neapolis (lines 41 and 46). Beyond these cases, we seem to have as complete an accounting as the early ninth century could produce.

2. Numbers and Populations of Palestinian Religious Houses

The lacunae in the text where the roll is damaged nevertheless pose a more serious problem. How many institutions disappeared with the lost edge of the roll, and how might that affect our overall picture? For Jerusalem, happily, there is no loss whatsoever. Tables 2.3–2.5 summarize the complete data on the personnel of the Christian religious establishments in and around the Holy City, beginning with the data on the Holy Sepulcher.

For the regions outside of Jerusalem, as table 2.6 shows, the enumeration has been lost or is unspecified for six or seven of the twenty one establishments discussed in the Memorial, that is, 28.5 or 33 percent.[21] The two certain monaster-

---

20 Leontius, *Vita Stephani Thaumaturgi* 83, 536B–C, and 131, 556A–B. In the former passage, a monk describes how the wayward monk had been with him when the narrator was (then) practicing the monastic life at Kastellion ("Τὸν μονήρη βίον . . . ἐν τῇ εὐαγεῖ μονῇ τοῦ Καστελλίου μετηρχόμην"), which certainly leaves open whether he was still doing so when he told the story. Compare the Arabic version, 45.2–3, trans. 71 (which renders the verb in the present and so changes the meaning "I practice the monastic life in the monastery of Kastellion . . ."). The second passage explains that monk's contact with Stephen by Stephen's retreat then to caves of Kastellion but makes no reference to a monastic community: rather, it simply identifies the caves in which St. Stephen was staying as those of Kastellion. The opening section of the Life, which survives only in the Arabic version, indicates that Kastellion was already declining around 750, if we may judge from the fact that at that date Stephen's uncle was made abbot of both Kastellion and Mar George of the Cave simultaneously (ibid., 9.3, p. 10). On Kastellion in general, see Vailhé, "Répertoire alphabétique [1]," 522–23 and, for its "relatively small" late antique structures, Hirschfeld, *Judean Desert Monasteries*, 46–49, and 52.

21 It is also at least possible that the lacuna at the end of line 36 which interrupts the description of the shrine of the Lord's Leap, a mile outside of Nazareth, enumerated personnel at that shrine and that the monastery of the Virgin whose monks are counted at the beginning of line 37 repre-

TABLE 2.3   Personnel of the Holy Sepulcher complex, about 808

Function and station	Priests	Deacons	Subdeacons	Canons	Monks	Other[a]
				Personnel		
General staff	9	14	6	23	41	
Custodians Sepulcher	2					
Custodians Calvary	1					
Custodians Chalice	2					
Custodians Cross, Face-Cloth	1	1				
Synkellos	1					
Total	16	15	6	23	41	61

Grand total of all personnel: 162[b]

[a]See table 2.4.   [b]The *Breve* explicitly excludes the three hostels from this enumeration.

ies that today are lacking numbers of monks were significant ones, the Old Lavra, also known as the monastery of Chariton, and the monastery of Choziba; Charlemagne's envoys were unable to obtain figures for two more monasteries near Jericho and gave none for the convent in Tiberias. Hypothetically, the religious establishment at Cana that figured in the lacuna could also have been a monastery but, if so, numerically it was likely not as large.[22] The size of the convent at Tiberias and the community at Neapolis are not specified. In their late antique heyday, the monasteries of Chariton and Choziba may have reached some forty to sixty monks at most.[23] They probably only decreased in size in the early Middle Ages.

---

sents a separate shrine, which would mean that we are lacking data on one more church. See chapter 11, textual commentary on these lines.

22   The restitution of *monachi* by Tobler and Molinier in the lacuna in line 37 of the Memorial is purely hypothetical. Wilkinson, *Jerusalem Pilgrims*, 291–92, mentions a monastery there, the sole evidence for which is Epiphanius. The text of Epiphanius, *Descriptio Palaestinae* 12, 81.12–16 with the apparatus, preserved in the Jerusalem manuscript does document an early medieval monastery. According to A. Külzer, this manuscript, Jerusalem, Patriarchike Bibliotheke, Tou hagiou Taphou, 97, reflects a text composed between 638 and 900, so we cannot be certain the monastery was active about 808. See *Peregrinatio graeca in Terram Sanctam: Studien zu Pilgerführern und Reisebeschreibungen über Syrien, Palästina und den Sinai aus byzantinischer und metabyzantinischer Zeit* (Frankfurt am Main, 1994), 14–17.

23   For rough estimates of the size of the communities based on the archaeological evidence, see Hirschfeld, *Judean Desert Monasteries*, 23 and 36. In view of the rest of the findings of this chapter,

TABLE 2.4 Details of other personnel
of the Holy Sepulcher, about 808

Function	Quantity
fragelites	13
candle bearers	12
patriarchal servants	17
praepositi	2
accountants	2
notaries	2
cellarers	2
treasurer	1
fountain man	1
porters	9
Total	61

As table 2.6 indicates, the largest of the typical communities, excluding the traditionally greatest houses of St. Sabas and St. Theodosius, counted about 35 monks; the smallest, 8.

From these numbers we can gain a rough sense of how many monks are missing from the damaged section. Estimating the missing values from the average of the attested sizes of communities in the Judaean desert (excluding the two giants) at least gives a rough idea of the likely order of magnitude of the total of religious communities of monasteries, convents, and cathedrals outside the Holy City.[24] Extrapolating from the known community sizes allows us to hypothesize

it seems unlikely that St. Chariton's would have been the rare Judaean monastery that was larger in the early Middle Ages than in late antiquity. Theophanes, *Chronographia* AM 6301, 1:484.16–17, is likely therefore referring to the spiritual greatness rather than the physical size when he ranks St. Chariton with St. Sabbas as "the two great lavras" (τῶν δύο μεγάλων λαυρῶν). The epithet *mega* or *megiston* appears to be a conventional one for Chariton: see below, chapter 11, textual commentary on lines 29–30, note 15. Should this assumption prove incorrect, the numbers and proportion of Judaean monks within the overall make up of the Holy Land church would be somewhat larger than I have estimated.

24 For the purpose of estimating the total monastic population, including the disproportionately huge St. Sabas and St. Theodosius—respectively, some four times and twice as large as the next biggest monastery in this group—would clearly skew the average unduly. The average size of the remaining recorded male monastic communities outside Jerusalem and the bishoprics can be calculated as 19.8 (i.e., the total 139 monks and abbots documented for St. Euthymius, 31; St. Gerasimus, 11; St. John the Baptist, 36; Nazareth, 12; Leap of the Lord/Virgin, 8; Heptapegon, 10; Sinai, 31; and divided by seven). For the bishoprics, the average size of the three communities of Tiberias, Mount Tabor, and Sebastia is 24, which we can hypothesize as the size of the missing community

TABLE 2.5 Ecclesiastical personnel of all Jerusalem churches, about 808

Church or location	Priests	Monks	Nuns	Other[a]	Total	Site no.
Holy Sepulcher	16	41		105	162	1
Holy Zion			2	17	19	2
St. Peter's				5	5	3
Praetorium				5	5	4
St. Mary Nea				12	12	5
St. Tathelea				1	1	6
St. George				2	2	7
St. Mary of the Sheep Pool			25	5	30	8
St. Stephen				2	2	9
Virgin's Tomb[b]		6	15	13	34	10
St. Leontius	1				1	11
St. James	1				1	12
Holy 40 ("St. Forty")	3				3	13
St. Christopher	1				1	14
St. Aquilena	1				1	15
St. Quiricus ("Cirycus")	1				1	16
St. Stephen	3				3	17
St. Dometius	1				1	18
St. John's birthplace	2				2	19
St. Theodore	2				2	20
St. Sergius	1				1	21
Sts. Cosmas and Damian, birthplace	3				3	22
Sts. Cosmas and Damian, where they healed	1				1	23
Ascension shrine				3	3	24
Teaching of the Disciples	1	3			4	25
Church of the Virgin				2	2	26
Hermits		35			35	
Convent, location unspecified			26		26	27
Sts. Peter and Paul in Bisanteo		35			35	28
St. Lazarus in Bethany	1				1	29
St. John, held by Armenians		6			6	30
Subtotal	23	85	68	67	243[c]	
Total, Sites 1 and 2–30	39	126	68	172	405[d]	

[a]This includes undifferentiated ecclesiastics, for example, at Holy Zion (no. 2), "including priests and clerics." [b]Apparently a double monastery. [c]Not including the 15 lepers.
[d]This grand total does not include either the patriarch and personnel of the three hostels (which the Breve explicitly excludes) or the 15 lepers cared for at St. Stephen (no. 17; see note c).

that monasteries of the Judaean desert alone comprised approximately 381 monks and abbots.[25] Using the same procedure to estimate the number of monks missing from the possible monastery at Cana, and totaling the figures for the various regions and churches, we can extrapolate that, beyond the 380 cenobitic monks positively documented in Judaea, Galilee, and Sinai, their total number in the entire Holy Land outside of Jerusalem may have reached as high as 544.[26] To the former figure should be added the three stylites of Bethlehem and Neapolis, for a documented total of 383 recorded monks, as tables 2.6 indicates, and an estimated total of some 547 monks. Adding the estimated 22 nuns missing from the entry for Tiberias gives a total maximum estimated monastic population of 569 outside of Jerusalem. Cathedral (some of whom were monks) and other clergy are also positively documented. Including the 4 bishops and a priest, therefore, as well as the cathedral clergy not already assigned to the maximal estimation of monks, and increasing that total by the 24 extrapolated for the missing Neapolis figures and by the same number for the apparently missing cathedral clergy of Diospolis, and one bishop, which the envoys seem to have missed, yields a final estimated maximum total of 631 religious of all descriptions for the entire Holy Land outside of Jerusalem.[27] This estimate may err somewhat on the high side, but it nevertheless provides a compelling order of magnitude.

While the roll's snapshot of churches outside Jerusalem does suggest a significant and, in some respects, vital Christian institutional life in Palestine at the moment the census was taken, the picture looks more somber when it is viewed in a broader chronological perspective. Two pieces of information set the tone, and that tone appears to harmonize with Einhard's judgment of the poverty of Christians living under the Muslims (chapter 1.1). The first is the failure or inability

---

of Neapolis and, probably, that of Lydda. For the convent in Tiberias, we have no choice but to use the Jerusalem figures. That might skew the hypothetical size of this convent upward, although it is also true that recent archaeology shows that Tiberias was flourishing at this time. See A. Walmsley, *Early Islamic Syria: An Archaeological Assessment* (London, 2007), 77–79. Assuming that the two female recluses at Holy Zion were a special case, the three convents average 22 nuns; including Holy Zion would drop the average to 17.

25 That is, 301 positively attested religious (i.e., 70 + 150 + 30 + 10 + 35 monks and 6 abbots) in the Judaean houses (table 2.6, nos. **32–40**), plus allowing for a maximum hypothetical 20 monks each for the two damaged Judaean entries, and the same number for the monasteries of Jericho and Pharan, where the envoys could not obtain information, that is, 301 + (20 × 4) = 381.

26 That is, the total of male cenobite monks outside of Jerusalem (380) documented in table 2.7, nos. **31–51**, plus the estimated average population of 20 monks each from the four Judaean monasteries which lack figures, and an additional estimated 20 monks for the establishment at Cana: 380 + 80 + 20 = 480. Finally, we can add the maximal possible number of monks (64) present among the undifferentiated personnel of Bethlehem (13), Tiberias (28), and Sebastia (23) that explicitly included monks, to arrive at the total of 544 as the estimated maximal number of male cenobites.

27 That is, 569 monks, stylites and nuns plus 5 bishops and 1 priest with 8 other documented ecclesiastics + (24 estimated ecclesiastics × 2) = 631. See table 2.7.

A Mediterranean Church in the Early Middle Ages

to repair Justinian's great Nea church in Jerusalem and the decayed state of the shrine of John the Baptist in Sebastia (lines 50–51 and 43–44, respectively). Although one could attribute their disrepair to Muslim strictures on Christian church building, the second indication—the state of the bishoprics of the Holy Land—confirms the general diagnosis. Late antique Palaestina Prima and Palaestina Secunda boasted some forty bishoprics. The Carolingian survey mentions only five, including Jerusalem (or six, including Diospolis), and one of the five had already been transferred to the monastery on Mount Tabor (table 2.6).[28] Are the others merely neglected by our Carolingian informants, or did they no longer exist as functioning ecclesiastical units by about 808? The fact that the surveyors report failure in documenting certain monasteries inclines me to think they did not miss much. The jejune evidence of the lead seals of Holy Land churches points in the same direction, for the sees documented by seals antedating the Crusades coincide with sees mentioned in the roll.[29]

The monasteries show a similar picture. At the outset of the last century, Siméon Vailhé used mainly written evidence to produce an inventory of all monastic establishments in the Holy Land. The result comprises 137 entries for the whole ancient and medieval history of the Holy Land.[30] This list has been criticized for erroneously counting some houses twice;[31] nevertheless, the numbers in late antiquity were big. For the Judaean desert alone, the most recent study, based on archaeological *and* written evidence, claims about sixty-five monasteries.[32]

28 On the bishoprics, see, for example, the list in F. M. Abel, *Géographie de la Palestine* (Paris, 1933), 2:200–201. M. Levy-Rubin, "The Reorganisation of the Patriarchate of Jerusalem during the Early Muslim Period," *ARAM Periodical* 15 (2003): 197–226, uses the subsequent episcopal lists to argue for a very large expansion of episcopal appointments, most of whom had no real pastoral charge, after the Carolingian survey.

29 The absence from this period of any reliably dated lead seals of Holy Land bishoprics, or monasteries for that matter, points in the same direction. The only possible contradictory evidence is a seal of a Christopher, metropolitan of Scythopolis, which has been uncertainly dated by its early twentieth-century editor to the seventh or eighth century, a date about which Laurent is quite reserved, since he did not see the seal or a reliable photograph of it. See *Le corpus des sceaux de l'Empire byzantin* (Paris, 1963–81), 5.2:401, no. 1570. Even if the date were reliable, the range does not imply the bishopric was still occupied in the ninth century: indeed, we now know that downtown Scythopolis, or Bet Shean, where a major shopping complex was built under caliph Hisham (724–743), was comprehensively destroyed by the terrible earthquake of 749. Y. Tsafrir and G. Foerster, "Urbanism at Scythopolis-Bet Shean in the Fourth to Seventh Centuries," *DOP* 51 (1997): 85–146, here 138–39; compare Walmsley, *Early Islamic Syria*, 87–88. The institutions of later but still pre-Crusade prelates documented by seals all figure on the roll. See the seals of a bishop of Tiberias from the early eleventh century in Laurent, *Corpus*, 5.2:403–4, no. 1572. Among monasteries, there is a mid-eleventh-century seal of St. Sabas, ibid., no. 1577; and a tenth- or eleventh-century seal of St. Euthymius, ibid., no. 1582.

30 Vailhé, "Répertoire alphabétique [1]," and, "Répertoire alphabétique des monastères de Palestine [2 and 3]," *ROC* 5 (1900): 19–48, 272–92.

31 Hirschfeld, "List of the Byzantine Monasteries," 4.

32 Idem, *Judean Desert Monasteries*, 10.

TABLE 2.6   Total explicitly recorded religious personnel of the churches
and monasteries of the Holy Land

Church	Bishop	Priests	Cenobitic Monks[a]	Hermits/Stylites	Nuns	Others[b]	Attested total	Site number
Jerusalem and environs		39	91	35	68	172	405	1–30
Judaean sites outside Jerusalem								
Bethlehem: Nativity and stylites			?	2[c]		15	17	31
Monastery of St. Theodosius			71				71	32
Monastery of St. Sabas			150				150	33
Monastery of St. Chariton (Old Lavra)			1 + ?				1	34
Monastery of St. Euthymius			31				31	35
Monastery of Choziba			1 + ?				1	36
Monastery of St. Gerasimus			11				11	37
Monastery of St. John the Baptist			36				36	38
Monastery of St. Stephen near Jericho			unkn				0	39
Monastery of Mount Pharan			unkn				0	40
subtotals Judaean sites			301	2		15	318	
Galilean sites								
Nazareth			12[d]				12	41
Monastery of the Virgin of the Leap of the Lord			8				8	42
Cana			?				0	43
Heptapegon			10				10	44
Twelve Thrones		1				2	3	45
Tiberias	1		?		unspec	30[b]	31	46–47
Mount Tabor	1		18				19	48
subtotals Galilean sites	2	1	48			32	83	
Samaritan sites								
Sebastia (Sebaste)	1		?			25[b]	26	49
Neapolis	1			1[c]		unspec[b]	2	50
subtotals Samaritan sites	2			1		25	28	
Egyptian site								
Sinai			31				31	51
Subtotals outside Jerusalem	4	1	380	3	?	72	460	
Totals, entire Holy Land	4	40	471	38	68	244	865	

Note: ? = number missing due to lacuna; unkn = text admits not knowing the number; unspec = text does not specify a number   [a]Including abbots.
[b]Includes undifferentiated totals, for example, of monks, or of monks and canons or clerics.   [c]Stylites.
[d]Accepting de Rossi's likely suggestion that the substantial community at Nazareth was a monastery (see chapter 11, textual commentary on lines 35–36).

TABLE 2.7 Total estimated religious personnel of the churches and monasteries of the Holy Land
(estimates or numbers including estimates are in italics)

Church	Bishop	Priests	Cenobitic Monks[a]	Est. max. cenobites	Hermits/Stylites	Nuns	Others	Est. total	Site number
Jerusalem and environs	*1*	39	91		35	68	172	*406*	**1–30**
Judaean sites outside Jerusalem									
Bethlehem: Nativity and stylites				*13*	2[b]		2	*17*	**31**
Monastery of St. Theodosius			71					71	**32**
Monastery of St. Sabas			150					150	**33**
Monastery of St. Chariton (Old Lavra)			1	*20*				*21*	**34**
Monastery of St. Euthymius			31					31	**35**
Monastery of Choziba			1	*20*				*21*	**36**
Monastery of St. Gerasimus			11					11	**37**
Monastery of St. John the Baptist			36					36	**38**
Monastery of St. Stephen near Jericho				*20*				*20*	**39**
Monastery of Mount Pharan				*20*				*20*	**40**
subtotals Judaean sites			301	*93*	2	0	15	*398*	
Galilean sites									
Nazareth			12[a]					12	**41**
Monastery of the Virgin at the Leap of the Lord			8					8	**42**
Cana				*20*				20	**43**
Heptapegon			10					10	**44**
Twelve Thrones		1					2	3	**45**
Tiberias	1			*28*		22	2	*53*	**46–47**
Mount Tabor	1		18					19	**48**
subtotals Galilean sites	2	1	48	*48*	0	22	4	*125*	
Samaritan sites									
Sebastia (Sebaste)	1			*23*			2	*26*	**49**
Neapolis	1				1[b]		24	26	**50**
subtotals Samaritan sites	2			*23*	1		26	*52*	
Egyptian sites									
Sinai			31					31	**51**
Non-Jerusalem sites missing from the roll									
Lydda	*1*						24	*25*	**51**
Subtotals outside Jerusalem	5	1	380	*164*	3	22	56	*631*	
Totals, entire Holy Land	6	40	471	*164*	38	90	228	*1,037*	

Note: Restored figures are indicated by italics.
[a]Accepting de Rossi's likely suggestion that the substantial community at Nazareth was a monastery (see chapter 11, textual commentary on lines 35–36).   [b]Stylites
N.B. The 15 lepers cared for by the church of Jerusalem have not been included in the personnel tallies.

Although some were very small indeed and not all were functioning simultaneously, comparison with the nine monasteries the roll documents in the same general area again proves a drastic contraction of monasticism after late antiquity.

It has been observed that, of approximately fifty monasteries of the Judaean desert whose names are known, "only six or seven have preserved their original names in one form or another" in Arabic.[33] The loss of even the names of the others in the local inhabitants' collective memory witnesses in yet another way the decline of the monasteries after the Islamic conquest. In fact, as table 2.8 shows, seven of the nine Judaean desert monasteries listed in the Memorial are precisely those whose names are more or less well preserved as Arabic place names, most of which allude in some way to a monastery.[34]

So too it is no surprise that in 818, when Theodore Stoudite, the embattled Byzantine champion of icons, sought support from the Christian religious communities of Palestine, he decided to send letters to the patriarch, to two monks of Jerusalem itself whom he had met previously when they had visited Constantinople, and to four monasteries of the Judaean desert that figure equally in the Memorial: St. Sabas, St. Theodosius, St. Chariton, and St. Euthymius. The abbot of Stoudios in Constantinople was in a position to know, and he presumably considered these the major houses of the Holy Land.[35]

The scale of the decline of monasticism in the Judaean desert is breathtaking. Of some sixty-five late antique monasteries, only nine seem to have existed in the early ninth century. This implies an overall decline of approximately 88 percent. Recent study of the fate of monastic institutions in Constantinople may put this collapse in perspective. There, the total number of monasteries has been estimated to have dropped from between 150 and 200 houses about AD 600 to around 50 a century later. The rate of decline thus may have been between 66 and 75 percent over the intervening years.[36] If the monastic decline in Constantinople in

---

33 Idem, "List of the Byzantine Monasteries," 2–3.

34 For the Arabic toponyms, see ibid., respectively, 26–28, 31–32, 10, 16–18, 29–31, 18–19, and 24–26; 35–36; 6. The derivation from the saints' names is clear in the case of Dosi, Saba, and Khureitun. I am indebted to Prof. Deborah Tor for an illuminating philological discussion of the Arabic *deir* (or *dayr*), which, in that part of the world, routinely refers to a monastery or Christian settlement. See, in general, D. Sourdel, "Dayr" *EI² Online*, consulted 17 October 2006.

35 Theodore Stoudite, *Epistulae* 276, 409–12; *Ep.* 279, 419.11–15; *Ep.* 277, 412.1–5, with apparatus on line 1; *Ep.* 278, 415.1–5, with apparatus on line 1, respectively. They seem to have been bundled with a letter to the patriarch of Alexandria (*Ep.* 275): see Fatouros's comment, ibid., 1:319*.

36 The valuable estimates come from P. Hatlie, *The Monks and Monasteries of Constantinople, ca. 350–850* (Cambridge, 2007), 219. They are based on his tabulation of Constantinopolitan monasteries between 350 and 850, ibid., 457–72, offering a more complete foundation for such an appraisal than the earlier effort of P. Charanis, "The Monk as an Element of Byzantine Society," *DOP* 25 (1971): 61–84, here 65, founded on the earlier historical topographical work of Raymond Janin. Hatlie considers Charanis's estimate to be more pessimistic than his own, although the numbers Hatlie adduces imply, like Charanis, a maximum decline of 75 percent.

TABLE 2.8 Monasteries in the Judaean Desert
recorded by the Memorial that have left traces
in Arabic place names

Monastery	Arabic toponym
St. Theodosius	Deir Dosi
St. Sabas	Deir Mar Saba
St. Chariton (Palaia Lavra)	Khan Khureitūn
St. Euthymius	Khan el-Ahmar
Choziba	Deir Mar Jiryis
St. Gerasimus	Deir Ḥajla–ʿEin Ḥajla
St. John Baptist	Qaṣr el-Yahūd
St. Stephen, Jericho	*none*
Pharan	ʿEin Fara

fact approached the vertiginous drop that indubitably occurred in the territory conquered by the Arabs, it would add a new dimension to the debate over the extent of the ancient capital's urban collapse. Conversely, so extreme a contraction in Constantinople might incline us to think that the decline in the numbers of monasteries which archaeology and the Basel roll document in the Holy Land was an acute manifestation of a broader phenomenon of ecclesiastical contraction across the eastern regions of the ancient world. Caution is certainly warranted, insofar as the argument about the numbers of monasteries at Constantinople has thus far been obliged to rest on the silence of a sometimes tenuous base of written sources.[37] Nevertheless, there can be little doubt that the general trend of numbers of monastic houses in the imperial capital was downward, and the qualitative evidence from the period seems equally to reflect a decline in the dynamism and standards of Constantinopolitan monasticism.[38]

What is true for the total number of Palestinian monasteries holds also for their size. St. Sabas had about 150 monks at an early stage and is thought to have gotten bigger, probably approaching 250 to 300 monks in the sixth century.[39] Archaeology seems to confirm the statement of the Life of Theodosius attributed to Theodore, bishop of Petra, that his house counted over 400 monks.[40] Even if that number were exaggerated, the community had clearly shrunk substantially to

---

37 Charanis, "Monk," 66.

38 Hatlie, *Monks and Monasteries*, 219–52.

39 Hirschfeld, *Judean Desert Monasteries*, 25 with note 21; 255. J. Patrich, *Sabas, Leader of Palestinian Monasticism: A Comparative Study in Eastern Monasticism, Fourth to Seventh Centuries* (Washington, D.C., 1995), 67, deduces the sixth-century figure from the archaeological and historical evidence.

40 Hirschfeld, *Judean Desert Monasteries*, 8–79; compare 265 n. 41. The number comes from Theodore of Petra, *Vita Theodosii coenobiarchae* (BHG 1776), 46.5–9.

reach the 70 monks of the early ninth century. A recent study considers that, at its late antique peak, Judaea's six large monasteries would have comprised from 100 to 400 monks, averaging about 150 monks; its twelve middling ones, about 50; and its twenty-five small ones, about 20.[41] A comparison with the size cohorts around 808 enumerated in table 2.8 points to a significant ratcheting down of the size of communities by the ninth century. In other words, in late antiquity, the monasteries of the Judaean desert alone may have boasted as many as 2,200 to about 3,000 monks, including hermits.[42] In aggregate terms, this is a far cry from the high total of 381 monks we can estimate for the same area about 808. By the ninth century, the monastic population of the Judaean desert had dropped to less than one-fifth (13–17 percent) of its late antique peak.

Some little-noticed but potentially valuable figures shed light on numbers of women monastics in late antiquity. When the Persians conquered Jerusalem in 614, they massacred many thousands of religious and laypeople who had taken refuge in the Holy City. Based on the report of the couple who organized the burials afterward, the contemporary account enumerates in some detail the bodies collected in various parts of the city and its environs. It claims that the total number of individuals buried exceeded 60,000.[43] According to this witness, the Persians removed 400 nuns from the convent on the Mount of Olives and raped them; some they also killed.[44] If this figure is plausible, it would signify that one convent in the early seventh century had almost six times the total population of Jerusalem nuns in the eighth century. Whatever we may think of these figures, we seem to be on rather solid ground with the excellent biography of Patriarch John the Almsgiver of Alexandria written by his close associates John Moschus and Sophronius of Jerusalem and known today through a pre-Metaphrastic epitome and another independently abbreviated version.[45] This work, which abounds in economic information, details how the patriarch used his considerable wealth to relieve the suffering of the survivors of the Persian conquest of Jerusalem, both

---

41 Hirschfeld, *Judean Desert Monasteries*, 78–79.

42 Ibid., 79, a figure that Patrich (*Sabas*, 9 n. 6) seems to imply might be on the low side. Patrich himself (9) estimates the monastic population of the Judaean desert before the great expansion of the sixth century at around 1,000–1,500 monks.

43 The surviving Arabic and Georgian versions of the contemporary Greek treatise on the fall of Jerusalem attributed to a monk of Mar Saba, variously identified as Strategius or Eustratius in the versions, enumerate over 60,000 burials of cadavers collected in specific monuments and sites from all over the city and its immediate environs. The treatise has long been recognized as an exceptionally precious witness to the topography of Jerusalem. See, in general, P. Peeters, *Recherches d'histoire et de philologie orientales*, SubsHag 27 (Brussels, 1951), 78–116. *Expugnationis Hierosolymae AD 614 recensiones Arabicae*, Recension A, 23.1–44, trans. 36–37; compare *La prise de Jérusalem par les Perses en 614*, 23.1–44, trans. 51–53.

44 *Expugnatio Hierosolymae*, A, 12.2, 14; compare *Prise de Jérusalem*, 12.1, 20.

45 See above, chapter 1, note 35.

A Mediterranean Church in the Early Middle Ages

TABLE 2.9 Size cohorts of Holy Land
monastic communities, about 808

Monks or nuns	Number of communities
100+	1
50–99	1
30–49	5
20–29	3
10–19	4
9 or fewer	4

Note: This tally accepts the identification of the community at
Nazareth (12) as monastic and counts the 6 monks and 15 nuns at the
Virgin's Tomb as one community of 21 religious. Note that map 2 does
not distinguish the different communities and sizes in Jerusalem.

those still in the Holy Land and those who had fled to Alexandria.[46] To the Holy
Land he sent enough money to redeem around a thousand nuns who survived
the horrific massacres but who had been taken captive by the Persians; he had the
women registered and restored to monasteries.[47] Although most of this section
of the Life of John concerns Jerusalem, the context could conceivably refer to the
entire Holy Land. Nevertheless, a total of nearly 1,000 who might have survived
the fall of Jerusalem is not at all implausible; just seventeen years earlier, Gregory I
had reported that 3,000 nuns were enrolled in the documentation of the Roman
church.[48] By this date Rome was not likely any more populous than Jerusalem.[49]
In any case, whether the ransomed nuns were from Jerusalem alone or from all
over the Holy Land, the comparison with the ninth century looks stark, for the
reported survivors amounted to nearly fifteen times the certain number of nuns in
Jerusalem about 808 and nearly twelve times our estimate of the total population
of women religious across the entire Holy Land (see below, chapter 3.3).

Another figure also derived from the lost Life of John the Almsgiver points in
the same direction. Although it is not entirely clear whether the number refers to
Palestinian refugees in the Egyptian metropolis or, possibly, to poorer clerics of
Alexandria, the abbreviated version of the Life states that 300 priests and deacons

46 This is so despite the fact that the pre-Metaphrastic epitomator displays a typical hostility
to numbers. See E. Lappa-Zizicas, "Un épitomé inédit de la Vie de S. Jean l'Aumonier par Jean
et Sophronios," *AB* 88 (1970): 265–78. The stylistically less ambitious independent abbreviation
proves that the lost Life contained even more concrete and numerical information.
47 *Vita Iohannis Eleemosynarii* (BHG 887v) 9, 23.25–28.
48 *Registrum* 7, 23, June 597, 477.86–98.
49 For example, J. Durliat estimates Rome's population at around 60,000 in 530, before the devastation of the Gothic wars. See *De la ville antique à la ville byzantine. Le problème des subsistances*,
Collection de l'École française de Rome, 136 (Rome, 1990), 110–23.

received financial support from the wealthy patriarch.[50] Even if the roll's lack of detail precludes us from obtaining an exact total of priests and deacons for the entire Holy Land about 808, the more detailed breakdown it offers for Jerusalem indicates a total of probably somewhat more than 71 priests and deacons for the nearly four out of ten recorded and estimated ecclesiastics (405 of 1,037, i.e., 39.1 percent—leaving aside the 15 lepers whose care by the Church was also budgeted in the Breve) in Palestine residing in the Holy City.[51] Whether the 300 subsidized priests and deacons from the Life of John the Almsgiver represented the local Alexandrian clergy or the fraction of Jerusalem or indeed Palestinian clergy who had escaped the horrific massacres and reached Alexandria, that number is nearly seven times the approximate total of comparably ranking clergy in Jerusalem about 808. The seventh-century figure again underscores the stark difference between the size of the priestly and diaconal cohorts of the great late antique churches of the region and that of the early Abbasid Holy Land. That stark difference also provides food for thought about the differing human numbers and dynamics of the ecclesiastical groups that produced and were presumably the primary audience for so much of the Christian literature written and read in late antiquity in contrast to the smaller world of the early Middle Ages. It invites also to reflect on the suitability and character of the new and old physical structures in which these differing populations served.

Whatever aspect of the Holy Land church we examine, decline is unmistakable relative to the late antique peak. The causes were multiple. Many scholars concur that the arrival of the Justinianic cycle of plagues caused or accelerated general demographic decline in the affected areas, which certainly included Palestine.[52] The seventh-century contraction of monastic houses in Constantinople has

---

50 *Vita Iohannis Eleemosynarii* (BHG 887v) 6, 21.34–22.13, and esp., *Vita Iohannis Eleemosynarii* (BHG 887w) 6, 275. Lappa-Zizicas ("Un épitomé inédit," 268–69) favors the interpretation that these measures in general concerned Alexandria's suffragans and, in the case of the 300 priests and deacons, the clergy of Alexandria itself. The Greek is indeed difficult—the editions of each version are based on only one manuscript—but the context seems to argue for a refugee population. In any case, 300 does not seem too high for the seventh-century Alexandrian clergy, in light of the numbers available from Constantinople (see table 2.1), and makes the same point about the reduced size of the Orthodox religious population of the Holy Land in the ninth century.

51 The Breve explicitly identifies 39 priests and 15 deacons. Allowing a minimum of 2 for the entries for shrines whose personnel is simply listed as "including priests and clerics" (inter presbiteris et clericis)—except of course for the church of St. Tathelea, which has only 1 person on its staff—yields an additional minimum of 17 priests (see tables 2.3 and 2.5).

52 Initial outbreak in Palestine: John of Ephesus, *Historiae ecclesiasticae fragmenta* Fragmenta E–F, 229.17–231.20. Compare the English translation of this passage as preserved in Syriac in *The Chronicle of Zuqnīn, Parts III and IV, AD 488–775*, 96–99. On the devastating impact there, see C. Dauphin, *La Palestine byzantine. Peuplement et populations*, BAR International Series 726 (Oxford, 1998), 514–18; and, in general, the papers in L. K. Little, ed., *Plague and the End of Antiquity: The Pandemic of 541–750* (Cambridge, 2007). A dissenting voice is J. Magness, *The Archaeol-*

also been viewed as reflecting at least partly the broader demographic contraction of Byzantine society and particularly of the capital.[53] In the 790s, a leading Palestinian ascetic ascribed a sharp decline in the quality of the local monastic observance to the devastation of the terrible earthquake of 749, and the destruction may have lessened the numbers of monks directly or indirectly.[54] The wave of Palestinian refugees that inundated Alexandria around 614 and the subsequent crisis among those who stayed in the Holy Land are manifest from the exceptional measures that John the Almsgiver devised to deal with both aspects of the problem.[55] We have seen how gravely the churches of Jerusalem are reported to have suffered under the Persian occupation, and the impact on the monasteries of the Judaean desert seems to have been equally heavy.[56]

Whether the refugees ever returned to Palestine or new recruits ever took the place of the killed and enslaved is unclear. The effects of the Muslim conquest, particularly under the Umayyads, have been variously judged.[57] Although it is not easy to disentangle immigration triggered by the Persian devastation from that sparked by the Arab conquest some twenty years later, there is no denying that one or both explain the seventh-century surge in the permanent migration of Levantine and especially Holy Land religious to the distant safety of Africa and Italy, a migration that resulted in the founding of the new monastery of St. Sabas in Rome.[58] And the flow seems not to have stopped even around 800.[59]

---

ogy of the Early Islamic Settlement in Palestine (Winona Lake, 2003), 196, 208, who argues that the details of the archaeological evidence do not support demographic decline in the later sixth and early seventh century such as has been ascribed notably to the plague. Compare also Walmsley, *Early Islamic Syria*, 36–37, and further references, above, chapter 1, note 1.

53 Hatlie, *Monks and Monasteries*, 216.

54 See below, chapter 8.2, note 22.

55 See, in addition to the passage discussed above, note 50, *Vita Iohannis Eleemosynarii* (BHG 887v) 9, 23.3–24.2; 11, 24.15–20; 12, 24.31–36; compare also 14, 25.17–21, along with the additional details in the *Vita* (BHG 887w) 9, p. 277; 11–12, p. 278.

56 See the summary account in Wilkinson, *Jerusalem Pilgrims*, 14–17, using the detailed description of the *Expugnatio Hierosolymae AD 614*. On the Persian massacres and the dispersion and restoration of the monastic communities, see Patrich, *Sabas*, 326–28; on the negative effects on the Judaean monasteries, Schick, *Christian Communities of Palestine*, 96.

57 Very negative for monasticism (Hirschfeld, *Judean Desert Monasteries*, 16–17) but not directly negative for pilgrimage (Wilkinson, *Jerusalem Pilgrims*, 17–21). The uncertain security conditions under the new regime encouraged a contraction of the outlying parts of the complex toward the central establishment of Mar Saba, and a decline in the number of monks. See Patrich, *Sabas*, 328–29.

58 Rome presents the clearest picture. See J.-M. Sansterre, *Les moines grecs et orientaux à Rome aux époques byzantine et carolingienne*, Académie royale de Belgique, Mémoires de la classe des lettres, Collection in 8°; 2nd ser., 66 (Brussels, 1983), 1:13–42; for some indirect but indubitable indicators of a Palestinian migration to Sicily and southern Italy, see M. McCormick, "The Imperial Edge: Italo-Byzantine Identity, Movement and Integration, A.D. 650–950," in *Studies on the Internal Diaspora of the Byzantine Empire*, ed. H. Ahrweiler and A. E. Laiou (Washington, D.C., 1998), 17–52, at 36–38.

59 See the story of Gregory Akritas, in McCormick, *Origins*, 197–98.

Furthermore, the debate about rates of conversion to Islam makes clear that, though opinions differ on the chronology, the trend was one of progressive conversion of Christians to Islam.[60] It has been little noticed that a Syrian apocalyptic writer of the late seventh century already testifies to the threat of apostasy weighing on local Christian communities at that early date.[61] Even if the absolute size of the population had remained the same, the Christian share in that population was at least beginning to diminish by 800, and so the local recruitment base for Christian institutions was necessarily contracting. In addition to the broader demographic and cultural contexts, a factor specific to the Holy Land reinforced the decline. Right from the beginning, Palestinian monasticism had been distinctively and deeply extraregional in its recruitment.[62] While individual monks certainly crossed the military and political lines separating Byzantium from the caliphate, the lasting hostility between the two powers surely hindered or discouraged the kind of large-scale involvement in the Holy Land of Constantinopolitans or residents of Asia Minor that we see from the fourth to the early seventh century.[63] And the Byzantine state, whence had flowed so much investment in Holy Land monuments and institutions, was economically but a shadow

---

60 R. W. Bulliet, *Conversion to Islam in the Medieval Period: An Essay in Quantitative History* (Cambridge, 1979), 104–15; with some updating: R. W. Bulliet, "Process and Status in Conversion and Continuity," in *Conversion and Continuity: Indigenous Christian Communities in Islamic Lands, Eighth to Eighteenth Centuries,* ed. M. Gervers and R. J. Bikhazi, Papers in Mediaeval Studies 9 (Toronto, 1990), 1–12; and R. W. Bulliet, "Conversion Stories in Early Islam," in ibid., 123–33. The critical discussion of M. G. Morony, "The Age of Conversions: A Reassessment," (ibid., 135–50), in the end confirms Bulliet's views. N. Levtzion, "Conversion to Islam in Syria and Palestine and the Survival of Christian Communities" (ibid., 289–311), offers some valuable insights into the broader process and phasing of the turn to Islam in the Holy Land. Schick (*Christian Communities of Palestine,* 158) generally confirms Bulliet's findings for Syria under the Umayyads. See also the general discussion in Eddé, Micheau, and Picard, *Communautés chrétiennes,* 160–70.

61 This part of Pseudo-Methodius's message was not retained in the near contemporary Latin translation, underscoring its specificity to the world that gave rise to the text. See H. Möhring, "Karl der Grosse und die Endkaiser-Weissagung: der Sieger über den Islam kommt aus dem Westen," in *Montjoie: Studies in Crusade History in Honour of Hans Eberhard Mayer,* ed. B. Z. Kedar, J. Riley-Smith, and R. Hiestand (Aldershot, 1997), 1–19, here 4, 5, and 10.

62 Hirschfeld, *Judean Desert Monasteries,* 12–13; J. Binns, *Ascetics and Ambassadors of Christ: The Monasteries of Palestine, 314–631* (Oxford, 1994), 91–95; and, with details, Dauphin, *La Palestine byzantine,* 158–65.

63 Thus the Stoudite monk Dionysius carried a letter from the Byzantine monastic leader Theodore Stoudite to the patriarch of Jerusalem in 818, and probably also the letters addressed to the monasteries of St. Sabas, St. Chariton, and two hagiopolitan monks, but seems to have had no intention of staying in the Holy Land. See Theodore Stoudite, *Ep.* 276, 409.81–12; compare 320*–23*; J. R. Martindale, ed., *Prosopography of the Byzantine Empire,* 1 *(641–867)* [CD-ROM] (Aldershot, 2001), "Dionysios 6," and F. Winkelmann and R.-J. Lilie, eds., *Prosopographie der mittelbyzantinischen Zeit* (Berlin, 1998), 1: no. 1346.

A Mediterranean Church in the Early Middle Ages

of its former self by around 800.[64] Only further research will indicate the extent to which the relative institutional decline of the Holy Land church stemmed from local, Christian demographic decline or redistribution and patterns of urban development detected in other areas of the late antique Levant. Certainly the disappearance of so many bishoprics is suggestive of significant developments in the towns. In any event, the dimensions of the change Charlemagne's inquest permits us to detect between about 600 and 800 are substantial. Beyond its importance in and of itself, that change casts a rare shaft of light on the homeside dimensions of the westward immigration of the Levantine elite that has hitherto been palpable chiefly in its lasting impact on Rome and its church and even on far-away England, as the biblical commentaries associated with Theodore of Tarsus and the school of Canterbury remind us.[65]

Yet it must be stressed that appraisal of this decline is affected by the terms of comparison. If there can be no question that the Holy Land church, in absolute terms, was greatly diminished as an institutional force with respect to the days of Justinian, that was equally true of virtually all Christian churches from Rome to the Levant. The decline and disappearance of Palestinian bishoprics seem generally comparable to those of the Balkans, if not to the less stark developments in Asia Minor over the same period, except that recovery occurred in both those areas.[66] If the churches of the Holy Land needed new roofs, many of those of the Byzantine empire were in an even worse state of disrepair: according to Charlemagne, his ambassadors had reported that some shrines there lacked roofs altogether.[67] Those of Rome and those of Lyons needed—and got—much reconstruction in the eighth century.[68] Certainly, whatever Charlemagne's ambassadors saw on their travels through the Byzantine Empire, the fortunes of monasticism improved dramatically at Constantinople in the course of the eighth and ninth centuries. The traditional vision of deep and far-reaching conflict between the eighth-century emperors and monks owes much to the monastic establishment's ideological repositioning after the collapse of the Iconoclast movement. More recent work makes clear that under Constantine V (741–775) monasticism in general did not suffer as drastically as once was thought.[69] A first "boom" seems to have occurred between

64 See the excellent concluding synthesis of A. E. Laiou, "The Byzantine Economy: An Overview," in *EHB* 3:1145–64, here 1145–47.
65 B. Bischoff and M. Lapidge, *Biblical Commentaries from the Canterbury School of Theodore and Hadrian*, Cambridge Studies in Anglo-Saxon England 10 (Cambridge, 1994).
66 G. Dagron, "The Urban Economy, Seventh–Twelfth Centuries," in *EHB* 2:393–461, here 397–400.
67 *Opus Caroli regis contra synodum (Libri Carolini)* 4.3, 494.33–495.6.
68 For Rome, see McCormick, *Origins*, 701; for Lyons, chapter 3.4.
69 M.-F. Auzépy, *L'hagiographie et l'iconoclasme byzantin*, Birmingham Byzantine and Ottoman Monographs 5 (Aldershot, 1999), 271–88; Hatlie, *Monks and Monasteries*, 446–47.

about 780 and 815, followed by another surge after 845. It has been estimated that by the end of the first expansion the number of active monastic communities in the capital was more than one hundred, that is, the estimated fifty or so houses thought still afloat around 700 more than doubled over the intervening century.[70] Again, even should the scarcity of evidence from Constantinople's seventh century make the apparent decline look worse than it was and hence the apparent recovery documented by the more complete evidence of the late eighth and ninth centuries seem better, the upward trend is certainly correct and presaged the golden age of middle Byzantine monasticism.

What about the Holy Land? If the decline between 600 and 800 is unmistakable, debate continues over its timing.[71] The reality of decline does not necessarily imply that the fortunes of the Palestinian church had gone downhill at an even rate since the peak. "Punctuated evolution" has a place in history. As far as the size of the patriarchal establishment is concerned, we may suspect that the situation in the early ninth century represented an improvement over the second half of the seventh century, when the patriarchal see itself was vacant, and there is considerable lack of clarity on the situation in the early eighth century.[72] So too we may suspect that between the Arab conquest and the arrival of Charlemagne's envoys, the fortunes of various Christian communities around the Holy Land changed in fairly complex ways. Those fortunes will have reflected at least in part the broader trends of the local economy and society.

Mosaic inscriptions attest the upkeep and renovation of the churches belonging to Christian villages in the Holy Land under the Umayyads and Abbasids, particularly in the earlier eighth century.[73] The one case for which we can com-

70 Hatlie, *Monks and Monasteries*, 320–21.

71 Hirschfeld (*Judean Desert Monasteries*, 16–17) suggests that the great break came with the Arab conquest. Careful scrutiny of the archaeological data, notably of church abandonment, led Schick (*Christian Communities of Palestine*, 117–38), to conclude that the decline of the Christian population was limited under the Umayyads but gained speed from the early Abbasids, in connection with broader economic trends. Magness (*Early Islamic Settlement*, 215–16) tends to set the overall decline of settlements later in the eighth and in the ninth centuries.

72 Gil (*History of Palestine*, 432–33, 456–57) and Schick (*Christian Communities of Palestine*, 325–27) summarize the data from various sources. See above, chapter 1.2, note 32, for speculation that the payment to the Arabs recorded in the Expenditures might reflect the size of the patriarchal establishment at the moment of the Conquest.

73 See most importantly the discussion of Schick, *Christian Communities of Palestine*, 112–19, who estimates that about one half of churches of all sorts in use before 602 are known to have continued in use until the ninth century (119). The evidence seems to me the strongest for the earlier eighth century. Thus of the seven new dated church mosaic inscriptions discussed by L. Di Segni, five date from the eighth century (four of which date between 701 and 725), one from the later seventh, and one from 785/86 or, less likely, 801/2, on her interpretation: "Christian Epigraphy in the Holy Land: New Discoveries," *ARAM Periodical* 15 (2003): 247–67. The clustering appears to signal a time which fostered Christian repairs or new building in the region; it coincides with the period when Walmsley, *Early Islamic Syria* (e.g., 69), detects accelerating economic and other change.

pare the size of the monastic population, that of St. John the Baptist near Jericho, suggests a subsequent improvement. When the Anglo-Saxon Willibald spent the night there in the mid-720s, he found about 20 monks.[74] The community of 36 reported by the Memorial almost three generations later represents an increase of 80 percent. If typical, it would signify a remarkable—and recent—improvement in the state of the monastic church in the Holy Land. The general pattern of Mediterranean communications likewise suggests that the Frankish monastery on the Mount of Olives and the seventeen nuns who had come to Jerusalem from Charlemagne's dominions were a new phenomenon. Carolingian pilgrimage supplied a new source of religious vocations, even as Charlemagne himself, as the very existence of the Basel roll underscores, represented a new source of financial support for the Holy Land church. At least theoretically, Christians were forbidden to build new churches or rebuild old ones. Perhaps the reported orders by the caliphs al Mahdi (775–785) and Harun al Rashid (786–809) to destroy newly built Christian churches testify to a reaction against the architectural consequences of an improvement of fortunes. In any case, Islamic jurists' prohibitions against the building of new churches seem to acquire new weight in the later eighth century.[75] Future archaeological research should shed new light on this tentative conclusion of an at least partial and temporary improvement in the fortunes of the Jerusalem church in the late eighth and early ninth centuries.

Nevertheless, wherever we can make a fairly clear comparison with the heyday of the Holy Land church in the sixth century, the overall trend is downward. This is so whether we look at the numbers of bishoprics, of monasteries, the size cohorts, or the aggregate numbers of religious. About forty bishoprics had shrunk to five or six around 808. Monasteries had disappeared at a comparable rate, and no monastery reached the size of the biggest sixth-century houses. For the best-surveyed area, the Judaean desert, the number of monasteries contracted from about sixty-five to nine. The aggregate number of the desert monks fell from somewhere in the vicinity of 2,200–3,000 to about 380. Thus, although the purchasing power of ninth-century expenditures—assuming that revenues equaled or surpassed outlays—seemed to mitigate somewhat the stark contrast of early medieval and late antique wealth in terms of absolute quantities of gold, the drastic difference in human size of the ecclesiastical establishment in the two periods militates against an optimistic interpretation of the evidence.

Comparing the relatively clear picture of the sixth century with that of 808 must not foster the impression that the stark rate of decline was necessarily

---

74 Hugeburc, *Vita Willibaldi* 4, 96.16.

75 On the destruction of illegally erected churches, see W. Hage, *Die syrisch-jacobitische Kirche in frühislamischer Zeit nach orientalischen Quellen* (Wiesbaden, 1966), 70. For prohibitions on church construction in Abū Yūsūf (†798), see Schick, *Christian Communities of Palestine*, 161–62.

regular. Nor should it blind us to the likelihood of partial recovery in some times and places across the long decades of the seventh and eighth centuries. The reasons for the decline and, likely, relatively small-scale resurgences will have been complex and deserving of closer scrutiny. We have noted the greater (though far from absolute) isolation of the Holy Land from the bulk of more distant lands that, under the unified conditions of the Roman Empire, had once supplied so many diverse streams of foreign pilgrims to populate the Holy Land's monastic institutions. The erosion by conversion of closer Christian populations within the caliphate reduced that source also of new professions. The imperial coffers of Constantinople and those far-flung populations had once been a key source of the wealth it took to maintain and keep attractive the myriad religious houses of the Holy Land.[76] As those flows of vocations and money dried up, the patriarchs of Jerusalem and indeed all the religious houses of Palestine were forced to rely mostly on the more meager resources available close to home, and this too played its role in constricting monastic life. Finally, surges in violence and disorder must have winnowed some communities, even as they drove others, like that of Mar Saba, to shrink toward its topographical center, as Joseph Patrich has put it.[77] Nevertheless, the story of decline over the long haul is only half the tale that the Basel roll tells. At least as important is the light it throws on the sociology of Christian religious life in the Holy Land as it existed at the dawn of the ninth century, and the comparative perspectives that beckon beyond the lost world of late antiquity, with the new and contemporary world of Byzantium and the Carolingian Empire.

76 Binns (*Ascetics*, 85–91) paints a vivid picture of the wealth that rolled into Palestine under the Christian Roman emperors.
77 Patrich, *Sabas*, 328.

. . . .

Chapter Three

TOWARD A COMPARATIVE SOCIOLOGY OF EARLY MEDIEVAL RELIGIOUS HOUSES

T HE UNIQUE QUANTITATIVE DATA preserved on the Basel roll illuminates aspects of what we might call the sociology of early medieval religious
life. It documents issues such as the spatial distribution of male and female religious communities as well as proportions of eremitical vocations, of female versus male religious houses, and of rural versus urban establishments. It even tells
us something about the ethnic or linguistic mosaic of prayer in the religious life
of the Holy Land. Comparing religious institutions there over time underscores
change in Palestine. Comparing the Holy Land's religious institutions with con-
temporaneous ones elsewhere about which we are similarly informed lets us delineate some salient features of religious life in the early Middle Ages. And it does so
as much for the places that we compare to the patriarchate of Jerusalem as it does
for the houses of Palestine. This approach throws into sharper relief the value of
the data from the roll for the comparative sociology of early medieval religious
institutions. The sizes of monastic communities in the ninth-century Holy Land
differ starkly from those of late antiquity, but that fact alone does not suffice for
an accurate historical appraisal of their state: we must ask how they compare to
similar communities in the Carolingian Empire and Byzantium. We will compare
more closely the data available on the roll with the good evidence we have for the
archiepiscopal religious communities of an exactly contemporary church in Burgundy about 813 and again about 830. That juxtaposition is particularly valuable
since it derives in part from a document that strikingly resembles those preserved
on the Basel roll and indeed was similarly prepared for Charlemagne for much the
same reason. Comparison will provide some unusual insights into the social com-
plexion of both Eastern and Western churches.

1. General Patterns within the Holy Land Church

The Basel roll shows us that the region's orthodox Christian religious life cen-
tered unmistakably on Jerusalem. Thirty of the fifty-one (59 percent) churches and

49

religious houses recorded on the roll are in Jerusalem and its immediate environs.[1] As far as people are concerned, nearly half the Holy Land's recorded Christian religious (405—not counting the 15 lepers—out of a documented but incomplete total of 865, i.e., 46.8 percent; see above, table 2.6) lived and prayed within a stone's throw of the Holy Sepulcher.[2] Even increasing the 460 documented religious residing outside of Jerusalem to 631, to account for the missing institutions (above, chapter 2.2), suggests that a minimum of 39.2 percent (405—406 if we add the patriarch who is not mentioned in the Breve—of a total of 1037, including the patriarch) of Holy Land religious lived in the shadow of the Holy Sepulcher.[3] By contrast, the religious communities of Samaria and Galilee lagged far behind the communities of Jerusalem and the Judaean desert, at least in number. Charlemagne's envoys knew of nine religious establishments in the former places, and the surviving parts of the report enumerate a total of 111 ecclesiastics of all descriptions in Galilee and Samaria (table 2.6)—12.8 percent of the 865 documented total of all Holy Land religious. Using the hypothetical sizes developed for the church and possible monastery at Cana, the cathedral at Neapolis, the convent in Tiberias, and the cathedral of Diospolis-Lydda, the estimated total for the northern region would be 202 (19.5 percent) of the total 1,037 estimated religious of the Holy Land, as corrected for gaps in the manuscript.[4]

The role of Jerusalem in the early ninth-century church was even more preponderant than these numbers suggest. With their documented 301 monks, the nearby monasteries of the Judaean desert lay within, at most, some thirty-five kilometers of the 405 religious of Jerusalem. In human terms, that might represent a maximal distance of a seven hours' walk. If we add to them the 17 religious of Bethlehem (less than ten kilometers distant), the total of 723 religious comprised 83.6 percent of the total documented 865 religious of the Holy Land.[5] More than eight out of ten of the Holy Land's documented religious lived well within a day's walk of Jerusalem. Although this percentage does not include the missing totals from the two key houses of Chariton and Choziba, both of which lay within twenty-five kilometers of the Holy City (see map 2), increasing all the figures

1   Thirty in Jerusalem (listed in table 2.5, minus the hermits and counting the Anastasis as one institution) and twenty-one outside (see table 2.6; one for each entry except for Tiberias, where the single entry also mentions a convent of women) recorded in the Memorial.

2   Note that the Jerusalem number does not include the three hostels and the patriarch whom the Breve excludes.

3   That is, 406 + 631 = 1,037 estimated Christian religious in the Holy Land, of which 406 constitutes 39.2 percent.

4   For the hypothetical sizes extrapolated for the five missing monasteries (20 each), two cathedral communities (24 each), and convent (22) throughout Samaria and Galilee, including Lydda, see above, chapter 2.2.

5   See entries **31–40** in table 2.6 and map 2. Compare the map of monasteries in Y. Hirschfeld, *The Judean Desert Monasteries in the Byzantine Period* (New Haven, 1992), xviii.

by the extrapolated missing numbers of religious does not substantially change the picture.[6]

This spatial pattern helps explain the particularly close connections of the patriarchate with the monasteries of Judaea. Those connections had played an important role in late antiquity and must have been reinforced in the difficult days of the Abbasid caliphs. We know, for instance, that around 800 the monastery of St. Sabas was bringing its supplies in from Jerusalem.[7] The privileged links of the monasteries, and particularly St. Sabas, with the patriarchate are clear, for instance, in the role Sabaite monks played at the Holy Sepulcher.[8] For instance, the patriarch Thomas, with whom the Carolingian ambassadors were dealing, seems to have begun his career as a monk at Mar Saba before becoming abbot of Palaia (Old) Lavra.[9] Within the patriarchate itself, according to the Breve, monks were at least a quarter of the personnel (41 of 162, 25.3 percent; see table 2.3). This presumably does not include monks who might have held orders from subdeacon to priest and who could therefore have been recorded under those categories in the Breve. At least one priest of the Anastasis attested around this time had in fact originally been a monk at St. Sabas.[10]

According to the tallies of the Breve, the religious residing in the Holy City and on the Mount of Olives included 91 individuals explicitly identified as monks, 68 nuns, and 35 hermits. That is, the explicitly monastic element comprised almost half (194 of 406; 47.8 percent) of the total religious population of the city. What was left of the episcopal hierarchy may have been no less monastic in its character. The bishop of Jerusalem himself had begun religious life as a monk, and Thomas

6 To see this, we add the 80 missing monks assigned to the Judaean monasteries of Chariton, Choziba, St. John the Baptist, and Pharan (map 2) to the religious definitely attested in Judaea (including Bethlehem) and at Jerusalem on the roll. The total of 804 is 77.5 percent of the estimated total size (1037) of the Christian ecclesiastical population of Palestine.

7 Stephen, *Martyrium XX Sabaitarum* 8, 6.24–25.

8 For example, the Sabaite monk Eustratius was an official at the Anastasis about 807: Leontius, *Vita Stephani Thaumaturgi* 24, 513E, and the Arabic version, 24.1, trans. 39, and who continues as the biographer's informant: 25.1–6 and 26.1–8, 40–42. Michael the Synkellos of the patriarch was equally a Sabaite. See *Vita Michael syncelli* (BHG 1296) 3, 48.19–50.22. See also below, note 10.

9 Leontius (*Vita Stephani Thaumaturgi* 136, 558A–B) describes the recently promoted patriarch as a former deacon and marvelous physician who had been in charge of the sick of the Holy City. The Arabic version, 64.6, trans. 101, garbles the chronology; compare 101 n. 260. Stephen (*Martyrium XX Sabaitarum* 15, 13.6–8, and 30, 23.21–24) refers to Thomas as a monk of St. Sabas, the best of physicians, who later became abbot of Palaia Lavra. Compare the *Commentarius praevius*, AASS Iulii 3 (1867): 529F–530A, and M.-F. Auzépy, "De la Palestine à Constantinople (VIIIe–IXe siècles): Étienne le Sabaïte et Jean Damascène," *Travaux et mémoires* 12 (1994): 183–218, here 185 n. 16.

10 Theodegetos, priest of the Anastasis about 807, had been a monk at Mar Saba. See Leontius, *Vita Stephani Thaumaturgi* 94, 541E; Arabic version, 50.1, trans. 78.

was not the only patriarch of the period to have come from the cloister.[11] No less significant, the Memorial (line 41) shows that another bishop had shifted his residence to a monastery on Mount Tabor, a move that probably testifies to the decay of whatever town had once held his see as well as to the monastic proclivities of local bishops.[12] Beyond the anecdotal evidence, the quantitative data confirm decisively the portrait of a patriarchal church intimately connected to and heavily influenced by its monastic context. The impact of the Palestinian church on the religious life of Byzantine Constantinople was just beginning to be felt in our period. In light of the cenobitic character of the contemporary Jerusalem church, the overwhelmingly monastic character of that Palestinian influence, which would reshape even Constantinople's cathedral liturgy, makes eminently good sense.[13]

The roll sheds unique light on what is usually an imperfectly documented facet of monasticism. For most churches, scholars are reduced to educated guesswork about female monasticism. Thanks to the roll, we know that at the beginning of the ninth century the Palestinian church counted a maximum of five convents out of the Roll's fifty-one documented churches and houses, that is, about one in ten (9.8 percent) religious institutions were female. And this is a maximum figure, which assumes that the two recluses at the Zion church were what remained of the convent near Zion known from other sources.[14] The compilers were able to count 68 nuns, all of them at Jerusalem; they noted an unspecified number in a convent at Tiberias. Women thus constituted about one-sixth (68 of 406; 16.8 percent) of the total religious recorded at Jerusalem in this period, and about half that fraction (7.9 percent) of the total recorded religious population of Palestine. Using the corrected figures developed above, the estimated total of 90 nuns would represent just under a tenth of the entire orthodox Christian religious establishment (90 of 1,037; 8.8 percent), a figure for individuals which is not out of proportion with that of female religious institutions. A comparative framework will further clarify the significance of the numbers of female religious (see below, p. 63).

11 For a Sabaite bishop of Lydda, see above, note 8, on Eustratius. The usurper patriarch Theodore, who evinced Elias II in the late eighth century, had been a monk at the monastery of the Spoudaion in Jerusalem: Leontius, *Vita Stephani Thaumaturgi* 44, 522B–C; Arabic version, 33.1–35.1, trans. 51–56. For Elias II, see, for example, R. Schick, *The Christian Communities of Palestine from Byzantine to Islamic Rule: A Historical and Archaeological Study*, Studies in Late Antiquity and Early Islam 2 (Princeton, N.J., 1995), 326.

12 F. M. Abel, *Géographie de la Palestine* (Paris, 1933), 2:205, possibly from Helenoupolis.

13 R. F. Taft, "Byzantine Rite," *ODB* 1:343–44; idem, "Liturgy," *ODB* 2:1240–41, with further references.

14 In or around 786, Michael Synkellos's mother and two sisters entered that convent. *Vita Michael syncelli* 2–3, 48.17–21.

One characteristic sharply distinguishes female monasticism from its male counterpart in the Holy Land: all five convents were urban.[15] We can deduce the breakdown of regular religious houses in terms of urban and rural locations. One tends to think of Palestinian monasticism as a desert phenomenon. Deserts seem pretty non-urban, even though, as we have seen, the links of most of the desert monasteries with towns, and especially Jerusalem, were strong and frequent. In fact, the majority of Palestine's monastic establishments (15 of 27, accepting Nazareth as a monastery; 55.6 percent) around 808 were located inside or right next to towns. Naturally, the fact that the five convents of women are exclusively urban plays a role, but even if we look only at male houses, nearly half are urban.

When we compare the numbers of houses with the numbers of monks, we see that many of the urban monasteries and convents were on the small side (table 3.1; average 19.5). The desert houses were large by comparison (average 38), which explains why a small majority of all regular religious individuals and a clear majority of all male monks were located away from towns. Nevertheless, more male monks than one might think resided inside or very near towns.[16] This was obviously true of Jerusalem and its environs, with its 91 monks as well as its 68 nuns; but there were also monks near (*prope*) Jericho, in Bethlehem, in Sebastia, in Tiberias, and probably in Nazareth.[17] A monastery a mile outside of Nazareth had 8 monks.[18] There are also grounds for thinking there was a monastery at Cana, although that site might have been more of a village than a town by this date.[19] We can combine these figures with the estimates for the missing monastery and convent populations to arrive at an estimated maximal total of 285 urban religious monks and nuns, as opposed to an estimated total of 420 monks—440 if we include Cana as rural—whom we can classify as rural and indeed mostly

15 All houses tallied in the Breve, including the convent with the 17 women from the Frankish Empire, who, we are reminded, served the Holy Sepulcher, were clearly considered part of Jerusalem by the compiler and should be reckoned as such.

16 On the phenomenon of specifically urban monasticism in Byzantium, see G. Varinlioğlu, "Urban Monasteries in Constantinople and Thessaloniki: Distribution Patterns in Time and Urban Topography," in *Archaeology in Architecture: Studies in Honor of Cecil L. Striker*, ed. J. J. Emerick and D. M. Deliyannis (Mainz, 2005), 187–98. For the Holy Land, see H. Goldfus, "Urban Monasticism and Monasteries of Early Byzantine Palestine: Preliminary Observations," *ARAM Periodical* 15 (2003): 71–79.

17 For St. Stephen near Jericho, the envoys could not obtain the number of monks (lines 34–35). In Bethlehem, Tiberias, and Sebastia, monks are lumped together with priests (sic) and clerics or canons in the total numbers of 15, 30, and 25 urban ecclesiastics, respectively. See table 3.1. As noted there (no. **41**), the 12 religious in Nazareth whose status disappeared in the lacuna were most likely monks. See also below, chapter 11, textual commentary on lines 35–36.

18 Table 3.1, no. **42**.

19 See chapter 11, textual commentary on lines 37–38.

desert.[20] The upshot is that almost four out of ten (39.3 percent) of all regular religious lived in or very close to towns around 808. The exclusively urban character of the Palestinian nuns naturally boosts this share somewhat: leaving the women aside, the proportion of male monks whom we can classify as urban drops to just under a third (30.7 percent).[21] In other words, however we count them, it is rather striking and unexpected to discover that even in the home of desert monasticism urban cloisters accounted for a large share of regular religious, whether we count by houses or by heads.[22] At least in the Holy Land around 808, urban monasticism was more important than one might suspect.

An equally precious shaft of statistical light falls on eremitical religious vocations. By the very nature of their religious calling in the wilderness or desert that their name (from *eremos*, "desert") recalls, hermits tend to be lost to statistics. The king's informants nevertheless carefully tallied the thirty-five hermits resident in cells located in various specified places on the Mount of Olives. Thus the eremitical life represented 8.6 percent of the Christian religious in the Holy City. This figure is probably a minimal one. As the report emphasizes, it lists only those hermits who reside or stay (*sedent*, line 19) distributed among their cells. The distributive sense of the words "per cellolas eorum" is clear and would have been so perceived by westerners more accustomed to cenobitic monasticism, underscoring the fact that this individualistic lifestyle was the least likely to lend itself to an inventory. For all of Palestine, the proportion shrinks by half or more if we accept the two stylites at Bethlehem and the one at Neapolis as hermits (38 of 865 documented religious, 4.39 percent; 3.7 percent of the corrected total of 1,037 ecclesiastics). Outside Jerusalem, Charlemagne's envoys located only the very stationary and spectacularly noticeable ascetics who perpetuated the late antique tradition of

20 Calculated as follows for urban monks and nuns: Jerusalem, 91 monks and 68 nuns; Jericho, estimated 20 monks; Bethlehem: a maximum of 13 monks from the unspecified religious group (see table 3.1, no. **31**); Nazareth, 12 probable monks and 8 monks a mile from Nazareth (table 3.1, nos. **41–42**); Tiberias, a maximum of 28 monks (table 3.1, no. **46**), and the estimated 22 nuns; Sebastia, 23 maximum monks (table 3.1, no. **49**), which comes out to 285 in total. This total likely errs somewhat on the high side, given the rather high numbers of our extrapolated community sizes and given that monks were probably not quite so dominant among the ecclesiastics of Bethlehem, Tiberias, and Sebastia as we have allowed. It nevertheless supplies a useful approximation. The total of non-urban monks is calculated from the estimated total for the Judaean desert (above, chapter 2.2), of 381 less the estimated 20 monks of St. Stephen's near Jericho, which we have classified as urban, plus the 10 monks of the Heptapegon in Galilee, 18 at Mount Tabor, the 31 of Sinai, and the 20 monks attributed to Cana. For the reasoning behind the extrapolated estimates of monks and nuns for the lacunas at Jericho, Cana, and Tiberias, see above, chapter 2.2.
21 That is, removing the 90 nuns from the 285 total urban regular religious, that is, leaving 195 urban male monks, as a proportion of the total of 635 cenobitic male monks of Palestine.
22 Confirming for this period the basic point of Goldfus, "Urban Monasticism," for the late Roman period.

TABLE 3.1 Maximal populations of twenty-seven cenobitic institutions in the Holy Land

Church or location	Recorded size of monastic community	Extrapolated community size	Urban?	Site no.
Jerusalem				
Holy Sepulcher	41	41	yes	1
Holy Zion	2 nuns	2	yes	2
St. Mary at the Sheep Pool	25 nuns	25	yes	8
Virgin's Tomb	6 monks, 15 nuns	21	yes	10
Shrine of the Teaching of the Disciples, Mount of Olives	3 monks	3	yes	25
Convent	26 nuns	26	yes	27
Sts. Peter and Paul in Bisanteo	35	35	yes	28
St. John, held by Armenians	6	6	yes	30
Outside Jerusalem				
Bethlehem	13 monks maximum[a]	*13*	yes	31
Monastery of St. Theodosius	71	71		32
Monastery of St. Sabas	150	150		33
Monastery of St. Chariton (Old Lavra)	1 abbot + ?	*21*		34
Monastery of St. Euthymius	31	31		35
Monastery of Choziba	1 abbot + ?	*21*		36
Monastery of St. Gerasimus	11	11		37
Monastery of St. John Baptist	36	36		38
Monastery of St. Stephen, Jericho	unknown	*20*	yes	39
Monastery of Mount Pharan	unknown	*20*		40
Nazareth	12[b]	12[b]	yes	41
Monastery of the Virgin at the Leap of the Lord	8	8	yes	42
Cana	?	*20*		43
Heptapegon	10	10		44
Tiberias	28 monks maximum[a]	*28*	yes	46
Tiberias convent	unspecified	*22*	yes	47
Mount Tabor	18	18		48
Sebastia	23 monks maximum[a]	*23*	yes	49
Monastery at Sinai	31	31		51
	Total	*725*		

Note: For the purposes of analyzing the monastic communities of the Holy Land, this table presents for the unspecified numbers of monks in mixed communities the maximal numbers consistent with the text. This produces slightly different subtotals from those developed in the other tables. See note a for further details. Numerals in italics are extrapolated; ? = number missing due to lacuna; unknown = text admits not knowing the number; unspecified = text does not specify a number.

[a]Bethlehem is reported to have had "15 including priests, clerics, and monks." Assuming the plurals are correct and represent a minimum of 2 clerics, this would make a maximum of 13 monks (for monks might have been priests). Similarly, Tiberias had a total of 30, including priests, monks, and "canons"; Sebastia, a total of 25, including priests, monks, and clerics.

[b]On the hypothetical identification of the community at Nazareth as monastic, see chapter 11, textual commentary on lines 35–36.

living on top of columns.[23] If hermits loosely associated with the cenobitic monasteries and lavras of Judaea escaped the Carolingian envoys or their informants or simply were lumped in with the cenobites in the enumeration, then the proportion of religious following the eremitical path would have been even higher. In any case, the significance of hermits looks like a distinctive feature of Holy Land religious life. Its continuing importance reflects the long-standing tradition of individualistic asceticism celebrated throughout the early medieval Christian world by the hagiographical works associated with the desert fathers.[24] As the languages in which they prayed show us, many if not all of the hermits around Jerusalem had come there on pilgrimage. This unique supply of highly motivated individuals perhaps combines with the enduring prestige of Holy Land eremitism to explain what looks like an exceptionally large proportion of hermits in this church.

The envoys' concern to classify by language of prayer offers insight into the ethnicity and international recruitment of Holy Land hermits in the early ninth century. That Greek should still dominate two generations after the death of John of Damascus is interesting but perhaps not surprising in light of the high quality of local Greek literary production around 800, exemplified by the remarkable Palestinian saints' lives that clarify and deepen the testimony of the Basel roll. The appearance of a Christian hermit who prayed in Arabic, however, heralds things to come.[25] It is surprising that, as the third largest group (14 percent), the Latins should tie with the Georgians, whose Holy Land presence in the period is well known.

S. D. Goitein thought that the ethnicities suggested by the hermits' languages of prayer allow us to gauge those of the city's broader Christian population.[26] I am skeptical that the proportions of hermits from different language groups closely reflect the entire religious *and* lay population of Jerusalem. On the face of it, 37 percent Greek speakers seems low but plausible for the total Christian population of the city. But that Latins should be more numerous than Armenians is striking and seems unlikely to correspond to the overall demography of early ninth-century Jerusalem. Nevertheless, the hermit list may provide a better indicator for the Christian cenobitic religious of the city. In fact, the exhaustive character of the Breve allows us to test this proposition by comparing the proportions

23 A. P. Kazhdan and N. P. Ševčenko, "Stylite," *ODB* 3:1971, for the continuing existence of stylites in the eighth and ninth centuries also in the Byzantine Empire.
24 See the observations on the enduring literary echo of this tradition in G. Philippart and M. Trigalet, "Latin Hagiography before the Ninth Century: A Synoptic View," in *The Long Morning of Medieval Europe: New Directions in Early Medieval Studies*, ed. J. R. Davis and M. McCormick (Aldershot, 2008), 111–29, at 127–28.
25 S. H. Griffith, "From Aramaic to Arabic: The Languages of the Monasteries of Palestine in the Byzantine and Early Islamic Periods," *DOP* 51 (1997): 11–31.
26 S. D. Goitein, "al-Ḳuds, A. History," *EI*² online, accessed 19 October 2006.

TABLE 3.2   Hermits' languages of prayer

Language of prayer	Quantity	%
Greek	13	37
Syriac	8	23
Latin	5	14
Georgian	5	14
Armenian	2	6
Arabic	1	3
unspecified	1	3
Totals	35	100

it reports for Latin, Armenian, and, to a certain extant, Greek religious and so gauge the plausibility of the extrapolation.

The Armenian figures clearly do not match. However, we can be certain that the Franks did not tally most Armenian religious in Jerusalem. They ignored the rival Armenian patriarchate that had existed from the seventh and eighth centuries, though Armenians seem to have been well-represented in the Holy Land in this period.[27] The Franks' aggressive vision of their own religious righteousness is unlikely to have inclined them to contemplate financing religious institutions whose orthodoxy they suspected. Thus too our documents ignore the Jacobite patriarch of Jerusalem and any religious establishments that may have been associated with him.[28] The isolated mention of Armenians at the church of St. John's may be an anomalous exception to the envoys' ignoring non-orthodox Christian establishments. The Breve's phrasing suggests contested possession of a shrine on which the Greek patriarch had claims. But the presence of Armenian Christians favoring Chalcedonian orthodoxy also probably cannot be ruled out at this date.[29]

Nevertheless, table 3.3 does offer some confirmation of the breakdown suggested by the hermits. We know from abundant anecdotal evidence that the

27 Schick, *Christian Communities of Palestine*, 326–27.
28 Ibid., 327.
29 See above, chapter 2.1, note 6, on the Latin phrasing of this entry for the church of "St. John, which the Armenians hold ("sanctum Iohannem quod tenent Armeni"; line 24), the ambiguous theological status of Armenians in Byzantine high society, and the persistence of a pro-Chalcedonian current of opinion. This church may be the shrine of the Baptist mentioned in the vicinity in late antiquity. In any case, both Armenian lists of shrines from the Fatimid period and the Armenian inscriptions that have been discovered on the site testify that the Armenian control of this church was permanent. See K. Bieberstein and H. Bloedhorn, *Jerusalem: Grundzüge der Baugeschichte vom Chalkolithikum bis zur Frühzeit der osmanischen Herrschaft*, Beihefte zum Tübinger Atlas des Vorderen Orients, Reihe B, Geisteswissenschaften 100 (Wiesbaden, 1994), 3:327–36.

Hermit language of prayer	%	Religious in Jerusalem, excluding hermits	
		Quantity	%
Greek	37	?	?
Syriac	23	?	?
Georgian	14	?	?
Latin	14	53[a]	14.3
Armenian	6	6	1.6
Arabic	3	?	?
unspecified	3	311	84.05
Totals	100	370	99.95

[a]That is, 35 monks, 17 nuns, and 1 recluse from Spain

"Greek" monasteries of Palestine welcomed orthodox religious of other ethnicities—individuals whose native language was Georgian, Syriac, and Arabic certainly figured among the ranks of monks of such houses as St. Sabas.[30] Aside from the hermit list, the roll does not bother to specify non-Western ethnicities, which indeed would have served no purpose for calculating the overall financial needs of various religious communities. The combined percentage of non-Western and non-Armenian hermits comes to a total of 80 percent. This compares well to the similar percentage of Jerusalem's religious of unspecified ethnicity, which is 84 percent (311 of 370). Taken with the convergence of the data on Latin hermits and Latin cenobitic monks and nuns, this in turn shows that proportions of linguistic groups recorded among hermits probably do furnish a rough benchmark of the analogous proportions among the broader group of Christian religious resident in the Holy City and its immediate environs. If so, then around 40 percent of Jerusalem's orthodox Christian religious spoke Greek, about a quarter spoke Syriac, about a seventh prayed in Latin, and the same number spoke Georgian, while under 5 percent of Christian religious could be identified as speaking mainly Arabic in the opening years of the ninth century.

30 See, for example, S. H. Griffith, "Greek into Arabic: Life and Letters in the Monasteries of Palestine in the Ninth Century," in *Arabic Christianity in the Monasteries of Ninth-Century Palestine* (Aldershot, 1992), VIII, pp. 117–38, here VIII, 126. For Georgian monks and their literary activities at St. Sabas between the eighth and tenth centuries, see G. Garitte, *Le calendrier palestino-géorgien du Sinaiticus 34 (Xe siècle)*, SubsHag 30 (Brussels, 1958), 17.

There is in any case no denying the Western numbers, and historians who contemplate the problem of long-distance contacts will have to take into account the surprising fact that, in the last years of the reign of Charlemagne and Harun al Rashid, some 14 percent (14.3 percent; 53 monks and nuns and 5 hermits out of 406) of all orthodox Christian religious resident at Jerusalem were Western Europeans. And although the Latin monastery on the Mount of Olives was but one-fifth the size of St. Sabas and half that of St. Theodosius, those two monasteries were exceptional—much larger than the other Greek houses of the Holy Land. In fact, at thirty-five monks, the Western establishment on the Mount of Olives was tied with the monastery of St. John the Baptist at the Jordan as the fourth largest monastery of ascertainable size in the Holy Land (see table 3.1).[31] It stood at the head of the second tier of local monasteries and constituted the largest single religious establishment in Jerusalem after the Holy Sepulcher complex itself. In this light, Charlemagne's interest in the church of the Holy Land takes on a more concrete physiognomy, and we begin to understand how it was possible that the Filioque controversy arose in 807 from Greek criticism of the Frankish creed at Christmas services in Bethlehem.

2. The Christian Religious Populations of the Holy Land in Medieval Context

Although no other contemporary church can be known in quite the same way as the patriarchate in Jerusalem, some comparisons are possible. It is worth emphasizing that the individual items of data that come to our attention are chronologically scattered. Change, however, need not have occurred only on the time scale of record preservation. When the records run more deeply, we can indeed observe sudden changes as well as gradual growth or decline in the numbers of religious houses or their populations. For instance, the contrast in Carolingian monastic populations before and after the foreign raids and civil wars of the ninth century seems as obvious as the surge in both statistics in England after the Norman conquest or the huge expansion in many parts of Europe that accompanied the religious and economic dynamism of the twelfth and early thirteenth centuries.[32] We

31   Among the monasteries for which the numbers are lacking, with some 40 to 60 monks at most, only Chariton and Choziba might have been larger in their late antique heyday. See above, chapter 2.2, note 23. They had surely followed the overall downward trend since then.
32   On the dramatic late Carolingian changes and later medieval peak, see B. Guillemain, "Chiffres et statistiques pour l'histoire ecclésiastique du moyen âge," *Le moyen âge* 59 (1953): 341–65, 348–49. On the Norman growth and peak, see D. Knowles, *The Monastic Order in England: A History of Its Development from the Times of St. Dunstan to the Fourth Lateran Council, 940–1216*, 2nd ed. (Cambridge, 1963), 425–26; D. Knowles, *The Religious Orders in England* (Cambridge, 1957), 255–62; and the summary tables in D. Knowles and R. N. Hadcock, *Medieval Religious Houses, England and Wales*, new ed. ([London], 1971), 488–95. See also U. Berlière, "Le nombre des moines dans les anciens monastères," *RBén* 41 and 42 (1929 and 1930): 231–61 and 19–42, respectively, here 42.33–34.

have already seen that in the Holy Land at least one monastery experienced considerable growth in the eighth century.[33] The scarcity of data on the size of contemporary Byzantine religious houses precludes close comparisons. Scholars have generally reacted skeptically to the most frequently cited figure, the 700 monks ascribed to the monastery of Stoudios in Constantinople.[34] However, it has reasonably been observed that this may just be an exaggeration referring to the whole confederation of Stoudite monks; Theodore himself refers to a community of more than three hundred monks, which is huge enough.[35] A tabulation of scattered data from the eleventh to the fourteenth centuries indicates that fifteen male monasteries whose communities can be estimated averaged fifty-nine monks each, an average that is swollen by the inclusion of one monastery, Bessai, which reportedly briefly attained 300 monks.[36]

The Carolingian envoys recorded the existence of twenty-seven communities in which cenobites were present, counting the male and female communities of the Virgin's Tomb as a single establishment, i.e., as some kind of double monastery, and accepting the monastic identification of the community at Nazareth (see table 3.1). For nine of them, the numbers of monks are imprecise or missing. The remaining eighteen break down into the size cohorts that are laid out in comparison to the distribution of community sizes documented from twenty-three houses for the entire middle and late Byzantine Empire (table 3.4).[37] The mathematical mode is the same, which suggests that, in both the Holy Land and the Byzantine Empire, monastic houses of males and females may have commonly comprised from 30 to 49 members. However, the second-ranking cohorts differ, since in Byzantium, houses comprising 50 to 99 religious shared this position with houses of 10 to 19. By contrast, in the Holy Land the analogous position was occupied by the small end of the spectrum, by houses of 10 to 19 members and by houses counting 10 or fewer persons. If houses of 10 to 29 members were combined for both Byzantium and the Holy Land, houses of this size would constitute the mode in both places. Finally, we should not attach too much importance to the apparent insignificance of very small monasteries in the Byzantine Empire. The fact that a ninth-

33 See above, chapter 2.2, note 74, on St. John the Baptist on the Jordan.
34 A. Kazhdan, A. M. Talbot, A. Cutler, "Stoudios Monastery," *ODB* 3:1960–61.
35 R. Cholij, *Theodore the Stoudite: The Ordering of Holiness* (Oxford, 2002), 44–45, with note 271. On the inclusion of other Stoudite establishments already among the 700, see A.-M. M. Talbot, "A Comparison of the Monastic Experience of Byzantine Men and Women," *Greek Orthodox Theological Review* 30 (1985): 1–20, at 19, table 2. Compare also P. Hatlie, *The Monks and Monasteries of Constantinople, ca. 350–850* (Cambridge, 2007), 324–25.
36 Based on Talbot, "Comparison," 19, table 2.
37 Ibid., 19–20, table 2. The total of 700 for eleventh-century Mount Athos combines the totals of all the monasteries on the peninsula and is therefore not included here; for female monasteries she includes both original and later sizes; I have used the later, higher of the two figures.

TABLE 3.4 Size cohorts of monastic communities:
Holy Land (ca. 808), Byzantine Empire (11th–14th centuries),
and Carolingian empire (ca. 750–ca. 850)

| | Number of monasteries | | |
| | | | |
No. of monks	Holy Land	Byzantine Empire	Carolingian Empire
100+	1	3	14
50–99	1	5	8
30–49	5	6	4
20–29	3	3	2
10–19	4	5	
9 or fewer	4	1	

Source: Talbot, "Comparison," 19–20, tables 2–3, and below, table 3.5.
Note that I have tallied the 6 monks and 15 nuns of the Virgin's Tomb
as one community. Were they separated, the cohort of 20 or more
would decrease by one and cohorts of 10 to 19 and 9 or fewer would each
increase by one.

century emperor had to outlaw monasteries with fewer than three monks or nuns
indicates that small numbers may simply be underreported in what is in any case
bound to be a very incomplete sample, given that we know of the existence of 562
monasteries and nunneries at Constantinople itself and in two major regions of
the empire, but possess so little data on their populations.[38]

If the general run of Holy Land monasteries would have appeared familiar in size to a contemporary visitor from Byzantium, chances are that a pilgrim
from Charlemagne's empire would have formed a different opinion. Although
the theme deserves a systematic study on its own merits, there is enough readily available material to give a provisional idea of Carolingian monastery sizes in
the decades surrounding the preparation of the Basel roll (table 3.5). Aside from
the striking fact that Carolingian Europe offers more quantitative data for a few
decades than we have for the last seven centuries of Byzantine history, even this
preliminary assembly of data makes clear that Carolingian monasteries tended to
be bigger than those of the contemporary Holy Land and of the later Byzantine
Empire. Although the predominance of the biggest monasteries and the absence
of the smallest cohorts among the Carolingian houses probably owe much to the
sample, Western Europe's overall tendency toward bigger communities is unmistakable and all the more convincing for the short time span under consideration.

38   Talbot, "Comparison," 4, with note 15, and 18, table 1.

TABLE 3.5 Populations of twenty-eight Carolingian monasteries

No. of monks	House	Date	Reference
21	Senones	750s?[a]	1: 64A1–A3
21	Münster in Gregoriental	ca. 823–35	1: 55A1–A4[b]
30	Cornelimünster	817	2: 19
32	Convent of St. Peter, Lyons	813–14	Table 3.7
33	Bèze	before 830	3: 69; cf. 80–81
44	Ettenheimmünster	ca. 800	4: 105[c]
52	*Buxbrunno*	ca. 762	4: 97–98
53	St. Faron	ca. 762	4: 97–98
56	St. Rambert	813–14	Table 3.7
61	Molosme	before 830	3: 68; cf. 80–81
76	Neuweiler	750–800	4: 108–9
77	Lobbes	850	2: 236
83	St. Bertin	ca. 820	2: 240
90	Île-Barbe	813–14	Table 3.7
106	Gorze	786–96	4: 110
ca. 110	Reichenau	824–25	5: 244
113	Jumièges	ca. 762	4: 97–98
123	Rebais	ca. 762	4: 97–98
127	St. Denis	838[d]	3: 112–19
131	St. Germain des Prés	ca. 823	3: 105
137	Niederaltaich	ca. 800[e]	1: 241A–D3
140	Psalmodi	ca. 820	2: 257
150	Hersfeld	ca. 769–75	2: 23
166	St. Gall	ca. 824–25	1: 10A1–11A3
220	St. Martin of Tours	818–20	3: 35–41
300	St. Riquier	ca. 800	2: 243
ca. 300[f]	Corbie	822	6
673	Fulda	825–26	7: 586–90

Sources referred to by number in this table: 1. Reichenau Memorial Book; 2. U. Berlière, "Le nombre des moines dans les anciens monastères," *RBén* 41 and 42 (1929 and 1930): 231–61, and 19–42, respectively; 3. O. G. Oexle, *Forschungen zu monastischen und geistlichen Gemeinschaften im westfränkischen Bereich*, Münstersche Mittelalter-Schriften 31 (Munich, 1978); 4. K. Schmid and O. G. Oexle, "Voraussetzungen und Wirkung des Gebetsbundes von Attigny," *Francia* 2 (1974): 71–122; 5. A. Zettler, "Zu den Mönchslisten und zur Geschichte des Konvents," in *Die Reichenauer Mönchsgemeinschaft und ihr Totengedenken im frühen Mittelalter*, eds. Roland Rappmann and Alfons Zettler (Sigmaringen, 1998), 233–78; 6. Adalhard of Corbie, *Statuta seu brevia* 3, 376.1–3; 7. K. Schmid, "Mönchslisten und Klosterkonvent von Fulda zur Zeit der Karolinger," in *Die Klostergemeinschaft von Fulda im früheren Mittelalter*, Münstersche Mittelalter-Schriften 8.2.2 (Munich, 1978), 2:571–639. Many of the figures from 3 and 4 derive also from the Reichenau memorial book but, where possible, I preferred to use them with the critical discussion in the studies cited. A house name in italics indicates a site that cannot be identified.

[a] See, for the date, Schmid and Oexle, "Voraussetzungen," 109.   [b] Ibid., 104 n. 33.

[c] The absence of overlap with the 762 list indicates that the list from about 800 is probably of living monks. Compare ibid., 105, with note 35.

[d] The 838 figure reflects the reunified community, after the return of the 50 monks who withdrew in 817 because of the rest of the community's failure to live up to monastic norms. See Oexle, *Forschungen*, 117–19.

[e] See, for the date, Schmid and Oexle, "Voraussetzungen," 102–3.

[f] Calculating the required food supply for his monastery, Adalhard observes that the population of Corbie fluctuated considerably and estimates that it never dropped below 300 and now (*modo*) they were fewer than 350. It is not completely clear to me whether this includes others than monks. See also the discussion of this passage in M. Rouche, "La faim à l'époque carolingienne. Essai sur quelques types de rations alimentaires," *Revue historique* 250 (1973): 300.

3. Women's Houses

The important question of the proportion of female to male monasteries has been investigated for some places in the Middle Ages. Alice-Mary Talbot reported that in Constantinople over the full 1,100 years of Byzantine history, just over a fifth of all documented religious houses were female (77 vs. 270 male houses; 22.2 percent). A partial survey of the provinces indicated that, over the same period, nunneries were comparatively rarer outside the capital, at 7 percent of all documented religious houses (17 vs. 225 male monasteries).[39] Günder Varinlioğlu found that over the whole Byzantine period, female houses constituted just under one-fifth of those in Thessalonica.[40] The final, beleaguered centuries of Byzantium are less jejunely documented than the earlier periods. At that time, convents seem to have risen to over a third of all religious houses in Constantinople (30 vs. 55 male houses; 35.3 percent).[41] For that same period, it is possible to calculate the percentage of individual abbesses and nuns recorded in a standard prosopographical reference work compared to their male counterparts, as 4 percent (84 nuns and abbesses vs. 2,035 monks and abbots).[42] The discrepancy between the proportions of individuals and houses surely reflects at least in part the well-known underreporting of women in most medieval records. And the evidence from Thessalonica seems to reinforce that of Constantinople, pointing to a markedly urban concentration of female houses in Byzantium.

David Knowles derived figures for different periods in the history of English religious orders. At the time of the Norman Conquest, he estimated that a fifth of houses were female (21.3 percent). In the half century that followed, the proportion sank to a tenth (10.8 percent). This age of rapid religious expansion manifestly did not favor females. The period from 1216 to 1350 marked the quantitative high point of English religious life. Relatively well documented, the spectrum of religious now included canons, canonesses, and the mendicants. Knowles's reckoning indicates that female religious institutions could have shrunk slightly from 14.9

---

39 Ibid., 2; compare 18, table 1. Another approach was that taken by D. de F. Abrahamse, who presents the ratio of female to male monasteries in the century in which they are first attested, that is, 6:6, 10:25, 9:18, and 6:23 for the eighth through eleventh centuries, respectively. See "Women's Monasticism in the Middle Byzantine Period: Problems and Prospects," *ByzF* 9 (1985): 35–58, at 36–37. I would guess that the eleventh is the most richly documented of these four centuries, that is, that in which the proportion might be least severely affected by the chance survival of evidence. If that is true, potentially at least, the eleventh century proportion of one female for every four male houses would indicate about 20 percent female houses, which coincides with Talbot's assessment for Constantinople over the full span of Byzantine history as well as that strangely familiar proportion of female-to-male representation that we encounter in England at the Norman Conquest and elsewhere also.

40 Varinlioğlu, "Urban Monasteries in Constantinople and Thessaloniki," 192.

41 Talbot, "Comparison," 1–2.

42 Ibid., 1.

to 14.1 percent of the totals of 981 and 1,028 houses. His efforts to reconstruct the possible sizes of various communities allowed him to estimate the overall numbers of religious personnel. From nearly a quarter (22.9 percent) of all 1,094 estimated monks and nuns in 1066, women religious declined to under a fifth (17.1 percent) of the estimated total of 2,575 male and female regular religious around 1100. The proportion of women stays in that vicinity until the eve of the Black Death, when they appear to have comprised 18.5 percent of the total of some 18,005 religious.[43] The fraction of all kinds of religious who were women would naturally be lower if we were to add into the equation the unestimated numbers of secular clergy.

Finally, a study of the monasteries founded in northern Italy throughout the early Middle Ages concludes that of the total of 169 new religious houses, nearly a quarter were created for women (40 of 167; 24 percent).[44] In sum, whether we look at Byzantium, medieval England, or early medieval northern Italy, women's religious houses were always fewer than men's; they seem to have constituted between a tenth and a quarter of the total of regular religious establishments. The Holy Land looks to be on the higher end of the spectrum. We have already observed that among Christian religious establishments of all descriptions, those which included women represented about one-tenth (above, p. 52). Looking at it from a strictly monastic perspective, the five women's cenobitic houses formed just under one-fifth (17.9 percent) of the cenobitic communities of the Holy Land known from the roll (see table 3.1).[45]

The Breve preserves the record of 68 women religious in Jerusalem, while the Memorial does not specify the number in the convent at Tiberias. Thus women represent 16.8 percent (68 of 405) of total Christian religious personnel at Jerusalem, and 7.9 percent of all 865 recorded religious in these documents. Correcting for missing data as above, the total numbers of female religious come to 90 nuns, or 8.7 percent of the Holy Land's estimated total orthodox religious establishment (90 of 1,037).[46] Within the world of cenobites, women constituted 12.6 percent

---

43 Knowles and Hadcock, *Medieval Religious Houses,* 494, unnumbered table, if I read this table correctly. The discrepancies between the numbers given for the same years at the beginning of one period and the end of the preceding one are difficult to understand. See the discussion of proportions in B. L. Venarde, *Women's Monasticism and Medieval Society: Nunneries in France and England, 890–1215* (Ithaca, 1997), 6–16 and 179–86. Note, however, that Venarde's research is geared toward studying new foundations of women's religious houses in medieval France and England rather than relative proportions of existing houses.

44 A. Veronese, "Monasteri femminili in Italia settentrionale nell'alto medioevo. Confronto con i monasteri maschili attraverso un tentativo di analisi 'statistica'," *Benedictina* 34 (1987): 355–416, here 360. This valuable study treats the period 568–1024.

45 That is, 5 houses represent 17.9 percent of the 28 distinct religious communities by gender of the 27 cenobitic houses documented in the roll: here the double community of monks and nuns at the Virgin's Tomb outside Jerusalem is counted twice, hence 28 communities rather than 27.

46 For the extrapolations of the missing numbers, see above, chapter 2.2.

of the directly documented total (68 nuns vs. 471 male for a total of 539 recorded cenobitic monks) for the whole Holy Land. In terms of corrected totals, nuns comprised 12.4 percent (90 nuns out of a total estimated cenobitic monastic population of 725) of the total number of cenobites in the Holy Land.[47] While these figures look generally comparable to what we find in Western Europe, they are much larger than what the preliminary prosopographical data indicate for late medieval Byzantium, and they further underscore that the discrepancy between the relatively large proportion of female houses in Constantinople at that date and the prosopographical data about individuals must be ascribed to underreporting of the latter. Finally, one further striking fact is that in Jerusalem, for which we have the complete figures assembled by Charlemagne's envoys, nuns constituted almost half (68 of 159; 42.8 percent) of all religious persons explicitly identified as cenobites.

This high proportion of women among Jerusalem cenobites reflects in part a pattern of their distribution in the Holy Land that we have already noted: the urban location of Palestinian convents. In Byzantium too convents were predominantly located in towns. But some at least took root in the holy mountain monastic centers otherwise dominated by male monks—at Galesios, Auxentios, and Olympos—perhaps in part to accommodate female relatives of male monks established in those centers.[48] Beyond the Greek-speaking world, early medieval women's communities formed in both towns and countryside of northern Italy. Nevertheless, there too women's houses clustered decisively and preferentially in towns, as table 3.6 indicates. The regional patterns vary within northern Italy. For instance, the western regions of the Po Valley show more rural monasteries. Similarly, the preferred location of new foundations changed over time: while newly founded female houses were overwhelmingly urban under the Lombards and again in the tenth and early eleventh centuries, town convent foundation slackened there during the period of Frankish dominance in the eighth and ninth centuries.[49] In France and England in the late eleventh and twelfth centuries, the pattern looks interestingly different. Between 1080 and 1170, newly founded nunneries avoided the cities: barely one in ten was located within five kilometers of a town, and the proportion dropped to below 9 percent from 1171 to 1215, even as towns expanded rampantly and, at least in England, the foundation of religious houses accelerated immensely.[50] Although both Byzantium and

---

47 The total is calculated as follows: in or around Jerusalem, 91 cenobitic monks and 68 nuns; elsewhere in the Holy Land, 380 documented monks, which should be increased by the extrapolated missing figures of 164 additional monks in the incompletely reported monasteries and other communities, and 22 nuns, on which estimates, see above, chapter 2.2.

48 Talbot, "Comparison," 2–4.

49 Veronese, "Monasteri femminili," 377–78.

50 Venarde, *Women's Monasticism*, 142–43, with table 4. Judging indirectly from table 4, unless a dramatic change had occurred since 1080, Prof. Venarde seems to be including houses distant up

TABLE 3.6   Urban versus rural
monastic foundations, northern Italy, 568–1024

Houses	Urban		Rural	
	Quantity	%	Quantity	%
Women's	31	77.5	9	22.5
Men's	57	44.9	70	55.1

Source: Veronese, "Monasteri femminili," 374–79.

northern Italy hint that the urban location of female monasteries we observe in ninth-century Palestine reflects a Mediterranean social and institutional matrix, unlike the Palestinian case, neither parallel is exclusively urban. One wonders therefore whether the distinctively urban character of women's religious institutions reflects some historical inheritance, dangerous conditions in the region's countryside as opposed to walled towns, the recent frequency of disturbances in Palestine, or some other cause.

These broad-gauged comparisons help clarify what was unique, and what less so, about the state of the Palestinian church at the beginning of the ninth century. They suggest the value in reaching across the sea for comparative evidence. We will conclude with a final, more closely focused first comparative analysis of the new data. Though distant in space, one contemporary church whose history also goes far back into Christian antiquity seems particularly propitious as a point of comparison: Lyons.

4. Two Early Medieval Churches: Lyons and the Holy Land

The scope of the evidence available on the religious population of Lyons in the early ninth century is narrower, but the data appear remarkably precise and accurate. Half comes from a source that is virtually contemporary with the roll, prepared for the same set of eyes, and for much the same reason. Around 809–12, the ancient town's archbishop, Leidrad, was approaching the end of a remarkable tenure. He wanted to obtain from Charlemagne continued support for the reform that the prelate had launched in Lyons. At almost the same moment that the documents from Basel were being compiled for the same ruler's attention, the aging archbishop prepared a kind of statistical overview of the state of the episcopal

---

to twenty-five kilometers when he refers (143) to almost half of all new nunneries being "within a few kilometers" of a town. For the accelerating foundation of religious houses in this period, see Knowles, *The Religious Orders in England*, 2:256–59.

churches of his diocese as background for his request.[51] The man's connections with the king were close enough that he had been summoned from his Bavarian home in Freising and entrusted with reforming one of the great sees of Gaul. Leidrad had played an important role in the heresy case of Felix, bishop of Urgel, in the strategic zone on the border of Muslim Spain, and it is possible that, as a younger man, he had ministered to the king in person, in the royal chapel.[52] In any case, alongside the very influential courtier Theodulf of Orléans, Leidrad had certainly served Charlemagne as a *missus dominicus* even before he assumed his duties as archbishop.[53] He also shared some sort of experiences with the great court figure Alcuin, who calls him a "partner" (*consocius*) and friend.[54] Leidrad was among the elite group who witnessed Charles's last will and testament.[55] Such close connections with the king suggest that Leidrad was not improvising when he decided that, to obtain Charles's help, he would have to provide a detailed reckoning of the state of his church. The parallel between the Basel roll and the situation at Lyons goes even further. To judge from the manuscript tradition, Leidrad's description of his church, its buildings, and its personnel also was followed by a financial statement, although this details the church's revenues rather than its expenditures.[56] The similarity in the historical context of the Basel roll is striking:

51 See Oexle, *Forschungen*, 135–37, on the motives for the document, and 134 n. 173, on the approximate date.

52 J. Semmler, "Zu den bayrisch-westfränkischen Beziehungen in karolingischer Zeit," *Zeitschrift für bayerische Landesgeschichte* 29 (1966): 344–424, here 402–15. B. Bischoff detected Leidrad's distinctive handwriting in Lyons manuscripts. See *Die südostdeutschen Schreibschulen und Bibliotheken in der Karolingerzeit* (Wiesbaden, 1960–1980), 1:84f. J. Fleckenstein suspected Leidrad's presence in the royal chapel. See *Die Hofkapelle der deutschen Könige*, 2 vols., Schriften der Monumenta Germaniae Historica 16 (Stuttgart, 1966), 1:105 n. 390. See also the careful discussion in Oexle, *Forschungen*, 134–35.

53 Theodulf of Orleans, *Versus contra iudices* 118–19, 496.

54 Alcuin uses the term five more times in his letters, and it seems to designate individuals who share a certain fate. In *Ep.* 10, 61.9 he refers to Felix of Urgel's associates; in *Ep.* 156, 286.25 he refers to himself as a *consocius* in salvation of his close friend Arn of Salzburg ("Meque tuae salutis consocium . . .") who needs the help of Arn's prayers; and similarly in *Ep.* 173, 286.28 he writes, "me tuae salutis unanimem filium, fratrem, consocium." The phrase *consocius salutis* is exceedingly rare but occurs in this sense in an anonymous Irish *Commentarium in Lucam* (8, 70.230), composed about 780–85, possibly in the circle of Virgil of Salzburg, and known in a manuscript copied about 790–800. Compare J. F. Kelly, ed., *Commentarium in Lucam*, CCSL 108C (1974), xv, on the origins of the work. Alcuin also refers to those who were sharing the tribulations of patriarch George of Jerusalem as George's *consocii*. Finally, he criticizes the powerful Adalhard of Corbie for not helping him, if not as a friend, then as a (spiritual) brother and *consocius*, whom Adalhard had himself introduced into the *familia* of Adalhard's abbey of Corbie, presumably through a prayer association (*Ep.* 237, 382.26). Is it a coincidence that Theodulf refers to Leidrad as his "sorte sodalis" (*Versus contra iudices* 117, 496)?

55 Einhard, *Vita Karoli* 33, 41.5.

56 Both documents are cited from the only satisfactory edition, by A. Coville, *Recherches sur l'histoire de Lyon du Vme siècle au IXme siècle (450–800)* (Paris, 1928), 283–88.

here too a detailed written report enumerates personnel and finances as a condition for significant royal support. The structural and contextual links between the two reports provide insight into how Charlemagne and his advisors actually governed their empire in the waning years of the glorious reign.

Another circumstance adds depth to our picture of Lyons. Less than twenty years after Leidrad sent his report to Charlemagne, lists of the living members of the same group of churches were entered into the memorial book of the abbey of Reichenau, allowing a second snapshot of the religious population of episcopal houses of Lyons which is precious on its own merits.[57]

The Lyons data are not comparable in every respect to that of the Basel roll. It includes only episcopal houses, that is, houses that were especially subject to the bishop's protection and tutelage, beyond his jurisdiction as ordinary of the place.[58]

---

57 On the Lyons lists, their contents, and approximate date of about 830, see Oexle, *Forschungen*, 52–63, with an edition of the lists, which are reproduced in Reichenau Memorial Book, 94A1–96C2 and 126A3–B2.

58 As Oexle, *Forschungen*, 146–57, has shown, the churches that Leidrad had reformed and reorganized enjoyed a special status under Leidrad's *mundeburdis et defensio*, likely modeled on Chrodegang of Metz's arrangements for Gorze and recognized by the payment of an annual census. It is conceivable that houses existed in Lyons beyond those Leidrad mentions, but that does not seem very likely. Every shrine documented in all the sources and archaeology relevant to late antiquity and the early Middle Ages down to about 900 is discussed by P.-A. Février, J.-C. Picard, C. Pietri, et al., "Lyon," in *Province ecclésiastique de Lyon (Lugdunensis Prima)*, ed. B. Beaujard, P.-A. Février, J.-C. Picard, et al., vol. 4 of *Topographie chrétienne des cités de la Gaule, des origines au milieu du VIIIe siècle*, 13 vols. (Paris, 1986), 15–35, at 22–35. The one possible exception might be the fifth-century cemetery basilica of St. Justus (Saint-Just), about which Leidrad is silent and which had 15 canons in the time of the Reichenau lists (on which see below, note 61). It is unclear whether the omission is due to the absence of personnel, the good state of the shrine, or some other reason. The recent publication of its excavation mentions no datable material or construction after the seventh century; the stratigraphy seems to move directly from a layer with sixth-century materials to one characterized by ceramic assigned to the tenth or eleventh century. See J.-F. Reynaud, *Lugdunum Christianum: Lyon du IVe au VIIIe s. Topographie, nécropoles et édifices religieux*, Documents d'archéologie française 69 (Paris, 1998), 87–135, esp. 130. If it was occupied in Leidrad's day, it could have comprised some 15 canons, judging from the Reichenau and later ninth-century evidence. See Oexle, *Forschungen*, 144–45, and Février et al., "Lyon," 27–28. Within the episcopal group of St. John, St. Stephen, and Holy Cross, it seems clear from Leidrad and the Reichenau lists of Lyons clergy that the canons of the cathedral resided in St. Stephen's, next to the cathedral of St. John. Leidrad does not mention the Holy Cross, and the archaeology leaves unclear whether this church was functioning in the Carolingian period (Février et al., "Lyon," 26). Leidrad reports that he rebuilt three churches, for which he does not mention any personnel: Sts. Nicetius (Nizier), St. Mary, St. Eulalia–St. George (ibid., 32–34). Given what Leidrad says about their state of decay, and that he states outright that St. Eulalia was a church where there had been nuns ("ubi fuit monasterium puellarum . . . quam . . . a fundamentis erexi"; Letter, ed. Coville, *Recherches*, 285), it seems quite likely that no one was attached to these churches at the time he sent his report to Charlemagne. For the divergence on the dating of the structures of St. Nizier between Leidrad and the sixth or seventh century, see Reynaud, *Lugdunum Christianum*, 197. The brief of Lyons's resources mentions no ecclesiastical personnel for the two hostels or hospices: Brief, ed. Coville, *Recherches*, 288. No activity had been attested at the funerary basilicas of St. Justus, St. Irenaeus, St. Laurent de

Although that probably has no consequences for the town of Lyons itself, it does mean that non-episcopal abbeys elsewhere in the diocese are not treated, including those as important as Nantua, Savigny, and St. Claude. In other words, what was being tallied was neither a geographical entity nor even, strictly speaking, a diocesan one but rather, as Otto Gerhard Oexle has shown, an institutional and personal one, that is, the group of churches subordinate to the archbishop of Lyons.

Furthermore, the church of the patriarchate of Jerusalem offers a fairly well-defined whole in terms of regional geography. Lyons's religious geographic context, by contrast, is more complex, given the close proximity of the rival see of Vienne, only about thirty kilometers downstream on the Rhone from Lyons. It is hard to imagine that the proximity did not somehow affect the distribution and size of the religious communities in both ecclesiastical provinces. In other words, the closest comparisons can be drawn between the ecclesiastical establishment of Jerusalem and its immediate environs and the episcopal town of Lyons rather than between the broader ecclesiastical provinces. As noted, Leidrad's report seems to represent all houses at Lyons itself in addition to two others dependent on the archbishop. Within these parameters, the documents offer a remarkably precise and, for Lyons itself, practically complete picture. What is more, less than a generation separates the Lyons and Reichenau documents.[59] This affords a comparison that reveals, remarkably close-up, both stability and marked change.

Let us begin by taking a closer look at the way the religious communities of Lyons were developing in these years. Such a view helps us remember that, wonderful though the details preserved on the Basel roll may be, they represent a snapshot, not a film; we must remain sensitive to the possibility of short-term change before and after the moment of recording. Oexle's analysis of Leidrad's report, the brief of revenues, and the Lyons entries in the Reichenau memorial book has made very likely that Leidrad's report supplies a kind of missing link between the reform promulgated by Charlemagne in 802 and the great reform council his successor convened at Aachen in 816. Leidrad's activity was clearly inspired by Chrodegang's canonial program implemented at Metz in the previous century (on which see below, p. 145). Leidrad had brought in a singer from Metz to train his own clergy

Choulans, and St. Michael between late antiquity and the late Carolingian period or later. Février et al., "Lyon," 29–31; cf. Oexle, *Forschungen*, 145, on St. Justus and St. Irenaeus. On St. Irenaeus, see also Reynaud, *Lugdunum Christianum*, 175–82. However the most recent archaeology indicates that the cemetery of St. Laurent continued in use down to the eighth century and perhaps beyond; the church might have been in use but was replaced by a chapel in the tenth century. See Reynaud, *Lugdunum Christianum*, 137–73, esp. 172–73. As Février et al. imply ("Lyon," 35), the silence of Lyons records about St. Martin of Ainay before the second half of the ninth century may suggest that it did not exist then. Compare Reynaud, *Lugdunum Christianum*, 196. For other churches, none of which show signs of life in Leidrad's day, see Février et al., "Lyon," 31–34. On the need for archaeological investigation of these shrines, see Reynaud, *Lugdunum Christianum*, 265.

59 Oexle, *Forschungen*, 143.

TABLE 3.7 Changes in religious personnel
of the churches of the archbishop of Lyons, early ninth century

Institution	Numbers		growth	% change
	ca. 809–12	ca. 830		
At Lyons				
archbishop	1	1	0	
chorbishops	2	2	0	
St. John Baptist	–	–		
St. Stephen, canons	52	67	15	28.8
Saint-Nizier, canons	–	20	20	
St. Mary	–	–		
St. Eulalia–St. George, ex-convent becomes canonial house ca. 830	–	19	19	
St. Paul, canons	24	25	1	4.2
St. Paul, poor people	[12][a]	–	n/a	
St. Peter, nuns	32	42	10	31.3
St. Roman, hospice	–	–		
St. Genesius, hospice	–	–		
Saint-Just	0?[b]	15	15?	100?
Île-Barbe, monks	90	99	9	10
Subtotal	**201**	**290**	**89**	**44.3**
Outside Lyons				
St. Rambert, monks	56	56	0	
Total	**257**	**346**	**89**	**34.6**

Sources: Leidrad, Letter to Charlemagne, and Brief, 285–88; Oexle, *Forschungen*, 55–58. Compare Reichenau Memorial Book, 94–96.
[a]The poor people reported as cared for by the church of St. Paul are naturally not counted among the totals of religious personnel in Lyons.   [b]See n. 61.

in the reformed chant. His aim was presumably to organize performance of the liturgy of the hours in the public setting of the cathedral of Lyons, thereby opening its spiritual benefits to a broader public than might hear the office chanted privately inside the monasteries of Leidrad's diocese. Oexle further judges that, based on the Reichenau lists of members of Lyons religious communities, less than two decades later the populations of the churches of Lyons either remained about the same or, in the case of St. Stephen's and the convent of St. Peter, increased by about a third. This growth he connects with the more substantial endowments of these two churches recorded in Leidrad's brief of revenues of religious houses in Lyons. This in turn suggests that the growth was planned in advance, in order to staff public liturgical offices in the cathedral and to produce the books required by those services and the newly invigorated ecclesiastical life of the diocese.[60]

Several highly interesting trends emerge from table 3.7. To understand what was happening at Lyons, we should leave aside the episcopal house of Saint-Rambert with its unchanging number of monks about fifty kilometers distant. On the other hand, it makes sense to include as part of the picture at Lyons the monastery on the Île-Barbe, which lay on the Saône about six kilometers upstream from the cathedral. In only two decades, the data in table 3.7 show a hefty increase in the overall size of the religious population. The additional eighty-nine vocations documented at Lyons about 830 constitute nearly a 50 percent increase with respect to the 201 ecclesiastics living in Lyons late in Charlemagne's reign.[61] Second, as Oexle has noted, this upward trend did not affect all religious institutions evenly. Table 3.7 shows that Saint-Nizier and possibly Saint-Just went from apparently nothing to twenty and fifteen, respectively, and St. Eulalia–St. George (of which it is not certain whether it was still a functioning convent before Leidrad's reform) may have grown from nothing to nineteen canons. These cases aside, growth was steepest at the cathedral, where the chapter increased by fifteen persons, or almost a third, and at the convent of St. Peter, where the number of nuns increased by about the same proportion. Oexle has plausibly linked this growth, in the former case, with the Carolingian canonial reform's emphasis on expanding performance of the public liturgy in the cathedrals. Also plausibly, but more speculatively, he connects the increase in nuns with the production of books needed for the ongoing religious reform.[62] The 10 percent increase among the monks of Île-Barbe presumably reflects the continuing dynamism of that newly reformed monastery, for which Leidrad had recruited the intervention of Benedict of Aniane and some 20 monks from Aniane itself. The latter are presumably already included in Leidrad's total of 90 monks at Île-Barbe.[63]

---

60 Ibid., 143–57, esp. 145–46.

61 Even were we to allow that Leidrad for some reason omitted an existing community at Saint-Just, this would probably only lessen the increase by some 15 religious and leave the overall growth at 36.8 percent in less than a generation. We might hypothesize a community of around 15 in Leidrad's time, if such a community even existed, on the basis of Oexle, *Forschungen*, 144–45, whose discussion indicates a stable-sized community for Saint-Just of 15 members about 830 and 14 about 868.

62 B. Bischoff, *Mittelalterliche Studien. Ausgewählte Aufsätze zur Schriftkunde und Literaturgeschichte*, 3 vols. (Stuttgart, 1966–81), 2:18–19, mentions no sign of a nuns' scriptorium. S. Tafel, "The Lyons Scriptorium," *Palaeographia Latina* 4 (1925): 62–64, reports no female names among the many manuscripts associated with Lyons in this period.

63 ". . . ita restauravi ut tecta de novo fierent et aliqua de maceriis a fundamentis erigerentur, ubi nunc monachi secundum regularem disciplinam numero XC habitare viderentur" (Leidrad, Letter, 286). Together with Ardo's implication that the reform coincided with the rebuilding, the reform clearly seems already to have occurred when Leidrad wrote. Compare Ardo: ". . . Leidradus Lugdunensium pontifex volens monasterium quod vocatur Insula-Barbara rehedificare, quaesivit

Male canons were clearly on the ascendant in Lyons for, if the reporting is complete, their absolute numbers nearly doubled in under two decades (table 3.7).[64] This reflects the continuing effects of Chrodegang's reform, reinforced by Charlemagne's program of 802 and then by the Aachen council of 816. Canons increased by about 7 percent as a proportion of the town's overall religious population, so that they were approaching 50 percent of it about 830 (37.8 percent under Leidrad, 45.2 percent two decades later). This canonial dynamism contrasts with the development of the monks, whose absolute numbers grew only slightly (from 146 to 155, or 5.8 percent, including the distant Saint-Rambert, whose numbers in any case did not change). Their share of the religious population at Lyons dropped from 44.8 percent to 34.1 percent, although recent growth connected with the reform of Île-Barbe may be masked, since Leidrad compiled his report after the reform. In any case, over the next twenty years, the sole remaining convent would show the highest growth rate (31.3 percent) of any house in or near Lyons, even though the overall share of women in the religious life of the episcopal center declined slightly (15.9 percent under Leidrad; 14.5 percent about 830). What is more, the proportion of active houses at Lyons that were female dropped from one out of four, or even two out of five (depending on how recently St. Eulalia had lost her community of nuns) under Leidrad, to one out of seven under his successor. One wonders whether this pattern of shrinking representation of convents within the overall framework of religious houses, even as the general proportion of nuns remained about the same, was limited to Lyons. Rather than purely organic growth and decline, the trend could reflect a consolidation of more nuns in fewer houses. If so, one is tempted to suspect a desire to impose tighter control over female houses, to con-

---

instanter qui ei initium bonae vitae ostenderent, et accepit siquidem electos ferme a grege 20 discipulos, quibus preposuit rectorem eosque Burgundiae partibus ad habitandum direxit. Quo, prestante Christo domino, nunc in sancta religione pollentes et florentes, pregrandis est turba adgregata monachorum" (*Vita Benedicti Anianensis* [BHL 1096], 24, 209.40–45). Oexle (*Forschungen*, 149–50) provides a useful discussion, and criticizes Josef Semmler and others for taking the long first sentence to mean that Benedict, rather than Leidrad, the grammatical subject of the sentence, chose Campio and sent him north to Burgundy with the Aniane monks. However, it does seem strange that Leidrad would have *sent* ("direxit") monks from Aniane to Burgundy, which awakens the suspicion that Ardo might carelessly have shifted the subject from Leidrad to Benedict, if the edition is reliable. Ardo's Latin is less than perfect. See F. Rädle, "Ardo von Aniane," *LMA* 1:915. One could perhaps imagine, on the other hand, that Leidrad came to Aniane, selected the reformers and did indeed send them to Lyons. Campio has been identified as a Lombard name. See H. Kaufmann, *Altdeutsche Personenamen. Ergänzungsband* (Munich, 1968), 77. Compare N. Francovich Onesti, *Vestigia longobarde in Italia (568–774). Lessico e antroponimia* (Rome, 1999), 205. In any case, the reforming monks from the Visigoth Benedict's Septimanian monastery help to explain the oft-noted presence of a "Spanish colony" among Lyons book users and producers in these years. See, for example, Bischoff, *Mittelalterliche Studien*, 2:18.

64 From 76 to 146, that is, 92.1 percent, assuming that no numbers are lacking from Leidrad's time. If we were to assume that some 15 canons were already established at Saint-Just (above, note 61), then canons still increased by 62.3 percent.

centrate the female religious as well, perhaps, as their resources, and so to reduce costs, or indeed, to achieve both ends.[65]

To return to our point of departure, what can we say about the Christian church of Jerusalem in the light of this remarkable data from a contemporary Frankish archiepiscopal center? Certainly Lyons contrasts with Jerusalem on a number of points. We have only a single snapshot of the composition of the religious establishment in Jerusalem, and we cannot rule out a priori that things could change as quickly in the Holy Land as they did in Burgundy. Even so, it seems difficult to believe from what we know about the long-term development of the Christian church in Palestine that its short-term trajectory even remotely resembled the dynamism that is evident in Carolingian Lyons and detectible across the Frankish Empire. And it is worth stressing that the Carolingian surge emerges sharply even though we are starting the comparison with figures from the *end* of the first reforming archbishop's reign: had we information from before the reform, the growth curve probably would look even steeper. We can only imagine the impact of stories of this dynamism in Jerusalem, where Frankish pilgrims' stories could be backed up by the eyewitness testimony of the Greek envoys from the Holy Land who perforce rode across Charlemagne's empire to reach the royal court. Those foreign envoys likely lodged in the Frankish Empire's flourishing abbeys and episcopal mansions in the course of their travels to the king.[66]

Still, Jerusalem was nothing to sneeze at. Its total religious population of more than 405 persons (not including the 15 lepers) was almost exactly double that of contemporary Lyons, and it would still have looked considerably bigger in comparison with the increased ecclesiastical population recorded at Lyons a couple of decades later. Monasticism seems obviously more important at Jerusalem than Lyons, numerically and culturally. The distinctive prominence of the canonial movement launched by Chrodegang of Metz and as implemented at Lyons by Leidrad explains this sharp difference. Although historians are prone to focus on monasticism, that difference usefully reminds us of the signal importance of the canonial movement in the Carolingian church, an importance detectible in the roll itself.[67] The proportion of women is remarkably similar in both churches: the 16.8 percent of religious who were women at Jerusalem is virtually identical with

65 See the general observations of C. de Clercq, *La législation religieuse franque de Clovis à Charlemagne. Étude sur les actes de conciles et les capitulaires, les statuts diocésains et les règles monastiques (507–814)*, Université de Louvain. Recueil de travaux, 2nd ser., 38 (Louvain, 1936), 296.

66 For instance, the monk of St. Sabas who accompanied other envoys to Charlemagne's court at Rome at Christmas 800. See *Annales regni Francorum* s.a., 112. As Ganshof notes, envoys enjoyed the same privileges as *missi dominici* in requisitioning food and shelter on official business. F. L. Ganshof, *The Carolingians and the Frankish Monarchy: Studies in Carolingian History*, trans. J. Sondheimer (Ithaca, 1971), 174.

67 See below, chapter 7.3, on how the roll assimilates the Greek cathedral clergy of the Holy Land with Frankish cathedral canons.

the percentage at Lyons under Leidrad and comparable to the slightly reduced proportion some twenty years later (15.9 percent and 14.5 percent, respectively). Although Lyons spotlights the urban location of the two convents mentioned by Leidrad, in this respect the broader picture of the province of Lyons differs from that of Palestine, for we know of at least one rural convent in the diocese that had been founded before Leidrad's day, the seventh-century priory of Cousance (*Cosancus*), and another, Our Lady of La Bruyère (*Brueria*), that arose in the ninth century.[68]

A second significant difference between the episcopal churches of Lyons and the Jerusalem church merits mention. We have already seen that Carolingian religious communities probably ran larger than those both of Byzantium and the Holy Land. Leidrad's episcopal houses confirm this suggestion. His five houses totaled 257 persons, for an average house size of about 51. The thirty shrines recorded for Jerusalem totaled 405 male and female religious personnel, for the much smaller average staffing of 13 or 14 ecclesiastics per shrine. Naturally this low number is due partially to the pilgrimage character of the Jerusalem church: many memorial shrines there had only skeleton staffs. Nevertheless, even leaving aside the substantial number of such churches (19, averaging 1.7 ecclesiastics) that had three or fewer ecclesiastics attached to them, and the cathedral complex of the Holy Sepulcher, at the other end of the scale, the remaining ten still average only 15.4 persons, compared to the analogous figure for Leidrad's churches at Lyons, minus the cathedral chapter of St. Stephen, of an average of 48.6 (or, including Saint-Rambert, 50.5). By around 830, Lyons's episcopal shrines, minus the cathedral chapter, were getting both more numerous and smaller. Yet they still averaged over twice the size of the larger Jerusalem communities (six houses totaling 220, an average size of 36.7; including Saint-Rambert, a total of 276, averaging 39.4 persons each). Looked at in a different way, the contemporary Carolingian church had fewer and significantly bigger groups. The well-documented case of Lyons confirms the inference drawn from more scattered data: a Carolingian visitor would have been struck by the predominantly smaller size of Palestinian monasteries. What difference this would have made for the monks' social experience of monasticism and the tenor of cenobitic life is an open and interesting question.

So what have we learned from this experiment in the comparative study of the populations of early medieval monasteries around the Mediterranean? Thanks to the careful work of Charlemagne's envoys and their informants, we have a clear picture of the situation in the Holy Land. Jerusalem dominated the religious establishments of the entire area, for nearly half of all Christian religious under

68 See M. Parisse and J. Leuridan, eds., *Atlas de la France de l'an mil. État de nos connaissances* (Paris, 1994), 74–75; and J. Beyssac, *Abbayes et prieurés de l'ancienne France*, vol. 1, *Province ecclésiastique de Lyon*, Archives de la France monastique 37 (Ligugé, 1933), 170; la Bruyère: ibid., 141.

A Mediterranean Church in the Early Middle Ages

patriarchal authority resided and prayed in and around the Holy City. Monasticism dominated Jerusalem and the patriarchate by sheer weight of numbers and physical proximity. As we have already noted, this would work important consequences on the long-term development of the Byzantine church, for the Palestinian influence on the medieval patriarchal church of Constantinople would be deep, enduring, and heavily monastic.

Along the same lines, the roll affords us rare insight into the significant presence of hermits, who comprise almost 9 percent of the total religious persons of Jerusalem about 808. Women too were a minority among religious vocations, accounting for 10 percent of houses and 8 percent of individuals across the entire patriarchate. This proportion increased significantly in Jerusalem itself, such that women constituted 16 percent of the total religious population of the town. Their traces in the surviving written sources are all the more enigmatically invisible for that real and substantial presence. In Palestine, their religious experience was exclusively urban. Although one can detect an urban tendency in Byzantine female monasticism, and indeed, also in western Europe at some times and places, in Palestine around 800 it was the only option. Finally, it is striking that the percentages of women religious in Lyons and Jerusalem were very similar. One suspects that this is not coincidence, particularly since they align with the general profile of female establishments that ranged between 10 percent and 25 percent of total religious houses in times and places as distant as early medieval northern Italy and high medieval England. But more research will be needed to determine whether the fluctuation of female representation in the written record in general remains in the early Middle Ages at around one sixth or one fifth. If so, one should at least start to ask why that representation appears at that level.

The size cohorts of Carolingian monasteries are strikingly larger than those of both Byzantium and the Holy Land. It is hard not to connect this with the demographic and cultural élan of the Frankish West in the eighth and ninth centuries. Nevertheless, in the same period, strong new growth is also unmistakable in the size and numbers of monasteries at Constantinople, a trend that has been connected both with the broader demographic tendency of Byzantine society and the improving internal dynamic of the monastic movement in the capital.[69] The comparative scrutiny of Lyons and Jerusalem underscores the great impact of the canonial institution in the Frankish West, at least in episcopal towns. After this comparative examination of aspects of the Holy Land church with its sisters in Byzantium and the Frankish Empire, let us turn to look more closely at the presence of the religious of the Frankish Empire in ninth-century Jerusalem.

69 Hatlie, *Monks and Monasteries*, 312–52.

Chapter Four

. . . .

THE CAROLINGIAN ESTABLISHMENTS
IN THE HOLY LAND

THE APPEARANCE OF WESTERN monastic establishments in the Holy
Land is one of the most surprising developments of a period often associated
with cultural and economic isolation. Considered together with other records, the
Breve allows us to ask what these houses were, where and when they came into
being, and what may have become of them.

1. European Nuns in Jerusalem

The Breve takes pains to point out that 17 of the nuns who served at the Holy
Sepulcher were from Charlemagne's empire (line 22). The odd number strengthens the impression that it was carefully obtained. The convent was mixed, since it
included 8 nuns who were not Westerners. That they served at the Holy Sepulcher
suggests that the convent was situated inside the city walls. If so, then the Breve
treats the convent at this point in the document because the nuns were westerners.
Nevertheless, the other three establishments mentioned in this section—which is
clearly demarcated on the roll by a significant space and the summary at the end
of line 24[1]—are either on the Mount of Olives or just beyond it, in Bethany. It is
therefore not impossible that the convent too was on the Mount, right outside the
city walls, across the Kidron Valley (the Valley of Jehoshaphat). Another convent
was certainly located outside the walls, in Gethsemane.[2] There had been two major
convents for women on the Mount of Olives in late antiquity, founded by Melania the Elder in the fourth century and Melania the Younger in the fifth.[3] One

---

1   See below, chapter 11, textual commentary on lines 21–23.
2   The female religious specified on the roll as resident in Jerusalem are the 25 nuns at the shrine
of St. Mary at the Sheep Pool (lines 11–12), and the 2 *inclusae* present at the church of Zion (line 9),
on whom, see above, chapter 3.1, note 14.
3   Wilkinson, *Jerusalem Pilgrims before the Crusades*, 2nd ed. (Warminster, 2002), 335.

of them may have been the very large convent whose 400 women were reported to have suffered terribly at the hands of the Persians in 614.[4] Whether it or some other late antique convent on the Mount overcame that catastrophe and the subsequent upheavals in the Holy Land is unknown, and thus it is unclear whether the house recorded in the Breve, if indeed it was located on the Mount of Olives, was a new foundation or a survivor from late antiquity.

2. The Monastery of Saints Peter and Paul on the Mount of Olives

Most scholars have recognized in the Breve's monastery of Sts. Peter and Paul "in Besanteo at the Mount of Olives"[5] the house of Western monks known from the Frankish sources. "Besanteo" seems to render phonetically the Aramaic place name *Bet Ṣanṭaya*, "the house of the locust trees."[6] This is certainly the church of St. Peter whose dedication was commemorated on 21 January in the early medieval liturgy of Jerusalem, especially since another document refers to the same anniversary as that of St. Paul's.[7] Beyond the Breve, this most unusual house is

4 See above, chapter 2.2, with note 44.

5 In the phrase "iuxta montem Oliueti," *iuxta* is used in its Late Latin sense, equivalent to *apud* or *ad* (see, for example, *ThLL* 7.2:751.38–55), as is clear from the other references to this house mentioned in this section.

6 J. T. Milik, "Notes d'épigraphie et de topographie palestiniennes," *RevBibl* 66 (1959): 550–75, at 553–55. Milik's observation on the use of *in* in the roll to indicate toponyms is well taken. Compare Milik, "Notes d'épigraphie et de topographie palestiniennes: IX. Sanctuaires chrétiens de Jérusalem à l'époque arabe (VIIe–IXe s.)," *RevBibl* 67 (1960): 564. Milik's hypothetical identification of this place with Wadi Qadum, a tributary of Qidron Brook (Nahal Qidron)—the Valley of Kidron (Qidron) separates the Mount of Olives from the Temple Mount—is rejected by Wilkinson (*Jerusalem Pilgrims*, 336). Vailhé's hypothesis that "Besanteo" was a corruption of "monastery of the Byzantines" is based on the phonetic similarity and the topography but otherwise seems to have little to recommend it. See "Répertoire alphabétique des monastères de Palestine [1]," *ROC* 4 (1899): 519. Compare K. Bieberstein and H. Bloedhorn, *Jerusalem: Grundzüge der Baugeschichte vom Chalkolithikum bis zur Frühzeit der osmanischen Herrschaft*, Beihefte zum Tübinger Atlas des Vorderen Orients, Reihe B, Geisteswissenschaften 100 (Wiesbaden, 1994), 3:415–16; and Milik, "Notes d'épigraphie et de topographie," 554–55. Vailhé supposed that this ninth-century monastery was therefore the same one that Moschus reports as having been founded by Abraham, archbishop of Ephesus, apparently on the Mount of Olives, in the sixth century, and which was known in the early seventh century as the unlocalized "monastery of the Byzantines," that is, "the Constantinopolitans" (John Moschus, *Pratum spirituale* 97, PG 87.3:2956D ["μοναστήριον, τὸ ἐπιλεγόμενον τῶν Βυζαντίων"]), which he further combined with the reference to the monastery of Abraham on the Mount of Olives (*Pratum spirituale* 187, PG 87.3:3064D).

7 Thus Milik, "Notes d'épigraphie, IX," 564. Compare the Jerusalem calendar as preserved in the tenth-century manuscript on Sinai, as well as the version of the tenth- or eleventh-century Georgian lectionary in Paris (B.N.F., ms. géorg. 3), *Le calendrier palestino-géorgien*, 137. If we were to hypothesize that the monastery was dedicated in Charlemagne's reign on this date—the anniversary of the Roman martyr St. Agnes—it would have fallen on a Sunday, which was favored for

known from a few mentions in Western sources and the surviving letter its community wrote in 808 to Pope Leo III.[8] It has occasionally been suggested that Sts. Peter and Paul was simply a minor late antique monastery that had continued to exist through the centuries. That seems unlikely, though, given the steep decline and disappearance of cenobitic communities that occurred in the intervening centuries (see chapter 2).[9] Another indication that the monastery was in fact a new foundation comes from a gloss that Bernhard Bischoff spotted in two manuscripts of canon law. The gloss's terse phrasing reflects Carolingian awareness of Western religious in the Holy Land and indicates it was a recent foundation. To explain his source's reference to the official Roman name, Aelia, for the refounded city of Jerusalem after its destruction by the Roman army, the Carolingian glossator wrote, "Aelia is the name of the place where there is *now* a monastery at the Lord's Sepulcher."[10] Bischoff was surely right that, from the pen of a Carolingian observer, such a statement could refer only to a new Western foundation in a land famous for its ancient monasteries. It is conceivable that Sts. Peter

church dedications, in 776, 781, 787, 798, and 804. The last two dates would be consonant with missions of Charlemagne to the Middle East. McCormick, *Origins of the European Economy: Communications and Commerce, A.D. 300–900* (Cambridge, 2001), 887, nos. 238 (AD 797), 888–89, nos. 245 and 248 (AD 799–800), and 891, no. 261 (AD 802–3).

8   *Epistolae selectae pontificum Romanorum* 7, 64–66. See below, chapter 8.2, esp. notes 44 and 45.

9   Milik, "Notes d'épigraphie, IX," 564, quite tentatively, on the basis of the dedication to St. Paul of a late antique monastery of St. Roman, celebrated on 30 April and 19 August in the Georgian calendar, followed, with equal or greater reserves, by Bieberstein and Bloedhorn, *Jerusalem: Grundzüge der Baugeschichte*, 3:415–16.

10   "Aelia nomen loci ubi nunc est monasterium ad sepulcrum domini." Bischoff, *Mittelalterliche Studien*, 3:239. The gloss smacks of a contemporary observation, and the unusual way of identifying Jerusalem by the existence of a new monastery there indicates the novelty and sensational if short-lived importance of the house. Bischoff identifies the monastery in question with the establishment on the Mount of Olives, since he refers to the monastic envoys of 799 and 800 to Charlemagne's court, one of whom is explicitly identified as being a monk from the Mount of Olives: *Annales regni Francorum* a. 800, 112. Sources in the know, including those royal annals (cf. also a. 826, 169), the monks themselves in their letter to Leo III, and the pope himself, correctly identify this monastery with the Mount of Olives (*Epistolae selectae pontificum Romanorum* 7 and 8, 66.22 and 37–38), not the Holy Sepulcher. But one can easily imagine that the 1,500 meters or so separating the Sepulcher from the Mount of Olives did not much matter to someone describing the situation from Frankland. The entry in the Reichenau Memorial Book, 103CD1, "Bonegesius reclusus in monte Oliueti," may simply be referring to a Latin hermit such as those the Breve records around 808 (lines 19–21; see above, chapter 3.1) and so illuminates neither this question nor that of the continued existence of the monastery on the Mount of Olives at the time it was written. The manuscripts that contain the gloss, Berlin, Deutsche Staatsbibliothek, Phillipps 1763 (shortly after AD 800) and Albi, Bibliothèque municipale, 38bis (s. IXmed.), seem to have been written in southern France. See H. Mordek, *Kirchenrecht und Reform im Frankenreich. Die collectio vetus Gallica, die älteste systematische Kanonessammlung des fränkischen Gallien; Studien und Edition*, Beiträge zur Geschichte und Quellenkunde des Mittelalters 1 (Berlin, 1975), 272 and 270, respectively.

and Paul on the Mount of Olives is one of the "very many monasteries" that, in the tenth century, the Byzantine emperor Constantine VII Porphyrogenitus credited Charlemagne with building in connection with his dispatch of "much money and abundant treasure to Palestine."[11] There is no reason to doubt that, whoever founded it, Charlemagne made gifts to this community that surely went beyond the books mentioned by the monks.[12] Its titular saints, Peter and Paul, trumpeted a Western identity to ninth-century Christians, as they do to a modern medievalist. The fact that, unlike the seventeen nuns who precede it, the monastery's Western character is not specified makes perfectly good sense in a report prepared for a king who was in regular contact with the house and who had just received its abbot at his court.[13] The patron saints, Charlemagne's benefactions to the house, and his personal acquaintance with the abbot all obviated the need to specify more about this abbey in a document prepared for the emperor's attention. These considerations only reinforce earlier scholars' recognition of this house mentioned in the Breve as the Western monastery situated on the Mount of Olives in the early ninth century.

The abbot, George, had originally been named Egilbald and, according to the royal annalist, came from "Germany" (*Germania*), that is, the Frankish lands east of the Rhine.[14] We may well think that the annalist met George and the monk Felix at Aachen in 807. The fact that the Frankish abbot from Palestine bore a religious name that was quite unusual in his home region signals that he probably assumed this religious name elsewhere.[15] The main shrine of St. George was in fact in Lydda, near Ramla and, whatever its difficulties, it was regularly visited

---

11 Constantine VII Porphyrogenitus, *De administrando imperio* 26, 1:108.8–9: ὅστις χρήματα ἱκανὰ καὶ πλοῦτον ἄφθονον ἐν Παλαιστίνᾳ ἀποστείλας, ἐδείματο μοναστήρια πάμπολλα.

12 *Epistolae selectae pontificum Romanorum* 7, 65.34–39.

13 The depiction of flourishing monasteries on the Mount of Olives offered by a Greek hagiographical novel composed at Rome in the early ninth century may owe something to knowledge of the Latin establishment, although there had been no shortage of monasteries in the late Roman period the novelist attempted to depict. See *Vita Gregorii Agrigenti* (BHG 707) 26, 176.4–177.13; compare Wilkinson, *Jerusalem Pilgrims*, 335–36.

14 *Annales regni Francorum* a. 807, 123–24. In this phase of the composition of the Royal Annals, *Germania* is used in contrast to Gaul: a. 801, 114, on an earthquake around the Rhine, affecting "Germania" and Gaul; also a. 803, 118 and index, 187. On the composition of the Annals, see W. Wattenbach, W. Levison, and H. Löwe, *Deutschlands Geschichtsquellen im Mittelalter: Vorzeit und Karolinger* (Weimar, 1952–73), 2:251–56.

15 For instance, the name does not appear in the abundant Carolingian onomastic material of Fulda, precisely the area this man is supposed to have come from. Only two Georges turn up anywhere in the Fulda evidence. One is in a fifteenth-century copy of a Fulda necrology and is identified as a *miles*, which does not sound like the ninth century in any case; the other wrote a charter in 994. See K. Schmid, *Die Klostergemeinschaft von Fulda im früheren Mittelalter*, Münstersche Mittelalter-Schriften 8 (Munich, 1978), 3:196, g 132.

by Western pilgrims. Given the Palestinian origins of the cult, it seems likely that Egilbald took this name in the Holy Land. This implies that he became a monk only during his pilgrimage—a not unfamiliar pattern.[16]

Acting as envoys of the patriarch Thomas, George and Felix had not come to Charlemagne's court alone. They traveled with the ambassadors of the caliph himself, Harun al Rashid, whose extraordinary gifts made such an impression on the Franks. Beyond the silks, perfumes, and unguents one might expect from the great international market that was Harun's Baghdad, the caliph sent Charles a spectacular tent and a brass water clock that rang out the hours.[17] Although the Royal Annals, the *Annales regni Francorum*, typically give no hint of the diplomatic business transacted, the embassy clearly marks some high point in relations between the two powers. Charlemagne's desire to impress the caliph in turn and, incidentally, his familiarity with the value of a fine textile in Baghdad come through clearly from his efforts to collect exceptional counter-gifts to send back to the caliph. At the same time, the preparations for the return embassy reveal how Charlemagne and his entourage understood his rulership to work: officials who enjoyed high office and royal favor were expected to help supply the king with the gifts that were indispensable to foreign policy, including with the most powerful ruler in the world, the caliph in Baghdad.[18]

The Memorial usually mentions each Holy Land monastery's abbot by name. The Breve's failure to refer to an abbot in its enumeration of the Western community points to an origin around 807, the period of the absence of Egilbald/George, who was in the West between the sailing season of 806 and his return to Jerusalem in the good weather of 808.[19] Egilbald's direct or indirect successor, abbot Dominic, traveled to the court of Charlemagne's son and successor, Louis the Pious, at Ingelheim, in June of 826.[20] This Dominic could well be the same person who, in 808, ranked high enough to sign in the first place the community's letter to Pope

16 On the cult, see, for example, A. Kazhdan and N. P. Ševčenko, "George," *ODB* 2:834–35. Arculf mentions the shrine (Adomnan, *De locis sanctis* 3.4.12, 230.49–231.54), as did Willibald and Bernard. For them, and the difficulties, see chapter 2.1.

17 *Annales regni Francorum* a. 807, 123–24. For further references, see McCormick, *Origins*, 893–94, no. 277.

18 *Formulae Salzburgenses* 62, 453–55, with the additional text recovered by Bischoff, *Salzburger Formelbücher* 2.2, 34 (cf. pp. 13–14), which adds the size of the tent and reveals Charlemagne's efforts to collect counter-gifts for Harun from his subordinates. The letter emphasizes that the king would especially like gold and *pallium*, since (construing the grammar strictly) the court knew that the latter was particularly expensive in Iraq. Given the origins of this formula collection, it seems highly probable that the very short letter (178 words) was sent to Arn, archbishop of Salzburg (785–821); the author—whose name has been removed—was an abbot who seems to have been acting on Charlemagne's behalf. Adalhard of Corbie is one plausible candidate.

19 McCormick, *Origins*, 893, nos. 271 and 277.

20 *Annales regni Francorum* a. 826, 169. Compare McCormick, *Origins*, 912, no. 396.

Leo.[21] We hear of no more abbots after that, and it is fair to wonder how long the monastery continued to exist. Some forty years after Abbot Dominic's visit to Ingelheim, the eyewitness Bernard the Monk makes much of Charlemagne's foundation of a hostel for Western pilgrims. Yet this Frankish observer, who throughout his travels displays considerable interest in all things monastic, says nothing about a Western monastery in his detailed description of the shrines and sights on the Mount of Olives.[22] The only plausible conclusion is that the monastery of Sts. Peter and Paul had disappeared by that date.

3. The Hostel of Charlemagne

The "Hostel of Charlemagne" is the third establishment of Western religious documented in the Holy Land in the Carolingian age. According to Bernard, who stayed there,

> We were received in the hostel (*hospitale*) of the most glorious emperor Charles, in which are received all who go to that place on pilgrimage and speak Romance. Adjacent to it is a church in honor of St. Mary, which has a most noble Bible [alternatively, "library"][23] thanks to the effort of the aforesaid emperor, with twelve houses, fields, vineyards, and a garden in the Valley of Jehoshaphat. In front of the hostel there is a market, for which

21 *Epistolae selectae pontificum Romanorum* 7, 66.21.
22 Bernard, *Itinerarium* 14–16, 316–17. According to a manuscript rubric, Bernard and his two companions were monks; Bernard himself refers to his traveling companions as "fratres in devotione caritatis" (1, 309), which may confirm this—although the rubric could have been inspired by these very words. *Deuotio* in the Carolingian period could refer to religious vows, for example, Alcuin, *Ep.* 184, 309.24–25. The expression *deuotio caritatis* comes from Bede. See, for example, *De templo* 1, 182.1416–18, or *In Marci euangelium expositio* 4.14, 617.857. Bernard's usage is probably shaped by Bede's homily on the feast day of Benedict Biscop, the Anglo-Saxon monastic leader and founder of Bede's own monastery of Wearmouth-Jarrow: "Qui enim terrenis affectibus siue possessionibus pro christi discipulatu renuntiauerit quo plus in eius amore profecerit eo plures inueniet qui se interno suscipere affectu et suis gaudeant sustentare substantiis eiusdem nimirum professionibus consortes qui se pro christo pauperem factum in suis domibus agrisque recipere et maiore prorsus quam uxor parens frater aut filius carnalis deuotione caritatis refouere delectentur" (*Homiliarum euangelii libri ii* 1.13, 91.83–90), which context makes the monastic connotation clear. Bernard is also very interested in monasteries wherever he goes. See, for example, *Itinerarium* 2, 310, on the abbot and size of the community of St. Michael in Gargano, "qui multis preerat fratribus"; the way he specifies the authority of patriarch Michael of Alexandria over "omnium episcoporum et monachorum et Christianorum . . .": 7, 312; or the monastic background of Patriarch Theodosius of Jerusalem: 11, 315, and so forth.
23 For the semantics of the alternative translations, see M. McCormick, "Textes, images et iconoclasme dans le cadre des relations entre Byzance et l'Occident carolingien," in *Testo e immagine nell'alto medioevo*, 2 vols., Settimane 41 (1994), 1:95–162, at 109 n. 26.

everyone who does business there pays two gold pieces per annum to the man who oversees it.[24]

What and where was this institution? Identifications have ranged from an ancient hostel founded, supposedly, by Gregory the Great, to the famous Crusader shrine of St. Mary of the Latins, *Sancta Maria Latina*. Relying on the pope's ninth-century biographer, Wilkinson has suggested that Charlemagne enlarged a hostel "provided by Gregory the Great not long before the Persian invasion of 614."[25] However, Gregory's letters themselves do not make clear whether such a hostel was ever founded—the amount of money Gregory sent is modest—and the ninth-century story looks like a careless exaggeration of the known papal letter.[26] Even if Gregory had founded such an institution shortly before the devastation of the Persian invasion, the general trend of the Holy Land church in the seventh century does not incline one to optimism about such a hostel's continued existence around two hundred years later.

As understood until now, the Breve's inventory of Christian establishments alludes only indirectly to the existence of hostels in the great pilgrimage center. Greater sensitivity to its wording in light of the historical development of early medieval Latin changes that. At the end of the list of the officers and staffed shrines of the Holy Sepulcher complex, the Breve totals the whole and then notes, "excepto ospitales iii." This has typically been understood as "except for the three guestmasters." Although it seems odd to add up a total number of persons and

24 Bernard, *Itinerarium*, 10, 314: ". . . et recepti sumus in hospitale gloriosissimi imperatoris Karoli, in quo suscipiuntur omnes qui causa devotionis illum adeunt locum, lingua loquentes Romana. Cui adiacet ecclesia in honore sancte Marie, nobilissimam habens bibliothecam studio predicti imperatoris, cum duodecim mansionibus, agris, vineis et orto in valle Iosaphat. Ante ipsum hospitale est forum, pro quo unusquisque ibi negotians in anno solvit duos aureos illi, qui illud provideat." Outside of biblical contexts, in Carolingian records *mansio* most frequently refers to the finding of or right to shelter or, especially, to a house (hence modern French *maison*). See, for example, Charles the Bald, *Capitulare missorum Suessionense*, MGH Capit 2: 269.7–9, no. 259.7; Hincmar of Rheims, Capitulary 5, 86.23; and *Capitula Franciae occidentalis*, 4, 4, ed. R. Pokorny, MGH Capitula episcoporum 3 (Hanover, 1995): 42.9.

25 Wilkinson, *Jerusalem Pilgrims*, 316, citing John Hymmonides' Life of Gregory the Great (BHL 3641), 2.52, PL 75:110A, which draws largely on the same excerpts of the pope's Register that we know today: "Haec quidem Gregorius intra vel extra urbem studio pietatis exercuit. Caeterum Probum religiosum abbatem cum multis pecuniis Jerosolymam destinavit, cujus instantia venerabile xenodochium constituit, et, tam ibi quam in monte Sina penes Arabiam, Dei famulis sub regimine Palladii constitutis, quotidiani victus et vestimenti copiam quandiu vivere potuit annualiter mittere procuravit." Compare Wattenbach, Levison, and Löwe, *Deutschlands Geschichtsquellen*, 468.

26 Gregory seems to express regret concerning an unclear decision he could not change about the inheritance that his abbot Probus had left to found a hostel in Jerusalem and sends along a mere 50*s* as a "benedictio paruula." *Registrum* 13.26 (February 603), 1027. Hymmonides apparently concocted his story of foundation and annual gifts to the Holy Land by combining this document with Gregory's two letters to Sinai of September 600, *Registrum* 11.1–2, ibid., 857–60.

then to add three more in this way, this is a legitimate translation of *hospitalis*, according to classical norms.[27] In classical Latin, the masculine or feminine noun *hospitalis* should be a substantivized adjective designating a person who is associated with a *hospitale*, an institution that welcomes strangers (*hospites*), from travelers to the destitute and the sick. However, there is no neuter in the Romance progeny of Latin, and the decline of the neuter gender in Late Latin led native speakers to conflate the forms *hospitalis* and *hospitale*. In Frankland, Gregory of Tours and the Salic Law both use the masculine singular (*hospitalem*) for the place or right of shelter.[28] The form *hospitalis* for the institutions that welcomed poor people and travelers occurs particularly (but not exclusively) in our period among Italian speakers of Latin. Thus Pope Hadrian I could write to Charlemagne about the hostels (*hospitales*) in the Alps that sheltered pilgrims traveling to Rome.[29] During the decade when other royal officials compiled the Breve, a capitulary promulgated in Italy by Charlemagne's son Pippin juxtaposed the term with *xeno-dochium* (spelled phonetically as *sinodochia*, "hostels") in the same sense.[30] Even closer to home, *hospitalis* was the favored term for hostel in the mouth of Adalhard of Corbie, Charlemagne's cousin, who had lived for many years in Italy and whose influence in the king's entourage in these years was of paramount importance.[31]

27 Thus Wilkinson, *Jerusalem Pilgrims*, 253.

28 Gregory of Tours, *Liber in gloria martyrum* 52, 75.5–6: "Fedamius . . . Cavillonensim urbem adiret, idemque apud basilicam . . . hospitalem habebat, ab abbate loci victus stipendia capiens"; *Pactus Legis Salicae* 55.4, 207.3–4: "aut hospitalem dederit," which the various sixth- through ninth-century recensions sometimes correct to *hospitalitatem*, *hospitium*, or *hospitale* (ibid., pp. 206–7); compare *ThLL* 6.3:3035.3–6. This and the Carolingian evidence disproves the idea of M. Bonnet, *Le latin de Grégoire de Tours* (Paris, 1890), 348, that Gregory's *hospitalem* in this case modified a noun that was understood.

29 *Codex Carolinus* 87, 623.27–28: ". . . una cum hospitales, qui per calles Alpium siti sunt, pro peregrinorum susceptione. . . ." Compare the Life of Leo III in the *Liber pontificalis*, ed. Duchesne, 2:28.5–6: ". . . hospitalem beato Petro apostolo in loco qui Naumachia dicitur a fundamentis noviter construens."

30 MGH Capit 1:209.14–15, no. 102.9: "Ut episcopi et abbates per sinodochia et monasteria eorum ospitalem, ubi antiquitus fuit, faciant et summopere curent, ut nullatenus praetermittantur." See also the capitulary of Louis II of 865, MGH Capit 2:94.6–9, no. 217.5: "senodochia autem sic, ubi sunt neglecta, ad pristinum statum revocent; hospitales vero pauperum tam in montanis, quam et ubicumque fuisse noscuntur, pleniter et diligenti cura restaurentur."

31 On Adalhard in these years, see B. Kasten, *Adalhard von Corbie. Die Biographie eines karolingischen Politikers und Klostervorstehers* (Düsseldorf, 1985 [1986]), 47–68; *Statuta seu brevia*, 10, 372.5: "Constituimus ad ospitalem pauperum cotidie dare panes . . ."; compare 22, 399.4: "ad utilitatem hospitalis." Adalhard's speech habit perhaps reflects his years in Italy; Italianisms seem to have helped delineate the extent of Adalhard's lost writing preserved in a work by Hincmar of Rheims. See below, chapter 8, note 8. Rimbert used the term in the same way in his Life of St. Ansgar: "Specialius tamen hospitalem pauperum in Brema constitutum habebat, ad quem decimas de nonnullis villis disposuit, ut ibi cum cotidiana susceptione pauperum aegroti quoque recrearentur" (*Vita Anskarii* 35, 69). Of course, Ansgar, Rimbert's teacher and master, had been a monk at Corbie, and Rimbert himself had warm relations with Corbie, to whose monks he dedicated the *Vita Anskarii*.

Contemporary usage therefore makes clear for us the meaning of this passage of the Breve. After enumerating the personnel of the patriarchal complex and totting up the total, the compiler notes that he has not counted the personnel associated with three hostels: "They add up to 150, not counting the three hostels."[32]

One of these hostels may well be the one founded by Charlemagne. Their inclusion at the end of the discussion of the staff of the Holy Sepulcher complex suggests that the hostels were reckoned somehow a part of the complex. The likeliest understanding is that they were physically close to these buildings, as one might expect of institutions established for pilgrims. In this connection, scholars have often thought that Charlemagne's new hostel was somehow connected with St. Mary of the Latins. This shrine, favored by Western pilgrims from at least the eleventh century, once stood on the site of the modern German Church of the Redeemer near the Anastasis.[33] The link is not impossible (see map 1 for the hostel's hypothesized location). The map of Golgotha drawn by the seventh-century pilgrim Arculf shows, just south of the Anastasis complex, a church of St. Mary, which has been hypothetically connected with the Carolingian hostel.[34] This church surely still existed when the Franks compiled the Breve, for the early medieval church calendar of Jerusalem mentions a liturgy celebrated there. Presumably its location within the Anastasis complex explains why the Breve compilers did not single it out.[35]

In this case, then, we might be hearing an echo of Adalhard's usage as it influenced his community. For Rimbert's Corbie connections, see, for example, M. Manitius, *Geschichte der lateinischen Literatur des Mittelalters*, Handbuch der klassischen Altertumswissenschaft 9.2 (Munich, 1911–31), 1:705. Conversely, Adalhard called the person who administered or served a hostel in this period "hospitalarius" (*Statuta* 10, 372.10, 14 etc.).

32 The hostels may well have been staffed in part by lay men and women, who were therefore not counted among the religious personnel. Furthermore, we might expect some of the staff to have come from the monastery of the Holy Sepulcher and therefore already to have been counted under that heading. In his contemporary report on the church of Lyons, Leidrad similarly omitted personnel for the two hostels whose revenues he enumerates (Brief, 288); so too there are no reports of special religious personnel attached to them in the spiritual confraternity lists of Lyons preserved in the Reichenau Memorial Book (94A–96D).

33 For example, S. Runciman, "Charlemagne and Palestine," *EHR* 50 (1935): 612–13; Wilkinson, *Jerusalem Pilgrims*, 316; and Bieberstein and Bloedhorn, *Jerusalem: Grundzüge der Baugeschichte*, 2:262.

34 Ibid., 2:262. Wilkinson, *Jerusalem Pilgrims*, 380–82, reproduces and discusses the sketches of shrines preserved by ninth-century manuscripts of Adomnan and Bede. He allows the possibility (365) that Adomnan's illustration of the Church of St. Mary shows the Nea Church, but the design itself—the church is shown inside the walls of the Anastasis complex and its doors face north— allies with the Nea's distance from the Anastasis and the clear Latin statement of Adomnan that the rectangular church of Mary adjoins the Anastasis ("Illi rotundae eclesiae . . . quae et anastassis, hoc est resurrectio, uocitatur . . . a dextera coheret parte sanctae Mariae matris Domini quadrangulata eclesia" [*De locis sanctis* 1.4, 190.4–7]) to rule out that interpretation.

35 On 11 August, as recorded in the tenth-century Georgian calendar on Sinai (St. Catherine's, MS georg. 34), *Le calendrier palestino-géorgien*, 83, with the commentary on that date on 299 and

A Mediterranean Church in the Early Middle Ages

Bernard's description does not precisely situate the hostel, although its location on a marketplace (*forum*) would fit a location south of the Anastasis complex.[36] His statement that the church of St. Mary had received a splendid Bible (or library) from the gift of Charlemagne could mean that it already existed in Charles's time. It is also conceivable that the gift came to St. Mary's from the monastery of Sts. Peter and Paul (see below). Beyond the shrine connected with the Holy Sepulcher, the only other possibilities inside the city according to the Breve's information about churches dedicated to the Virgin would be the ruins of the Nea Church or the church of the Virgin's birthplace, St. Mary of the Sheep Pool; outside Jerusalem, there was Mary's Tomb in Gethsemane or the church on the Mount of Olives, near the Ascension church. Although Bernard's phrasing is not conclusive, it seems less likely that he was referring to a site outside the city walls.[37] All in all, the Breve's inclusion of the mention of the hostels in the section on the Holy Sepulcher joins with the market Bernard mentions in front of Charlemagne's hostel to make the immediate vicinity of the Holy Sepulcher the most attractive possibility. In fact, analysis of the ceramics and stratigraphy of a trench sunk on this site beneath the present-day Lutheran Church of the Redeemer has indicated construction activity in the eighth or ninth century that has been tentatively linked to Charlemagne's hostel.[38]

---

on 22 June: 257. See also Milik, "Notes d'épigraphie, IX," 359–60, who confirms that its location was in some way elevated.

36   Although, *pace* Wilkinson (*Jerusalem Pilgrims*, 316), "situated on the edge of the main forum next to a Church of St. Mary," Bernard's Latin (*Itinerarium* 10, 314) does not *necessarily* locate the church next to "the main forum." The indefinite subject of "est forum" means simply that "there is a market" in front of the hostel. This *could* reinforce the location near the Holy Sepulcher, since the late Roman forum and the early Arab and medieval markets were indeed situated there. See the maps in M. Avi-Yonah and H. Geva, "Jerusalem: The Byzantine Period," in *NEAEHL* 2:769; and D. Bahat, M. Ben-Dov, H. Geva, et al., "Jerusalem: Early Arab to Ayyubid Periods," in *NEAEHL* 2:787, 788.

37   "De Emmaus pervenimus ad sanctam civitatem Ierusalem, et recepti sumus in hospitale. . . ." (*Itinerarium* 10, 314). The variant version of Bernard, from an apparently lost manuscript in Rheims preserved by Jean Mabillon, reads, "De Ramula ad Emmaus castellum, de Emmaus ad sanctam civitatem Hierusalem. Ibi habetur hospitale, in quo suscipiuntur. . . ." (*Acta sanctorum ordinis s[ancti] Benedicti* 2 [Venice, 1734]: 473). Both versions imply that Bernard stayed *in* Jerusalem. For him, the Valley of Jehoshaphat and Gethsemane clearly lay *outside* of Jerusalem. See *Itinerarium* 13 (ed. Tobler and Molinier, 316): "Exeuntes autem de Ierusalem, descendimus in vallem Iosaphath, que abest a civitate milliario, habens villam Gethesemani . . ."; compare Mabillon's redaction: *Itinerarium* 12, 474: "De Hierusalem in valle Josaphat miliari, et habet villam Gethsemani. . . ." Although the Latin is not as clear as one might wish, it seems nevertheless that both Bernard and Christian Druthmar locate only the farms belonging to the hostel in the Valley of Jehoshaphat (see below, note 42).

38   J. Magness, review of K. J. H. Vriezen, I. Carradice, and E. Tchernov, *Die Ausgrabungen unter der Erlöserkirche im Muristan, Jerusalem (1970–1974)* (Wiesbaden, 1994), in *BASOR* 298 (1995): 87–89; compare Bieberstein and Bloedhorn, *Jerusalem: Grundzüge der Baugeschichte*, 2:263.

A location south of the Holy Sepulcher strengthens the possibility of a topographical connection between the church next to the hostel and the later church of St. Mary of the Latins in that same general vicinity.[39] But did the Carolingian hostel survive long enough to become that later medieval church? In the absence of direct evidence, the hostel's financial viability offers one clue on its survival. As we have already seen, Bernard the Monk's description of his visit to the Holy Land details the status in 867 of the endowment Charlemagne had created to finance the hostel. It took the form of revenues deriving from a dozen houses with fields, vineyards, and a garden, located in the Valley of Jehoshaphat (or Kidron), to which Bernard seems to add the rents accruing from merchants who had businesses in the market in front of the church of St. Mary of the Latins. This last sort of financial arrangement had deep roots in the region in late antiquity and continued to thrive in our period.[40]

Within just a few years of Bernard's visit and careful report on the finances of the hostel, the situation had taken a serious turn for the worse. Christian of Stavelot composed in the later years of the ninth century, possibly after 880–81, a remarkably literal and historical commentary on the Gospel of Matthew. In it he draws on the testimony of travelers from the Holy Land and confirms and deepens Bernard's information about the hostel's land holdings.[41] According to Christian,

39 For a possible connection between Charlemagne's hostel and St. Mary of the Latins, see Runciman, "Charlemagne and Palestine," 612–13; Wilkinson, *Jerusalem Pilgrims*, 316; and Bieberstein and Bloedhorn, *Jerusalem: Grundzüge der Baugeschichte*, 2:262–63.

40 Bernard, *Itinerarium* 10, 314, quoted above, note 24. Bernard does not explicitly state that the market rents, or some part of them, benefited the hostel, but it is difficult to imagine why otherwise he would have mentioned this financial detail. Fees from nearby markets were a traditional way of financing urban churches in contemporary Byzantium. Thus the tax revenues of 1,100 shops had been allocated to the church of Constantinople in late antiquity, and a surviving document from the tenth century shows that the practice continued: N. Oikonomides, "Quelques boutiques de Constantinople au Xe s.: Prix, loyers, imposition (*Cod. Patmiacus* 171)," *DOP* 26 (1972): 353–54. An eighth-century papyrus preserves the list of annual rents of shops and houses located in the block of an Egyptian church. A. Grohmann, *From the World of Arabic Papyri* (Cairo, 1952), 161. The practice was taken over by the Muslims. J. Pedersen, "Masḏjid," *EI*² 6 (Leyden, 1991): 671–72. It also helped finance Jewish institutions in the Holy Land in the eleventh century. M. Gil, "Dhimmī Donations and Foundations for Jerusalem (638–1099)," *Journal of the Economic and Social History of the Orient* 27 (1984): 156–74, e.g., 171.

41 Christian's mention of the ongoing conversion of the Bulgars dates the work to after about 866, and his information on the loss of the hostel's revenues further dates his composition after Bernard's visit in 867. For Christian's contacts with the Middle East: M. McCormick, "Les pèlerins occidentaux à Jérusalem, VIIIe–IXe siècles," in *Voyages et voyageurs à Byzance et en Occident du VIe au XIe siècle*, ed. A. Dierkens, J.-M. Sansterre, and J.-L. Kupper (Geneva, 2000), 289–306, at 289. Christian's prefatory letter to his *Expositio super Librum generationis* dedicates the work to the communities of Stavelot and Malmédy in a way that seems to indicate that he was no longer at either monastery. See *Epistola dedicatoria* 53.55–54.79, where he insists that someone who once knew their virtue could never be separated from their love, and so forth. Although Huygens has doubted the identification (*Expositio* 8), this Christian might be the homonymous dean

thanks to "that king's" love for Charlemagne, the hostel had held estates (*villae*) at the biblical site of the Potter's field, Aceldama, which has consistently been located in the Hinnom Valley, south of the Holy Zion church. Hence, he writes, this place was now called "Hostel of the Franks."[42] The estates are presumably the twelve houses and appurtenances that Bernard the Monk locates in the adjoining Valley of Jehoshaphat and which he indicates belonged to the hostel, thanks, he notes, to the efforts of Charlemagne.[43] Most important, Christian indicates that, at the time he was writing, the hostel no longer owned these estates, and its staff and the pilgrims were reduced to relying on alms.[44] The loss of the hostel's landed endowment certainly signals a serious financial crisis.

Another little-studied record of Carolingian communications with the Holy Land throws a shaft of light on that crisis. In 881 Elias, patriarch of Jerusalem, sent two Western monks to Europe in order to raise funds for the churches of the Holy Land. The letter he entrusted to them tells us that because a local ruler was or had become a Christian, the patriarch had unexpectedly had a chance to repair a number of churches that were in poor shape. Since he lacked cash to pay for the repairs, he had borrowed the money, using as collateral the church's olive groves, vineyards, and even liturgical vessels. Now, because he was unable to repay his creditors, he was faced with losing all of these if Western Christians did not send subsidies.[45]

(*decanus*) at Stavelot who appears in a charter dated 880–81; thus, if the hints of the dedication reflect a permanent absence, the treatise will postdate that charter. *Recueil des chartes de l'abbaye de Stavelot-Malmédy*, no. 40, 1:102.20–21. The charter would be the latest datable event in Christian's life.

42 "Tunc fuit in sepulturam peregrinorum et modo idem ipse locus Hospitale dicitur Francorum, ubi tempore Karoli uillas habuit, concedente †illo† rege pro amore Karoli; modo solummodo de elemosina Christianorum uiuunt et ipsi monachi et aduenientes" (Christian of Stavelot, *Expositio* 27, 498.94–98). *Illo* here might be the equivalent of the English "N." when a name is not known; however, it reads poorly, and could be a corruption. P. Riant offers the plausible conjectural emendation: *Ismaelitico rege*. "La donation de Hugues marquis de Toscane, au Saint-Sépulcre et les établissements latins de Jérusalem au Xe siècle," *Mémoires de l'Académie des inscriptions* 31 (1884): 151–95, at 155 n. 4.

43 Elsewhere Christian uses *uilla* to refer to villages, estates, and towns. See, for example, *Expositio* 1, 77.472–73, where—revealingly for the economy of early medieval Europe—Christian assumes the food supply granted to Joachin (Jehoiakim), king of Judah, and designated in the Vulgate as *annona* or *cibaria* (4 Reg. 25:27–30; Jer. 52:31–34) took the form of *uillae*: "et dedit ei uillas et constituit cibos mensae eius"; compare ibid., 8, "Capharnaum uilla magna erat in Galilea . . . ," 181.78–79; and ibid., 27, "Et recte de uilla ueniebat. *Villa*, Grece 'pagos' et inde pagani dicuntur," 506.284–85.

44 "Modo solummodo de elemosina Christianorum uiuunt et ipsi monachi et aduenientes" (*Expositio* 27, 498.98).

45 "Tum divina providentia gestum est, ut Princeps hujus climatis . . . Christianus factus, hanc primitus legem dederit ut Ecclesiae Dei a Christianis reaedificarentur atque recuperantur . . . Quapropter . . . ad has renovandas atque resarciendas totius virtutis animum prorsus armavimus. Et quoniam sumptus ad tantum perficiendum opus nequaquam nostros habere potuimus, alienos quaesivimus. . . . oliveta, vel vineas, atque ipsa earundem sanctarum Ecclesiarum sacrata vasa in

No less than other orthodox churches of the Holy Land, the Latin Christian religious would have fallen under the patriarch's jurisdiction, so it is not at all impossible that the real property of Charlemagne's hostel was among the church lands used in this way. If so, we do not know whether they were ever recovered.

Who staffed the hostel? Here we must begin by observing that Bernard clearly thought that his readers would want to know about the Western establishment in Jerusalem, and we have already seen that for an informant who rarely missed an opportunity to mention monasteries or monasticism, the omission of the Frankish monastery from his description of the Mount of Olives is strong evidence that it had ceased to exist by 867. This interpretation is reinforced by Christian's testimony. When he explained that the Frankish hostel had lost its landed revenues, he pointedly observed that "now *both the monks and* the travelers (et ipsi monachi et aduenientes) live exclusively from the alms of Christians."[46] The hostel in his day was the home of a community of monks and it is difficult to imagine another Western monastic community in Jerusalem beyond the one documented in the Breve. Those monks resided on the Mount of Olives in 808 and, apparently, still in 826.[47] All of this suggests that the Frankish monastery on the Mount of Olives moved to or combined with the hostel inside the city walls sometime between 826 and 867.

Some assume that apparent topographical continuity makes probable the identity of the ninth-century Frankish hostel with the eleventh-century Amalfitan shrine of St. Mary of the Latins and the hospital that was originally associated with it. That hospital later would give rise to the military order of the Hospitalers.[48] Evidence that the hostel still existed in the tenth century would make such continuity with St. Mary of the Latins more plausible. Two arguments might have seemed to help sustain such a contention. An enigmatic lead seal once seemed able to point in that direction but now turns out to come from a later and different establishment. The enigmatic Greek seal of "Hadrian, priest of the monastery of the Latins," which appeared on the market in Beirut, was supposedly discovered at Antioch. The obverse shows the Virgin, and the seal was dated on stylistic grounds

---

pignera tradidimus: et adhuc tantam pecuniam non accepimus, unde saltem illas utcunque resarcire valeremus. . . ." (Elias III of Jerusalem, *Epistola*, 363–64). See, on the letter, McCormick, *Origins*, 956–57, nos. 680 and 684. On the Christian governor, and the generally favorable state of Palestine for Christians under the Egyptian dynast Ahmad ibn Tulun, see M. Gil, *A History of Palestine, 634–1099*, trans. E. Broido, 2nd ed. (Cambridge, 1997), 307–8.

46 See above, note 44.

47 On the monks' letter of 808, see below, chapter 8.2. The *Annales regni Francorum*, a. 826, 169, identify Dominic as "abbas de monte Oliveti."

48 In support of institutional continuity, see, for example, Runciman, "Charlemagne and Palestine," 612. Bieberstein and Bloedhorn (*Jerusalem: Grundzüge der Baugeschichte*, 2:262) allow for continuity but emphasize that the eleventh-century church of the Amalfitans was practically a new foundation. See further below, note 55.

to the tenth century.[49] Closer scrutiny has shown however that the legend should be read "The Mother of God of Adrianople monastery of the Latins" and the seal's date is now assigned to the last third of the eleventh century.[50]

So the continued existence of a Carolingian hostel now hinges solely on a charter dated 29 October 993. This act indicates that St. Mary of the Latins existed already at this date. It could conceivably therefore be the same as the Carolingian hostel last attested a little over a hundred years before. By this document, Hugh, margrave of Tuscany, and his wife "Julitta" (Juditha) supposedly conveyed various properties in central Italy to the Holy Sepulcher and Sancta Maria Latina. The charter survives only in a rather unpromising form, as a figurated original in Marseille, that is, a copy assigned to the eleventh century that was prepared in such a way as to make the reader think it was the tenth-century original.[51] The personalities mentioned in the charter seem indeed to have moved in the same circles, many of the small places it mentions in central Italy can be identified, and many of the formal diplomatic features of the document correspond to those attested in genuine original charters of Hugh.[52] About this document, nevertheless, scholars

---

49 V. Laurent, *Le corpus des sceaux de l'Empire byzantin,* 2 vols. (Paris, 1963–81), 5.2:389, no. 1559, with p. 458, on a second copy.

50 *Les sceaux byzantins de la collection Henri Seyrig,* ed. J. C. Cheynet, C. Morrisson, and W. Seibt (Paris, 1991), 189, no. 282, with pl. XIX, no. 282, where the beginning of the letter pi that justifies the restoration of <A/Δ>PIANOYΠ<O/Λ>EOC is clearly visible. The editors observe that an Adrianopolitan monastery dedicated to the Virgin, with an abbot named Hugh, is documented in the twelfth century.

51 First published by Edmond Martène and Ursin Durand, *Veterum scriptorum et monumentorum historicorum, dogmaticorum, moralium, amplissima collectio* (Paris, 1724) 1:347–49 (and not in their *Thesaurus novus anecdotorum* [Paris, 1717], *pace* Wilkinson, *Jerusalem Pilgrims,* 316). Paul Riant republished the pseudo-original from Saint-Victor of Marseilles along with a facsimile and defended its substantial genuineness while admitting that it had been tampered with. See "La donation," where, 160–61, the crucial passages read: "offero tibi Deo et gloriosum Domini Sepul<crum, i>n Hierusalem" . . . "donamus Sancto Sepulcro <Domini in> Hierusalem, et tibi Warino, abbati, atque consanguineo tuo Gi<selberto> inde inde (!). Quę autem . . . offerimus, . . . faciendum exinde presenti die illi qui nunc et per tempore serviunt monachi in Hierusalem ad opus illorum peregrinorum, qui vadunt et veniunt de Hierusalem, ut ipsi inde vivant et monachi qui sunt in Sancta Maria Latina in Hierusalem, censum quod Dominus dederit recipiant ad usum omnium peregrinorum, qui vadunt et revertentur ad Sanctum Sepulchrum Domini. . . ." Along with the problematic syntax, the fact that the first phrase seems to convey the gift to the Holy Sepulcher and the second to a different institution, St. Mary of the Latins, appears troubling, although Western donations—of the twelfth century—did not always clearly distinguish the two institutions. See R. Hiestand, "Die Anfänge der Johanniter," in *Die Geistlichen Ritterorden Europas,* ed. J. Fleckenstein and M. Hellmann, Vorträge und Forschungen 26 (Sigmaringen, 1980), 31–80, 47–48.

52 Hugh was certainly in contact with Gerbert of Rheims, who famously encouraged Western magnates to support the Christians in the Holy Land (*Ep.* 28 [early 984?], in *Die Briefsammlung Gerberts von Reims,* 51–52). Gerbert asked Hugh for help with Bobbio in 986 (*Ep.* 83, 112). Although the identification by Riant, "La donation," 179–83, of the act's "tibi Warino, abbati" with Guarinus, abbot of Cuxa in Catalonia, has been doubted by A. Falce, *Il marchese Ugo di*

---

are divided, or at least some doubt the charter's genuineness. Until a specialist of central Italian diplomatic can dispel the suspicions that the document has been tampered with, the survival of Charlemagne's hostel into the tenth century must remain only plausible, not probable.[53]

In any case, careful scrutiny of the evidence for the origins of the Amalfitan church and its male and female hostels shows that St. Mary of the Latins was in effect founded or refounded a few years before 1071, and the hospices were established shortly before about 1080.[54] Even if there had been an awareness of some kind of topographical continuity with Charlemagne's hostel, and even admitting the controverted genuineness of Hugh of Tuscany's donation charter, there seems little reason to imagine any institutional or personal continuity that could have survived the destruction of Christian institutions in Jerusalem under Caliph al Hakim in 1009–10.[55]

To conclude, we know nothing about possible successors to the 17 Western nuns established at Jerusalem. We may nevertheless suspect that Western female monasticism experienced a fate similar to that of their Western countrymen's house. The Frankish monastery on the Mount of Olives seems to have ceased to exist or to have fused with the Frankish hostel between 826 and 867. That hostel probably was inside the early medieval walls of Jerusalem and close to the Holy

---

Tuscia (Florence, 1921), 108–9, a Cuxa specialist finds it plausible. He observes that Hugh's sister was married to the doge of Venice, Peter IV Candiano, who was murdered in a power struggle, and that Guarinus was instrumental in restoring her brother-in-law to power in 978. P. Ponsich, "Saint-Michel de Cuxa au siècle de l'an mil (950–1050)," *Les cahiers de Saint-Michel de Cuxa* 19 (1988): 24–25 and 30. Furthermore, Guarinus seems to have been in Italy in June 993, when he obtained a bull (Jaffé, *Regesta*, 1: no. 3850) from Pope John XV (985–996). Many of the local place names seem to fit. See Riant, "La donation," 175–76, and Falce, *Il marchese Ugo*, 112. Finally, the formulary of the suspect act adheres pretty closely to that of Hugo's writing office, judging from W. Kurze, *Monasteri e nobiltà nel Senese e nella Toscana medievale: studi diplomatici, archeologici, genealogici, giuridici, e sociali* ([Siena], 1989), 184–85, who presents the key features of his acts from originals of undoubted genuineness.

53 Although Riant ("La donation"), Falce (*Il marchese Ugo*, 106–13), and A. Calamai (*Ugo di Toscana. Realtà e leggenda di un diplomatico alla fine del primo millennio* [Florence, 2001], 120–21) accept the genuineness of the charter, an eminent Holy Land specialist and one of central Italian diplomatic both have reservations. See Hiestand, "Die Anfänge der Johanniter," 33 n. 11; and Kurze, *Monasteri e nobiltà*, 183, respectively.

54 William of Tyre gives a fairly detailed account of its foundation in *Chronicon* 18, 4–5, 814–17. For the establishment of St. Mary of the Latins a few years before 1071 and the hospital shortly before about 1080, see Hiestand, "Die Anfänge der Johanniter," 36–37; compare A. Luttrell, "The Earliest Hospitallers," in *Montjoie: Studies in Crusade History in Honour of Hans Eberhard Mayer*, ed. B. Z. Kedar, J. Riley-Smith, and R. Hiestand (Aldershot, 1997), 37–54, here 38–42.

55 For a potential awareness of some sort of continuity with an earlier establishment in the bull of Paschal II of 19 June 1112, see W. Holtzmann, "Papst-, Kaiser- und Normannenurkunden aus Unteritalien," *Quellen und Forschungen aus italienischen Archiven und Bibliotheken* 35 (1955): 46–85, at 50. For the effective absence of continuity, see Hiestand, "Die Anfänge der Johanniter," 33–34.

Sepulcher. It was still in existence, although financially beleaguered in the last three decades of the ninth century. Whether or not it survived until the late tenth century and notwithstanding its possibly identical or nearby location, the written sources attest no visible institutional or personal continuity with the establishment of St. Mary of the Latins of the later eleventh and twelfth centuries.

Chapter Five

. . . .

LATE ANTIQUE MONUMENTS
AND EARLY MEDIEVAL PEOPLE
OF THE HOLY LAND

THE VISUAL AND TACTILE QUALITY of the descriptions left by contemporary travelers to the Holy Land impresses the modern reader of late ancient
and medieval literature. For their time, pilgrim narrators went to extraordinary
lengths to help readers visualize the holy places: descriptions of colors, sketch
drawings, even measurements occur among their accounts. Clearly, they antici-
pated that their readers would want to imagine in palpable detail the sights and
shrines that bore witness to the birth of their religion.[1] The counts of personnel
preserved in the roll are a very different matter. So too the architectural details
recorded there, by their nature and, as I will show, by their precision.

This chapter focuses on the second document preserved on the Basel roll, the
Memorial of the Monasteries which are in the Promised Land outside of Jerusalem. Resolving the long-standing riddle of the mysterious measuring unit used by
Charlemagne's envoys will unlock the Memorial's evidence on some of the greatest architectural monuments of late antiquity. Along with insight into the preoccupation of Charlemagne and his entourage with a certain aspect of large
buildings, the Memorial's information on the still-standing shrine of the Nativity
will supply the key for understanding the measurements the king's envoys brought
back to him—and now to us. The Memorial also makes an important contribu-
tion to understanding the early state of the Zion Church. Its evidence allies with
recent archaeological discovery to inform our knowledge of those lost buildings
of Jerusalem with new precision. We will look carefully at how—with Procopius's
sixth-century account, the Madaba Map, and recent archaeological research—
the Memorial illuminates a lost Justinianic monument, the great Nea shrine of

---

1 On this quality of pilgrim narratives, see, in general, J. Richard, "Les relations de pèlerinage
au moyen âge et les motivations de leurs auteurs," in *Wallfahrt kennt keine Grenzen: Themen zu
einer Ausstellung des Bayerischen Nationalmuseums und des Adalbert Stifter Vereins, München*, ed.
L. Kriss-Rettenbeck and G. Möhler (Munich, 1984), 143–54, at 147. On the drawings, see, for example, Bede, *De locis sanctis* 2.2, 256, or 2.5, 258, using Adomnan. On the measurements, see table 5.1.

the Virgin. The results of these three different investigations invite careful scrutiny of the Memorial's detailed but complicated evidence about the dimensions of the most important late antique church in the Holy Land, Constantine's complex at the Holy Sepulcher. First, however, let us look at the modest but new information on the prelates of early ninth-century Palestine that we can obtain from the Memorial.

1. People in the Roll

The documents copied on the Basel roll throw a few rays of light on Holy Land prosopography in this very dark period.[2] They do not name every key person mentioned. The omission of the patriarch and the failure to name the *synkellos* of Jerusalem may appear more surprising than they really are. Since everything about these documents indicates that they constitute a practical dossier for the Frankish emperor's plan to finance the Christian establishment of the Holy Land, there was little point to naming the patriarch and his foremost collaborator: the intensive communications of the period 799–810 would have made their names well known to the Frankish court.[3] In any case all prosopographical data are confined to the Memorial.

That document names most of the abbots and bishops of the churches it catalogs. It does not, however, refer to a *hegoumenos*, or abbot, of Mar Saba. The omission may have arisen from a mechanical error in the copying of the roll. Alternatively, the silence could stem from Mar Saba's prominence and special relations with what one might call its daughter house, St. Sabas of Rome, whose local importance will have made it quite familiar to the Frankish court.[4] There is no

2 For what is known to date, see especially the sparse sigillographic evidence collected in V. Laurent, *Le corpus des sceaux de l'Empire byzantin,* 2 vols. (Paris, 1963–81), 5.2:392–413, and 5.3:297–98, as well as the Holy Land seals scattered among *Les sceaux byzantins . . . Seyrig,* 160–93, none of whose establishments occur in the roll. See also the very spotty episcopal lists—including the names of bishops as edited by Tobler and Molinier—compiled by G. Fedalto, *Hierarchia ecclesiastica orientalis. Series episcoporum ecclesiarum christianarum orientalium* (Padua, 1988), 2:1014–39.

3 It seems likely that the patriarch was so obvious a personality that he was not counted among the personnel of the patriarchate, although he is referred to indirectly, in connection with his candle bearers, his servants, and the *synkellos* "who manages everything under the patriarch" (Breve, lines 4–5 and 7). A less likely interpretation would be that the survey was conducted during a hypothetical period between the death of the patriarch George, which occurred on a 7 April of 807 or of an earlier year, and the accession of the patriarch Thomas, which must have occurred before his embassy to Charlemagne in 807. On the embassy, see above chapter 4.2.

4 There is insufficient room on the damaged part of the roll for the name of the abbot of Mar Saba. A possible Roman intermediary between Mar Saba and the Frankish court in these years may have been the Greek Peter, *religiosus egumenus,* who was one of Pope Leo III's envoys to Charlemagne between 801 and 814 and whom Theodore Stoudite called "archimandrate of Rome." J.-M. Sansterre has identified him as the abbot of St. Sabas in Rome, although it is not impossible

evidence of an abbatial vacancy of the great Palestinian monastery at this time. Local hagiography identifies Basil as hegoumenos of Mar Saba in 794 and as commissioning the *Martyrdom of the Twenty Sabaite Monks* between 797 and 807. He is presumably the same Basil to whom, between 809 and 811, Theodore Stoudite wrote about the Moechian affair in Constantinople.[5]

The edition of Tobler and Molinier printed the names of two abbots and three bishops. The Judaean abbot with an anachronistic Latin name is manifestly erroneous. Careful analysis of the text, its formulas, and its handwriting corrects this error and produces the abbot's true name, even as it yields the names of two more Palestinian abbots. One of the three bishop's names is also incorrect in previous editions.

On the roll, the name of Elias, abbot of the monastery on Mount Sinai is clear; all editions give it correctly. According to my understanding of the damaged text,[6] which follows here de Rossi, the name "Basil" (line 27) most likely refers to the abbot of the monastery of St. Theodosius "in the desert" (in illo erimo), that is, Deir Dosi. Similarly, de Rossi correctly identified as its abbot the "Iohannes" mentioned just before the number of monks at the monastery of St. Gerasimus, even though later editors thought otherwise.[7] Previous editors have not recognized that the abbot's name that they read as "Laetus" is in fact not a complete name, but the end of a name that began in the lacuna that immediately precedes it. Moreover, the third letter has been misread as an *e*, although it is clearly a *c*. The restoration is therefore an easy one: <Teofi>lactus, and we can be sure that Theophylactus was hegoumenos of Choziba around 808.[8] The damaged part of the roll has unfortunately completely lost three more abbots' names: that

---

that he headed another of the many Greek houses in the city. *Les moines grecs et orientaux à Rome aux époques byzantine et carolingienne* (Brussels, 1983), 1:79–80. See also Leo III, *Epistolae X 9* (Jaffé, *Regesta*, 1: no. 2528), 101.5–12; and Theodore Stoudite, *Ep.* 35, 1.100.19–21. On St. Sabas on the Aventine Hill in this period, see, in general, Sansterre, *Les moines*, 1:22–29, and passim. For monks from Jerusalem at Rome in the Carolingian period, see, for example, M. McCormick, *Origins of the European Economy: Communications and Commerce, A.D. 300–900* (Cambridge, 2001), 223, table 8.6.

5   Leontius, *Vita Stephani Thaumaturgi*, 183, 580C; compare the Arabic version, 80.2, trans. 129. He is also mentioned in the opening section, preserved only in the Arabic version (ibid., 2.1, trans. 3) as well as in Stephen, *Martyrium XX Sabaitarum* 1, 1.14–2.18, for the date of which, see below, chapter 8, note 18. Theodore Stoudite's letters addressed to the abbot of Mar Saba in 818 (*Ep.* 555, 2:849–52; *Ep.* 277, 2:412.1–5) do not name him. See also J. R. Martindale, ed., *Prosopography of the Byzantine Empire 1 (641–867)* [CD-ROM] (Aldershot, 2001), "Basilios 134," to which the references in Leontius and Stephen should be added.

6   See chapter 11, textual commentary on line 27.

7   Tobler and Molinier (Breve, 303) took the name as a reference to John the Baptist's baptizing there, even though the monastery is several kilometers from the present course of the Jordan. See chapter 11, textual commentary on lines 31–32.

8   See chapter 11, textual commentary on line 31, for the detailed justification.

of the Palaia Lavra, or St. Chariton, who seems to have had a very short name, as well as those of St. Euthymius and of the monastery of St. John the Baptist, near the Jordan.[9]

Finally, the Memorial names Basil as bishop of Sebastia (line 45) and Theophanes ("Teophanius" in the manuscript) as bishop of Mount Tabor (line 41).[10] A third prelate has entered history under a false name: the bishop of Tiberias, identified in previous editions as Theodore, was in fact named Theophilus, as the letter traces preserved on the manuscript make clear (line 40).[11] None of these bishops seem to be known so far from other documents. Theophilus of Tiberias must be a successor of Basil, former monk of Jerusalem and associate of the intruder patriarch Theodore, who had been administrator or bishop of Jericho and who was bishop of Tiberias when he visited St. Stephen before 794.[12] The Memorial did not identify a fourth bishop, of Nablus (line 46).

2. Charlemagne and the Architectural Dimensions of Holy Land Monuments

Analysis of the roll's date and circumstances indicates that it is connected with a royal meeting held at Aachen in October 810, which treated sending money to restore the churches of Jerusalem (below, chapter 8). This is entirely borne out by the unusual information supplied by the documents as clarified by the new edition. The selection of buildings on which the Memorial reports and the nature of the things measured on those buildings differ distinctively from the typical pilgrim literature of the early Middle Ages. Correctly understanding the measurements supplied by the Memorial takes us a step further toward appreciating the unique character of the roll in that those measurements are considerably

---

9   The available space (line 30) indicates that the abbot of St. Chariton had a short name, such as Elias or T(h)omas; the damage seems too extensive to afford insight into the length of possible abbots' names for the monasteries of St. Euthymius or St. John the Baptist (lines 30 and 33). For details, see chapter 11, textual commentary on the corresponding passages. The monastery of St. John the Baptist figures in Leontius, *Vita Stephani Thaumaturgi* 62, 528B; compare the Arabic version, 37.2, trans. 60. The shrine of St. John the Baptist on the Jordan was usually locked, and one had to go to get the key from the *prosmonarios* of the monastery located above it. See the Greek life, 85, 537E; Arabic version, 46.1–5, trans. 72–73.

10   See above, chapter 2.2, note 28, on the significance of the bishop residing in a monastery.

11   See chapter 11, textual commentary on this line for discussion. Fedalto, *Hierarchia ecclesiastica orientalis*, 2:1038, should therefore be corrected.

12   Leontius, *Vita Stephani Thaumaturgi* 58, 527D; compare the Arabic version, 33.1–4, 51–54, and 35.1–12, trans. 56–58. The manuscript colophon of the Uspenskij Psalter, Saint Petersburg, National Library of Russia, MS gr. 216, records another bishop of Tiberias, Noe, who ordered Theodore, deacon of the Anastasis, to copy this manuscript in AD 862. M. Vogel and V. Gardthausen, *Die griechischen Schreiber des Mittelalters und der Renaissance*, Beihefte zum Zentralblatt für Bibliothekswesen 33 (Leipzig, 1909), 136.

---

more accurate and informative than hitherto appreciated. The consequences are important both for our knowledge of lost Holy Land monuments and for understanding the purpose behind the roll.

The Memorial supplies measurements of only four monuments. At first blush, the data on the numbers of steps leading up to the shrines at Sinai and in Jerusalem might seem fairly typical pilgrim fare, for other Holy Land descriptions accounts also count them.[13] But significant differences emerge from a comparison of the Memorial's data with the most similar detailed accounts—those of the seventh-century Armenian Guide, of the Gaulish bishop Arculf as preserved in Adomnan of Hy, and of the eleventh-century Spanish pilgrim Hyacinth.[14] Table 5.1 summarizes their data on the churches documented in the Memorial.

The Memorial lists measurements for only a few structures, albeit key ones, including at least one building that was in ruins and that the other witnesses ignore. And, as table 5.1 shows, for those structures it gives measurements corresponding to the perimeter of buildings or their major structural elements (the dome of the Resurrection shrine). The notion that these measurements were merely meant to allow the person for whom the roll was intended to imagine the size of these structures is rudely dissipated by the way in which the Memorial (line 56) sums up the different spaces recorded for the Holy Sepulcher complex: "their *roof* altogether is ninety-six dexters in length, thirty across."[15]

I have never encountered a pilgrim's account that records measurements for the roofs of shrines. Indeed, the typical pilgrim's account differs both in what it measures and how it does so. Pilgrims tended to focus on the most sacred spots and objects within shrines, and they often improvised units of measure, relating distance and size in terms of paces, arms, palms, and thumbs. For instance, Adomnan's informant, Bishop Arculf, supplied measurements only for the Sepulcher shrine itself inside the Resurrection complex and for the bronze disk through which one could reach to collect relic dust in the church of the Ascension.[16]

---

13   For example, the Armenian Guide 7, 166; Epiphanius, *Descriptio Palaestinae* 10, 79.20: "2,340 steps." Compare, for Sinai, ibid., 7, 75.15, where either the number 7 or the translation of βασμίδιον proposed by E. Trapp, W. Hörandner, J. M. Diethart, et al., eds., *Lexikon zur byzantinischen Gräzität besonders des 9.–12. Jahrhunderts* (Wien, 1993–), 1:269, must be wrong.

14   Hyacinth, *Descriptio Terrae Sanctae*, ed. J. Campos, "Otro texto de latín medieval hispano. El presbítero Iachintus," *Helmantica* 8 (1957): 77–89. Campos dated the text to the ninth or tenth century, essentially on paleographical (he assigns the script to the tenth century) and linguistic evidence. M. Biddle assigns the script to the eleventh century and, convincingly, argues that the way Hyacinth describes the Holy Sepulcher reflects the structure as it was rebuilt after the destruction by al Hakim in 1009. "The Tomb of Christ: Sources, Methods and a New Approach," in *"Churches Built in Ancient Times": Recent Studies in Early Christian Archaeology*, ed. K. Painter, Occasional papers from the Society of Antiquaries of London 16 (London, 1994), 140 n. 14; cf. 106–8.

15   Line 56, "tectum in integrum habet in longo dexteros xcvi, in aduerso xxx."

16   On the disk in the Ascension Church, see Adomnan, *De locis sanctis* 1.23.6–8, 200.25–35.

TABLE 5.1 Measurements of three Holy Land churches, as recorded by the Memorial, compared to various Holy Land pilgrim reports

Structure	Measurements				Item
	Memorial	*Armenian Guide*	*Adomnan*	*Hyacinth*	
Nativity Church, Bethlehem	"length": 38 dexters; "on the upper extremity, at the transept": 23 dexters; "the other extremity": 17 dexters	200 ells long and 100 ells wide		space where the manger was: three paces long and two and one-half wide	1
Church of the Holy Sepulcher	dome: 53 dexters; "around": 107 dexters from the Holy Sepulcher to Calvary: 27 dexters; from Holy Calvary to where the Holy Cross was found: 19 dexters Total roof surface, including Holy Sepulcher, Holy Calvary and church of Constantine: 96 dexters long, 30 dexters across	dome: 100 ells high and 100 ells wide from the [Constantinian] Martyrium to the Resurrection: 20 ells Golgotha: 10 paces from the Resurrection			2a
shrine of the Holy Sepulcher, inside the Church			can hold nine standing men; roof is a foot and a half higher than a man who is not short; floor is three palms higher than floor of church	door: two cubits high and one and one-half wide	2b
Sepulcher itself		length of a man	seven feet long; Arculf measured it with his hand Christ's shroud: eight feet long	four arm lengths and two thumbs long, four palms high, four palms wide.	2c
Zion church	39 dexters long, 26 across	100 ells long, 70 wide			3

Sources: Memorial, item number 1: lines 52–53; number 2a: lines 53–56; number 3: lines 56–57. Armenian Guide, item numbers 1 and 2b, trans. Wilkinson, 166; numbers 2a, 2c, and 3: ibid., 165. Adomnan, item number 2b: *De locis sanctis* 1, 2, 6, ed. L. Bieler *CCL* 175 (1965): 187,28–30 and 1, 2, 8, 187,37–40: number 2c: 1, 2, 10, 188,51–52 and 1, 9, 16, 194,80–81. Hyacinth, *Descriptio Terrae sanctae*, item number 1: 80,43–44: number 2b: 81; number 2c: 81,74–76.

Adomnan reports Arculf's estimates of how many people could fit into the special shrine surrounding the Holy Sepulcher and of the size of the Sepulcher or Christ's shroud. Hyacinth actually describes how he measured, for instance, Jesus's table, although he chose to record the dimensions of only the most sacred spaces—the space where the manger had been inside the Nativity Church in Bethlehem and the actual size of the Holy Sepulcher and of its doorway.[17] The Armenian Guide is closer to the Memorial, in that it gives data for more buildings.[18] The Memorial, strikingly, gives no measurements whatsoever for the main goal of all pilgrims—the shrine of the Holy Sepulcher.

Adomnan, the Armenian Guide, and other pilgrim accounts report measures of venerated elements of various shrines, not roofs or overall floor plans. The very nature of the numbers supplied by the various witnesses differs. Pilgrims often relate the sizes they report as estimates. Arculf, for instance, reports how many standing men could fit in the shrine of Christ's tomb, and Hyacinth paced off the space that had held the manger in Bethlehem. The Armenian Guide's obviously rounded figures (e.g., 10, 20, 50, 70, 100, 200) contrast sharply with the precise and detailed measurements of the Memorial (e.g., 17, 19, 23, 27, 30, 96, 107).

The principle of selection also bears examining. The Memorial reports on the most important monuments, but they are only four in number, and they are not given in any particular order. In fact, the first entry concerns a ruin, and it alone offers any kind of explanatory note, identifying the structure as a gigantic "church of Saint Mary, which the earthquake . . . sank into the earth." Holy Land specialists concur that this entry refers to Justinian's great Nea Church in honor of the Virgin. The document's specification that it is determining the roof size of the Anastasis complex and its explicit description of the ruined state of the Nea awaken the suspicion that its figures are in fact concerned with construction and repair, that is, precisely the purpose implied by the 810 meeting (see chapter 8.1). Moreover, the Anastasis complex certainly needed and received repairs during this period.[19] The next set of measurements in the Memorial strengthens that suspicion. It gives the Bethlehem Nativity Church's measurements and number of columns, without further explanation. It is possible that, like so many other Holy Land structures, this church too suffered damage in the tremendous 749 earthquake. Finally, we have no information on the state of the Zion Church about

17 Hyacinth counts the columns and goes on to say that he measured "all these," that is, Jesus's table, and his bath also, although he does not write down the measurements (*Descriptio Terrae Sanctae*, 80.42–44 and 61–64).

18 On its date, see Wilkinson, *Jerusalem Pilgrims before the Crusades*, 2nd ed. (Warminster, 2002), 16–17. In addition to specific holy spots within churches and those shrines listed in table 5.1, the Armenian Guide, trans. Wilkinson (166) gives measurements for the church of the Ascension and the shrine of Jesus's baptism at the Jordan.

19 See below, chapter 8.2, on Eutychius's account of repairs to it.

A Mediterranean Church in the Early Middle Ages

800, although we do know that, around 786, the mother and two sisters of the *synkellos*, the patriarch's closest advisor, retired to the monastery there, and it received much of the family property.[20]

So the Memorial's measurements differ in kind and preciseness from those of pilgrim accounts. How they differ, moreover, suggests a purpose other than visualizing and remembering the holy places that lay behind the pilgrim texts. The measurements recorded in the Memorial strongly suggest that its compilation has to do with the integrity of the buildings—an interpretation confirmed by the observation of the total roof size. Two of the four monuments, the Holy Sepulcher and the Nea Church, certainly needed repairs in the period. We know nothing of the physical state of the third monument, the Nativity Church at Bethlehem, or the fourth shrine, the Zion Church. The deduction that the person who ordered the Memorial was concerned with what we may call the physical plant of pilgrim sites in the Holy Land is only comforted by the precision and accuracy of the figures that can be verified. This accuracy has not so far been fully appreciated.

Only occasionally have the measurements given by the Memorial received detailed scrutiny.[21] Perhaps that is because, at first glance, those which can be verified appear inaccurate. But more careful scrutiny uncovers a delightful surprise, which runs counter to modern opinions about early medieval indifference to numeracy—opinions not contradicted by the roll's apparent mathematical error of the sum of personnel at the Holy Sepulcher.[22]

The Holy Sepulcher is widely believed today to preserve the basic features and dimensions of the original central-plan structure built by the emperor Constantine. Nevertheless, aspects of its reconstruction are not without controversy, and the Memorial's enunciation of what it measures is not unambiguous.[23] Only the Justinianic Basilica of the Nativity in Bethlehem is today intact and indisputably

---

20 *Vita Michael Syncellae* (BHG 1296) 2–3, 48.14–22; for the date, see the introduction, ibid., xiv.

21 The most detailed treatment remains that of T. Tobler, who attempted to deduce the Memorial's measurement unit on the assumption that the Anastasis rotunda or its foundations in the nineteenth century were identical with those of the ninth century. He deduced that a *dexter* corresponded to three Rhenish feet, or one meter. See *Descriptiones Terrae Sanctae ex saeculo VIII, IX, XII et XV* (Leipzig, 1874), 385–91. H. Vincent and F. M. Abel used the Nativity Church to deduce the length of the dexter as 1.485 meters. *Jérusalem. Recherches de topographie, d'archéologie et d'histoire* (Paris, 1912–26), 2:456. For the true solution, see below. Finally, Dr. Oren Gutfeld has made good use of the Memorial's data in his recent dissertation on the Nea Church. See below, note 43.

22 See the stimulating discussion of numeracy in A. Murray, *Reason and Society in the Middle Ages* (Oxford, 1985), 141–57, which has spurred further research and brought greater depth and nuance to the nevertheless unimpressive picture of early medieval numeracy. See, for example, R. Sonntag, *Studien zur Bewertung von Zahlenangaben in der Geschichtsschreibung des früheren Mittelalters. Die Decem Libri Historiarum Gregors von Tours und die Chronica Reginos von Prüm* (Kallmünz, 1987).

23 On the circumference of the rotunda of the Anastasis, see below, p. 112.

---

in much the same shape as it was in the early ninth century: it has appeared to more than one scholar as the best starting point.[24] That fact allows us to test the measurements supplied by the roll against the actual monument; but to use the roll's data to recover with confidence the dimensions in modern equivalents of lost monuments, we need to understand the nature of the measurement in question. The significance of such a test will not be lost on archaeologists who wish to consider the roll's data when it comes to investigating the traces of three of Jerusalem's most important late antique monuments: the great shrine of the Tomb of the Lord, the Zion Church, and the gigantic Justinianic shrine to the Virgin. Israeli archaeologists' discovery of part of a fourth monument, the Nea shrine, creates an unusual opportunity in this respect, as we shall see.

The name of the measure in question, *dexter*—used in the plural, *dexteri*, in our text—is attested sporadically in Carolingian documents from the territory of present-day France and Switzerland. It occurs primarily in Old French and Old Provençal and derives from classical Latin *dextans* (itself derived from *de sextans*, i.e, five-sixths of a unit of measurement).[25] Benjamin Guérard identified a series

---

24 Vincent and Abel, *Jérusalem. Recherches de topographie*, 2:456; Bieberstein, "Der Gesandtenaustausch," 157 n. 37.

25 The word's phonetic similarity to the adjective *dexter, dextra* appears to explain the abusive incorporation of the *r*. For this and the derivation, see W. von Wartburg, *Französisches etymologisches Wörterbuch. Eine Darstellung des galloromanisches Sprachschatzes* (Bonn, 1922–2003), 3:61, s.v. "dextans." It is unclear whether the sporadic occurrence of *dexter* in Latin is an accident of preservation or attestation; the measure is a fairly small one, and so perhaps not as useful for the needs of most surviving eighth- and ninth-century documents that mention boundaries. It will be interesting to test this case when the original early medieval charters of France are all available in a general online concordance. See, for example, *Cartae Senonicae* 5, 187.24, a collection of formulas compiled from documents in use at Sens between 768 and 775. See also the following instances: an act of 817 concerning the region of Arles ([B.] Guérard, *Cartulaire de l'abbaye de Saint-Victor de Marseille* no. 163, 1:191); Irmino's Polyptych of Saint-Germain des Prés, from the 820s (Breve 9.247, 248, and 262, pp. 82–83, which are, curiously, the only occurrences in this great inventory); and an act of 889/90 of Bishop Aimericus of Chartres (transmitted in the *Cartulaire de l'abbaye de Saint-Père de Chartres*, 1:16). The term occurs also in the passion of the patron saints of Zurich preserved in a manuscript of the late eighth century (*Passio Felicis, Regulae et sociorum* [BHL 2887], 9, ed. Iso Müller, "Die frühkarolingische Passio der Zürcher Heiligen," *Zeitschrift für Schweizerische Kirchengeschichte* 65 [1971]: 132–87, here 143). Compare too C. Du Cange, *Glossarium mediae et infimae latinitatis*, ed. L. Favre (reprint, Paris, 1938), 3:93 s.v. "Dextri." It is also attested in Carolingian Catalonia. See M. Bassols i Climent and I. [= Joan] Bastardas, *Glossarium mediae latinitatis Cataloniae* (Barcelona, 1960–86) 1:917–19, for which reference I thank Dr. Nathaniel Taylor. The earliest attestation cited there is from 924. My friend Thomas N. Bisson, whose command of the abundant new archival material is without compare, kindly assures me that the term came to Catalonia with the Carolingians. The use of *dextri* in two Merovingian diplomas of 643–48 and 670 (MGH DD Mer 1, nos. 81, and 108, 207.8 and 279.17), probably does not take us back any further than the eighth century. The former act has certainly been tampered with, and the latter, though genuine, was reworked such that it is wiser for now to accept both diplomas' exact wording only for the period between 768 and 814, when they were forged or reworked. See T. Kölzer, *Merowingerstudien*, 2 vols., MGH, Studien und Texte 21, 26 (Hanover, 1998), 1:15–23 and 90–95;

A Mediterranean Church in the Early Middle Ages

of texts and equivalencies that showed that the Carolingian dexter consisted of 5 Roman feet (29.6 cm). Thus a dexter equals 1.48 meters.[26] Leaving aside for a moment the length of the nave of the church at Bethlehem, which poses a special problem beyond the reading of the last letter or raised point, a comparison with the interior measurements of the church uncovers an apparent inconsistency. At the equivalence proposed by Guérard, the transept should be (23 dexters × 1.48 m =) 34.04 meters long, while the width of the front of the building should be (17 dexters × 1.48 m =) 25.16 meters. In fact, the interior measurements of these features are 36 meters and 26.8 meters, respectively.[27] If Guérard's analysis of the metric equivalence of the dexter is correct, then there are two possibilities: the measures are wrong, reflecting the supposed lackadaisical early medieval attitude toward quantification, or they are based on a different unit.

The latter is the correct solution. I would suggest that the Carolingian ambassadors lacked the foresight to include a Frankish measuring rod in their packs for the long trip to the Middle East. Would it not have been logical for them to reconstitute on the spot a Carolingian dexter? Having forgotten to pack a Frankish measuring rod, would they have noticed that the local, Byzantine foot (*orguia*) was 1.6 cm longer than the Roman foot they used at home, five of which constituted the dexter? The Byzantine foot measured 31.23 centimeters, yielding a "Byzantinized" dexter of 1.5615 meters.[28] If this unit is used as the multiplier, the Memorial gives the measurements of the transept as 35.9145 meters and the front as 26.545 meters, a variance from the actual measurements of 8 centimeters and 25 centimeters, respectively, that is, a disparity of less than 1 percent from the actual measurements.[29]

The nave of the Nativity Church measures 53.2 meters in length; neither unit gives a satisfactory equivalent.[30] However, the measurements for the Holy

---

against a proposed correction to *dextrorsum*, see M. Hélin, "Dexter et dextri," *Bulletin du Cange. Archivum latinitatis medii aevi* 28 (1958): 161–64. The word does not occur in the capitularies, at least to judge from the detailed indexes of Boretius and Krause, MGH Capit and eMGH5; in the indexes of the charters of Pippin III, Charlemagne, Lothar I, Lothar II, Charles the Bald, Charles III, Pippin I, and Pippin II; or in the Lombard charters made available online at "Quellen zur Langobardengeschichte" at http://www.oeaw.ac.at/gema/lango.htm. The single occurrence in the charters of Odo in 891 is a passage that may have been interpolated: *Recueil des actes d'Eudes, roi de France (888–898)*, ed. Robert-Henri Bautier (Paris, 1967), 118.16; compare 114.

26   That is, 29.6 cm × 5 = 1.48 m. See Guérard's *Cartulaire de l'abbaye de Saint-Père*, clxxiii; compare the introduction to his edition of Irmino's Polyptych of St. Germain des Prés, 1:956–60, where he presents various early medieval texts on measurements and shows the word is equivalent to *passus*, that is, five *pedes*.

27   A. Ovadiah, *Corpus of the Byzantine Churches in the Holy Land* (Bonn, 1970), 37; on the method of measuring, 15–16.

28   E. Schilbach, "Pous," *ODB* 3:1708.

29   As supplied by Ovadiah, *Corpus*, 37. The variances are of 0.2 percent and 0.9 percent, respectively, that is, within a tolerance not uncommonly admitted by twenty-first-century architects.

30   38 × 1.48 m = 56.24 m; 38 × 1.5615 m = 59.337 m.

Sepulcher complex make clear that, for the envoys, the roof was a main concern. It was only natural then that the Bethlehem measurement also include the narthex, for it too was roofed. If the Franks measured to include the narthex, which is 6 meters deep, the total length would be 59.2 meters, or some 13 centimeters off, a variance of 0.2 percent, closely conforming to the transept measures.[31] The convergence of the measurements of Charlemagne's *missi dominici* with the surviving structure is nothing short of remarkable. This raises the exciting possibility that the work of those ninth-century envoys can be used to recover the dimensions of the lost or controverted late antique monuments of Jerusalem. At the very least, archaeologists and architectural historians will need to consider these data very carefully. Let us next look at a set of measurements concerning a controverted monument.

The fourth church, whose measures the envoys furnished was the "mother church" of all churches, the Zion Church, on the western side of the *cardo*, the main north-south axis of Jerusalem, across from the ruins of the Nea shrine (see map 1). The manuscript readings and building features are straightforward: it was 39 dexters long and 26 dexters wide ("in longo habet dexteros xxxviiii, in transuerso xxvi"), or, by the Byzantine foot, 60.9 meters by 40.6 meters.[32] In varying states of repair, the late antique church stood on this spot down to the Crusader period, when the Western conquerors tore down and replaced its ruins. The demolished church appears to have been a basilica that linked two venerated pilgrim sites. Its northwestern corner was remembered as the site where the Virgin died; annexed to its southeastern corner was a very ancient structure, venerated at least since late antiquity as the site of the Last Supper and the first Pentecost and which modern scholars have hypothetically connected with the early Judaeo-Christian community of Jerusalem.[33] Two different reconstructions of the basilica have been proposed. The older of the two estimated the size and plan of the late antique church from the size and placement of what were identified as foundation walls discovered in a series of sounding trenches opened in 1899 on the part of the site that belonged to German Catholics.[34] Two decades later, the biblical archaeologists Hugues Vincent and Félix Marie Abel proposed a different reconstruction, derived from the German publication and the examination of at least some of the

31 Modern photographs of the structure seem to indicate that the present roof does not cover the thickness of the wall between the narthex and the nave, which is about one meter thick (thus Ovadiah, *Corpus*, 37). The long section of W. Harvey, *Structural Survey of the Church of the Nativity, Bethlehem* (London, 1935), drawing D, gives a wall thickness of 110 centimeters.

32 Lines 56–57.

33 B. Pixner, "Church of the Apostles Found on Mt. Zion," *Biblical Archaeology Review* 16, no. 3 (1990): 16–35; 60; compare, for example, H. Geva in M. Avi-Yonah and H. Geva, "Jerusalem: The Byzantine Period," *NEAEHL* 2:778.

34 H. Renard, "Die Marienkirche auf dem Berge Sion in ihrem Zusammenhang mit dem Abendmahlssaale," *Das heilige Land* 44 (1900): 3–23.

Germans' notes.[35] According to the earlier, German reconstruction of Heinrich Renard, the late Roman, multi-aisled basilica measured around 61 meters by 40 meters.[36] Vincent and Abel arrived at a different reconstruction. They reckoned the late antique structure to have been 60–62 meters by 34 meters.[37] Consensus today seems to favor the earlier, German interpretation of the data.[38] Both reconstructions agree on the length. Vincent's range includes the measurements supplied by the Memorial as we have interpreted them, while Renard's estimate of about 61 meters could scarcely be closer to the 60.9 meters of the Memorial. Only Renard's estimate, however, fits the Memorial's width within 60 centimeters, or 1.5 percent. In sum, the Memorial now fits very nicely one interpretation of the archaeological evidence and thereby confirms the modern consensus that favors Renard's reconstruction of the late antique Zion Church. At the same time, this new convergence reinforces the conviction that the measurements recorded on the Basel roll must be taken seriously. Let us now turn to its testimony on the biggest church in the Holy Land.

"In Jerusalem, he [emperor Justinian] dedicated a shrine to the Mother of God, to which no other can be compared."[39] This, the Nea Church of the Virgin, Procopius indicates, was one of Justinian's greatest building projects. That is saying something, given the attention Procopius had devoted to the Hagia Sophia. The Nea anchored the southern part of the main thoroughfare and essential processional way of the pilgrimage city. The importance of great liturgical processions in the late antique city and the exemplary role of Jerusalem and its throngs of pilgrims certainly encouraged Justinian to expand that street.[40] The approximately 200 meters that have been excavated reveal a spectacular cardo with porticoes supported by 5-meter high columns that linked Justinian's great new church with the main shrine, the Anastasis, or Resurrection complex, of the Holy Sepulcher. The terrain obliged Justinian's architects to build gigantic supporting vaults so that, in Procopius's words, part of the Nea building was "founded on mighty rock, and

35 Vincent and Abel, *Jérusalem. Recherches de topographie*, 2:432–37, in which the tensions between the original German team and the French specialists appear quite clearly.

36 Renard, "Die Marienkirche," 17; compare the plan on 18–19. Renard's dimensions are based on the segments of foundations identified on the plan; he reinforced them by his educated guess of the meaning of the dexters reported in the Memorial (13). He reasoned that dexter must come from "right foot," and should therefore equal one pace, which he estimated at 150 cm. He therefore calculated the Memorial's reported size of the church as 58 to 60 m long and 39 to 40 m wide.

37 Vincent and Abel, *Jérusalem. Recherches de topographie*, 2:436.

38 H. Geva in Avi-Yonah and Geva, "Jerusalem: The Byzantine Period," 778; compare Bieberstein and Bloedhorn, *Jerusalem: Grundzüge der Baugeschichte* 2:120.

39 Procopius, *De aedificiis* 5.6.1, 162.5–6; on which description, see Y. Tsafrir, "Procopius and the Nea Church in Jerusalem," *Antiquité tardive* 8 (2000): 149–64.

40 J. F. Baldovin, *The Urban Character of Christian Worship: The Origins, Development, and Meaning of Stational Liturgy* (Rome, 1987), 83–102; on the archaeology of the *cardo*, see, with further references, Tsafrir, "Procopius," 156–62.

part floated in the air."[41] Historians and archaeologists could only dream about this lost Justinianic monument and its complex of hospitality structures for visiting pilgrims on the southern part of that late Roman street until, from 1970 to 1982, Nahman Avigad discovered and excavated parts of the ruins of the Nea Church in the Old City's Jewish Quarter.[42] Unfortunately, this archaeological work was never adequately published. Nevertheless, the new understanding of the measures recorded in the Memorial sheds more light on the Nea building and compels a revision of the conventional wisdom about its size and configuration within the reconstructed urban topography of late Roman Jerusalem.

The measures of the Nea Church are both complicated and rewarding to interpret, especially since recent and ongoing work is deepening our understanding.[43] A number of facts converge to secure the identity of the Justinianic structure: the huge scale of the parts of the western end of the church that were uncovered, the stupendous supporting substructures, the location on the late Roman cardo, the building's correspondence with a large structure on the Madaba Map's depiction (see fig. 4), the discovery of Justinian's commemorative inscription in the cisterns that formed the substructures, and the possibility that the church's qualifier "Nea" may have derived from the place name for that "new" part of the city in late Roman times.[44] Although the plan has been reconstructed with various degrees of confidence and estimated measures have been published, much in them remains hypothetical.[45]

Charlemagne's envoys were certainly not measuring the roof of the Nea, since, they observe, the church had been destroyed by an earthquake. They seem rather to have measured the walls or foundations of the church itself, presumably on the assumption that Charles would want to consider rebuilding the church. The Breve's report that twelve ecclesiastics still staffed the Nea shows that, notwithstanding

41 Procopius, *De aedificiis* 5.6.8, 163.1–3.
42 N. Avigad, *Discovering Jerusalem* (Oxford, 1984), 229–46; compare N. Avigad, "Excavations in the Jewish Quarter of the Old City of Jerusalem, 1970," *IEJ* 20 (1970): 135–40; N. Avigad, "A Building Inscription of the Emperor Justinian and the Nea in Jerusalem (Preliminary Note)," *IEJ* 27 (1977): 145–51; and N. Avigad and H. Geva, "The Nea Church," *IEJ* 32 (1982): 159. See also Avi-Yonah and Geva, "Jerusalem: The Byzantine Period," here, H. Geva, "The Nea Church," 776–77.
43 In particular, Yoram Tsafrir's study of Procopius's description and Dr. Oren Gutfeld's doctoral dissertation (Hebrew University, Jerusalem) carefully scrutinize the written mentions, excavations, and unpublished excavation records for this great building. I am grateful to both my old friend Prof. Tsafrir and Dr. Gutfeld for their generous discussion of our respective findings and collegial sharing of their materials. When Dr. Gutfeld's work will be published, it will surely supersede all earlier materials.
44 See the works cited in notes 42 and 43.
45 See, for example, A. Ovadiah and C. G. de Silva, "Supplementum to the Corpus of the Byzantine Churches in the Holy Land," *Levant* 13 (1981): 222: "It is difficult to reconstruct the plan of the church" and "These two walls hint at a special plan."

the destruction, it had not been entirely abandoned.[46] The Memorial reports that the church was 50 dexters "in length, through the middle" and, if the damaged text is reliable, 35 dexters "on one extremity" (in uno fronte).[47] Using the new understanding of the dexter, this implies a huge building, measuring 78.08 meters in length by 54.65 meters in width, probably on its most accessible, western facade. Neither figure fits the published archaeological information. Let us examine them in turn.

Published modern accounts estimate the length of the Nea Church as either 115 meters or around 100 meters. The Memorial flatly contradicts both, since it reports a length "through the middle" (in longo per medium [line 52]) of 50 dexters, which works out to 78.08 meters. Comparison suggests that the modern estimates are too high. At 115 meters, the Nea would have ranked among the most gigantic churches built under the Roman Empire. It would surpass, for instance, most of Rome's huge basilicas of late antiquity: it would have been more than 15 percent bigger than Rome's cathedral church of the Lateran Basilica and a third larger than St. Mary Major. A Nea Church of these dimensions would have rivaled even the extraordinary lengths of old St. Peter's and St. Paul outside the Walls.[48] In fact, in the Holy Land context, a nave 78 meters long would seem impressive enough, outclassing by nearly a third the estimated 60 meters of the central nave of Constantine's basilica at the shrine of the Holy Sepulcher, making the Nea the biggest church in Jerusalem.[49] The excavator deduced a length of 115 meters for the Nea Church by tacitly identifying as the church's facade a "doorway" or "threshold" uncovered at about that distance west of the Nea's apses.[50] The threshold's

46 The term chosen to describe the destruction is somewhat unusual. Overwhelmingly, Late Latin and Medieval Latin used the Memorial's word *demersit* in the sense of "sank" for something or someone sinking in water or, very rarely, of sinking into mud or into an abyss. Occasionally *demergo* was used for "fall down." See O. Prinz and J. Schneider, *Mittellateinisches Wörterbuch bis zum ausgehenden 13. Jahrhundert* (Munich, 1967–), 3:281.14–33. In the former case, the ruins of the church might have appeared to the Frankish observers to have sunken into the earth, perhaps into the massive cistern vaults that underpinned the southeastern part of the church.

47 *Fronte*: compare the similar expression "in alio fronte" (line 53) for the Nativity Church. For the readings of the numbers in our edition, see chapter 11, textual commentary on these lines.

48 The Lateran measured 98.5 meters in length, including the apse, which measured 8.8 meters deep. R. Krautheimer, *Corpus basilicarum christianarum Romae: The Early Christian Basilicas of Rome (IV–IX cent.)* (Vatican City, 1937–1977), 5:74. St. Mary Major measured 73.5 meters, including the walls but not the apse (ibid., 3:46); St. Peter's, 119.3 meters, including the apse (ibid., 5:286); and Saint Paul's, 128.38 meters (ibid., 5:150).

49 See V. C. Corbo, *Il Santo Sepolcro di Gerusalemme. Aspetti archeologici dalle origini al periodo crociato*, 3 vols. (Jerusalem, 1981–82), 2: tav. 3, for Constantine's nave.

50 Although he does not explicitly state this, Avigad's accompanying plan indicates that he must have estimated the length of the Nea by identifying the foundations of a 5.4 m wide "doorway," or "threshold," uncovered "about 116 m" to the west of the apses, with the western end of the structure. Compare Avigad, *Discovering Jerusalem*, 232 ("doorway whose original width was 5.4 meters"), and Avigad, "Building Inscription," 146 ("an associated marble floor and a large threshold").

connection to the church whose apses were rediscovered is based on the fact that it is parallel to that distant wall, and that ceramic evidence dates it as "Byzantine," that is, in the terminology of Holy Land archaeology, to the fourth to seventh centuries A.D.[51] While it is certainly tempting, and indeed plausible, to link the apparently impressive entrance foundations to the west with the Nea church, nothing compels us to identify them as the western wall of that church and reject the testimony of the Memorial on the shrine's length.

In his later account, Avigad himself implicitly identifies this structure as the wall of a narthex, since he says the church would "have been about 116 meters long (including the narthex)."[52] Even this hypothesis would be very difficult to reconcile with the Memorial, for the gigantic 30-meter-deep narthex that would imply seems incredibly big, even for a church the size of the Nea. By way of comparison, the immense inner narthex of the mighty Hagia Sophia in Constantinople measures only 12 meters deep, including the walls, and that church's two narthexes together total only 19.5 meters.[53] If the threshold foundations are indeed part of the Nea complex, they are more likely one of the several entrance structures Procopius describes. A nave extending westward some 78 meters from the likely position of the hypothetical central apse, delimited by the southeast corner and the northern apse, would leave about 60 meters for the succession of structures that, Procopius tells us, shaped the approach to the great shrine.[54] From a methodological point of view, it is agreeable to note that after I had worked out this length of 78 meters for the central nave, Oren Gutfeld informed me that his study shows that the western end of the northern wall W20 (on which, see below) appears to turn to the south; he suspected that this could mark the western end of the nave.[55] If so, he would calculate the length of the basilica as 74 meters on the inside and 78 meters on the outside. It is hard to imagine more remarkable, independent confirmation of the essential accuracy of the roll's evidence as we have interpreted it.

The famous mosaic map of the Holy Land discovered in the pavement of the church at Madaba, Jordan, is the essential visual source for the topography of Jerusalem around 600 (see fig. 4).[56] It offers a highly schematized depiction of the

51 Avigad, *Discovering Jerusalem*, 232; Avigad, "Building Inscription," 146, citing the Hebrew publication for the ceramic.

52 Avigad, *Discovering Jerusalem*, 232.

53 According to the magnificent plans prepared by my late friend R. L. Van Nice, *Saint Sophia in Istanbul: An Architectural Survey* (Washington, D.C., 1965–86), pl. I.

54 *De aedificiis* 5.6.22–25, 164.21–165.11. Bieberstein and Bloedhorn, *Jerusalem: Grundzüge der Baugeschichte*, 2:293, arrive at a similar explanation. Compare Bieberstein, "Der Gesandtenaustausch," 157–58 n. 37, and the discussion of Tsafrir, "Procopius," 162–63.

55 See above, note 43.

56 See figures 4 and 5. The map can also be conveniently studied on the Franciscan Web site devoted to "The Madaba Map": http://www.christusrex.org/www1/ofm/mad/index.html. On the

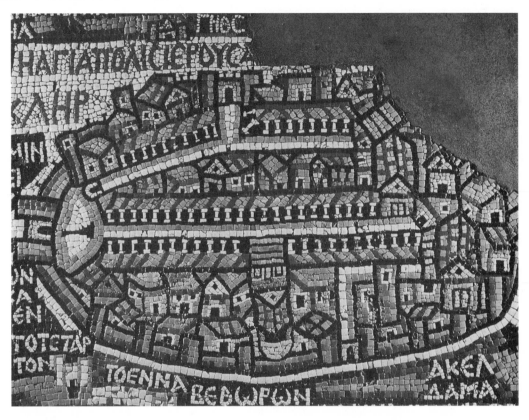

FIGURE 4
The Madaba Map, detail: Jerusalem. Madaba, Jordan (photo courtesy of the Archive of the
Studium Biblicum Franciscanum—Jerusalem)

church that scholars universally identify as the Nea and shows what looks like
a single nave basilica with double doors opening directly on to the cardo (fig. 5).
Procopius's detailed description, however, indicates that the map simplifies the
topography of the complex, since he states quite clearly that the church proper
was preceded by two porticoes, the second, or outermost, of which was called the
narthex, a four-sided colonnaded atrium with impressive doorways, a magnificent
propylaeum, or entrance vestibule, featuring an arch of breathtaking height supported by two columns, and two hemicycles on either side of the street leading
to the shrine.[57] This last detail suggests that the church was not perpendicular

<hr />

date, see J. Russell, "The Palaeography of the Madaba Map in the Light of Recent Discoveries:
A Preliminary Analysis," in *The Madaba Map Centenary 1897–1997*, ed. M. Piccirillo and E. Alliata
(Jerusalem, 1999), 125–33.

57　*De aedificiis* 5.6.22–25, 164.21–165.11. For an encounter in the "courtyard" (ἐν τῷ μεσαύλῳ) of
the Nea, see John Moschus, *Pratum spirituale* 131, PG 87:2996B–C, with the comments of Vincent
and Abel, *Jérusalem. Recherches de topographie*, 2:918 n. 1.

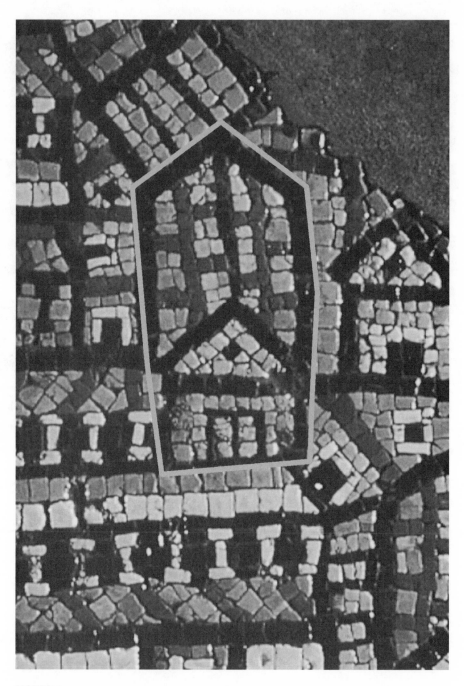

FIGURE 5
The Madaba Map, detail: the Nea Church. Madaba, Jordan (photo courtesy of the Archive of the Studium Biblicum Franciscanum—Jerusalem)

A Mediterranean Church in the Early Middle Ages

to the cardo, which in fact appears to be the case.[58] However one configures this imposing succession of courtyards and porticoes, it seems plain that they required some considerable space between the cardo, whose route is archaeologically documented, and the main nave of the Nea Church. The newly interpreted data from the Memorial about the length of the church indicate that these entrance structures spread over the several dozen meters between the cardo and the western wall of the church, itself 78 meters west of the apse.

The Memorial likely gives us more insight into these entrance structures. It begins its description of the ruined church with another measurement of length, "on both sides," 34 dexters ("habet mensuram de ambobus lateribus in longe" [line 51]), which works out to 53.09 meters.[59] These measures cannot refer to the nave since they are 25 meters shorter than the unambiguous length of the church down the middle, which, we have just seen, finds remarkable archaeological confirmation. Because they occur at the outset of this entry, and we can easily imagine that the envoys approached the church from the main thoroughfare, the cardo, these measures may well designate the entrance structures between the street and western wall of the church. The space separating the probable course of the cardo and the western wall of the church as we identify it could certainly accommodate 53 meters of such structures.[60]

Finally, the Memorial's testimony on the Nea's width is a little complicated. As de Rossi read the now-damaged passage, the ruined church measured 35 dexters, or 54.65 meters, "on one extremity" (in uno fronte xxx<v> [line 51]).[61] The reading and translation of the second measurement is quite clear: "through the middle, across,[62] 32" (per medium in aduerso, xxxii [line 52]). Thirty-two dexters comes to 49.97 meters. Now, the literature and the excavator's occasionally cloudy reports identify the church's width as 57 meters (presumably an exterior measurement)

58 For the oblique relation between the ruins of the church and the cardo, see, for example, the map in Avi-Yonah and Geva, "Jerusalem: The Byzantine Period," 769.

59 Although today it is difficult to make out the third digit of "xxxiiii," the number was clear to de Rossi. See chapter 11, textual commentary on lines 51–52. The only other hypothetical reading that the other letters would allow would be "v" (i.e., "xxviiii"), which would make the side measurements even shorter.

60 In favor of this interpretation is the plan of the site in Avigad, *Discovering Jerusalem*, 233, fig. 279, which indicates that the cardo should lie about 60 meters west of what we have identified as the western wall of the Nea. Should these measures refer instead to the main basilica, they would suggest that the building had an unusual plan, with lateral naves on both sides that were 25 meters shorter than the central nave.

61 The last digit is known only from de Rossi's edition. See chapter 11, textual commentary on lines 51–52.

62 For the meaning of *in aduerso* as "across" or "width-wise," compare its use for the total roof dimensions of the Holy Sepulcher–Constantinian basilica complex, line 56: "illorum tectum in integrum habet in longo dexteros xcvi, in aduerso xxx."

and 52 or 51.9 meters (explicitly identified as an interior measurement).[63] These measurements will likely give some pause to scholars working only from the published materials. The archaeological investigation uncovered the southeast corner of the building; however, the partial excavation of the northeast apse did not reach the northeastern corner. The published reconstruction assumes that the north wall of the eastern end, with its inscribed apse, was exactly symmetrical to the fully recovered south corner. This assumption appears to find support in a segment of the northern wall of the shrine shaded in the same fashion as the other excavated elements drawn with the church and depicted in the published plans as perfectly aligned with the hypothetical continuation of the northeast corner.[64] However, none of the reports clearly explains what that stretch of northern lateral wall is and how it came to light. Thanks to Gutfeld's research, it has become clear that this northern wall was discovered accidentally in the 1970s. Designated "W20" in the unpublished excavation materials, it was inspected by Avigad and measured.[65] Thus the interior measurement, at least at that point in the church's plan, seems secure.

How can an archaeological width of 52 meters be reconciled with the two different width measurements recorded by the Memorial? The fact that the author bothered to take a separate measurement of the width "in uno fronte" in itself shows that the width of the structure at this point differed from that in the middle of the church. The implication is that, if de Rossi read this number in the manuscript correctly, the front of the church was two meters wider than the main building. This front presumably refers to a narthex or other outer structure of the church.

The second measurement, of the distance "through the middle, across" corresponds to the central part of the church itself, that is, the general area whose width is supplied by the 1970s discovery of northern wall W20. Thus the figure reported by the Memorial errs by just under two meters. The source of the error seems obvious, given how easily copyists, then and now, mistake Roman numerals. Only one dropped minim or vertical stroke would have sufficed to turn "xxxiii" dexters into the "xxxii" that now figures on the Basel roll, which is, as we shall see, an early administrative copy of the original (see chapter 8). Adding the metric equivalent of that one dexter to the recorded 32 dexters would yield a width for the central nave of the Nea of 51.53 meters, that is, once again, a 0.01 percent error from the

63 Geva estimated 57 meters ("Nea Church," in Avi-Yonah and Geva, "Jerusalem: The Byzantine Period," 777); Avigad, 52 meters (*Discovering Jerusalem*, 234); and Bieberstein and Bloedhorn, 51.9 meters (*Jerusalem: Grundzüge der Baugeschichte*, 2:293).

64 See Avigad, *Discovering Jerusalem*, 233, fig. 278 (cf. 230); and Geva, "Nea Church," in Avi-Yonah and Geva, "Jerusalem: The Byzantine Period," 776.

65 Personal communication from Dr. Gutfeld.

reported measurement of 52 meters. In sum, if we can accept a small mistake in one of the Roman numerals recording the dimensions of Justinian's great Nea shrine of the Virgin, the Memorial gives us the building's exact width and length within 0.01 percent tolerance as 78.08 meters long by 51.53 meters wide. These new measurements correspond to and correct the interpretation of the archaeological data. The entrance structure visible to the Franks was 2.65 meters wider than the nave of the church. A last measurement, 53.09 meters "long on both sides" cannot be correlated to any of the structures so far brought to light. Its place in the description suggests that this structure was part of the entrance buildings described by Procopius, and there is space enough for it between the newly identified western wall of the Nea and the probable course of the street. Future archaeological exploration will likely provide more details.

Given these repeated indices of the accuracy of the measurements transcribed in the Memorial, one turns with anticipation toward the data on "the rotunda" (illa alcuba) of the Holy Sepulcher, even as one savors the thought that the Arabic word for cupola (the source of our "alcove") was first heard in Christian Europe at a meeting of Charlemagne's advisors at Aachen in 810.[66] The recent archaeological consensus maintains that the central part of the present-day church of the Holy Sepulcher preserves the plan of the great late antique rotunda.[67] However, there are two problems. The first arises from the irregularity of the church plan in its present state. Spaces between columns, for instance, vary between 103 and 145 centimeters, and the columns in the rotunda do not form a perfect circle:[68] one cannot simply apply the formula for calculating the circumference of a circle to estimate the rotunda's outer or inner measurements. The second question arises from the question of what exactly they measured when the envoys reported, "The church of the Sepulcher of the Lord: around, 107 dexters" (illa ecclesia de sepulchro Domini: in giro, dexteros cvii [lines 53–54]). Lexical scrutiny of the crucial term *in giro* shows that this figure, equivalent to 167.08 meters, measures some kind of perimeter.[69] Since the other measures seem to have been taken from the

66 On the significance of this detail for understanding how the documents on the Basel roll were compiled, see further, below, chapter 7.2.

67 A. Ovadiah and C. G. de Silva, "Supplementum to the Corpus of the Byzantine Churches in the Holy Land (Part II)," *Levant* 14 (1982): 122–70, here 134–38, with full bibliography.

68 See the plan of the rotunda as measured in 1896–1911 in Vincent and Abel, *Jérusalem. Recherches de topographie*, 2:108, fig. 39.

69 "Around" translates *in giro* better than "in circumference," even though the term is often used of objects that may have been, or certainly were, circular—for example, the paten whose edges were decorated with jewels by Pope Sergius I (687–701): "Hic fecit patenam auream maiorem, habentem in gyro gemmas ex albis et in medio ex iacynto et smaragdo crucem. . . ." (*Liber pontificalis*, ed. Mommsen 214.18–20). Agnellus (*Liber pontificalis ecclesiae Ravennatis*, 27, 72, etc., 291.30 and 327.24) prefers the phrase "per in giro" in similar circumstances. A diploma of Charlemagne

internal spaces of buildings, it is likely that this was done also in the church of the Holy Sepulcher. We do not know how exactly the irregular eleventh-century dome and, especially, the surrounding structures follow the fourth-century building plan in all its detail; nor do we know what Charlemagne's envoys included in the perimeter of the Constantinian structure. Even so, the reported 167 meters, though larger than the present structure, looks plausible enough to be taken into account in future efforts to reconstruct the late antique building.[70]

The data on the rotunda seem more clear cut: "the dome, 53 [dexters]" (illa alcuba, liii [line 54]), that is, 82.76 meters. It is possible that the Franks climbed up on the roof and measured the dome in this way. More likely, they walked around the outside of the columns that delineated the rotunda and measured the circumference with a cord. The rotunda's irregularity and the exact configuration of the eastern end of the central part of the church as Charlemagne's envoys would have encountered it remain a subject of discussion. Working from the available plans of the presumed Constantinian rotunda, the circumference around the outside of the columns comes to about 73–75 meters.[71] This falls short of the close fit

---

(MGH DD Kar 1: no. 81, 117.9), 16 July 774, at Pavia for St. Martin of Tours, "in giro Bergamasci," does not help much. A suggestion that the term's semantic range extends beyond circles comes from the way in which Childeric II's diploma for the monasteries of Stavelot and Malmedy renders the words of its model, in the name of Sigibert III, "ut girum girando in utrorumque partibus monasteriorum mensurentur ..." (MGH DD Mer 1: no. 81, 207.7–8, supposedly of AD 643–647/48) as "tam in longum quam in traversum"—"both in length and in breadth" (DD Mer 1: no. 108, 279.8). On the Carolingian circumstances of these reworked diplomas, see above, note 25. See also the rather vaguer usage of DD Mer no. 150, an original of Childebert III (3 April 697), 377.48. And see, from the ninth century, the biblical commentary of Paschasius Radbertus, who used the term to describe a railing that ran all around the edge of the roof of Solomon's temple: "Porro in Palestina consuetudo est architecturae quod et in templo Salomonis fuisse probatur ut desuper per totum plana habeatur atque in gyro iuxta quod lex precepit cancelli deambulatorii ne forte aliquis inde labatur incautus. ..." (*Expositio in Mathaeo*, 3, 251.553–56). Finally, the term *in giro* is used in the sense of "perimeter" in the early medieval measurement treatises published by Guérard, *Polyptyque de l'abbé Irminon*, 1:957–60. The upshot is that the Jerusalem structures whose (roof) measurement is reported in the Breve need not have been circular in shape.

70 Measuring along the edge of the walls of the plan of the present structure as drawn by Vincent and Abel (*Jérusalem. Recherches de topographie*, 2:108, fig. 39), I came up with a figure of approximately 150 meters.

71 It is regrettable that there seem to be no published large-scale architectural drawings of one of the most important monuments in Christendom. The regularity of the measurements depicted by Corbo, *Il Santo Sepolcro*, 2: tav. 3—all column bases are displayed as 1.5 m, and all intercolumnar spaces save two, as 2 meters; the other two are both depicted as 2.5 m—invites skepticism. The scale of the plan in Vincent and Abel (*Jérusalem. Recherches de topographie*, 2:108, fig. 39) is too small to allow a highly accurate measurement. Nevertheless, they report exact measurements for a number of spaces and column bases presently in situ which are far less regular than Corbo's. Using the two exactly measured widths of external faces of columns that they supply and accepting the internal measurements to stand for the missing external measurements (even though the two cases in which they are supplied show that this results only in an approximation) and finally assigning to the unspecified external intercolumnar spaces values in centimeters based on those reported in

that the Memorial's other measurements have generally supplied. In view of these measurements' general accuracy and our imperfect knowledge of the predecessor of the present building, this circumference appears close enough, once again, to make the Carolingian figures worthy of renewed scrutiny by specialists of this exceptionally complicated structure.

This section of the Memorial continues with two measurements documenting distances within the Resurrection complex. The distance from the Holy Sepulcher to Holy Calvary, the rock outcropping traditionally identified as the place of Jesus's execution, Golgotha, was 27 dexters, or 42.16 meters (line 54). The distance from there "to where the Holy Cross was found" (identified with the apse of Constantine's basilica)[72] was 19 dexters, or 29.67 meters (line 55). Again, the measurement looks plausible.

The report on the buildings of the Holy Sepulcher complex concludes with a summary of the total surface area, which contains a crucial clue. It makes clear the intent with which these measurements were taken: "including the Holy Sepulcher and Holy Calvary and Holy Constantine: their roof altogether is 96 dexters in length, 30 across" (lines 55–56). Thus the total dimensions of the roof for the entire complex were reported as 149.90 meters in length by 46.85 meters in width. Once again, the measurements seem compelling: they fall within the two leading estimates of the overall length and breadth of the complex (including also the courtyard of the rotunda), as deduced from the remains, the texts, and the topographical evidence.[73]

. . . .

In sum, the three cases—the transept, nave, and front of the Church of the Nativity—in which its measurements can be checked in straightforward fashion against an intact monument, show that the Basel roll reports precisely and accurately the dimensions of the structures it documents within a tolerance for error of under 1 percent. For the Zion Church, the Memorial reports dimensions that accord

---

a few cases and extrapolated from reported numbers for the equivalent space on the plan, yields a larger circumference, of around 75 meters.

72 According to the sixth-century pilgrim guide to Jerusalem: "Et inde intrans in aecclesiam sancti Constantini. Magna ab occidente est absida, ubi inuente sunt tres cruces. Est ibi desuper altare de argento et auro puro...." (*Breviarius de Hierosolyma*, Forma a, 1, 109.10–16). For a detailed discussion of evidence about this spot, see R. Aist, *The Christian Topography of Early Islamic Jerusalem: The Evidence of Willibald of Eichstätt (700–787 CE)* (Turnhout, 2009), 71–107, which appeared only after this study was in press.

73 C. Coüasnon, *The Church of the Holy Sepulchre in Jerusalem* (London, 1974), whose (very small) plate VIII suggests that from the rear apse of the rotunda to the front of the Constantinian Basilica was a total of about 143 meters and that the latter was about 42 meters wide. Corbo, *Il Santo Sepolcro*, has a larger scale drawing (tav. 3), which indicates about 150 meters by 52 meters for same dimensions.

TABLE 5.2   Dimensions of Holy Land shrines recorded in the Memorial,
calculated to the nearest centimeter

Church	Text	Dexters	Meters
Nativity	"in length"	38	59.34
	"on the upper[a] extremity, at the transept"	23	35.91
	"on the other extremity"	17	26.55
Zion	"in length"	39	60.90
	"across"	26	40.60
Nea	"on both sides . . . in length"	34	53.09
	"on one extremity"	35	54.65
	"through the middle, across"	32	49.97
	"in length, through the middle"	50	78.08
Holy Sepulcher complex			
Church of the Tomb	"around"	107	167.08
Rotunda	"the dome"	53	82.76
Distance within the complex	"From the Holy Tomb to Holy Calvary"	27	42.16
	"From Holy Calvary to where the Holy Cross was found"	19	29.67
Total roof surface "including the Lord's tomb, holy Calvary, and Holy Constantine"	"in length"	96	149.9
	"across"	30	46.85

[a]"Upper" here is used in the familiar Latin sense of "eastern"; see below, chapter 10, note 73.

within 1.5 percent with the reconstruction proposed by the German excavation of 1899. For the greatest lost monument of Jerusalem, Justinian's Nea Church, the Memorial challenges the published reports of the latest archaeological discoveries but finds remarkable confirmation in ongoing research into the correct interpretation of the architectural observations of the 1970s. Finally, its testimony vindicated on every point where it can be checked, the measurements the Memorial offers on the constituent parts of the late antique complex that marked the Holy Sepulcher seem to fit approximately but not exactly what scholars have deduced—or assumed—about the present and past dimensions of this complex monument.

This at least opens the question of whether the structures measured in 800 were identical to what is visible today.

In any event, all this confirms that the new understanding of the mysterious unit of measurement used in the Basel roll is accurate. Though they gave it a name from home, the Franks used a measuring rod or cord based on the local Byzantine foot, and they seem to have taken their measurements with an accuracy that contradicts common prejudices about the early Middle Ages and numeracy. Charlemagne's envoys proceeded with care and skill, for they had a practical purpose in documenting these dimensions. Measurements of roofs do not reflect pious curiosity. Rather, roofs are the single most important element to the enduring architectural integrity of any established building. The person who ordered this document wanted to know the roof sizes of the main churches of Jerusalem for the same basic reason that he wanted to know how many individuals were members of the orthodox Christian religious houses of ninth-century Palestine. These measurements would allow one to estimate the cost of repairs or restoration and so ensure the continued longevity of these great shrines or, in the case of the Nea, of rebuilding a badly damaged structure that was still partially functional since it was still staffed. Barring textual corruption, we have recovered in the Basel roll accurate dimensions of the greatest buildings of late antique Jerusalem as they could still be measured around AD 800. Archaeologists and historians of late antique architecture will now be able to ponder the data summarized in table 5.2, and to confront them with detailed and unpublished archaeological reports and, indeed, in due time, with the structures still buried beneath the Holy City as archaeologists exhume them from ancient oblivion.

The great emperor's intervention in faraway Palestine was not a casual affair, but carefully prepared and calculated in terms of needs. Alongside this fact, we must remember that over half a hundred westerners were permanently resident in the Holy City in the first decade of the ninth century and constituted 14 percent of the city's Christian religious establishment—and one of the most influentially connected parts at that. Furthermore, Charlemagne apparently intervened in similar fashion on behalf of the churches of Egypt and Africa, and even ransomed Greek monks enslaved by raiders on Pantelleria off the coast of north Africa.[74] All of these facts taken together tell of a Frankish king's truly extraordinary ambition in a world in which, around AD 800, more life and more movement linked the northern Frankish homeland to the ancient centers of Mediterranean civilization than has hitherto been reckoned. Such indeed is the implication of the existence

---

74 For Charlemagne's support of the churches of Egypt and Syria, see below, chapter 9. For his ransoming in 806 of the Greek monks of Pantelleria sold as slaves in Spain, see McCormick, *Origins*, 893, no. 272.

of the documents transcribed on the Basel roll for this exceptional ruler and his entourage. But it is time now to turn to the internal and external evidence on which this assessment of the roll and its content is founded, to the way in which this extraordinary record has come down to us, to share with the reader the technical evidence that allows us to judge when, where, how, in what sort of Latin, by whom, and for whom these remarkable records were composed.

Part Two

. . . .

THE DOCUMENTS

P ART ONE HAS TOLD THE STORY that emerges from the documents in the Basel roll about the historical development of the Christian church in the Holy Land, about the wealth of that church, and about the demography of its personnel in a local and comparative perspective. It has clarified and tabulated the physical dimensions of its greatest buildings. Part two tells the story of the roll itself. How did it come to us; where, when, and why was it copied; and above all how, when, and why did it come into existence? Close scrutiny of the document will reveal some of its secrets, and authorize more confident use of its precious evidence. We will begin with the discovery and previous editions of the roll, and proceed to describe the physical document and consider what its handwriting suggests about its origin. Answering these questions raises new ones, and deepens the testimony of the roll. The nomenclature of the three different records transcribed on the roll is not banal, and the search for parallels will clarify the nature and context of these documents. Where and how exactly the author or authors got their unique information remains a mystery. Studying the language and organization of the roll will serve the dual purpose of shedding some light on that crucial question, even as it will give us the tools needed to interpret the tricky usage of everyday Latin in a working administrative context, and of making plain the foundations of the analyses of part one. These investigations, finally, will position us to address the fundamental question of when and why the documents copied on the Basel roll came into existence, and what that tells us about how, in the final years of his life, an early medieval ruler ran his empire.

Chapter Six

▪ ▪ ▪ ▪ ▪ ▪ ▪ ▪ ▪ ▪ ▪ ▪ ▪ ▪ ▪ ▪

THE BASEL ROLL

1. The Discovery

THE CLASSICIST FRANZ DOROTHEUS GERLACH (1793–1876) seems to have discovered the roll containing the documents and frequently called *Breue commemoratorium de illis casis Dei* after the slightly corrected name of the first record transcribed. The professor and, from 1829 to 1866, librarian of the University of Basel (Switzerland) removed the parchment from the binding of an unspecified book.[1] No record was kept of the volume from which the fragments came, so the historical link to this precious document's provenance has probably been severed forever. In his analysis, de Rossi presumed that the book came from one of the great monasteries of the region.[2] Today the document bears the shelf

---

1   There is slight uncertainty about which Basel scholar actually found the document. G. B. de Rossi states that Gerlach removed the document from a binding. See "Un documento inedito sui luoghi santi di Gerusalemme e della Palestina," *BACr* 3 (1865): 81–88, at 83. Tobler, on the contrary, attributes the removal to "the unforgettable Wackernagel," who must be Lachmann's student, Wilhelm Wackernagel (1806–1869), a distinguished Germanist at the University of Basel from 1833 to 1869. See *Descriptiones Terrae Sanctae ex saeculo VIII, IX, XII et XV* (Leipzig, 1874), 355. On Gerlach, see J. Mähly, *Allgemeine Deutsche Biographie* (1875–1912; reprint, Berlin, 1967–71) 9:14–15; and E. His, *Basler Gelehrte des 19. Jahrhunderts* (Basel, 1941), 51–57. For Gerlach's career as librarian, see A. Heusler, *Geschichte der Öffentlichen Bibliothek der Universität Basel* (Basel, 1896), 63–64, and 71–73; and A. Staehelin, *Geschichte der Universität Basel, 1818–1835*, Studien zur Geschichte der Wissenschaften in Basel 7 (Basel, 1959), 181. On Wackernagel, see, for example, His, *Basler Gelehrte*, 113–24.

2   I discussed this point with Dr. Martin Steinmann, then keeper of manuscripts, during my visit to Basel in 1986 and confirmed it in a letter in 1993. In fact, most of the University Library's manuscripts and many of its early printed works came from the late medieval collections of the religious houses of Basel. See Heusler, *Geschichte*, 9–11; compare G. Meyer and M. Burckhardt, *Die mittelalterlichen Handschriften der Universitätsbibliothek Basel: Abteilung B: Theologische Pergamenthandschriften* (Basel, 1960), 1:xiii–xvi and de Rossi, "Un documento inedito," 83, who may have had some information from the discoverer, although he presents his presumption as founded on an examination of the entire two-volume collection of fragments assembled by Gerlach. Compare his statement that another Basel document he published was removed from the cover of a book. G. B. de Rossi, "Basilea. Testamento inciso in marmo sopra un sepolcro," *BACr* 1 (1863): 94–95, here 95;

mark N I 2, Bll. 12 u. 13 in the Public Library of the University of Basel (Öffentliche Bibliothek der Universität Basel). As we shall see, the paleography of the roll strengthens the general plausibility of de Rossi's presumption and a neglected note jotted on the roll confirms his monastic surmise.

Unfortunately, the most recent and widely used edition is the worst one ever made. The great specialist of the Christian epigraphy and archaeology of Rome, Giovanni Battista de Rossi (1822–1894), first edited the texts found on the roll, in what today we would call diplomatic fashion, in 1865.[3] Nine years later the Swiss physician and historian of the Crusades Titus Tobler (1806–1877) published the documents anew. He produced what he himself calls an audaciously corrected critical text to facilitate its use by historians. Tobler mitigated any erroneous corrections by also printing and inviting the reader to use a very good diplomatic transcription prepared for him by the philologist and head librarian of Basel University Library, Ludwig Sieber (1833–1891).[4] Most recently, Auguste Molinier (1851–1904) simply ignored the diplomatic transcription; he reprinted only Tobler's "corrected" text under both of their names in 1880.[5] Karl Schmid (1923–1993) observed serious deficiencies in this version and foresaw a new critical edition

de Rossi writes (e.g., "Un documento inedito," 85) as though he personally examined the manuscript of the roll. He either traveled to Basel or received it in the mail on loan, as was not uncommon in the nineteenth century and even still in my student days in Belgium. Further research in de Rossi's papers, preserved in the Vatican Library, might uncover the precise circumstances of his knowledge of the roll. On his papers, see P. Saint-Roch, *Correspondance de Giovanni Battista de Rossi et de Louis Duchesne: 1873–1894*, Collection de l'École française de Rome 205 ([Rome], 1995), 5; de Rossi was presumably in Basel on his Rhine trip of 1858, and he may have stopped there again when passing through Switzerland in 1862 or 1865. See P. M. Baumgarten, *Giovanni Battista de Rossi, der Begründer der christlich-archäologischen Wissenschaft. Eine biographische Skizze* (Cologne, 1892), 22–24 (the German original offers details lacking in the "expanded" Italian translation: P. M. Baumgarten, *Giovanni Battista de Rossi, fondatore della scienza di archeologia sacra. Cenni biografici*, trans. G. Bonavenia [Rome, 1892]). If so, it may be that he had time only for a cursory examination of the original, and shortcomings in his notes (see his own remark on p. 87, on [his] line 36, which honors him) or memory might explain one or two of his less compelling judgments. On the dispatch of foreign manuscripts to de Rossi in Italy, see Baumgarten, *Giovanni Battista de Rossi*, 26–27.

3   de Rossi, "Un documento inedito."

4   Tobler's two versions of the text: *Descriptiones Terrae Sanctae ex saeculo VIII, IX, XII et XV*, 77–84 ("corrected" text), and 364–68 (Sieber's diplomatic transcription, followed by a lengthy commentary). On Sieber's work, see 356–57. On the audacious corrections and the need to consult the transcription, see 363. Tobler and Sieber carefully studied de Rossi's edition (see e.g., Tobler, 356–57), and their diplomatic edition marked a substantial advance. On Tobler, see K. Furrer, *Allgemeine Deutsche Biographie* 38 (1897; reprint, Berlin, 1971), 395–402. On Sieber, see A. Bernoulli, *Allgemeine Deutsche Biographie* 34:179–80.

5   T. Tobler and A. Molinier, eds., *Itinera hierosolymitana et descriptiones Terrae Sanctae bellis sacris anteriora et latina lingua exarata*, 2 vols. (Geneva, 1877–85), 1.2:301–5. Molinier made only some minor spelling changes, for instance, substituting the *e-caudata* for the diphthong *ae*—without manuscript evidence.

under his direction. It has not appeared, as far as I know.[6] None of the editions is free of error. Of the four, however, Sieber's forgotten diplomatic transcription offers far and away the best published version of the text. Tobler's "corrected" text makes dozens of tacit emendations to the text according to a nineteenth-century vision of classical Latinity. Worse, it silently changes all place names to their classical equivalents. Given the standards of his age, this was a venial sin, since Tobler foresaw that the reader could easily discover the changes by consulting the accompanying diplomatic transcription. Molinier's failure to reprint or even mention the diplomatic transcription that accompanied Tobler's "corrected" text or otherwise to alert the reader to these extensive changes to the text has obfuscated precious testimony on the circumstances of the documents' origin. Readers who did not have the possibility of comparing Molinier's text with his source had no way of detecting this. With the exception of the studies of Schmid and Borgolte, all substantive work done on the document since 1880 has been based on the defective edition of Tobler and Molinier.

2. Codicology and Paleography

The roll at present consists of two pieces measuring 30 by 26 centimeters and 30 by 26.5 centimeters. They were originally one continuous sheet of parchment. Their left halves still fit together well, although at the point where they once were joined most of the right half is gone.[7] The edges show signs of mold. The document is written on one side in the roll format favored for administrative records or memorandums. It is written on the flesh side, which is where the ruling was also applied. Prickings are visible in the left margin 3 millimeters from the edge, spaced at 10 millimeter intervals. At present, sixty long lines of text survive; of these, substantial amounts of twelve lines (lines 28 and 30–40) have been lost due to a large segment of ruined parchment that has disappeared; the text, moreover, has been trimmed on the right edge. Between trimming and darkening of the parchment, the ends of many lines have lost a varying number of letters.[8] Material glued to the

---

6   Schmid, "Aachen und Jerusalem: Ein Beitrag zur historischen Personenforschung der Karolingerzeit," in *Das Einhardkreuz. Vorträge und Studien der Münsteraner Diskussion zum arcus Einhardi*, ed. K. Hauck (Göttingen, 1974), 137 n. 54; I am grateful to the late Prof. Karl Schmid for informing me by letter about the existence of this unpublished edition, prepared under his direction.

7   It may be that when de Rossi saw the document, the two pieces were attached back-to-back, so that he concluded that it was written on both sides and failed to realize that the bottom of Bl. 1 fits into the top of Bl. 2, making the lacuna much smaller than he postulated; compare de Rossi, "Un documento inedito," 83. By 1874 Tobler (*Descriptiones Terrae Sanctae*, 356–57) found de Rossi's description inexplicable. See also next note.

8   Many small horizontal slits were cut into the top and two sides of the sheet at two-millimeter intervals after the text was transcribed. They apparently served for sewing; some traces of cord

verso of the roll for reinforcement impeded examination. I thought I could perceive a modern cursive note written toward the center of folio 1ᵛ.

The main script is a beautiful, expert Caroline in dark brown ink (see the full-size pull-out plate). It slants slightly to the right and displays rather high ascenders and descenders. Words are irregularly but extensively separated. Although the general aspect is rather roundish, certain letters—particularly *n*, *m*, and occasionally the rather large bow of *d*—show a slight angularity. The verticals of *n* and especially *m* look more slanted to the right than the ascenders of other letters. Straight *d* overwhelmingly predominates, as does uncial *a*; the *cc* form of *a* becomes relatively common only toward the end of the text; it occurs both closed (*faran*, line 35) and open (*mariae*, line 37), that is, with and without the top stroke. *E-caudata* (*ę*) and *a-e* in the æ ligature occur rarely; the latter is once written interestingly in combination with *m* (in *gethsaemani*, line 21); *ae* is common. *I-longa* is frequent at word beginnings. The sign & occurs often in words; *s-t* ligature is used regularly. The form *cct* (that is, *at*) seems to occur once. One senses that the author is trying to avoid the *r-e* ligature, and fails twice (*erexit* and *honore*, lines 32 and 37). The attack stroke frequently takes a triangular form. The letters *x*, *y* (dotted), and *z* all respect the two-line space. The bow of *h* is small; that of *b* tends to be left open, as does the lower bow of the elegant *g*, which is well to the right of the upper bow.

Abbreviations are rare; they include *nomina sacra*; *prb* (nominative singular), and *prbris* or *prbri*, regularly, in the plural, with the abbreviation sign through the shaft of the *b*;[9] the superscript *-us* sign in *ei(us)*; and nasals. Of particular interest, given that this hand has been assigned to an upper Rhenish script tradition, the scribe used *-b;* and *-q;* to abbreviate *-bus* and *-que*, respectively. Bischoff observed that Reichenau, a leading scriptorium in the same script area ("Schriftprovinz"), shifted from that style of abbreviating to the new fashion of abbreviating *-b·* between about 822 and about 838. This is one hint that the roll was copied before the new abbreviation triumphed in the regional scribal tradition, presumably around those dates.[10]

A handsome rustic capital that avoids the kind of mannerisms associated with the scriptorium of Reichenau serves as an emphasis script.[11] Capitals help to dis-

---

survive on the right edge. This sewing might have been connected with the roll's use as a binding; it is conceivable that to form a stronger binding, the two pieces were once sewn back-to-back. This would explain de Rossi's statement that the document was written on both sides of a single sheet (see previous note).

9   W. M. Lindsay, *Notae Latinae: An Account of Abbreviation in Latin MSS. of the Early Minuscule Period (c. 700–850)* (Cambridge, 1915), 436–37. Among his examples, that of Wolfenbüttel, Herzog-August-Bibliothek, Weissenburg 81, copied apparently at Wissembourg in 772, shows the most similar range of abbreviations. See E. A. Lowe, *Codices latini antiquiores: A Palaeographical Guide to Latin Manuscripts Prior to the Ninth Century*, 12 vols. (Oxford, 1934–72), 9: no. 1393.

10   Bischoff, *Mittelalterliche Studien*, 2:38.

11   Ibid., 2:37.

tinguish sense units; so too punctuation, which consists of a raised point for minor stops and a distinctly subscript comma or semicolon-like sign for major stops; blank spaces at line ends mark the biggest stops of all. Great care was devoted to the execution of the numbers and the raised points that set them off from the text, notwithstanding the apparent arithmetical error in line 8.[12]

In response to a query from Karl Schmid, the late Bernhard Bischoff (1906–1991) attributed the script to the upper Rhine region and dated it to the second quarter of the ninth century. He also drew attention to similarity of format with the celebrated Murbach roll, a copy of the decisions of the reform council apparently transcribed at the gathering itself at Aachen in 816.[13] I had the privilege of discussing this script with Prof. Bischoff in person in 1986. I asked him if he would consider paleographical grounds for dating the script a decade or two earlier, in light of the perplexing codicological situation that his dating made of the roll a copy, for neither of us could then imagine an explanation for why such a copy would be made in the same roll format as the presumed original.[14]

Despite a number of differences in detail, the general aspect of the script of the pontifical of Freiburg-im-Breisgau, Universitätsbibliothek, MS 363, bears comparison with the Basel roll. Bischoff assigned this clear, regular hand also to the upper Rhine ca. the second quarter of the ninth century and noted that it was already at Basel in the ninth century.[15] It too slants to the right and extensively

12 A feature of the numbers that I cannot recall having seen elsewhere is that they are often preceded by *two* raised points and followed by the usual single point; the point following the number is usually higher than the point that precedes the number. The two raised points before the number may represent a normal punctuation mark followed by the point marking setting off the number.

13 Schmid, "Aachen und Jerusalem," 138 n. 57, where Bischoff is quoted as identifying the hand of the Basel roll as follows (I have incorporated in square brackets the subsequent correction added to this quotation by K. Schmid, *Gebetsgedenken und adliges Selbstverständnis im Mittelalter. Ausgewählte Beiträge. Festgabe zu seinem sechzigsten Geburtstag* [Sigmaringen, 1983], 530 n. 58): "Dass die Schrift einem alemannischen Skriptorium des 9. Jahrhunderts angehört, bestätigt Bernhard Bischoff am 10. Juli 1971 in Münster. Für seine Bestimmung der Schrift 'oberrheinisch, 2. Viertel des 9. Jahrhunderts,' [und seinen Hinweis auf die Überlieferungsform] 'Nähe zu den Murbacher Statuten,' möchte ich auch an dieser Stelle herzlich danken." I cannot explain why a vaguer and different opinion about the Basel roll is recorded in B. Bischoff, *Katalog der festlandischen Handschriften des neunten Jahrhunderts (mit Ausnahme der wisigotischen)*, vol. 1, *Aachen-Lambach* (Wiesbaden, 1998–2004), 64, no. 294: "IX. Jh., 2. Hälfte," with no regional attribution. The Murbach Statutes are preserved on a roll that may well stem from discussions of monastic reform at Louis the Pious's court in 816; it is now Colmar, Archives départementales du Haut-Rhin, Grand document 139. See H. Mordek, *Bibliotheca capitularium regum Francorum manuscripta*, MGH Hilfsmittel 15 (Munich, 1995), 112; compare Bischoff, *Katalog der festlandischen Handschriften*, 203, no. 901.

14 He promised to reexamine the question and let me know if he changed his mind. Although we corresponded subsequently, he never indicated a change of opinion on this issue.

15 Bischoff, *Katalog der festlandischen Handschriften*, 272, no. 1289; for an illustration, see A. Bruckner, *Scriptoria Medii Aevi Helvetica: Denkmäler Schweizerischer Schreibkunst des Mittelalters*, vol. 12 (Geneva, 1935), Tafel 1<d>.

separates words. Other less expert hands from this region also show general affinities with the script of the Basel roll, although the roll's writing is uniquely polished and expert.[16]

I have found no paleographical evidence that militates for an earlier origin than Bischoff's dating to the second quarter of the ninth century (or than the second half of that century, for that matter). The paleographical dates suggested by Bischoff do not square with other data from this dossier, which must have originated before 814. Nevertheless, the use of parchment tends to confirm Bischoff's paleographical judgment since we would expect that the original administrative document, written on the shores of the Mediterranean, at that date would have used papyrus.[17] If Bischoff's date ca. 825–50 is correct, then the Basel roll must be a slightly later copy of the original; it is, however, a copy whose roll format shows that it was intended for administrative, not literary, purposes. We shall return to this riddle.[18]

Finally, various hands dating approximately from the later ninth to the eleventh centuries scribbled pen trials between some lines of the roll.[19] Two of these

16 Although certainly and distinctively a generation or so earlier by its multiple alternate letter and ligature forms, another upper Rhenish script, the list of Saxon hostages *Indiculus obsidum Saxonum*, St. Paul in Lavanttal, Stiftsbibliothek, 6/1 (ed. MGH Capit 1:233–34, no. 115), also bears comparison with the hand of the Basel roll. Probably written in 805 or 806, it records the hostages who were entrusted to Haito, bishop of Basel and count Hitto. It could conceivably stem from Basel also. Some traits worth noting with respect to the script of the Basel roll include its general vertical or right-leaning uprights, the (surprising at this date) predominance of uncial *a* and word separation, and the straight *d*. On the document, see A. Kosto, "Hostages in the Carolingian World (714–840)," *Early Medieval Europe* 11 (2002): 123–47, here 142–45. I am grateful to Prof. Kosto for sharing a photograph of this remarkable document. Finally, a note added on p. 29 of the Gospel Book of Saint-Ursanne, Porrentruy, Bibliothèque cantonale jurassienne, MS 34, which lists some tributaries of the church of Saint-Ursanne in a hand that the catalogers assign to the tenth century, displays a script that appears related to that of the roll. Although it is likely a few generations later than the roll, it was surely written in the diocese of Basel. The manuscript, along with the catalog, can be viewed at *e-codices: Virtual Manuscript Library of Switzerland*, http://www.e-codices.unifr.ch/de/bcj/0034/029.

17 The papal and Byzantine chanceries of course were then still using papyrus for correspondence. Even from Italy, Charlemagne's envoys might write home on papyrus, as proved by a document sent to him from Benevento in 788 (*ChLA* 16 [1986], no. 629). On papyrus use in the Mediterranean about 800, see McCormick, *Origins of the European Economy: Communications and Commerce, A.D. 300–900* (Cambridge, 2001), 704–8.

18 See below, chapter 8.3.

19 By their very nature as jottings, such pen trials are often roughly written and difficult to interpret. In addition to those discussed in the following note and a few isolated letters, the Basel roll displays between lines 42 and 43 a few words and letters "ut q(uid) d(eus) & u uota" (or "r rota"), of which the first three words are a scriptural tag (Psalm 73:1), and *quid* is irregularly abbreviated as *q* with a kind of superscript *i* rising from the bow. "In nomine" was written between lies 43 and 44 and again between 45 and 46. Between lines 35 and 36, someone has written the letters "mo" in the special *litterae elongatae* used for the initial lines of charters.

scribbles hint at where the roll went after it had served its initial administrative function. Between lines 48 and 49, a ninth- or tenth-century hand wrote "a abba" in Caroline minuscule with the exaggerated long ascenders often used in contemporary charter hands. The appearance of a monastic title "abbot" could point to a monastic environment of some sort. But monasteries of course are not the only places that produced charters mentioning abbots. Stronger evidence of monastic provenance comes from the pen trial written in an unskilled hand of the later ninth or tenth century between lines 24 and 25: "uoluptas habet pena(m) necessita<s>" (pleasure has its punishment, constraint . . .)—an unmistakable quotation from the Rule of St. Benedict: "Uoluptas habet poenam et necessitas parit coronam" (pleasure has its punishment, constraint wins a crown).[20] A monastery following the Rule of St. Benedict is far and away the most likely place where such a quotation from the Rule might appear. We can easily imagine that the nearly proverbial expression was on the tip of a learner's tongue and might come up as he laboriously exercised his handwriting and pen nib against real parchment (rather than the stylus and wax tablet of more ephemeral jottings). It is, then, highly likely that once the roll had served its administrative function—as we shall see—at the royal court of Louis the Pious or his son Louis the German, someone from the court deposited it in a monastery in the Basel region. It might well have remained there until it passed into the collection of the University and Public Library.

3. The Three Documents: Organization and Nomenclature

To date, scholars have treated the text of the Basel roll as a single document. This is inaccurate: internal and external characteristics make clear that we have here a dossier consisting of three separate documents produced at the same time as part of the same investigation. A kind of *explicit* in emphasis script, titles, initial letters, spacing at the end of lines, differing contents, differing statistical precision, and, I think, differing informants distinguish these documents. The first text has given to the whole the name by which the roll is commonly cited: *Breue commemoratorii de illis casis Dei uel monasteriis qui sunt in sancta ciuitate Hierusalem uel in circuitu*

---

20 Benedict of Nursia, *Regula* 7.33, 49. The translation is that of Leonard J. Doyle, *St. Benedict's Rule for Monasteries* (1948; reprint, Collegeville, Minn., n.d.), 24. Benedict took the words over unchanged from the Rule of the Master 10.44, 1:428.98–9. Notwithstanding the Master's (and Benedict's) attribution of the phrase to scripture, it comes from a late antique hagiographical text, the Passion of Anastasia (BHL 401) 234, or one of its constituent parts, the Passion of Agape, Chionia, and Irene of Thessalonica (BHL 118) 9, 250B, when the legendary martyr explains to her pagan tormentor that prostituting her will not pollute her soul. The expression appears to derive ultimately from the rather more appealing expression of the fourth-century African Optatus, bishop of Milevis: "Denique uoluntas habet poenam. necessitas ueniam" (*Contra Parmenianum Donatistam* 7.1, 160.5–6). On the Master's use of *scriptura* for a broader swath of Christian literature than the Bible, see A. de Vogüé's discussion, *La règle du maître,* 1:214–20.

eius: "An inventory memorandum of God's houses and monasteries that are in the Holy City of Jerusalem and its environs."[21] As we have seen in the first part of this book, the *Breve commemoratorii de illis casis Dei* describes the staff of the patriarchate of Jerusalem and enumerates the personnel of the religious houses of the Holy City and its immediate environs; it also identifies the ethnic background of certain hagiopolitan religious.

The second text, *Memoria de illis monasteriis quae sunt in extremis Hierusalem in terra promissionis* (Memorial of the monasteries that are in the Promised Land outside of Jerusalem) consists of two parts. The first surveys Christian religious establishments in the Holy Land beyond Jerusalem. Without transition it proceeds from the end of a typical description of the monastery known today as St. Catherine's at Mount Sinai to a list of architectural statistics, starting with the number of steps associated with the Sinai shrine and concluding with the dimensions of the church of Zion in Jerusalem. In its present state, the last three lines of the Basel roll preserve the beginning of a third text. The *Dispensa patriarchae . . . per . . . annum*, "The Patriarch's Expenditures," lists the annual expenditures of the patriarchal establishment in Jerusalem. The roll breaks off after the first six or seven entries.

The documents are laid out in simple fashion, much like other administrative records of the same period that also survive in roll format, for instance the Munich fragment (ca. 813) of Charlemagne's Capitulary no. 143 (Munich, Bayerische Staatsbibliothek, Lat. 29555/2), the *Descriptio mancipiorum ecclesie Massiliensis* of around 813, and the Murbach roll.[22]

On the Basel roll, the first record's title is not distinguished by emphasis script, but its conclusion is clearly demarcated by a kind of *explicit* in rustic capitals ("Isti in Hierusalem sunt . . ."). Subdivisions within the first document are indicated by space left at the end of such units and, less regularly, by initial emphasis letters: they demarcate five subsections, of which the first treats the personnel of the patriarchate and the Holy Sepulcher complex. The second details those of the other three great Passion shrines; the third, the remaining shrines inside and just north of the city walls of Aelia Capitolina; and the fourth, shrines in the Kidron Valley (Valley of Jehoshaphat) and environs. At least two of the three establish-

---

21   All citations are from the critical edition printed below, chapter 10. For my translation of the words *Breue commemoratorii*, see below, chapter 11.

22   On the Munich roll, see H. Mordek, "Karolingische Kapitularien," in *Überlieferung und Geltung normativer Texte des frühen und hohen Mittelalters. Vier Vorträge, gehalten auf dem 35. Deutschen Historikertag 1984 in Berlin*, ed. H. Mordek, Quellen und Forschungen zum Recht im Mittelalter 4 (Sigmaringen, 1986), 25–50, here 33–35, with a photograph. The Marseilles roll is imperfectly edited in *Cartulaire de l'abbaye de Saint-Victor de Marseille*, 2:633–54. A reduced photograph appears in Å. Bergh, *Études d'anthroponymie provençale*, vol. 1, *Les noms de personne du Polyptyque de Wadalde (a. 814)* (Göteborg, 1941).

ments recorded in the fifth subsection were on the Mount of Olives or just beyond it; two also had western religious, so that either might explain the grouping of these entries. The second document, the Memorial, shows no formal subdivisions beyond those suggested by punctuation and initial letters. More than half of its final line is left blank, marking the break before the *Dispensa*, whose remnant also displays no formal subdivisions.

Each document treats the individual items according to the same formula: the location or name of a shrine is occasionally supplemented with an indication of saints buried or venerated there or a reference to other circumstances, such as state of repair; names of prelates follow, then types of clergy (e.g., priests, monks, nuns), sometimes distinguished according to their dignities, and, finally, their numbers. A subtotal—which seems erroneous—is given for the patriarchal establishment in Jerusalem (see above, table 2.3; cf. text, line 8, and page 219). In addition, the documents usually furnish the names of bishops or abbots, where appropriate. For the architectural measurements (table 5.2), the Memorial identifies structures, followed by subdivisons and the measurements of each. For the patriarchal expenses, an item of expenditure is followed by the sum. All of this is analogous to ordinary Carolingian practice, as documented for instance by the *Breuium exempla,* Charlemagne's model document for inventorying royal properties.[23]

Tables 2.3 and 2.4 show that the patterns of the numbers of religious personnel in the Breve and Memorial diverge. The Breve seems to enumerate religious personnel more precisely. Thus at the Holy Sepulcher, the Breve reports quite varying totals of separate categories (priests, deacons, subdeacons, etc.): 9, 14, 6, 23, 13, 41, etc. The pattern holds for virtually the entire Breve, for instance, 26 nuns; 17 nuns from Charlemagne's empire, etc. Nonetheless a few numbers that appear rounded either reflect reality or suggest an occasional estimate. That we are looking at estimates rather than actual counts seems most plausible for the numbers of nuns at the church of the Virgin at the Sheep Pool and the lepers (line 12). In both cases, one can understand that the envoys or their informants were unable or unwilling actually to count the individuals. In the Memorial, on the other hand, almost all the totals of religious personnel look rounded off. It stretches belief to assume that, saving stylites and four churches, all religious houses inventoried outside of Jerusalem and its suburbs were populated by communities numbering in multiples of five.[24] We must therefore conclude that the authors of these documents were

23   For example, c. 30, ed. MGH Capit 1:255.10–26; or Brühl, 53.42–54.16. Anyone can now look at the manuscript itself thanks to the excellent digital site of the Herzog-August-Bibliothek: http://diglib.hab.de/mss/254-helmst/start.htm.

24   The exceptions are the 12 in the unidentified Galilean establishment (line 36), the 8 monks of the Virgin's shrine a mile from Nazareth (line 37), 3 at the shrine of the Table (line 40) and the 18 monks under bishop Theophanes at Mount Tabor (lines 41–43).

more careful or better informed in the Holy City itself, whereas for the country-side, they were mostly content with estimates.

The names the first two documents bear are not banal. In Carolingian usage, *breue* has a wide spectrum of meanings. In administrative parlance it generally means a "summary," a list or catalog of persons or things; it can also mean "report."[25] The second word, without the prefix (i.e., *memoratorium*), occurs occasionally in Italian acts of the eighth and ninth century; it is sometimes combined with *breue* or its variants and means something like "memorandum," "record."[26]

Charlemagne's court seems to have used *commemoratorium* in 788 or 789 to designate a diplomatic memorandum submitted to the pope.[27] The unprefixed form designates a capitulary of Charlemagne from 807 or thereabouts and seems

25 Prinz and Schneider, *Mittellateinisches Wörterbuch* 1:1576.65–69 and 1577.20–69. See, for instance, the use of the form *breuis* in Adalhard's *Statuta* on the management of the abbey of Corbie (e.g., *Statuta seu brevia*, 365.1, 19, 393.21, etc.). A tenth-century manuscript (Paris, B.N.F., lat. 13908, apparently from Corbie itself), titles the *Statuta* themselves a *Breue* (ibid., 365, app. on line 1; cf. p. 357). On Adalhard's role in Charlemagne's entourage, see above, chapter 4.3. See too below, note 35, on a memorandum by his half brother, Wala.

26 For example, *Codice diplomatico longobardo* no. 70, 1:214 (original of 739, Lucca): "Memoraturium facio ego Ursu uouis neputi mei de morganicapu matri uestre"; ibid., no. 252, 2:332: 24 April 771, "Notitia breuis memoratorio pro foturis temporibus, in corum praesentia recepit Autpert actor domni regi de uilla Lauchade." Compare p. 333, the original of which is preserved in the Archivio di Stato, Milan. Another *memoratorium* from the Po Valley in 852 concerns a transaction "ad urbem curte domni imperatoris (*Codex diplomaticus langobardiae* no. 179, 302–3). A legal enactment on the *magistri commacini*, or builders of Lombard Italy, ascribed to kings Grimwald or Liutprand, is called "Item memoratorio de mercedes comacinorum" in the Lombard laws. *Die Gesetze der Langobarden*, 324. *Breue memoratorium* is used for a type of private act in the duchies of Spoleto and Benevento; see H. Brunner, *Zur Rechtsgeschichte der römischen und germanischen Urkunde* (Berlin, 1880), 14–17, with examples from 821 and 837 as well as from southern Italy. *Memoraturium* is used in *Codex diplomaticus Cavensis* no. 38, 1:57 (AD 854); no. 52, 1:65 (two documents, 857), etc. Compare H. Bresslau and H. W. Klewitz, *Handbuch der Urkundenlehre für Deutschland und Italien*, 3rd ed. (Berlin, 1958), 1:51; O. Redlich, *Die Privaturkunden des Mittelalters* (Munich, 1911), 27; and A. de Boüard, *Manuel de diplomatique française et pontificale* (Paris, 1929–52), 2:169. See also the suggestive combination of words at the conclusion of a long list (*notitia*) of people in *Codice diplomatico longobardo* no. 154, 2:76 (15 May 761, Lucca; eighth-century copy, Lucca): "in hoc ordine eos commemoraui in hunc breue." So far I have found no examples of the combined and prefixed form *breue commemoratorii* among Italian documents.

27 *Codex carolinus* 85 (Jaffé, *Regesta*, 1: no. 2467), 621–22. The pope's phrasing suggests that the term comes from the document itself or the words used by Charlemagne's ambassador: ". . . inter responsionis suae verba obtulit nobis commemoratorium, ut asserebat, vestre excellentie exaratum" (621.12–13). Compare 622.4, where Hadrian calls it "commonitorium illud." I disagree with the deduction in J. F. Niermeyer, C. van de Kieft, and G. S. M. M. Lake-Schooneebek, *Mediae Latinitatis lexicon minus* (Leyden, 1993), 211, s.v., that the term here means "protocol" in the sense of transcript of an election: on the contrary, it is clearly a memorandum of Charlemagne, spelling out his position on this issue (cf. Hadrian's reference to Charlemagne's statement about the patriciate in that document, *Codex carolinus*, 622.4–6).

to come from or be put in Charlemagne's mouth.[28] *Commemoratorium* also occurs, occasionally, in Frankish private documents from the same period and later that involve high-ranking persons with probable or certain court connections, such as counts.[29]

The words *breue* and *commemoratorium* combine to designate six private acts involving Freising between 760 and 819. Interestingly, they cluster between 804 and 808, and three of those four manifestly concern royal counts and a direct appeal to Charlemagne and his representatives.[30] The earliest surviving document to use *breue commemoratorium* in precisely the same way as the roll to designate a memorandum concerning a catalog of things was written up at the abbey of Werden, a place with close links to Charlemagne, probably at some point between 796 and 837. Werden was of course founded by an associate of the king who had been entrusted with the mission to the Saxons, Alcuin's Frisian student Liudger (d. 26 March 809), bishop of Münster. Although this *breue commemoratorio*

28 "Memoratorium qualiter ordinavimus propter famis inopiam. . . ." Capitulary no. 48, ed. MGH Capit 1:134.25. F. L. Ganshof accepted the customary date. See *Was waren die Kapitularien?* trans. W. A. Eckhardt and B. W. Franz (Darmstadt, 1961), 165. A. E. Verhulst, however, wondered whether it could be connected with the famine addressed in Charlemagne's letter to Ghaerbald, bishop of Liège. See "Karolingische Agrarpolitik. Das Capitulare de Villis und die Hungersnöte von 792/93 und 805/06," *Zeitschrift für Agrargeschichte und Agrarsoziologie* 13 (1965): 175–89, at 183. On Ghaerbald's possible links with the Jerusalem mission, see below, chapter 8.2.

29 *Die Traditionen des Hochstifts Freising* no. 226, 1:209 (17 October 806), sons of Count Droant and Judith: "Notitia vel commemoratorium de traditione. . . ." *Commemoratorium* also designates a document from Passau dating between 806 and 813: see *Die Traditionen des Hochstifts Passau*, ed. M. Heuwieser (Munich, 1930), no. 63, 53. A *<co>mmemoratorium* concerns testamentary dispositions of the wealthy and court-connected widow Erkanfrida in 853: *Urkunden- und Quellenbuch zur Geschichte der altluxemburgischen Territorien* no. 89, 1:87. The editor's restoration is surely correct. Plate III, facing 192, reproduces his photograph of what is presumably one of the originals in roll format, Berlin, Staatsbibliothek, Lat. fol. 729. The last stroke of the first *m* is clearly visible. On the couple's court connections with Louis the Pious, see *Urkunden- und Quellenbuch*, 1:84 n. 3 and 85 n. 5. For another, later Passau occurrence, see below. Early in the sixth century, Eugippius (*Epistola ad Paschasium* 2, 148) used *commemoratorium* to refer to his biography of St. Severinus. This text would experience a broad diffusion in Bavaria, documented by a manuscript tradition that began no later than 903. See, for example, Eugippius, *Vita Severini*, xxii.

30 *Die Traditionen des Hochstifts Freising* no. 16, 1:44 (17 November 760); no. 197, 1:187–90 (16 June 804), a transaction whose early stage had involved several prominent members of the court; no. 213a, 1:201–2 (ca. 804–8), involving count Helmuuinus; no. 224, 1:208 (14 July 806); no. 232b, 1:214–15 (29 September 806 or 807), a first-person *notitia* of the priest Otker describing how he went to Charlemagne to complain about Count Cotehrammus's violent seizure of his property and returned with the emperor's *missi* to obtain the restitution the act describes; no. 410, 1:353 (18 April 819); for a seventh occurrence, apparently from about 842, see below. This means that the use of the term is certainly of Carolingian date. The wording could conceivably come from Cozroh, the compiler of the cartulary before 854, but it is difficult to see why he would have used the word so sporadically. On the date of the manuscript (Munich, Hauptstaatsarchiv, Hochstift Freising, Lit. 3a), see Bischoff, *Die südostdeutschen Schreibschulen*, 1:112–13.

inventories swine feeding grounds, the title resembles the first Basel document down to the definite article.[31] A similar use appears in an undated document copied in the Freising cartulary, probably in 842 or 843.[32] So the term is Carolingian, its use appears to cluster in milieus connected with the royal court and in the same years as the documents preserved on the Basel roll were composed, and, semantically, the closest contemporary parallel is that of the abbey of Werden, whose abbot and founder had close links with the royal court. The application of the term to other kinds of documents is best attested in Bavaria, also at that same time, and typically, in documents that concern people with links to the court.

The second document has a title that is no less striking: *Memoria*. This is not a common term for early medieval records. The standard lexica inventory no examples prior to the tenth century, and when *memoria* does occur, it tends to designate a private act of the *notitia* type.[33] I have encountered a like use of the word only once in Carolingian administrative parlance. A north Italian manuscript from the first third of the ninth century seems to have been a Carolingian count's personal law book. It contains a series of orders imparted by the emperor Lothar to his counts at Corteolona, near Pavia, in 822 or 823. In this case the heading reads, "Memoria quod domnus imperator suis comites [sic] precepit" (*Memoria* that the lord emperor commanded to his counts).[34] An intriguing analogue

---

31 "Breue commemoratorio de illa pastione quod nos habemus de ambas partes Rura in Hesi et in Uagnesuuald," *Die Urbare der Abtei Werden a.d. Ruhr*, no. 1, 3.13–14. The personal names in this inventory recur among the acts pertaining to Werden between the years 796 and 837, when Liudger's family controlled it, whence its probable date. Compare ibid., 3–4, app. The script of the segment of the cartulary containing this document (Leyden, B. Univ., Voss. Qu. Lat. 55, fol. 48) was originally dated simply to the ninth century by Bernhard Bischoff. See K. A. de Meyier and P. F. J. Obbema, *Codices Vossiani Latini*, vol. 2, *Codices in Quarto*, Codices manuscripti 14 (Leyden, 1975), 138. Bischoff, *Katalog der festlandischen Handschriften*, 2:58–59, no. 2220, finally assigned it to Werden, possibly around 900. On Liudger, his kinsmen, and the Carolingian court, see esp. Schmid, *Gebetsgedenken*, 203–335; and W. Stüwer, *Das Erzbistum Köln. Die Reichsabtei Werden an der Ruhr*, Germania sacra, n.F., 12.3 (Berlin, 1980), 296–98.

32 The inventory of the treasury and property of Bergkirchen bei Jesenwang was drawn up when Freising took control of this church. See B. Bischoff et al., eds., *Mittelalterliche Schatzverzeichnisse*, Veröffentlichungen des Zentralinstituts für Kunstgeschichte 4 (Munich, 1967), 23–24, no. 12; compare *Die Traditionen des Hochstifts Freising*, no. 652, 1:550–51. See also a fragmentary inventory of lands held by Passau bishops since the time of Charlemagne in the early tenth-century section of the Passau tradition book, *Die Traditionen des Hochstifts Passau*, no. 79, 1:66. On the script, see also Bischoff, *Die südostdeutschen Schreibschulen*, 2:3.

33 See, for example, F. Blatt, ed., *Novum glossarium mediae Latinitatis ab anno DCCC usque ad annum MCC*, M–N (Copenhagen, 1959–69), 358.24–34.

34 MGH Capit 1:318.27, no. 158; on the title, compare ibid., 317. On the manuscript (St. Paul im Lavanttal, Carinthia, Archiv des Benediktinerstiftes, 4/1) and its comital connection, see R. McKitterick, *The Carolingians and the Written Word* (Cambridge, 1989), 59 n. 82; compare A. Bühler, "Studien zur Entstehung und Überlieferung der Kapitularien Karls des Grossen und Ludwigs des Frommen," *Archiv für Diplomatik* 32 (1986): 305–501, here 343–44, and 376 n. 247. For detailed descriptions, see B. Krusch, *Die Lex Bajuvariorum: Textgeschichte, Handschriften-*

---

comes in a memorandum called *Breue memorationis*, drawn up around 834–36 by Wala, the half-brother of Adalhard of Corbie and also a onetime advisor of Charlemagne, for his monastery of Bobbio.[35] The common threads in the nomenclature of the first two Holy Land documents point to the Carolingian court.

Notwithstanding their circumscribed differences, nothing suggests that the Breve, the *Memoria*, and the *Dispensa patriarchae* do not share a common origin. Beyond their physical survival together as part of a group of records consigned to one roll, they treat complementary aspects of the physical, financial, and personnel status of the churches under the patriarchate of Jerusalem. Some internal characteristics, and particularly the names by which they are called, recur in records connected directly or indirectly with the Carolingian court. A distinctive peculiarity of language in any event unites all three documents and obliges us to turn to a close examination of that aspect of their testimony.

kritik und Entstehung mit zwei Anhängen, Lex Alamannorum und Lex Ribuaria (Berlin, 1924), 80–87; and Mordek, *Bibliotheca capitularium*, 685–95.

35   Ed. Josef Semmler, *Corpus consuetudinum monasticarum*, 1:421.1.

. . . .

Chapter Seven

THE LANGUAGES AND SOURCES
OF THE BASEL ROLL

T HE LANGUAGE OF AN EARLY MEDIEVAL SOURCE calls for comment from two perspectives. The most primal is the simple understanding of the text. In this era of linguistic flux, language usage often does not conform to the canons of Latin grammar as revived or invented in the Italian Renaissance. The salient features of the roll's language need mentioning to ensure correct understanding of the text and to explain why the editor believes (or not) the testimony of, in this case, the sole surviving manuscript witness. The second perspective—of shared linguistic features that indicate common authorship among a group of documents—is more subtle but potentially no less rewarding. The language of the Breve, the Memorial, and the Expenditures deepens the other evidence concerning the circumstances of their genesis and transmission. It is also interesting to consider whether the rapid advances in the revival of classicizing Latin spread into such writing as served a practical role in the nitty gritty of Carolingian administration. Beyond that, sensitivity to the way a writer uses the language may help us spot tics of style, jargons, or preferred expressions that tip us toward his or her milieu or personal associates. No one who has practiced deeply the records of Italy on the one hand and the Carolingian heartland on the other around 800 will doubt that many—probably most—people writing Latin in these two areas used different handwritings and that they also used the language differently. Close attention to the language of our sources may also shed more light on the specific linguistic circumstances in which Charlemagne's envoys acquired the data the Basel roll preserves. That in turn will bolster or diminish our confidence in those data, even as it illuminates the operational procedures of *missi dominici* in a distant land and culture. Though the advent of large-scale computerized databases is making this kind of philological analysis more of a science and less of an art, the readily available material for administrative or diplomatic sources lags behind those for literary sources. On that score we have no choice but to rely mainly on the traditional tools of the trade. The result will naturally be improved and corrected by those using superior instruments in the years to come.

1. Late Popular Latin

An expert scribe wrote the Basel roll. He (assuming it was a he) uses, in general, a version of the reformed Carolingian orthography promoted by Alcuin and others. We know that the synthetic passive forms were dead, and deponents had mostly disappeared from the spoken language, which was then perched on the watershed between Popular Latin and Proto-Romance.[1] The classicizing language espoused by Carolingian scholars perhaps has left traces in the three deponent verb forms that occur in the text. Nevertheless, two (*nasci* with *dignatus est*) come in a stereotyped phrase about the Incarnation abundantly attested in the church fathers, the liturgy, and even in a contemporary letter from the Frankish monks of the Mount of Olives to Pope Leo III; our texts' perfect deponents (*natus fuit* etc.) survive to this day in French and Italian.[2] *Locutus est* is the only other deponent.[3]

Beneath the polished veneer lurks the living language of late Popular Latin. While Carolingian scribes zealously corrected obvious vulgarisms of spelling in earlier texts, they often left intact Proto-Romance features of word choice and syntax.[4] The Basel roll offers a particularly clear example of this phenomenon, insofar as the expert Alemannian scribe probably recognized and corrected common phonetic errors in the ordinary Latin words of his exemplar, although he did miss the correct aspiration when he wrote or kept *ospitales* for *hospitales*. Less familiar proper names escaped his classicizing vigilance and still display the phonology of Proto-Romance. Thus he mistakenly took "sancto Quaranta" (line 15) for a proper name, when in fact it is the Proto-Romance form for "sancti Quadraginti," that is, he created a "St. Forty" as opposed to the "Forty Saints." So too he failed

---

1   See, for example, V. Väänänen, *Introduction au latin vulgaire*, 3rd ed. (Paris, 1981), 128 and 129–30.

2   Lines 25–26, "In sancta Bethlem, ubi Dominus noster Iesus Christus nasci dignatus est de sancta uirgine Maria"; "nasci . . . dignatus est" and close variants occur fifteen times in Augustine and three times in Gregory I, according to the CLCLT-5. Among Carolingian liturgical books, "dignatus es nasci de virgine," not to mention similar formulas, occurs, for example, thrice in the Sacramentary of Autun, as well as in the Sacramentary of Gellone (CLCLT-5). See also similar formulas in the Carolingian supplement to the Gregorian Sacramentary as well as the Gelasian Sacramentary, conveniently cataloged in J. Deshusses and B. Darragon, *Concordances et tableaux pour l'étude des grands sacramentaires* (Fribourg, 1982), 3.3:150. Monks of the Mount of Olives: "in die natalis Domini in sanctam Bethleem in sancto praesepio, ubi noster Dominus . . . pro mundi salute nasci dignatus est. . . ." (Leo III, *Epistolae selectae pontificum Romanorum* 7, 65.1–2); *Natus fuit* etc. occurs in lines 12, 16–17. Compare French *est né* and Italian *è nato*, on which, see P. Flobert, *Les verbes déponents latins des origines à Charlemagne* (Paris, 1975), 584–85.

3   Line 42: "locutus cum Moysi et Elia fuit"; line 47: "locutus est," which of course occurs hundreds of times in the Vulgate.

4   On this remarkable and far-reaching phenomenon of "automatic" scribal correction in the Carolingian period, see E. Löfstedt, *Il latino tardo. Aspetti e problemi*, trans. C. Cima Giorgetti (Brescia, 1980), 12–13.

to recognize that "sancto Sertio" was in fact a popular phonetic deformation for "Sergio" (line 16) and left the vulgar form "sancto Legontio" for "sancto Leontio" (line 14).[5] *Spania* slips in for the correct Latin *Hispania* (line 23). So too for an important point of historical testimony. Because it was ambiguous, the correcting scribe of the Basel roll probably mistook the Breve's statement about not counting the personnel of the three hostels (*ospitales*) to refer to three persons working in a hostel and did not correct the masculine to the neuter.[6]

Syntactical and lexical features of late Popular Latin or Proto-Romance are frequent. The definite article *ille, illa* (whence French *le, la*), and so forth occurs a dozen times in the first two documents.[7] The ungendered relative pronoun *qui* appears right at the beginning (line 1) as the subject of a clause in reference to feminine and neuter antecedents; thereafter, classical usage is observed or restored. *Quod* occurs thrice as the direct object referring back to inanimate antecedents that are grammatically feminine or masculine (lines 11, 24, 50) in both the Breve and the Memorial.[8] *Excepto* functions as a preposition and governs the accusative.[9] Gender confusion includes a *sepulchrum* that is *uenerabilis* (line 13), masculine *frons, frontis*, and a *monasterium* that seems at times neuter, masculine, or feminine.[10] As in Romance, the infinitive is used with *ad* (line 50, *ad subire*) where classical Latin would have deployed the gerund.[11] The author of these reports uses *inter* as a copulative, so that *inter . . . et* means "including . . . and," and he generally construes *inter* with the ablative. This unusual usage with the ablative occurs in all three documents and underscores their common origin.[12]

---

5   *Sertio* reveals of course that the person who wrote the original document softened the *g* followed by an *i*. See Väänänen, *Introduction au latin vulgaire*, 54–55. For the vulgar insertion of a *g* in *Legontius* to avoid hiatus, see P. Stotz, *Handbuch zur lateinischen Sprache des Mittelalters*, Handbuch der Altertumswissenschaft 2.5 (Munich, 1996), 3:213–15. *Colunas* (line 53) could represent the Popular Latin and Proto-Romance assimilation of *mn* (cf. Väänänen, *Introduction au latin vulgaire*, 62); however, elsewhere the scribe of the Basel roll wrote *columnis* (line 26) and *colum<na>* (line 46), so we cannot rule out a simple slip of the pen.

6   See above, chapter 4.3.

7   Lines 1, 2, 20, 25, 27, 44 (twice), 46, 50, 53 (twice), 54. Compare Väänänen, *Introduction au latin vulgaire*, 121–22.

8   Väänänen, *Introduction au latin vulgaire*, 125. Another telling example of the scribe's correcting may well occur at lines 51 and 52. Describing the measurements of the Nea Church, the scribe first seems to have let slip the late vulgarism of a preposition modifying an adverb: *in longe*; a line later, he may have caught the mistake, and corrected before he copied as *in longo*. The scribe then used *in longo* three more times in four lines. On the late date of such an expression, see *ThLL* 7.2:1651.54–63.

9   Lines 8, 9. Compare Väänänen, *Introduction au latin vulgaire*, 167.

10   Ibid., 103–5; certainly neuter: lines 2–3, 33, and 34, and so forth; feminine: 22; masculine: *eum* (modifying *in monasterio*), and so forth.

11   Väänänen, *Introduction au latin vulgaire*, 139.

12   Lines 9, 10, 14—is "inter inclusas . . ." (14) a scribal correction?—17, 26, 45, 58. On this construction, see A. Uddholm, *Formulae Marculfi. Études sur la langue et le style* (Uppsala, 1953),

Lexical features show the same Late or Popular Latin flavor. "In exemplo sancti Symeonis" meaning "on the example of St. Symeon" has a classical pedigree; religious houses are *casae Dei*, and the diminutive *gradicula* replaces the simple form *gradus*.[13] *Habet* is used indefinitely ("there is").[14] *In aduerso* is synonymous with *in transuerso*, in the sense of "across." A mile is a *milium*, possibly echoing the Greek *million*, itself borrowed from Latin. *In extremis* means "outside of," corresponding to a use attested only in medieval Italian.[15] *Dispensa* seems not to be used in its typical Carolingian way as a feminine noun referring to "provisions," or "victuals," but to mean "expenditures" (from *dispendo*; cf. Prov. *depensa*; Fr. *dépens*, or *dépense*; Ital. *spesa*).[16] Though the word *ascensa* has left traces only in Italian, the fact that the term entered the Roman liturgy in the expression *Ascensa Domini* (the Ascension) guaranteed its familiarity among the Franks.[17] Another clue may come from the word *fabricatura* in the sense of "building account" or "structural expenses." In the Frankish world, the term meant "jewelry" or "metal work," that is, some kind of clearly movable wealth.[18] In the Expenditures, it means "building." That sense seems to find an early medieval parallel only in

---

diss. 126–28; compare W. Meyer-Lübke, *Grammaire des langues romanes*, trans. E. Rabiet (New York, 1923) 3:262–63, par. 217. One assumes with wonderment that it is only coincidence that the one case where Uddholm (128) has identified the structure (albeit with the accusative) in Einhard's *Vita Karoli* 16, 19.23–24 concerns precisely Charlemagne's envoys, who had in 806 taken an initial set of donations to the Holy Sepulcher and returned with Harun al Rashid's gifts, "inter vestes et aromata et ceteras orientalium terrarum opes ingentia illi dona direxit." See McCormick, *Origins of the European Economy: Communications and Commerce, A.D. 300–900* (Cambridge, 2001), 893–94, nos. 271 and 277. Adalhard of Corbie uses the same construction in his *Statuta* 10, 374.6; it recurs in a court-related set of annals associated with Lorsch from precisely these years (*Das Wiener Fragment der Lorscher Annalen*, 34.25) and in an act drawn up by Rudolf for a donation of a Roolf at Lorsch, *Codex Laureshamensis* no. 681, in 782. The *Memoria* also uses *inter* with the accusative to refer to spatial relations ("between," line 55).

13 On "in exemplo," see *ThLL* 5.2:1348.17–23. For diminutives in the sense of positives, see Väänänen, *Introduction au latin vulgaire*, 90.

14 Ibid., 128, no. 296.

15 S. Battaglia and G. Bàrberi Squarotti, *Grande dizionario della lingua italiana*, 21 vols. ([Turin], 1961–84), 5:468, s.v. "estremo," no. 3.

16 See G. Körting, *Lateinisch-romanisches Wörterbuch. Etymologisches Wörterbuch der romanischen Hauptsprachen*, 3rd ed. (New York, 1923), 357, no. 3020.

17 Ibid., 103, no. 3922; compare *ThLL* 2:759.3–16, and Ansegisus, *Collectio capitularium* 1.158, 514.9.

18 *Liber historiae Francorum* recensio B 13, 259.23; Arbeo of Freising, *Vitae sanctorum Haimhrammi et Corbiniani* recensio B (BHL 2538) 35, 80.11; and abundantly in the Merovingian and Carolingian collections of formularies for legal documents, for example, *Formulae Andecavenses* 32, 14.32 and 40, 17.34; *Marculfi formulae* 1.12, 50.14, 2.10, 82.11, and 2.14, 84.18, and so forth; and *Formulae Turonenses* 14, 143.5. Compare *Cartae Senonicae* 25, 196.12: "de fabricaturia"; *Formulae salicae Lindenbrogianae* 7, 271.36–272.1; and *Collectio Flaviniacensis* 8, 477.1. Charlemagne's son-in-law, Angilbert, used the word in the same sense. See *De perfectione et dedicatione Centulensis ecclesiae*, preserved in Hariulf, *Chronique de l'abbaye de Saint-Riquier* 2.10, 69.

northern Italy.[19] Similarly, the most likely restoration of *pactum* in line 28 is redolent of Italy.[20]

Given this linguistic picture, there can be little doubt that the person who originally wrote up the account spoke a late Popular Latin that was essentially Proto-Romance. The same person surely wrote all three documents, since even the brief surviving segment on the expenditures of the patriarch uses an unusual structure (*inter . . . et*) that recurs repeatedly in the other two documents, and the general features of the language of all three documents are the same. Within the system of late Popular Latin, the overall language of these documents is coherent and suggests that the same westerner wrote or dictated them. There are recurrent hints of an Italian connection in some of the words used. Given the preservation of Proto-Romance phonetic spellings in places where the copyist of the roll could not recognize them, we may suspect that the original he copied showed a less classical orthography and morphology.

2. Talking in Greek and Arabic

By their very nature, these documents had to have been composed in Jerusalem and the surrounding area. The westerner who created these extraordinary documents was dealing with the patriarchal church of Jerusalem at a moment of crucial linguistic change, for Greek was beginning to experience competition from Arabic. In fact, the documents transcribed on the Basel roll capture that moment of transition.

The traditional language of the orthodox church in the Holy Land appears in two words of the first document and, probably, one of the second. The patriarch's escorts are identified by the technical term *fragelites*, which attestation joins the Late Greek hapax *phragellitai* and, for the first time, reveals that term's true meaning. This word, which incorporates the Latin loanword φραγέλλιον (*phragellion*, from *flagellum*, "whip") and the Greek suffix for agent, was manifestly coined in the Greek-speaking world of late antiquity. Thanks to its occurrence in the Breve, we can now see that *phragellitai* is not a marooned survivor among Greek names for staff members of late Roman officials, as imagined until now. *Phragellites* is rather a technical term associated with the staff of the shrine of the Holy Sepulcher between the seventh and the ninth centuries. The etymology suggests a rather

---

19   In the will of Andreas, archbishop of Milan (Milan, 11 January 903), who transformed his own residential complex into a hostel or hospice, including the chapel, the bath, spaces, courtyard, garden, and all the other buildings and structures (presuming we have a neuter plural rather than a missing final *s* in this twelfth-century copy) there: *Codex diplomaticus Langobardiae* no. 402, 676B: ". . . atque balneum cum areas in qua extant, curte et orto, omnia simul tenente, et omnes edificias vel fabricatura inibi constructas. . . ."

20   See below, chapter 11, textual commentary on line 28.

forcible form of crowd-control from the boom days of late antique religious tourism: these are the "whip-men" on the patriarch's staff.[21] The Breve equally gives the Greek title of the patriarch's closest collaborator, the *synkellos* ("the one who shares a cell with"), and correctly identifies his influential administrative role.[22]

The second document refers to the monastery of St. Theodosius "in illo erimo," that is, "in the desert." Latin had borrowed *eremus* from Greek monasticism centuries earlier and the spelling *erimus* was not unknown in Late Latin.[23] That it appears here in the midst of otherwise reformed Carolingian spelling might as well echo the Late Latin sound of a loan word as the medieval and modern Greek pronunciation of the original Greek word. In any case, *erimo* escaped the corrector's vigilance in the same way as the saints' names mentioned above. A second Greek word occurs in the second document and, though damaged, it is certainly part of a toponym that has hitherto been obscured by erroneous reading and emendation: "in Pal<eo monasterio>." Here the descriptive name of the monastery of St. Chariton—"the old monastery"—reflects the way it was commonly referred to in Palestine: ἡ παλαιὰ λαύρα; similarly, its monks were called *palaiolauritai*. Our Greekless writer has mistaken the adjective παλαιός, παλαιά, παλαιόν for a proper name.[24]

More subtle traces of interaction with Greek-speakers in the Holy Land come in what look like linguistic calques. Here a rare Latin word, or a rare use for a

---

21   Line 4. This in turn allows us to correct the Greek dictionaries and an interpretation in the writings of the seventh-century Holy Land monk and exile John Moschus. The only other attestation of the word adduced hitherto has come, with a minor spelling variant, from Moschus, *Pratum spirituale* 49, PG 87.3:2904C. Here Moschus describes how a vision prevented a late Roman official of Germanic extraction, Gibimer, *dux Palaestinae*, from entering the Holy Sepulcher. The bystanders attempted to investigate, discovered the miraculous nature of the occurrence, and convinced the duke to renounce his monophysite communion on the spot. The bystanders were the *skevophylax* Azarias and the *phragellitai* (here spelled φραγγελιταί). Because the incident concerned an imperial official, Herbert van Rosweyden erroneously deduced that the term must refer to the duke's lictors (ibid., 3112C note 11). The Breve proves, on the contrary, that, just like the skevophylax, phragellitai were members of the patriarch's staff particularly associated with the shrine of the Holy Sepulcher. Correct accordingly, for example, G. W. H. Lampe, *A Patristic Greek Lexicon* (Oxford, 1961), 1489, s.v. It remains a hapax in the *Thesaurus linguae Graecae*, which I checked online on 24 December 2007. An alternative interpretation might connect these officials with the Passion relic of the whip with which Christ was scourged. But why, among the other Passion relics—the sponge, the lance, crown of thorns, and so forth—similarly preserved in the Anastasis shrine, would one single out this relic to name officials? The phonetic variant *phrangel(l)ion* for *phragellion* is a banal late Greek vulgarism, as a quick consultation of its attestation in the *Thesaurus linguae Graecae* confirms. On Gibimer, see A. H. M. Jones, J. R. Martindale, and J. Morris, *The Prosopography of the Later Roman Empire* (Cambridge, 1971–92), 3:536.

22   Line 7. See, for example, A. Papadakis, "Synkellos," *ODB* 3:1993–94.

23   *ThLL* 5.2:747.48.

24   Line 29. See below, chapter 11, textual commentary on this line. Similarly, the writer probably rendered phonetically the Greek name for the church of the Virgin at the Sheep Pool, known in Latin by the Greek-derived form "Probatica piscina" (see, e.g., John 5:2). Our writer's *Probatici* accurately renders the medieval Greek pronunciation of the final vowel of Προβατική.

Latin word, appears to echo Greek. Thus the patriarch's *conputarii* are obviously accountants of some sort, and the word is an ancient and, almost, medieval hapax in this sense.[25] It is nonetheless a good rendering of the patriarch's *logothetai*.[26] Although "qui sub patriarcha omnia corrigit" ("who manages everything under the patriarch") can be grasped from within Latin, the expression is unusual in this sense and is likely also an awkward rendering of a Greek term.[27]

Given the evidence the census itself provides on the languages of prayer of Christian religious in Jerusalem and the impact of Greek we have just detected, the presence of Arabic seems more surprising. Yet it is undeniable that to describe the vault of the Holy Sepulcher itself, the Memorial uses an Arabic technical term for a dome above a tomb; the term is transcribed with the Arabic definite article as *alcuba* (Ar. *al-ḳubba*; cf. "alcove").[28] Once again this document affords us an exceptional insight: a glimpse of the rise of Arabic in and around Christian milieus of Jerusalem who also still spoke Greek in the opening years of the ninth century, a phenomenon hitherto detectible only in the more rarified ambiance of the languages chosen for scholarly composition.[29] We shall return to the significance of this in a moment.

That the envoys relied on Arabic speakers in drawing up the Memorial is unmistakable, once we return to the authentic testimony of the manuscript itself. Three times Tobler and Molinier tacitly changed the forms of proper names as they appear in the manuscript by "restoring" them to their classical Greek and Latin equivalents. In fact, the Basel roll does not give two famous holy sites in Samaria their classical Greek names of Sebaste and Neapolis; rather, it offers forms

25 *ThLL* 3:2175.51–54, documenting only one occurrence, in Columban of Bobbio's letter to Pope Gregory I, mentioning the "most wise . . . Irish calculators" of the ecclesiastical computus, that is, the calculation of the date of Easter "Hibernicis . . . sapientissimis componendi calculi computariis" (*Epistola* 1, 6.4). A search performed on CLCLT-5 reinforces this observation. The *computarium* containing the names of deceased grandees handed over by a dying queen Mathilda in 968, according to the *Vita Mathildis* (BHL 5683) 13, 138.7, is clearly something different and has been interpreted as "calendar": compare Prinz and Schneider, *Mittellateinisches Wörterbuch* 2 (1999): 1127.71–1128.5.

26 Compare A. Kazhdan, "Logothetes," *ODB* 2:1247.

27 *Corrigere* was often used incorrectly to render Greek κατορθόω and cognates, in the sense of "carry out well." See S. Lundström, *Lexicon errorum interpretum Latinorum*, Acta Universitatis Upsaliensis, Studia Latina Upsaliensia 16 (Uppsala, 1983), 53; and Lampe, *A Patristic Greek Lexicon*, 735, s.v., sense 3b. Other possibilities behind the *corrigere* might be ἐπευθύνειν or ὁ (συν)διέπων. Certainly a contemporary monk of Mar Saba—so closely linked to the patriarchs in this period—used the latter verb to mean "to administer" a monastery. See Stephen, *Martyrium XX Sabaitarum* 30, 23.23.

28 E. Diez, "Ḳubba," *EI*² 5:289–96; cf. Latin *cupa*.

29 See S. H. Griffith, "Greek into Arabic: Life and Letters in the Monasteries of Palestine in the Ninth Century," in *Arabic Christianity in the Monasteries of Ninth-century Palestine* (Aldershot, 1992), VIII, pp. 117–38; and Griffith, "From Aramaic to Arabic: The Languages of the Monasteries of Palestine in the Byzantine and Early Islamic Periods," *DOP* 51 (1997): 11–31.

reflecting their medieval and modern Arabic names: "Sabastia" and "Naboli."[30] The clincher comes in the names of the hermits from the Caucasus living on the Mount of Olives. In Molinier's edition the text identifies them as *Georgiani*, which suggests that this information also did not originate with Greek speakers, since they called Georgians *Iberoi*. Actually, the roll has quite a different reading: it twice identifies these hermits as *Iorzani* (lines 19 and 21). The initial semivowel is, in this instance, a common hyperurbanism inspired by the initial sound *dz*—Proto-Romance speakers who used correct Latin spelling were accustomed to hear, for example, the sound that became in Italian *già*, and write *ia(m)*. This means that our envoys heard the hermits identified as *dzorzani*, which they rendered *iorzani*. What they heard corresponds to the contemporary Arabic name for Georgia, *al-Djūrzān* and proves that we have here the results of oral testimony rendered from Arabic into Proto-Romance.[31]

Thus there can be no doubt that Arabic as well as Greek was spoken in the course of the Frankish *missi dominici's* investigation in the Holy Land. The combination of the two may seem unusual, but each in fact reflects a particular aspect of what the envoys encountered. Greek terms concern the organizational hierarchy of the Sepulcher, whereas Arabic ones concern its physical plant and the identities of hermits and towns outside of Jerusalem. Does the surprising use of an Arabic term for the dome that marks the holiest site in Christendom suggest that the subaltern personnel of the patriarchate were already Arabophones? Or could it rather hint that our author was escorted by Arabic speakers, whether they had accompanied him to the Middle East from home or joined him as "minders," perhaps assigned by the caliph to accompany and watch the foreign ambassadors? The latter explanation would fit the Arabic accent of the identification of the holy men in the area around Jerusalem. But it probably does not account for the discussions of the architecture of the Holy Sepulcher, presumably conducted in and around the building itself.

It is likely that in this connection the Franks had some dealings with an individual mentioned in a contemporary Palestinian saint's life. Eustratius had formerly been a monk at St. Sabas. Around 807 he had become *basilikarios* of the Anastasis shrine. This rare word seems to designate a kind of sexton, that is, an

---

30 E. Honigmann, "Sabastiyya," *EI*[2] 8:670–71; F. Buhl and C. E. Bosworth, "Nābulus," *EI*[2] 7:844–45. For the Greek forms, see, for example, George of Cyprus, *Descriptio orbis Romani*, 51.1014–15. George was a seventh-century geographer whose work survives in a compilation ascribed to the ninth century that may have undergone some revision. See A. Kazhdan, "George of Cyprus," *ODB* 2:837.

31 V. Minorsky and C. E. Bosworth, "al-Kurdj," *EI*[2] 5.1:487; on the phonetic phenomenon in question from a Late Latin perspective, see Väänänen, *Introduction au latin vulgaire*, 53–54. The phenomenon extended beyond Italy, for Amalarius of Metz notes it in Gaul around 800. *Epistola* 1.1, *Amalarii episcopi opera liturgica omnia* 2:386.11–13.

official in charge of a church's physical plant.[32] A clue to the choice of an Arabic word for the dome of the Holy Sepulcher may come from a twelfth-century Greek manuscript preserved in the monastery of St. Catherine's on Mount Sinai. It transmits a "rule" of uncertain date for the monastery of St. Sabas. The rule shows numerous points of contact with the teachings of St. Sabas himself (d. 532), the founder of Holy Land cenobitism, although its reference to the saint's tomb indicates that the transmitted version dates from after his death. Most scholars allow that it preserves much older materials but that the present form dates to the Crusader kingdom, that is, the twelfth century. The twelfth-century date for this form of the text rests on a mention in the oldest manuscript of "Franks," apparently monks, and apparently of somewhat controversial orthodoxy, attending eucharistic services at St. Sabas alongside Georgians and Syrians. The presumption was that "Franks" could refer only to the Crusader period.[33]

Given what the Basel roll reveals about the substantial Frankish monastic presence in the Holy Land around 800, the mention of Frankish monks in the Rule of St. Sabas scarcely imposes a date later than that for this interpolation. Indeed, concerns about their orthodoxy arose during a liturgical service there and were levied by a certain monk John, "who was [formerly] of the monastery of St. Sabas." Although it is unclear whether this refers to St. Sabas in Rome or Palestine, John attacked the Frankish monks in Jerusalem and triggered an investigation by the patriarchal establishment, itself closely connected with the monastery of Mar Saba.[34] In other words, the mention of "Franks" in no way precludes the

---

32 Eustratius had been a disciple of St. Stephen Thaumaturgus before becoming βασιλικάριος. Leontius, *Vita Stephani Thaumaturgi* 24, 513E; Arabic version 24.1, trans. 39.

33 Ed. A. Dmitrievskij, "Kinovial'nijya pravila prep. Cavvij Osvyaščennago, vručennijya im pred končinoju preemniku svoemu igumenu Melitu" [The cenobitic rule of St. Sabbas, transmitted on his decease to his successor higoumen Melitos], *Trudij Kievskoj Dukhovnoj Akademii* 31, no. 1 (1890): 170–92. Dmitrievskij's opinion is clear from his title. He identified the mention of Georgians and Franks as later interpolations (180 n. 1 and 181 nn. 1–2). Eduard Kurtz reprinted and improved the edition in his review in *BZ* 3 (1894): 167–70. He distinguished what he considered to be interpolations into the original rule, for instance, the mention of the saint's tomb (169.17–18) and St. Sabas's speaking of the Franks in the Holy Land (169.12) since they arrived only in the eleventh century. Although Kurtz cautiously observes that one cannot provide peremptory proof that the emended text is exactly as it came from the hands of the saint, he clearly thought that was the case, aside from the putative interpolations; he refers to it as "this interesting document of ascetic literature from the early sixth century" (ibid., 168). J. P. Thomas, A. C. Hero, and G. Constable also seem to suspect that most of the document is much older than the eleventh or twelfth century commonly deduced from the mention of Franks. See *Byzantine Monastic Foundation Documents: A Complete Translation of the Surviving Founders' Typika and Testaments* (Washington, D.C., 2000), 4:1314 n. 1. G. Fiaccadori, "Proleitourgia," *La parola del passato* 44 (1989): 39–40, however, observes another probable interpolation, which is paralleled only in the eleventh century.

34 *Epistolae selectae pontificum Romanorum* 7, 64–66; compare McCormick, *Origins*, 894, no. 279. See further, below, chapter 8.2.

possibility that much of the text of the Rule reflected in this Sinai manuscript could be as early as the ninth century or indeed, as its editors have thought, considerably earlier.

What is interesting for our purpose is that, to avoid dissension within the community of Mar Saba, the Rule lays down the basic principle that the hegoumenos will always be a Greek-speaker but that all positions connected with the monastery's practical business—such as stewards (*oikonomoi*)—will go to "Syriac" speakers, because they are so good at business in their homelands.[35] If this principle were already established in the ninth century and carried over to the patriarchal establishment in which the monks of St. Sabas played so important a role, then it could explain the mixture of Greek and Arabic according to the type of information Charlemagne's envoys were soliciting. Local "Syriac" speakers were probably actually speaking the language scholars now call "Christian Palestinian Aramaic," formerly termed "Christian Syriac." The Carolingian envoys would have heard Greek insofar as they talked with the patriarch and his highest collaborators and a Semitic language when they dealt with multilingual individuals in charge of the buildings or went out into the countryside around the Holy City. Such Christian Palestinian Aramaic speakers are thought to have begun speaking the cognate language of Arabic soon after the Islamic conquest, and it is easy to imagine that they would have used the Arabic word for this architectural feature, the more so given the looming presence of the great Muslim shrine of the Dome of the Rock but a few hundred meters away.[36]

In sum, the language of the three documents transcribed on the Basel roll reveals a complex but passably clear picture. The author spoke Proto-Romance, although the Basel roll's spelling and some grammatical features adhere to the classicizing ideal promoted by the Carolingian revival. The Breve shows unmistakable signs of the passage of information from the Greek, while the Memorial preserves irrefutable traces of Arabic. Aside from these two concessions to the linguistic world of the Middle East, there is nothing about the documents that would be out of place among the texts that have survived from Carolingian royal administration. But it is possible to go one step further.

3. Echoes of the Court

We have already seen that one of the names of the documents, *commemoratorium*, and even *breue commemoratorii* recalls documents connected with people

---

35 Ed. Kurtz, 170.52–58.

36 For a specialist's thoughtful and learned discussion of this issue, I am indebted to my friend and colleague, Prof. Sidney H. Griffith, of the Catholic University of America. See, in general, Griffith, "From Aramaic to Arabic," with further references.

associated with the Frankish court in the early ninth century. Two further linguistic features point in the same direction.

At first glance, the roll's "custodes qui assidu<e> praeuident sepulchrum Domini presbiteri ii . . ." (guardians who constantly watch over the Holy Sepulcher) seems to misuse *praeuideo* ("foresee," "provide"). In fact, *praeuidere* in the sense of "watch over" or "take care of" is common in the lingo of Carolingian royal administration in the decades around 800, where it is often construed with a direct object and means "administer," "run," "look after."[37] *Praeuidere* is, for instance, a veritable linguistic tic of the author of the *Capitulare de villis*, which seems to have been composed at the royal court around 794.[38] The same usage recurs in the 790s in the Royal Annals and in capitularies that emerged from royal meetings at Thionville and Nijmegen in late 805 and early 806. In the latter case, the speaker, who was worried about church roofs, used it three times in eleven lines.[39] Adalhard of Corbie, so prominent then in Charlemagne's entourage, seems to use the word in this sense in the guidelines for managing the royal monastery of Corbie which he composed late in life, in January 822.[40] The usage persists in the royal writing office and elsewhere early in Louis the Pious's reign.[41]

37 This meaning, which seems to confuse *praeuidere* with *prouidere*, is clearly derived from the widely attested Carolingian usage of *praeuidere* in the sense "to look carefully into" or "look after something," usually construed with a dependent clause. For instance, the only use of *praeuidere* in this sense in Boniface's letter collection occurs in a letter drafted by Pippin III's entourage and sent to Lul (*Die Briefe des heiligen Bonifatius und Lullus* 55, 254.19–20). Compare, for example, Pippin III, Capitulary no. 14.6 (Verny, 755), MGH Capit 1:34.29–31, and below, note 39.

38 *Capitulare de villis*, MGH Capit 1:82–91, *praeuideo*: 83.22, 25, 35; 84.6, 13, 32; 85.19, 29, and so forth. Historians have generally judged inconclusive philological efforts to confirm Alfons Dopsch's view on linguistic grounds that the author of the *Capitulare de villis* was from southern France; the more recent consensus is that the mixed linguistic features of the text reflect the multiregional milieu of the royal court. See W. Metz, *Zur Erforschung des karolingischen Reichsgutes*, Erträge der Forschung 4 (Darmstadt, 1971), 8–19.

39 A few telling examples: *Annales regni Francorum* a. 788, 82 (composed at the court in the 790s): "fuit missus Wineghisus una cum paucis Francis, ut praevideret eorum omnia, quae gessissent." Capitularies nos. 44.7 and 49.4, respectively, MGH Capit 1:123.14–18: ". . . ad Bardaenowic, ubi praevideat Hredi, et ad Schezla, ubi Madalgaudus praevideat; et ad Magadoburg, praevideat Aito; et ad Erpesfurt, praevideat Madalgaudus; et ad Halazstat, praevideat item Madalgaudus; ad Foracheim et ad Breemberga et ad Ragenisburg praevideat Ottulfus, . . ."; and 1:136.11, 17, and 21. For Charlemagne's special interest in roofs and the possibility that he is the speaker, see below.

40 He does so in a curiously hesitant way, if these are his words and not a gloss. In *Statuta seu brevia* 21, 396.20, he uses *prouideant*, but at 397.8 he uses "prouideat et preuideat"; see also 98.13–14. The work is explicitly dated in its rubric (365.1–4). On Adalhard's influence in the royal entourage in the last decade of Charlemagne's life, see above, chapter 4, note 31.

41 Louis the Pious: BM 546 for Stavelot-Malmedy (814): *Recueil des chartes de l'abbaye de Stavelot-Malmedy*, 1:69, no. 26; BM 547 for Lagrasse (814): PL 104:993D; BM 568 for Micy (815): PL 104:1015B and 1015C; BM 610 for St. Germain d'Auxerre (816): PL 104:1040B. It is fascinating that the usage spilled over into the labored hexameters of the court poet Ermoldus Nigellus (*In honorem Hludowici Pii* 3.11, 98.1264), which evidence hints that the poet may indeed have been

A technical term of the church also points in the same direction. When describing the ecclesiastics attached to the various churches of the Holy Land, the documents on the Basel roll use pretty standard terminology: *presbiteri, diacones, clerici, monachi,* and, once—but see below—*canonici,* that is, canons. This last category had originated in Frankish cathedrals. It designated ecclesiastics living in community who did not follow a monastic rule but who lived according to the canons and performed the liturgy not in the seclusion of a monastery but in the public circumstances of cathedrals and other churches frequented by the faithful.[42] Alongside the monastic movement, the canonial institution played a critical role in the Carolingian ecclesiastical renewal. This was the case right from the time of Chrodegang's (d. 766) exemplary reform of the church of Metz to the culminating establishment of a normative rule for canons at Aachen in 816, the meeting that produced the Murbach roll already mentioned. In the years around 800, canons and their lifestyle were a hot topic in the highest circles of the Frankish Empire.[43]

It is interesting that the Western visitors to the Holy Land applied the Frankish term to a religious institution similar to one in their homeland. It is even more interesting that the Breve uses an unusual combination of terms to designate those who served the Holy Sepulcher: *clerici canonici.* Alone, either *clericus* or *canonicus* is banal in ecclesiastical Latin before 900. Together, they occur extremely rarely before that date and not much thereafter. In fact, the whole of patristic Latin down to 900 as inventoried by the usual online databases and a few other promising tools produces only eight occurrences.[44] The earliest is in a Merovingian council. All the others are Carolingian. The expression shows up in Charles the Bald's Edict of Pîtres (867). It appears in a diploma of Charlemagne supposedly issued at Aachen in 802. Actually the diploma was forged at Le Mans around

---

the same man as the Hermoldus attested in the king of Aquitaine's writing office. The use recurs in an anonymous text that describes a lost, forged Merovingian diploma and was composed in the same period to advance the pretensions of St. Denis, itself closely linked with the court through its abbot, the powerful archchaplain Hilduin. Here the term refers to Dagobert's fictitious merchant Solomon, who was in charge of collecting tolls at the northern gate of the Île de Cité, Paris, *Gesta Dagoberti* 33, 413.4–8: ". . . portam ipsius civitatis . . . quam negociator suus Salomon eo tempore praevidebat. . . ." Compare the usage in the capitularies above, note 39.

42 For these two elements of the canonial institution, see, for example, the Council of Mainz, AD 813, 9, ed. A. Werminghoff, MGH Conc 2.1 (1906): 262.25–263.2, and the Council of Tours, 813, 23, ibid., 289.25–31; compare O. G. Oexle, *Forschungen zu monastischen und geistlichen Gemeinschaften im westfränkischen Bereich,* Münstersche Mittelalter-Schriften 31 (Munich, 1978), 155. For a succinct overview, see R. Schieffer, "Kanoniker," *LMA* 5 (1991): 903–4. See also C. de Clercq, *La législation religieuse franque de Clovis à Charlemagne. Étude sur les actes de conciles et les capitulaires, les statuts diocésains et les règles monastiques (507–814),* Université de Louvain, Recueil de travaux, 2nd ser., 38 (Louvain, 1936), 296–97.

43 See, in general, Oexle, *Forschungen,* 148–57.

44 I base this on the Patrologia Latina database, the online AASS, CLCT5, eMGH5, and the very detailed indices to the MGH Concilia 1–4 and Capitularia.

857–63 but possibly reworked a lost genuine charter.[45] Five more attestations cluster in the reign of Charlemagne. Again, they connect closely with the royal court itself, since they come from the *Admonitio generalis*, the great reform capitulary of 789, as well as from the pen of the royal emissary Arn of Salzburg (ca. 798), from Charlemagne's *missi dominici* visiting the area around Aachen (ca. 806), and from two of the reform councils organized by the emperor in 813.[46] Yet another attestation that has not entered the electronic files occurs in the 820s, but from a pen that takes us right back to same time and place: again, it is Charlemagne's cousin Adalhard: he used the term in his Statutes for Corbie.[47] Inverted, the expression *canonici clerici* recurs in Leidrad's brief of the revenues of the church of Lyons, a document whose general kinship with those of the Basel roll we have already observed.[48]

It is striking to see the expression in the *missi*'s capitulary dated around 806. It is even more striking when we consider the origins of the document. Wilhelm Eckhardt closely analyzed the text and its transmission, and François-Louis Ganshof followed his conclusions. Eckhardt shows that this document was prepared not by the king but by the four *missi*, in connection with the letter they dispatched to the counts of their district, their *missaticum*, instructing the counts to prepare for the *missi*'s impending arrival. The *missaticum* clearly included the bishopric of Liège, in whose territory Aachen then probably lay. Various textual features hint that the capitulary was composed at the imperial court, at Nijmegen in March 806.[49] But there is more. At the last minute, one of the leaders of this mission had to withdraw because of ill health. He was replaced by none other

---

45 Council of Orleans, AD 538, 12, ed. C. de Clercq, CCSL 148A (1963), 119.133; *Edictum pistense, a. 864*, 30, MGH Capit 2:323.11–12; MGH DD Kar 1, no. 265 (supposedly of 802), 386.13–16. For the deduction that the forgery did not derive from a lost genuine diploma, and the range of dates proposed, see ibid., 385; and W. Wattenbach, W. Levison, and H. Löwe, *Deutschlands Geschichtsquellen im Mittelalter: Vorzeit und Karolinger* (Weimar, 1952–73), 5:594. Nevertheless, the appearance of an expression so closely linked with the court milieu in exactly these years suggests to me that the forger may indeed have consulted a lost genuine diploma from that period.

46 The *Admonitio generalis* 77, MGH Capit 1:60.31–33, no. 22, offers the least compelling case: "Ut illi clerici, qui se fingunt habitu vel nomine monachos esse, et non sunt, omnimodis videtur corrigendos atque emendandos esse, ut vel veri monachi sint vel veri canonici," where *canonici* implicitly modifies *clerici*. The others are straightforward: Arn, *Instructio pastoralis* 7, 199.25; MGH Capit 2:323.11–12; *Capitulare missorum speciale* 30, MGH Capit 1:103.30–31, no. 35 or, better, ed. W. A. Eckhardt, *Die Kapitulariensammlung Bischof Ghaerbalds von Lüttich* (Göttingen, 1955), 84, c. 6; and the passages of the councils Mainz and Tours of 813, cited above, note 42.

47 "Haec sunt quae clericis nostris canonicis suprascriptis . . . dari debent" (Adalhard of Corbie, *Statuta seu brevia* 9, 371.7).

48 Brief, ed. Coville, *Recherches*, 287–88; see also above, chapter 3.4.

49 Eckhardt, *Die Kapitulariensammlung*, 25–34, 68–70. The letter is edited in ibid., 99–102, preferable to MGH Capit 1:183–84, no. 85. Eckhardt suspects that it was composed or transmitted by the *missi* via the writing office of Bishop Ghaerbald of Liège. On capitulary no. 35, compare Ganshof, *Was waren die Kapitularien?* (Darmstadt, 1961), 107 n. 280.

than Adalhard of Corbie, Charlemagne's deeply influential cousin, whose tracks we have already encountered more than once in exploring parallels to the characteristic nomenclature and language of the documents preserved on the Basel roll. Adalhard was joined by someone named Hrocculf. As we will discover in the next chapter, Hrocculf was no stranger to Charlemagne's relations with the Middle East.

One final point bears mentioning in connection with the Holy Land documents and the deliberations of Charles's entourage at Nijmegen that spring of 806. Ganshof has shown that yet another capitulary, the *Capitula de causis diversis*, reflects those discussions.[50] This document presents itself as voicing the words of Charlemagne: the royal "we," verbs of command, and the jussive subjunctive echo from its opening words, "We will and we command." Toward the end, the spoken language slips quietly into the classically written text.[51] Charles orders his *missi* to examine all of the benefices in their territories and how they were being maintained and to look especially into the churches, starting with their roofs and continuing right down to the floors, the decoration, their lighting and liturgy ("in luminariis sive officiis"). The voice of the experienced administrator rings clear. Anyone who has dealt with the maintenance of a building knows that the roof comes first; if it goes, the building follows in short order.

Whether or not we are actually hearing the king's voice here, we surely catch a glimpse of Charlemagne's practical nature in the king's obvious interest in the state of church roofing. Nor is this royal interest in roofs isolated, for this king was not content to worry about roofs in his own empire: he also knew about roofs in the empire of his Byzantine rivals. The sarcasm is palpable in Charlemagne's belligerent riposte to the Byzantines' second ecumenical council of Nicaea, when he noted that he did not need lessons about honoring churches from an empire in which many shrines lacked not only lighting and incense but even roofs, as his

---

50   MGH Capit 1:135–36, no. 49; F. L. Ganshof, "Observations sur la date de deux documents administratifs émanant de Charlemagne," *Mitteilungen des Instituts für österreichische Geschichtsforschung* 62 (1954): 83–91, here 84–87.

51   "Volumus atque praecipimus..." (c. 1, 135.36). The author enjoins his counts not to neglect their duties of meeting with the subjects for the sake of the hunt but to do with his subjects as "we are accustomed to do" with the counts (135.38). With *praecepimus* and *iniungimus*, we have here four verbs of command in five lines. J. L. Nelson notes the frequency of *praecipimus* and *volumus* in MGH Capit 1:145–46, no. 58, where she plausibly detects the voice of Charlemagne himself. "The Voice of Charlemagne," in *Belief and Culture in the Middle Ages: Studies Presented to Henry Mayr-Harting*, ed. R. Gameson and H. Leyser (Oxford, 2001), 76–88, at 80. It seems unlikely that Charlemagne actually spoke in the classical grammar most of Capitulary no. 49 displays. However, the spoken forms of the vernacular break through in the final lines, in vocabulary and even in syntax, since the Romance *passé composé* (past participle plus the auxiliary verb *habeo*) replaces the Latin perfect: "... qui suum beneficium habeat condrictum aut districtum. Similiter et illorum alodes praevideant ... quia auditum habemus, quod aliqui homines illorum beneficia habent deserta et alodes eorum restauratos" (c. 4, 136.20–23).

own and his father's ambassadors to Constantinople had told him.[52] The king specifically addressed the repair of the roofs of his own empire's churches at the council that he convoked to discuss the Nicaea meeting in June 794.[53] In fact, Charles had promised Pope Hadrian to help replace the roof of St. Peter's by shipping him tin (*stagnum*) for that purpose, as the pope pointedly reminded him in the 780s.[54] A construction notice in the *Liber pontificalis* indicates that the king delivered on that promise, and the patriarch of Grado seems similarly to have owed new lead roofing to the Frankish ruler.[55] One grasps why the obsequious Leidrad specifically insists over and over on his repairs to the roofs of the churches of Lyons in the justification of his episcopate that he sent to Charlemagne.[56] The old bishop and former courtier knew that the king from whom he was seeking support always worried about the state of church roofs. Clearly, it was no accident that Charlemagne's personal envoys to the Holy Land went to the trouble of measuring the roofs of the main shrines of Jerusalem and Bethlehem. They were acting on orders from their king.

A second aspect of the decisions recorded in the 806 capitulary illuminates what we might call the operational or administrative context of the documents preserved on the Basel roll. In 806 the local officials were enjoined to put all the information they gathered on revenues and roofs in an inventory (*in brevem mittat*) and swear to it. The *missi* were to deliver the resulting inventories (*ipsos breves*) to the emperor.[57] We have perhaps not appreciated enough how much the drawing up of all these inventories of imperial properties and churches across the Frankish Empire constituted an extraordinary moment in the administrative history of early medieval Europe. It surely reflected, at least in part, the thinking of Charlemagne and his advisors about his succession and the division of his property, which he had promulgated but weeks before.[58] This is the historical context in which the same human group would soon command, and receive, another *breve*,

52 *Opus Caroli regis* 4.3, 494.33–494.6, composed in the years leading up to the council of Frankfurt: ibid., 3–10.

53 Council of Frankfurt 26, ed. A. Werminghoff, MGH Conc 2.1:169.4–7: "Ut domus ecclesiarum et tegumenta ab eis fiant emendata vel restaurata, qui beneficia exinde habent. Et ubi repertum fuerit per veraces homines, quod lignamen et petras sive tegulas, qui in domus ecclesiarum fuerint et modo in domo sua habeat, omnia in ecclesia fiant restaurate, unde abstracte fuerunt."

54 Charlemagne had promised a thousand pounds of tin, and Itherius, his envoy and abbot of St. Martin of Tours, had promised another thousand. *Codex Carolinus* 78, 610.20–30.

55 McCormick, *Origins*, 701.

56 "... maximam ecclesiam ... a novo operuerim. ... Similiter ecclesie Sancti Stephani tegumentum de novo reparavi ... unam [domum episcopalem], quam operui. ... unam in honorem sancte Eulalie ... de novo operui. ..." (Letter, 285–87).

57 MGH Capit 1:136.9–29, no. 49.4; compare the letter of the *missi dominici* of April 806, c. 3 (Eckhard, *Die Kapitulariensammlung*, 101), instructing counts to *inbreviare*—that is, presumably, to "draw up a *breve* listing"—those who were recalcitrant in discharging the imperial commands.

58 *Divisio regnorum*, 6 February 806, ed. MGH Capit 1:126–30, no. 45.

an equally remarkable testament to Charlemagne's will to describe, to count, to inventory, to restore the "houses of God," in this case, across the sea in Palestine. Only this one has survived, whereas all of the others have been lost or preserved only indirectly, for instance, as models, in the form of the *Brevium exempla*, or as extracts embedded in a local polyptych as, for example, the extract of the Imperial Polyptych that survives in the polyptych of the Alpine bishopric of Chur.[59] Let us, by way of conclusion to this part of our investigation, look more closely at how Charlemagne's representatives gathered that information across the sea.

4. Languages, Sources, and Orality

The observations about the language of documents deepen our understanding of what kind of sources Charlemagne's envoys used to compile their report. The Arabic form of several proper names proves that they did not use written Greek sources in these parts of the Memorial. Loanwords and peculiar phrasing make a Greek layer undeniable in the Breve. Nonetheless, in the Breve, the synkellos comes toward the end, when we would expect him to figure in second place in the hierarchy of the hagiopolitan patriarchal establishment. This break with precedence argues that no written source was copied for this section. In the world of late Rome and Byzantium, as in the contemporary Roman church, rank was a cardinal feature of social and administrative life. Official, administrative documents scrupulously observe precedence when presenting lists of individuals or groups.[60] Yet that is not the case here. A written record emanating from the Greek church of the Holy Land could scarcely allow one of the highest ranking persons in the patriarchal establishment to be listed almost at the bottom of the hierarchy.[61] The implication must be that the Breve's portrait of the patriarchal establishment of Jerusalem was based on *oral* inquiry and discussion with Greek speakers.

What of the churches of Jerusalem? The order in which they appear does not seem to reflect a strict ecclesiastical order of precedence, aside from beginning with manifestly the first church, the Holy Sepulcher and, perhaps, the ancient Zion Church in second place. Opinions have varied whether the recording of the churches in this part of the roll reflects their real topographical order. The stakes are significant. If, as some have maintained, the Breve follows a strict topographical order, perhaps reflecting the actual itinerary of the *missi dominici* through Jerusalem and its environs, that would allow us to situate more or less

---

59   Imperial Polyptych ("Reichsurbar"), 375–96.
60   See, for example, McCormick, "Taxis," *ODB* 3:2018.
61   Compare J. Darrouzès, *Recherches sur les ὀφφίκια de l'Église byzantine*, Archives de l'Orient chrétien 11 (Paris, 1970), 17–19.

exactly the unlocalized shrines it documents.[62] Denying such a reliable geographic sequence of shrines, others have excluded the possibility of reaching beyond speculation.[63]Analyzing the cases when the Breve moves from one known place to another clarifies the matter. Sequence seems not to be observed for the two churches of Sts. Cosmas and Damian, one of which stood in a known location inside the city wall of Jerusalem and the other of which very probably lay outside the wall, in the Valley of Kidron (Jehoshaphat).[64] At this point, the Breve is discussing shrines that seem mostly to lie in the Valley of Kidron and on the Mount of Olives, but one might view this clear break in sequence as an exception stemming from the common dedication of the two churches.[65] The first three shrines in the Breve do seem to follow a geographic order, in that the report proceeds from the Holy Sepulcher some 700 meters south to the Zion Church before continuing about 225 meters to the southeast to the church of St. Peter's denial which, at this date, still lay within the late Roman walls of Jerusalem (see map 1).[66] Following several unlocated shrines and one known site, we find ourselves in the northern part of the city at the shrine of the St. Mary at the Sheep Pool. From there, one could imagine the Breve's author proceeding about 550 meters west to St. Stephen's Gate (Gate of the Column), and then through the gate and some 350 meters north to St. Stephen. Although the order seems satisfactory enough, the churches share only a general location in the northern part of the city and its suburbs (see map 1).

62   J. T. Milik exemplifies this approach. See, e.g., Milik, "Notes d'épigraphie et de topographie," 555, where, based on the subsequent entry, he locates the Frankish monastery on the eastern slope of the Mount of Olives. For the traditional circuits by which pilgrims visited Jerusalem's sites, and which seem to find a general reflection in our document, see Aist, *Christian Topography*, 217–28.

63   Thus, emphatically, K. Bieberstein and H. Bloedhorn, *Jerusalem: Grundzüge der Baugeschichte vom Chalkolithikum bis zur Frühzeit der osmanischen Herrschaft*, 3 vols., Beihefte zum Tübinger Atlas des Vorderen Orients. Reihe B, Geisteswissenschaften 100 (Wiesbaden, 1994), for example, 3:416, on "St. Quaranta"; compare 407 on both St. Aquilina and St. Christopher.

64   See chapter 10, notes 28 and 29.

65   Although the urban shrine of Cosmas and Damian is mentioned first, the previous shrine of known location, three shrines earlier, is St. John's birthplace, on the slope of the Mount of Olives, and the next set, right after the extramural church of Cosmas and Damian, was also on the Mount of Olives.

66   See the map of Jerusalem in the early Arab period in Bahat, Ben-Dov, Geva, et al., "Jerusalem: Early Arab to Ayyubid Periods," in *NEAEHL* 2:787; compare G. Avni, "The Urban Limits of Roman and Byzantine Jerusalem: A View from the Necropoleis," *Journal of Roman Archaeology* 18 (2005): 373–96, esp. 392–93, and my map 1. Nevertheless it may seem odd that the Breve first goes from the Zion Church to that of St. Peter and only later returns to the Nea, via an unlocated shrine. If this in fact reflects an itinerary, it is possible that Charlemagne's envoys did not go to Zion via the old cardo, the main street, on which the ruined Nea stood, and in front of which they would have passed on this route. They may rather have gone south on the street behind (just east) of the Holy Sepulcher if it continued so far south, for it aligns approximately with the Zion Church on the map as drawn in *NEAEHL* 2:787. See also the discussion of the Nea and Zion dimensions and topography, above, chapter 5.2.

The very next entry seems to start over, for it now focuses on shrines east and south from the Jericho Gate. If the recording actually mimicked the author's movements from shrine to shrine, this might imply that he backtracked past the neighborhood of the Sheep Pool and then went out of the city to Gethsemane and the Virgin's Tomb. After St. Leontius, which can be located only generally in the Valley of Kidron, the Breve reaches the church of St. James, some 450 meters south of the Virgin's Tomb. Although one or even two (St. John's birthplace, surely, and St. Stephen, maybe) of the next nine sites are known to have been somewhere on the Mount of Olives, they allow no certain conclusions about exact geographic sequence. After the two churches of Sts. Cosmas and Damian already discussed, we come to three more monuments whose locations are known today, the shrine of the Ascension, the church where Jesus taught the disciples (on the site of the great Eleona shrine), and the church of St. Mary. Here the order is certainly not geographic. It starts in the middle of the three monuments, at the then most remarkable church in the vicinity, that of the Ascension, before moving about 100 meters southwest to the church of Jesus and the disciples, and next doubling back about 200 meters to the northeast to the Virgin's church. After enumerating the hermits scattered, apparently, around the Mount of Olives and on the stepped streets up its slopes, the document mentions the convent of uncertain location with the Western women and the Frankish monastery of Sts. Peter and Paul, situated somewhere else on the Mount of Olives (see chapter 4.2). From there the document proceeds southeast to Bethany, which lies about a kilometer from the last certainly located shrine, the church of the Virgin on the Mount. The final establishment again appears to contradict a strictly topographical order, since the church of St. John held by the Armenians has been identified 1,200 meters northwest of Bethany and just 300 meters east of the Ascension. In sum, even though it seems in general to organize the shrines in rough spatial groups—the Sepulcher and places in the southern part of the walled city, the northern city and immediate environs, the shrines outside the walls and to the east and the south, perhaps reflecting the general topography of the Kidron Valley and the Mount of Olives as well as the customary pilgrim circuit through the city—the Breve clearly does not observe a strict geographic sequence of shrines. While the place of a shrine in the document may hint at its general location, it provides no precise evidence on topography.[67]

The Memorial's list of towns outside of Jerusalem that could have been episcopal sees shows little sign of the established precedence of the ecclesiastical geography of the Middle East, at least as it was attested on the eve of the Arab conquest. For example, given their respective church precedence, we would have expected

67 The one possible caveat would be if the sequence of shrines followed street, road, and path networks that are at present invisible to us, as, for instance, for the possible route from the Holy Sepulcher to Zion discussed in the previous note.

that Neapolis-Nablus precede Sebaste-Sabastia.[68] Since both sees belonged to the old Roman province of Palaestina I, we would further expect them to precede Tiberias, which belonged to Palaestina II.[69] In fact, the Memorial has it the other way around in both cases. By the twelfth century, the number of sees had shrunk, but the outlines of the old precedence system remained visible, as table 7.1 makes clear: at that time Neilos Doxopatres gives the same order of the same bishoprics that had obtained in the seventh century.

The fact that the Memorial disregards precedence when listing the towns strongly argues that this document too does not derive from a written administrative record of the patriarchate of Jerusalem. Rather, the order in which the Frankish report enumerates the sees is roughly geographical (see map 2). The first circuit begins at Bethlehem and proceeds along a known footpath to the monastery of St. Theodosius (Deir Dosi) before continuing along the same path to St. Sabas (Mar Saba). Whether the westerners doubled back to Jerusalem and then headed east on the road to Jericho for the remaining sites or reached the Jericho road directly from St. Sabas, the rest of the circuit seems natural for an eastbound traveler on the Jericho road.[70]

The second circuit begins with the most important shrine, Nazareth and its environs, possibly out of geographical order. It then follows a plausible itinerary from north to south starting from Heptapegon and the shrine associated with the multiplication of the loaves and fishes and the Sermon on the Mount, on the northwestern shore of the Sea of Galilee (Lake Kinneret). The list moves south toward Jerusalem, via Tiberias, Mount Tabor, Sebastia, and Neapolis. Sinai is simply tacked on at the end, as well it might be, given its distance from Jerusalem, and there is no way of telling whether the envoys actually traveled there in a separate excursion. If not, someone else supplied them with the number of steps which pilgrims ascended to climb the mountain identified as the site where Moses received the Ten Commandments.

The language of the documents preserved on the Basel roll yields several insights into their genesis, and therefore their interpretation. Although at first blush these texts look quite classicizing, deeper scrutiny of the scribe's zealous and skilled corrections allows one to detect the pulse and forms of the living language

68 George of Cyprus, *Descriptio orbis Romani*, 51.1014–15.

69 Ibid., 52.1036.

70 On the Romano-Arab road system, see, for example, *Tübinger Atlas des Vorderen Orients*: G. Schmitt, J. Wagner, and R. Rademacher, Map B V 17.2, "Die römischen Provinzen Palaestina und Arabia (70–305 n. Chr.)" (Wiesbaden, 1988); and G. Reeg and F. Hüttenmeister, Map B VI 16, "Israel nach der rabbinischen Literatur" (Wiesbaden, 1984). For the network of paths, Y. Hirschfeld, *The Judean Desert Monasteries in the Byzantine Period* (New Haven, 1992), 205–12, with his maps 1 (p. xviii) and 5 (p. 206).

Site	Memorial ca. 808	George of Cyprus, 7th c.	Neilos Doxopatres, 12th c.
Nazareth	1		17
Tiberias	2	Palaestina II, 8	11
Mount Tabor	3		18
Sebastia	4	Palaestina I, 18	9
Neapolis	5	Palaestina I, 17	8

Sources: George of Cyprus, *Descriptio orbis Romani*, 51.1014–15 and 52.1036; [des] Nilos Doxopatres, *Taxis ton patriarchikon thronon armenisch und griechisch*, ed. Franz Nikolaus Finck (Vagharshabad [= Echmiadzin], 1902), 17.38–18.5. The order is the same as that in the text printed by H. Gelzer, "Ungedruckte und wenig bekannte Bistümerverzeichnisse der orientalischen Kirche," *BZ* 1 (1892): 245–82, here 253. See, in general, on the sees in the Byzantine and Arab period, Abel, *Géographie*, 2:199–205; R. de Vaux, "Une mosaïque byzantine à Ma'in," *RevBibl* 47 (1938): 227–58, here 251–55; and Levy-Rubin, "Reorganisation of the Patriarchate." On the medieval sigillographic evidence for the churches of the patriarchate of Jerusalem, see V. Laurent, *Le corpus des sceaux de l'Empire byzantin*, 2 vols. (Paris, 1963–81), 5.2:392–413.

of very late Popular Latin, or even Proto-Romance. The result is no idle game of philological virtuosity, for the recognition of this textual reality authorizes us, for instance, to conclude against all previous scholarship that the Breve does indeed document the existence of three different hostels in Jerusalem around 808. At least one shared linguistic rarity confirms that the same person wrote all three documents. There are strong hints of an Italian connection. Clear traces of Arabic and Greek show that the author obtained information from people who spoke those languages and who used words or names that the author simply transliterated. Even more interesting, there is no sign that he used official, written administrative records: the information recorded in at least the Breve and the Memorial came from first- or secondhand experience and oral inquiries.

Finally, and no less preciously, we have in the three documents, in an administrative copy at most only a few decades younger than the original, the actual raw materials generated by Carolingian administrators in action. We can almost hear the Frankish envoys asking the questions, almost see which places they actually bothered to visit in person, and those for which they were content with estimates at secondhand. Surely on that day when it was presented to Charlemagne and his closest advisors for discussion and decision, the roll embodied the very real role of writing in the operations of this early medieval king. Yet all that it does not say, all that was ascertained for it beforehand or explained afterward viva voce, or all that was obvious to those who produced it and used it make us mindful of the cardinal role of orality—assisted and perhaps structured by lists like these—in the dealings of the great king and his men.[71]

The concern with roofs was a long-standing one for Charlemagne. But the sustained drive to inventory, to list, and to count was one that peaked around 806 in the royal entourage. Whether we look at the nomenclature of the documents or their subtle linguistic tics, it is probably no accident that we are brought back to the royal entourage, to Charles himself and to his cousin, Adalhard of Corbie. The internal testimony of the very language of these records confirms what their content implies. The recurrence of jargon then trendy in a particular human milieu and documented in texts attributed to Charlemagne or Adalhard of Corbie of course does not imply that Charlemagne or Adalhard themselves went to the Holy Land and wrote these records. But those who did go were their associates, close enough to have shared their tics of language and thought. The person who wrote our three documents spoke with—and like—the most powerful men in the Carolingian Empire. For observing Carolingian royal governance in action, we have here one of the most remarkable testimonies that will ever be found.

71 Compare the discussion of J. L. Nelson, "Literacy in Carolingian Government," in *The Uses of Literacy in Early Mediaeval Europe*, ed. R. McKitterick (Cambridge, 1992), 258–96, esp. 272–82 and 284–85.

Chapter Eight

. . . .

THE DATE, PURPOSE, AND
CONTEXT OF THE DOCUMENTS

T HE NOMENCLATURE AND EVEN THE LANGUAGE of the roll evince multiple connections with the Carolingian court, and the document itself dates
from the final, imperial period in Charlemagne's rule. Eminent specialists have
judged these years a time of failure, decomposition, and stalemate. The overarch-
ing ambitions of the upstart conqueror of Europe to transform his ill-understood
empire outstripped the woefully underdeveloped institutions and instruments of
governance at his disposal. That produced a crushing burden of business without
the means to deal with it.[1] The picture of paralysis gains verisimilitude from what
we can discern of the aging king's declining health.[2] The notion of a king attempting to intervene in the life of a distant patriarchate seems to clash with this picture.

But is the picture right? A strong case has been made that the king's efforts to
pursue his plans in the last thirteen years of his reign seem in some respects even
more vigorous than in previous decades. If he slowed down, it may have been only
in the last year or two of his life.[3] For, in addition to Charles's energetic pursuit
of religious reform, ranging from the high Trinitarian theology of the Filioque in
809, itself triggered by conflict among Frankish and Greek monks in Jerusalem,
to the invigorated improvement of local church life organized under five regional

---

1   The position held preeminently by F. L. Ganshof, "L'échec de Charlemagne," *CRAI* (1947) :
248–54, and F. L. Ganshof, "La fin du règne de Charlemagne. Une décomposition," *Zeitschrift für
Schweizerische Geschichte* 28 (1948): 433–52, as well as H. Fichtenau, *The Carolingian Empire*, trans.
P. Munz (Oxford, 1963), 177–87.
2   Einhard (*Vita Karoli* 22, 27.3–6) notes that Charlemagne suffered from frequent fevers in the
last four years of his life and, at the end, limped in one foot. The biographers of Louis the Pious
emphasize the old king's steeply declining health, but only in 813: "senuerat enim valde" (Thegan,
Gesta Hludowici imperatoris 6, 180.11). Walking to and from the palace at the moment of coronation, Louis had to help hold up his father (ibid., 184.11–13). The Astronomer (*Vita Hludowici imperatoris* 20, 340.19–342.16) claims that Charlemagne's advisors were already trying to get Louis to
act preemptively in or around 811, as his father declined.
3   See J. R. Davis, "Patterns of Power: Charlemagne and the Invention of Medieval Rulership"
(PhD diss., Harvard University, 2007), 33–43, 113–16, and esp. 420–39.

councils convened simultaneously in 813—the largest conciliar effort in Charles's entire reign—his last decade witnessed almost a frenzy of royally sponsored efforts to reform, to count, collect, and document institutions, revenues, and names.[4] Thus in the royal *memoratorium* we have already cited in connection with the meeting at Nijmegen in the spring of 806:

> And so we will and command that, in each territory (*pagus*), our *missi* try to look after (*praevidere*) all the benefices that our own men and those of others are seen to have, how, after our announcement, they have been restored or ruined. . . . And how it is, let every *vicarius* in each county look after (*praevideat*) this in his area of responsibility (*in suo ministerio*) together with our *missi*, and as he is able to swear this, let him put it all as he will have found it in an inventory (*brevem*), and let them bring these inventories (*ipsos breves*) to us.[5]

Or in a capitulary attributed to 811:

> Let our *missi* investigate diligently and have written down, each in his own district (*missaticum*), what each person has as a benefice and how many men have holdings (*quot homines casatos*) in the benefice.

and

> Let not only the benefices of bishops, of abbots, abbesses, and counts, or our vassals but also of our own fiscal estates be written down, so we can know how much of our own we have in the district (*legatione*) of each.[6]

Only a bit of debris of Charles's vast efforts to count, record, and document the wealth of Frankland have survived, the *Brevium exempla* and *Capitulare de villis* chief among them.[7] It is perhaps no accident that the last phase in the king's drive

4   For the meetings and the debate surrounding the Filioque controversy see, in addition to discussion and further references below (note 46), the texts and discussion in *Das Konzil von Aachen 809*, ed. H. Willjung. On the 813 councils, see, for example, W. Hartmann, *Die Synoden der Karolingerzeit im Frankenreich und in Italien*, Konziliengeschichte, Reihe A, Darstellungen (Paderborn, 1989), 128–40. Hartmann rejects (128–29) the idea of paralysis at the top in these years.

5   MGH Capit 1:135–36, no. 49.4, here 136.9–19. On this capitulary and its powerfully suggestive language, see above, chapter 7.3, note 51.

6   MGH Capit 1:176–77, no. 80.5 and 7, here 177.1–3 and 177.6–8. On the date, see, for example, F. L. Ganshof, *Was waren die Kapitularien?* trans. W. A. Eckhardt and B. W. Franz (Darmstadt, 1961), 167.

7   See, in general, K. Verhein, "Studien zu den Quellen zum Reichsgut der Karolingerzeit [1]," *DA* 10 (1954): 313–94, and "Studien zu den Quellen zum Reichsgut der Karolingerzeit [2]," *DA* 11 (1955): 333–92; and W. Metz, "Zur Geschichte und Kritik der frühmittelalterlichen Güterverzeichnisse Deutschlands," *Archiv für Diplomatik* 4 (1958): 183–206. The *Brevium exempla*, a model for doing just that on royal estates, is generally dated to shortly after 800. See Verhein, "Studien

to inventory and record the details of wealth and its use coincides with the ascendancy of Charlemagne's cousin. As we have seen, Adalhard's linguistic usage finds echoes in some features of the roll's documents that suggest a link to his circle. In any case, he has left us one of the most remarkable accounts of the management of a great abbey in the already cited *Statuta seu brevia*; his effort to document in writing the organization and workings of the Carolingian court lives on in the famous *De ordine palatii*, the treatise Hincmar of Rheims drew from a generation later.[8] Whatever the precise role of Adalhard in this momentous turn of monarchy, the three documents consigned to the Basel roll must now take their place with these other relics of the royal urge to record, revealing to us the same drive to count, write down, and manage, extended now halfway across the world, to the most sacred shrines of the most sacred soil in Christendom. And we may be confident that these documents emanate from the same circle of Charlemagne's collaborators.

The documents preserved on the Basel roll belong to the extremely varied records of royal governance known as the capitularies. Their name derives from the fact that, formally, many of them are divided into chapters (*capitula*). Nevertheless, their format, under Charlemagne, ranges from carefully crafted pronouncements that evoke an edict to items on an agenda for a forthcoming or recent meeting. All are linked in some way to meetings and decisions of the king, and this is surely the case of the documents copied on the Basel roll. It is true that the internal evidence linking the documents to the court is suggestive rather than peremptory. The names of the documents themselves find echoes in this same Frankish court or in milieus connected with it (above, chapter 6.3). The roll format of the documents, the statistical nature of their contents, and the fact that their author stated that he

---

[2]," 344–48, and esp. 388–89, where he prudently concludes that it was written between 801 and 810–15. The *Capitula de causis diversis* 4, ed. MGH Capit 1:136.9–33, no. 49, commands the king's *missi* to report on the state of all benefices and to bring the written reports (*breves*) to the ruler. Ganshof, *Was waren die Kapitularien?* 165, assigns it to 806. See too Leidrad's detailed report, discussed above, chapter 3.4.

8   Hincmar himself states this and testifies (*De ordine palatii*, 54.218–21), that when he was an adolescent he knew or at least had seen Adalhard. Hincmar was at the court in the 820s in Hilduin of St. Denis's entourage. See also J. Fleckenstein, "Die Struktur des Hofes Karls des Grossen im Spiegel von Hinkmars 'De ordine palatii'," *Zeitschrift des Aachener Geschichtsvereins* 83 (1976): 5–22. On the extent of Hincmar's dependency on Adalhard's lost treatise, see, further, B. Kasten, *Adalhard von Corbie. Die Biographie eines karolingischen Politikers und Klostervorstehers* (Düsseldorf, 1985 [1986]), 72–79. The relationship can be relatively well circumscribed, based particularly on the telling linguistic and other features detailed, notably, in the dissertation of J. Schmidt, "Hinkmars *De ordine palatii* und seine Quellen" (Diss., Frankfurt am Main, 1962), cited at 72 n. 172. The survival of distinctively Lombard or Italo-Latin expressions in Hincmar's text combines with its nature to argue that Adalhard composed his treatise either during his probable regency for King Pippin of Italy, soon after 781, or for his certain regency for King Bernard, from 810 to 814: Kasten, *Adalhard von Corbie*, 79.

had *failed* to obtain data about two monasteries proves that this was no pilgrim's description of whatever a traveler encountered but rather the execution of a charge enjoined upon the authors.[9] Other than the imperial court, no other authority or milieu in Frankland between 800 and 814 would have been interested in or capable of organizing such an administrative survey of Christian Palestine.

It may be objected that the Basel roll presents no explicit authorial statement, that it lacks any form of the diplomatic apparatus of Carolingian imperial precepts and so cannot be certainly associated with Charlemagne's official business. The objection would be unfounded, for the documents consigned on the Basel roll are not public instruments conveying privileges or narrating the resolution of disputes. They are administrative documents—part of a dossier manifestly assembled for internal purposes, namely, to assess the financial needs and resources of the Christian churches in the Holy Land. The content of such documents was determined by their aim and their very specific audience of decision makers, who already knew the basic facts. Thus they do not attempt to identify or explain many things that a historical record, geared to a future audience with uncertain knowledge of the situation, would normally treat. A probing analysis of the external and internal characteristics of the first version of a capitulary of 813 and the decisions of the Aachen synod of 816 emphasizes that it is precisely characteristic of such royal documents to be "plain and lacking in any protocol." Rather, the validity of a capitulary owed more to the "material authenticity, that is, the regular appropriateness of the content."[10] This is all the more true for a document that is certainly a dossier prepared to help make decisions rather than the formal writing up of the decision itself. Only after Charlemagne, under Louis the Pious and Charles the Bald, do the formal characteristics of capitularies begin to contribute toward their authority.[11] Of comparable documents indubitably associated with Charlemagne's royal administration, we might cite the *Brevium exempla* or, even more germane, the original sheet preserving the beginning of the script by which Charlemagne's ambassadors were to conduct their audience with Pope Hadrian I in 784 or 785:

---

9 *Memoria* line 35: "In istis duobus, nescimus quanti sint." On this character of the roll, see already de Rossi, "Un documento inedito," 83; compare Tobler, *Descriptiones Terrae Sanctae ex saeculo VIII, IX, XII et XV*, 359. For more on the probable set of questions that underlay the roll, below, chapter 8.2.

10 H. Mordek, discussing the Murbach roll (Colmar, Archives Départementales du Haut-Rhin, Grand Document no. 139), mentioned above in connection with the Breve's format: "schlicht und ohne jedes Protokoll" and "die sachliche Authentizität, d.h. . . . . die inhaltliche Ordnungsgemässheit." "Karolingische Kapitularien," in *Überlieferung und Geltung normativer Texte des frühen und hohen Mittelalters. Vier Vorträge gehalten auf dem 35. Deutschen Historikertag 1984 in Berlin*, ed. H. Mordek (Sigmaringen, 1986), 25–50, here 32–36, quotations at 35. See, further, J. L. Nelson, "Literacy in Carolingian Government," in *The Uses of Literacy in Early Mediaeval Europe*, ed. R. McKitterick (Cambridge, 1992), 258–96, here 283–84.

11 Mordek, "Karolingische Kapitularien," 36.

neither carries any explicit indication of its royal origin, and neither can be imagined in any other circumstance.[12]

1. Date and Purpose of the Documents on the Basel Roll

Bischoff's paleographical dating of the document to about 825–50 implies that the Breve's reference to nuns "from the empire of Lord Charles" (line 22) can refer only to Charles the Great after the imperial coronation and before his death on 28 January 814.[13] This dates the original composition of the document securely to the period 801–14. Despite their apparent promise, persons referred to by name in the dossier provide no more certain date: the episcopal and abbatial lists, as indeed our general knowledge of the patriarchate of Jerusalem in these years, are too incomplete to help.[14] "The earthquake" (ille terrae motus [line 50]) that destroyed Justinian's Nea Church appears more promising, since such a way of referring to a natural event might seem to suggest a recent occurrence. Seismic activity in the region, however, was frequent, and the recording of it was spotty enough that our knowledge is certainly incomplete.[15] Holy Land specialists have connected the seism that damaged the Nea Church with the great earthquake of 18 January 749, although no specific evidence has come to light linking that earthquake with the collapse of the Nea among the scarce documents from contemporary Palestine.[16]

12   The script's manuscript witness is Paris, B.N.F., lat. 9008. See MGH Capit 1:225, no. 111; reproduced in ChLA 17 (1984), no. 655, on which, see D. Bullough, "Aula renovata: The Carolingian Court before the Aachen Palace," Proceedings of the British Academy 71 (1985): 267–301, at 277 n. 1. On this type of diplomatic document, called commonitorium in the West, see M. McCormick, "La lettre diplomatique byzantine du premier millénaire vue de l'Occident et l'énigme du papyrus de Paris," in Byzance et le monde extérieur, Byzantina Sorbonensia 21 (Paris, 2005), 135–49, here 141. On the Brevium exempla and royal administration, see Verhein, "Studien [2]," 384–86.

13   Even allowing for a very late dating of the script of the Basel roll (see above, chapter 6.2, notes 13 and 14), there would be no reason to associate the document with the brief imperial reigns of Charles the Bald (875–877) or Charles III (881–888), who are not known to have taken any initiatives involving the Holy Land.

14   For the list of patriarchs in this period, see G. Fedalto, Hierarchia ecclesiastica orientalis. Series episcoporum ecclesiarum christianarum orientalium (Padua, 1988), 2:1002. For the prosopographical data of the roll, see above, chapter 5.1.

15   On the shortcomings of the chief repertories of earthquakes, see K. W. Russell, "The Earthquake Chronology of Palestine and Northwest Arabia from the 2nd through the Mid-8th Century A.D.," BASOR 260 (1985): 37–59. Russell's criticism of D. H. Kallner-Amiran, "A Revised Earthquake Catalogue of Palestine," IEJ 1 (1950–51): 223–46, is well founded in this case. The major earthquake that, according to Kallner-Amiran, "Revised Earthquake Catalogue," 226, damaged the Nea and the al Aqsa mosque in 808, turns out to derive from an erroneous reading of F. M. Abel, Géographie de la Palestine (Paris, 1933), 1:53, who cites the Breve, there dated to 808, as evidence for the quake of "746."

16   For an attribution to the "746" seism, see, for example, J. Wilkinson, Jerusalem Pilgrims before the Crusades, 2nd ed. (Warminster, 2002), 332. For the correct date, see Y. Tsafrir and G. Foerster, "The Dating of the 'Earthquake of the Sabbatical Year' of 749 C.E. in Palestine," Bulletin of the

Other quakes are attested for the eastern Mediterranean in 796–97 and 802–3.[17] They or some unrecorded quake could conceivably have affected the Holy Land, including the Nea shrine, as indeed has been recently maintained.[18]

Nevertheless, the extreme earthquake of 749 still seems to me the most plausible cause for the destruction of the Nea. Although over half a century in an area of significant seismic activity might seem a long time for one quake still to be "*the* earthquake," that event was truly of exceptional violence and destructiveness. This is physically visible from the porticoes of Scythopolis (Beth Shean) it knocked down, which were still lying in situ when archaeologists unearthed them. It also damaged the al Aqsa mosque in Jerusalem as well as many synagogues and

---

School of Oriental and African Studies 55 (1992): 231–35, which uses a coin hoard sealed by the great earthquake that devasted Beth Shean (Scythopolis) shortly after 31 August 748 to clarify the partially contradictory testimony of the Greek, Arabic, Hebrew, and Syriac sources.

17   Al Tabari (*The Early 'Abbāsī Empire*, 2:219, 255) records earthquakes in AH 180 (AD 796/97) in Egypt and in AH 187 (802/3) in Cilicia.

18   K. Bieberstein believes an earthquake in 797 probably knocked down the Nea Church. "Der Gesandtenaustausch zwischen Karl dem Grossen und Hārūn ar-Rašīd und seine Bedeutung für die Kirchen Jerusalems," *ZDPV* 109 (1993): 152–73, here 157 n. 36. He bases this on a short text printed by Wilhelm A. Neumann in his substantial review of Titus Tobler, *Descriptiones Terrae Sanctae* (Leipzig, 1874), in *Theologische Quartalschrift* 56 (1875): 521–31, here 528–29. This anonymous text (inc. "In diebus Geor<g>ii patris") claims that a terrible earthquake hit Jerusalem in the first year of George's patriarchate, which Bieberstein dates as 797–807. Unfortunately, much is uncertain about the patriarchate of Jerusalem in these centuries, including George's dates. For the most reliable summaries of the contradictory evidence, see Joseph-Marie Sauget, "Giorgio, patriarca di Gerusalemme," *Bibliotheca sanctorum* 6 (Rome, 1965): 536–37; and D. Bundy, "Georges 41," *Dictionnaire d'histoire et de géographie ecclésiastiques* 20 (Paris, 1984): 624–25. The enigmatic *In diebus Georgii* is small help here. Its date and place of origin are unknown; it appears to display knowledge of events in Palestine around this time, but offers a chronology that seems impossible in at least some respects. As the superior versions of the text show, the author seems to know some details about the martyrdom by fire of some of the monks of Mar Saba and the violence done to many others by Arab attackers. See R. Priebsch, *Diu vrône Botschaft ze der Christenheit: Untersuchungen und Text*, Grazer Studien zur deutschen Philologie 2 (1895; reprint, 1976), 68.11–69.15 (from Munich, Bayerische Staatsbibliothek, clm 21557, fol. 103, twelfth century); or P. Jaffé and W. [G.] Wattenbach, *Ecclesiae metropolitanae Coloniensis codices manuscripti* (Berlin, 1874), 110 (from Cologne, Dombibliothek, Cod. 70, fol. 203r, eleventh century). However, this text situates the martyrdom in year five of George's patriarchate (i.e., possibly 801–2?), whereas the monk of Mar Saba who identifies himself as an eyewitness and who convincingly claims to be writing down the martyrdom for his own abbot seems unequivocally to situate the event in the patriarchate of George's predecessor, Elias II (Stephen of Mar Saba, *Martyrium XX Sabaitarum* 2, 2.19–25), and George is stated to have succeeded Elias in Leontius's *Vita Stephani thaumaturgi* (49, 524B; Arabic version, 33.17, trans. 54–55). The dates explicitly given by Stephen of Mar Saba have been challenged by A. Kazhdan, L. F. Sherry, and C. Angelidi, *A History of Byzantine Literature (650–850)* (Athens, 1999), 169–71, who prefer 788. The most obvious interpretation of the chronological synchronism given by Stephen corresponds to AD 797. In sum, *In diebus Georgii* seems to testify to a serious earthquake in the Holy Land around AD 800, but its chronological indications are difficult to reconcile with the contemporary Greek evidence.

other churches in the region.[19] Judging from its mighty surviving remains and the terracing that underpinned it, the Nea Church was as stout as it was big.[20] For Charlemagne's envoys to have reported that so mighty a structure was "ruined" or "broken" and "sank to the earth" ("quod ille terrae motus fregit et in terram demersit" [lines 50–51]) suggests a temblor of exceptional power, such as the 749 event.[21] Finally and most conclusively, a Palestinian author writing in exactly the years when the Franks visited Jerusalem proves that the terrible event was then still remembered in this way. Leontius of Mar Saba depicts his master, Stephen the Wonder Worker, as speaking between around 790 and 794 very graphically and without further qualification of the devastating impact "of the great earthquake" (apo tou megalou seismou) on the quality of Palestinian monasticism.[22] Thus the destruction of the Nea very likely occurred in 749. It takes us no closer to a proximate date after which the roll was composed.

Similarly, the Memorial's reference to attacks of "Arab bandits" (Sarraceni latrones) on the monks of the monastery of St. Theodosius appears more promising than it turns out to be. The security situation in the Holy Land was fairly troubled in these decades, and there are multiple reports of sporadic violence. However, the fact that the document highlights an attack on St. Theodosius while it does not mention the apparently more devastating attack and martyrdoms at Mar Saba, documented in the contemporary Martyrdom of the Twenty Sabaite Monks, appears perplexing. Two explanations are possible. The simplest stems from the position of the words in lines 27–29 of the Memorial:

> In the monastery of St. Theodosius, which was the first one built in that desert: 70 monks; Basil <is over them>. Saracen bandits burned the monastery and killed <many with cruel fire>, and others, <on account of the ransom, demolished> to the ground two churches dependent on that monastery. In St. Sabas, 150 monks.[23]

19　See Tsafrir and Foerster, "Dating of the 'Earthquake,'" for all of these points, and further references. For other archaeologically documented devastation that has been connected with this earthquake, see R. Schick, *The Christian Communities of Palestine from Byzantine to Islamic Rule: A Historical and Archaeological Study* (Princeton, N.J., 1995), 126–27.

20　On this building, see above, chapter 5.2.

21　For the translation of *demergo*, see above, chapter 5.2, note 46.

22　Leontius, *Vita Stephani thaumaturgi* 173, 576A–B; Arabic version: 75.7, trans. 123, where, as the editor notes (123 n. 314), the Arabic translator has misunderstood the Greek. The context makes clear that Stephen is referring to the 749 event, which he would have experienced at around age twenty. Leontius had earlier noted (*Vita Stephani thaumaturgi* 115, 549F) that in this section he was setting out his own experiences with the saint in the last four years of the holy man's life.

23　Angled brackets mark my conjectural restorations of the damaged text. See below, chapter 10, for the Latin text and chapter 11, textual commentary on these lines, for the detailed discussion of the restorations.

It is conceivable that the note on the destruction is inserted in the wrong place, either by the author's error or a scribal mistake that inverted the order of the last two sentences, and that the account of the burning of the monastery and martyrdom of the monks actually should refer to St. Sabas and the events of 797. Certainly, Arab bandits on that occasion burned at least part of the monastery. When the monks refused to pay a 4,000-dinar ransom to keep the bandits from burning the monastery church, they killed many monks by lighting a fire at the entrance to a cave shrine where the monks had taken refuge.[24]

It is also possible that the attack recorded by the Memorial was more recent than that attack on Mar Saba.[25] Given the St. Sabas author's attention to attacks on other monasteries, we might accept that the silence of the Greek Martyrdom about further martyrdoms at St. Theodosius is significant. If so, that could well suggest a later terminus post quem since troubles that also affected apparently even more monasteries, including St. Theodosius, broke out in connection with the general violence that spread across the caliphate at the death of Harun al Rashid on 24 March 809. Although written at Constantinople, Theophanes' *Chronographia* is an excellent source for the Holy Land and mentions that the "churches of the holy city of Christ our God were made desolate as well as the monasteries of the two great *lavras*, namely that of Sts. Chariton and Kyriakos, and that of St. Sabas, and the other *koinobia*, namely those of St. Euthymius and St. Theodosius. The slaughter resulting from this anarchy, directed at each other [i.e. the Muslims] and against us [sc. the Christians] lasted five years."[26] Theophanes reports similar violence again in 812/13.[27] If we were to connect the reference in the Memorial of the monasteries to the murder of some monks of St. Theodosius with the mention of the desolation of the same monastery (along with three others) by Theophanes in 809, then the Memorial would have been composed after that event.[28]

24 The bandits set fire to the monastery, although St. Sabas's miraculous intervention may have limited the damage. See Stephen, *Martyrium XX Sabaitarum* 15, 13.9–29; on the ransom, 28, 22.6–12; on smoke and fire against the monks who hid in the cave church, 31–36, 24.3–26.27.

25 The *Martyrium*, written from a Sabaite perspective, nevertheless also refers to attacks on and burning at St. Chariton's monastery (5, 4.26–5.1; 15, 14.6–9); and, possibly, St. Euthymius's 18, 15.22–31, if one corrects 15.29, ὑμῖν, to the homophonous ἡμῖν, which the general context and the last line might suggest.

26 Theophanes, *Chronographia* AM 6301 (= AD 809), 1:484.14–19; translation from Theophanes, *The Chronicle of Theophanes Confessor: Byzantine and Near Eastern History, AD 284–813*, trans. C. Mango, R. Scott, and G. Greatrex (Oxford, 1997), 665.

27 Theophanes AM 6305, 1:499.15–28, specifically naming St. Chariton and St. Sabas as well as the "other monasteries" that were made desolate. Nevertheless, Theophanes likely exaggerated the extent of the damage. S. H. Griffith, "Greek into Arabic: Life and Letters in the Monasteries of Palestine in the Ninth Century," in *Arabic Christianity in the Monasteries of Ninth-Century Palestine* (Aldershot, 1992), 117–38, here 117–20.

28 Thus Bieberstein, "Der Gesandtenaustausch," 168–69, who then dates the document to about 809. However, he further concluded that the roll could not have been written before about 802–7

Nevertheless, our information about the Holy Land religious houses is sufficiently incomplete, the Memorial seems to limit the violence to only one house rather than the four mentioned by Theophanes, and the atmosphere of violence in the decade following 797 is sufficiently palpable that it would be unwise to press the connection too strongly.

A terminus ante quem comes from outside the Basel roll.[29] Analysis of the roll's testimony invites the conclusion that the selection and presentation of the material it records is best explained by a program of financial support and physical reconstruction conceived from a Frankish royal perspective. Confirmation of this view comes in a Carolingian capitulary known from a ninth-century collection based on the records of Sens. It indicates that in late 810 Charlemagne met with his officials at Aachen to discuss "the alms that had to be sent to Jerusalem on account of God's churches that need to be repaired." This agenda item seems to emphasize the dispatch of the wherewithal for repairs rather than determining what needed fixing.[30] As the eminently comparable document compiled for Charles's attention

---

since the document mentions "a convent of seventeen nuns that Charlemagne established at the Holy Sepulcher," and Charlemagne could not have founded such an institution before his first embassy to Harun al Rashid in 797–802 but at the earliest during or on the basis of the second embassy of 802–7. Nothing indicates that Charlemagne founded the convent of nuns who served at the Holy Sepulcher. On the contrary, the Breve implies it was not a Carolingian house, since it mentions that it had 26 nuns, of whom only 17 came from the empire of Lord Charles and served the Holy Sepulcher: "Monasteria puellarum xxvi, de imperio domni Karoli quae ad sepulchrum Domini seruiunt deo sacratas xvii" (A monastery of virgins: 26, from the empire of Lord Charles 17 consecrated nuns who serve at the Sepulcher of the Lord). That they served the Holy Sepulcher does not necessarily imply that the convent was situated there. See further, chapter 4.1. On the form *monasteria*, see below, chapter 11, textual commentary on lines 21–23.

29 Although Tobler (*Descriptiones Terrae Sanctae ex saeculo VIII, IX, XII et XV*, 358) seems to have been the first to mention the capitulary under discussion here in the context of the roll, he does not directly connect them; similarly, Bieberstein ("Der Gesandtenaustausch," 168 and 169), where there does, however, appear to be an implicit link. Karl Schmid makes a cautious connection in "Aachen und Jerusalem. Ein Beitrag zur historischen Personenforschung der Karolingerzeit," in *Das Einhardkreuz. Vorträge und Studien der Münsteraner Diskussion zum arcus Einhardi*, ed. K. Hauck, Abhandlungen der Akademie der Wissenschaften in Göttingen, Philologisch-historische Klasse, 3rd ser., 87 (Göttingen, 1974), 122–42, at 138. H. Vincent and F. M. Abel went the farthest in stating that the Basel roll was likely compiled by an imperial envoy in order to establish an annual budget, which they connect with the 810 capitulary. *Jérusalem. Recherches de topographie, d'archéologie et d'histoire* (Paris, 1912–26), 2.4:938.

30 MGH Capit 1:153–54, no. 64.18, "De elemosina mittenda ad Hierusalem propter aecclesias Dei restaurandas." This capitulary is preserved in two manuscripts, Paris, B.N.F., lat. 9654, and Vatican City, B. Apost., Pal. lat. 582, which reflect a collection assembled in the Sens area, probably under the aegis of the archbishop; this part of that collection stems from a still earlier collection assembled in the last years of Charles or the first of Louis the Pious. See A. Bühler, "Studien zur Entstehung und Überlieferung der Kapitularien Karls des Grossen und Ludwigs des Frommen," *Archiv für Diplomatik* 32 (1986): 305–501, at 369–72; compare Mordek, *Bibliotheca capitularium*, 562–63 and 780–81. The rubric of both manuscripts states that these topics were "commonita" (given as instructions?) in the palace at Aachen in year 10 of Charles's empire. Since c. 12 treats those who

---

in exactly those years by Leidrad of Lyons has suggested, those who knew the king knew what to expect when they went to him seeking support: he would want a clear enumeration of costs.[31] This implies that Charlemagne already possessed the report on the state of the churches of the Holy Land by the autumn of 810. As we have seen, the data recorded on the roll fit the known parameters of Charlemagne's interest in the physical plant of his churches right down to the measurements of the roofs of the great shrines of Jerusalem. By these lights, the documents on the Basel roll will have been composed during a mission to the Holy Land that occurred between 801 and 810. The type of thinking behind the documents and some quirks of language find a particularly close context in the years around 806. The embassies of this period help narrow this further, as we shall see.

In addition to measuring roofs that might need replacing, a practically minded early medieval king might want to know something about individual churches' relative and total financial needs. In Carolingian terms, food was the bottom line, and counting the religious personnel of the various churches of the Holy Land was the first step in determining those churches' relative and total financial need. Once again we can turn to the looming presence of Charlemagne's cousin Adalhard for light. When, in the exceptionally bitter volcanic winter of January 822, the aging abbot drew up a detailed guide to the management of his great monastery, he started by enumerating its personnel and the rations to which they were entitled in order to calculate the annual food requirements of his house.[32] Adalhard's influence at Charlemagne's court was peaking in the period when the Basel roll was commissioned.[33] The detailed lists of numbers of members of the various religious communities of the Holy Land recorded in the roll would allow an advi-

---

had failed to mobilize for military service, BM 451 reasonably deduces that these issues were treated after Charlemagne's return to Aachen that year, that is, between October and 25 December, the imperial anniversary. In Carolingian Latin, *restaurare* can mean "to restore" in the general sense of "return to original state" or "reform"; with the concrete plural of "churches" as its direct object, it obviously refers to some kind of building activity. Compare, for example, the report Leidrad of Lyons sent to Charlemagne at this same time, and discussed above, chapter 3.4, on his efforts "De restauracione . . . ecclesiarum" (Letter, 285); this means repairs involving masonry and roofs, cloisters, foundations, a palace, and other kinds of rebuilding, as the details make clear: ibid., 285–87.

31 See above, chapter 3.4.

32 Adalhard of Corbie, *Statuta sive brevia* 1–3, 365–76; compare 377.20–23. For that winter, see M. McCormick, P. E. Dutton, P. A. Mayewski, and N. Patterson, "Volcanoes and the Climate Forcing of Carolingian Europe, A.D. 750–950," *Speculum* 82 (2007): 865–95, here 882. Like Adalhard's Statutes, most of the supply records analyzed by M. Rouche explicitly or implicitly start by counting heads. See "La faim à l'époque carolingienne. Essai sur quelques types de rations alimentaires," *Revue historique* 250 (1973): 295–320.

33 Kasten (*Adalhard von Corbie*, 47–68), according to whom Adalhard returned from the court to Italy in connection with the death of King Pippin on 8 July 810 or, at the latest, early in 811 (68). Adalhard was a significant presence in Charlemagne's entourage from 802, at the latest (ibid., 56–57).

The Documents

sor like Adalhard to estimate the annual cost of feeding those communities. On top of that, the author of the documents got access to the accounts of the patriarch himself, for he recorded the annual expenses of the patriarchate in the final, partially damaged segment of the roll: "Expenditures of the patriarch, including for priests, deacons, monks, clerics, and the entire congregation of the church <for one> year: 700 solidi, and the patriarch, 550 solidi; for the church fabric, 300 solidi. . . ." (lines 59–60).

The accounts of annual expenditures by the patriarchate and by any other institutions that may have been included in the now lost part of the roll would have allowed Charlemagne and his advisors to verify and calculate the resources and needs of the Holy Land church. We have already seen that Charlemagne also created a permanent resource base for the hostel he founded for pilgrims (above, chapter 4.3). Our new translation of the roll allows the clear possibility that Charlemagne's hostel existed already when the document was compiled.[34]

In terms of Charlemagne's own experience of his life cycle, the mention of repairs to churches of the Holy Land in the autumn or early winter of 810 coheres well with what Einhard relates about the ruler's last years. By way of introducing his famous account of Charlemagne's last will and testament, the king's secretary describes, probably as an eyewitness, Charlemagne's effort to distribute his wealth in the last three years of his life. That will, with its detailed provisions for future distributions of Charles's wealth, was established very early in 811 and thus within months of the meeting that had the repair of the Holy Land churches on its agenda.[35]

2. Count Roculf and the Filioque Controversy

The language, conceptual framework, and nomenclature of the three surviving documents prove that they did not originate in the archives of the patriarchate of Jerusalem. They are the work of westerners who spoke Proto-Romance and collected most of the information orally from Greek and Arabic-speaking informants (above, chapters 6 and 7). It seems improbable that they were compiled at the initiative of westerners resident in the Holy Land and acting on their own authority. The Muslim authorities were concerned to detect spies and control the movements of foreigners within their territories. This makes it highly unlikely that westerners traveling from town to town compiling a census of Christian clergy and

---

34 Line 8: "excepto hospitales iii." See above, chapter 4.3, for details.
35 Einhard, *Vita Karoli* 33, 37–41. On the circumstances, see M. Innes, "Charlemagne's Will: Piety, Politics and the Imperial Succession," *EHR* 112 (1997): 833–55. For the date, deduced from the movements of some of the will's witnesses, see BM 458. For more on the signers and their role in Charlemagne's empire, see K. Brunner, *Oppositionelle Gruppen im Karolingerreich*, Veröffentlichungen des Instituts für Österreichische Geschichtsforschung 25 (Vienna, 1979), 69–95.

clambering over major monuments to measure the size of aging roofs could have done so without explicit approval of the caliphal authorities in Baghdad.[36] The collaboration of Arabic speakers is proved by linguistic features of the Memorial. This brings us to the likelihood that the reports preserved in the Basel roll were connected with one of Charlemagne's embassies to Harun al Rashid. Is it possible to link the three documents preserved on the Basel roll with a particular Carolingian mission to the Levant?

Three or, more correctly, four such expeditions are recorded in the period in question. Since the two earliest embassies left before the imperial coronation, they will not have identified the seventeen western nuns as being "from the empire of Lord Charles" (de imperio domni Karoli [line 22]). If we do not hypothesize an unrecorded embassy between late 808 and 810, the embassy of Radbert, which left in 802 or 803 and returned to Europe in the summer of 806 would appear a likely candidate. According to Einhard, this mission carried donations (donaria) for the Holy Sepulcher.[37] Radbert himself died en route, but the Arab ambassadors who carried the caliph's response arrived safely at Aachen, bringing spectacular gifts to Charles. They were accompanied by George-Egilbald, abbot of the Latin monastery on the Mount of Olives, and the monk Felix. Finally, there is Pope Leo III's mysterious mention of two individuals named Agamus and Rocculf who reached Italy from Palestine in 808, before the end of August, and who are generally regarded as private travelers rather than royal envoys.[38] In fact, these travelers require closer scrutiny, for their status and identity have hitherto been obscured.

That scrutiny has to begin much closer to home, with the official tour of an inspection district (missaticum) that included Aachen and Liège in the spring of 806 and whose envoys, we have seen (above, chapter 7.4), used the unusual term clerici canonici that recurs in the Basel roll. Charles had initially entrusted the mission to Rado, Fulrad of St. Quentin, and Unroch. Because of ill health,

---

36 Eighth- and ninth-century travelers report their difficulties on this score with caliphal authorities. Thus Willibald and his fellow pilgrims were imprisoned as spies in 723 or 724 (Hugeburc, *Vita Willibaldi* 3, 94.6–95.15). So too Bernard in 867 needed to obtain a kind of safe-conduct (*Itinerarium* 7, 312).

37 Einhard, *Vita Karoli* 16, 19.11–25; Borgolte, *Der Gesandtenaustausch der Karolinger mit den Abbasiden und mit den Patriarchen von Jerusalem*, Münchner Beiträge zur Mediävistik und Renaissance-Forschung 25 (Munich, 1976), 81–83.

38 M. McCormick, *Origins of the European Economy: Communications and Commerce, A.D. 300–900* (Cambridge, 2001), 891, R261; 893, R271; and 894, R279. For the earlier embassies, see ibid., 887, R238; 890–91, R254–6, of 797–801; and 888–89, R245 and 248, of 800. The recording in court histories of embassies, at least to Constantinople, is demonstrably imperfect. M. McCormick, "Diplomacy and the Carolingian Encounter with Byzantium down to the Accession of Charles the Bald," in *Eriugena: East and West. Papers of the Eighth International Colloquium of the Society for the Promotion of Eriugenian Studies*, ed. B. McGinn and W. Otten (Notre Dame, 1994), 15–48, here 42 n. 49.

Rado was replaced by two men. One was Charlemagne's cousin and éminence grise Adalhard of Corbie, whose influence only increased as the ruler aged and his health declined.[39] The second replacement was Hrocculf.[40] This layman is very likely to be identified with the homonymous count ("Hruoculf") who held fiscal land next to the cathedral in Tournai in 817. As is well known, the way early medievals spelled the two roots that composed most Germanic names fluctuated greatly, and this man's name is no exception.[41] Though the distinctive name itself is not extremely rare, the date, the rank, and the fact that, as was often the case, he was landed in the area of his *missaticum*, all strengthen the identification.[42] The fact that Hrocculf kept such distinguished company and served alongside Adalhard and that he was landed in the *missaticum* that at least bordered on Aachen itself explains that the count was of sufficiently exalted status and availability to witness Charlemagne's will, probably early in 811.[43] Hrocculf clearly enjoyed the trust of Charles and must be seen as a close collaborator of the all-powerful Adalhard. And this takes us right back to the Breve, or at least to Charlemagne's relations with the patriarchate of Jerusalem.

For the conclusion appears to me inescapable that the Hrocculf who rode into Liège with Adalhard and the others on that spring day of 806 was none other than the identically named Roculfus, Charlemagne's "faithful servant" (fidelis serviens) who stopped in Rome and paid a visit to Pope Leo III while returning home from Jerusalem some twenty-four months later, in the spring or summer of 808. We learn of that visit from a papal letter to Charlemagne himself, the precise significance of which has hitherto remained unclear.

39 On Adalhard in these years, see Kasten, *Adalhard von Corbie*, 47–68; on this mission, 60–61.

40 Ed. Eckhardt, *Die Kapitulariensammlung*, 99; compare MGH Capit 1:183. Both manuscript witnesses seem to derive independently from the archetype (this is the implication of Eckhardt, *Die Kapitulariensammlung*, 12–13): the lost tenth- or eleventh-century manuscript from Saint-Hubert in the Ardennes, known only through the edition of Edmond Martène and Ursin Durand, *Veterum scriptorum et monumentorum historicorum, dogmaticorum, moralium amplissima collectio* (Paris, 1733) 7:12B–28D, and the twelfth-century manuscript Berlin, Staatsbibliothek, Lat. F. 626 (once the property of the College of the Jesuits at Louvain, Belgium, and hence possibly also from the same region). They both corrupt slightly the name of Hrocculf: "... Fulradus, Unrocus, Senhrocculfus missi domni imperatoris," creating a form that is nonsense in terms of early Germanic names. "Senhrocculfus" reflects later scribes' common difficulty in separating the unseparated words of the archetype and the frequent confusion of *n* and *u*. The correction to "seu Hrocculfus" is banal. Compare, for example, the reading of the Berlin manuscript, c. 5, p. 101, "certetur defacte fiant" for "certe tarde factae fiant."

41 For the components of the name, see below, note 59.

42 BM 658; PL 104:1070B–71B, on count Hruoculfus. See also M. McCormick, "Prosopography of Travelers in the Early Medieval Mediterranean," in preparation.

43 See Einhard, *Vita Karoli* 33, 41.10–11, where he signs last and is implicitly identified as a count; cf. BM 458 for the date; and McCormick, "Prosopography." Brunner (*Oppositionelle Gruppen*, 83) assumes that Roculfus is identical with the count.

This brief missive is transmitted to us along with, and itself mentions, a letter sent to Leo by the Frankish monks who resided on the Mount of Olives.[44] The monks' letter to Leo provides the key to the date as well as crucial background for understanding Hrocculf's voyage to Jerusalem, for it stems from the initial clash that sparked the Filioque controversy that today, twelve centuries later, still separates the churches of Rome and Constantinople. Although it has been argued that the letter was invented by the eleventh-century forger Ademar of Chabannes, whose manuscript once preserved it, that is certainly not the case, and there is no reason to suspect the letter's authenticity.[45] A certain John, formerly of the mon-

44 *Epistolae selectae pontificum Romanorum*, nos. 7 (monks) and 8 (Pope Leo III, Jaffé, *Regesta*, 1: no. 2520), from Étienne Baluze's (†1718) edition of a lost manuscript: Stephanus Baluzius, *Miscellanea*, 7 [= *Miscellaneorum liber septimus*] (Paris, 1715): 14–17. Léopold Delisle's careful investigation of the history of the present-day Berlin, Staatsbibliothek, Phillipps 1664, an autograph manuscript of Ademar of Chabannes (†1034), showed that this codex combined at least three separate manuscripts, which in the late seventeenth century were still in the treasury of St. Martial of Limoges: no. 79, the modern fols. 40–57, and nos. 143 and 144, corresponding, respectively, to the Berlin manuscript's fols. 58–83 (Ademar's reworkings of three works of Theodulf of Orleans; see P. Brommer, MGH Capitula episcoporum 1 [Hanover, 1984]: 78–79; and S. A. Keefe, *Water and the Word: Baptism and the Education of the Clergy in the Carolingian Empire* [Notre Dame, 2002], 2:278; cf. V. Rose, *Verzeichniss der lateinischen Handschriften der Königlichen Bibliothek zu Berlin*, vol. 1, Die Handschriften-Verzeichnisse der Königlichen Bibliothek zu Berlin 12 [Berlin, 1893], 1:199–200; 202); and to fols. 83–170 (Ademar's collection of materials relevant to church synods, which is truncated). L. Delisle, "Notice sur les manuscrits originaux d'Adémar de Chabannes," *Notices et extraits des manuscrits de la Bibliothèque Nationale et autres bibliothèques* 25, no. 1 (1896): 241–358, here 244–76. By comparing the seventeenth- and eighteenth-century descriptions of these various states of the manuscripts, Delisle (272–75) was able to show that the combined manuscript lost its last six folios in Holland, where it had been purchased by the bibliophile G. Meerman from the sale in 1764 of the Jesuits' Parisian Collège de Clermont, and that those last six folios had contained an "Epistola Caroli Magni ad Alcuinum" and an "Epistola Leonis ad Carolum imperatorem" as well as some sermons. The "Epistola Leonis" was the letter of Pope Leo III to Charlemagne that accompanied the letter of the monks of the Mount of Olives, both of which, as Baluze stated in the list of texts that opens his vol. 7 (unpaginated), came to him from a manuscript of St. Martial of Limoges. The lost witness to a letter of Charlemagne to Alcuin raises an intriguing possibility since only two such letters are known: the one published as Alcuin's *Ep*. 144, 228–30, about the names of Septuagesima, Sexagesima, and Quinquagesima Sundays, inviting Alcuin to join the king in the spring, and *Ep*. 247, 399–401, severely criticizing Alcuin for sheltering a fugitive cleric who had been condemned by Theodulf and favorably comparing Theodulf's conduct to Alcuin's. Given the other Theodulfian material in the manuscript, it is tempting to think that the lost folios had *Ep*. 247, which otherwise seems to be transmitted by only one manuscript, and—understandably, given its negative tone—outside of the main collections of Alcuin's correspondence. There seems to be no discussion of this manuscript in the posthumous work of the late and lamented D. Bullough, *Alcuin: Achievement and Reputation* (Leyden, 2004), whose account does not reach the period in which this letter was written.
45 D. F. Callahan has argued mainly on the basis of similarities of content that Ademar of Chabannes forged this letter. "The Problem of the 'Filioque' and the Letter from the Pilgrim Monks of the Mount of Olives to Pope Leo III and Charlemagne: Is the Letter Another Forgery of Adémar of Chabannes?" *RBén* 102 (1992): 75–134. Scrutiny of Callahan's arguments, of the letter's language, and of independent witnesses both to the facts of the controversy and the details of the

astery of St. Sabas, had accused the Frankish monks of heresy and sought to bar them from the traditional Christmas service at the Nativity shrine in Bethlehem. In the ensuing, bitter conflict, the Franks protested that they would die on the spot rather than be expelled from the shrine. During an investigation convened the following Sunday, 2 January 808, at the Holy Sepulcher, the Frankish monks and the archdeacon of the Jerusalem church mounted the pulpit and declared their conformity with the beliefs of the patriarchate and the Holy See. Nevertheless, the investigation revealed that the monks' Creed included the troublesome expression *filioque* ("and from the Son"), the equivalent of which was lacking in comparable Greek texts of the Creed. Since the monks had heard exactly this form in Charlemagne's royal chapel in the presence of Pope Leo III, and since similar wording could be found in orthodox books that the Frankish emperor had given the monks, they wished to receive explicit confirmation and support from the pope that their creed conformed to that of Rome.[46]

The problem of course was that it did not. The controversial words had been added to the Nicene-Constantinopolitan Creed since the sixth century in parts of Latin Christendom, including the Carolingian Empire and had already needed defending in Friuli by Paulinus of Aquileia in 796.[47] They did not appear in the Creed as it was chanted in the churches of Rome. And so Leo had a major controversy thrust upon him by the burgeoning contacts between Eastern and Western Christendoms. At first he dodged addressing the discrepancy directly and affronting the king whose main force had recently restored him to power: instead, he sent a copy of the Roman creed to the Frankish monks at Jerusalem and forwarded their letter to Charlemagne. Now the large Greek monastic establishment at Rome was closely linked to that of the Holy Land, and the Jerusalem controversy seems to have made enough impact in his own bishopric that Leo felt obliged to respond in the most public fashion possible.[48] In what can only be a response

---

letter, leads me to a different opinion. The language of the letter is clearly early medieval and very different from Ademar's beautifully accomplished classicizing Latinity. Moreover, the Frankish monks' role in triggering the controversy (and therefore the letter) is attested by the contemporary Byzantine *Vita Michael Syncellae* (BHG 1296), 6, 54.30–56.28 (although not explicitly situated in the Holy Land). On the composition and reliability of this work, likely composed at Constantinople before 867, see ibid., 5–17. Finally, Ado of Vienne (†875) appears to have known the letter, since his chronicle (PL 123:132D–133A) refers to John, monk of Jerusalem, as having precipitated the Filioque controversy.

46 *Epistolae selectae*, 7. For the date, see below. The origins of the Filioque controversy have elicited a substantial bibliography. For the historical theology, see B. Oberdorfer, *Filioque: Geschichte und Theologie eines ökumenischen Problems*, Forschungen zur systematischen und ökumenischen Theologie 96 (Göttingen, 2001), esp. 143–50, on the theological and liturgical background that made the question such a loaded one for Charlemagne and his advisors.

47 Ibid., 145–46.

48 On the links between early medieval Rome and the Holy Land, see J.-M. Sansterre, *Les moines grecs et orientaux à Rome aux époques byzantine et carolingienne*, Académie royale de Belgique,

to the controversy, the pope caused two large silver disks to be raised in St. Peter's, bearing the Roman text of the Creed in Greek and Latin. He had a third silver disk with the same Creed hung in St. Paul Outside the Walls. Pope Leo III's official biography mentions the hanging of the disks among other expenditures that independently have been dated to the first indiction, that is, the Byzantine fiscal year running from 1 September 807 to 31 August 808. The news from Jerusalem must therefore have reached him in the spring or summer of 808.[49] The Roman text lacked the controversial addition, as we know from the manuscript evidence and the ensuing difficulties between Charlemagne and Leo.[50]

In the brief letter apprising Charles of the problem in the Holy Land that accompanied that of the Frankish monks, the pope also mentions that two men returned to Rome from the Holy Land bringing Leo a letter from Thomas, patriarch of Jerusalem. They apparently traveled separately from the messenger who brought the Frankish letter to Rome.[51] The pope explicitly identifies these men as Charlemagne's "faithful servants, Agamus and Roculfus." Leo reports that the patriarch had asked him to commend these envoys to Charles, which Leo was glad to do, asking the emperor to show the mercy (*misericordiam*) he displayed toward

Mémoires de la classe des lettres, Collection in 8°, 2nd ser., 66 (Brussels, 1983), 1:9–51; compare McCormick, *Origins*, 223. The Frankish monks' letter itself reveals the personal web then linking Jerusalem and Rome, for it explicitly indicates that their chief tormentor, the Greek monk John, formerly of St. Sabas, was known to "your [sc. Leo III's] servant *hegoumenos* Theodoulos."

49 This section of Leo's Life consists almost exclusively of extracts from the papal accounts organized by indiction of disbursement. See *Liber pontificalis*, ed. Duchesne, 2:26.18–20 and 28–29; and H. Geertman, *More veterum. Il Liber Pontificalis e gli edifici ecclesiastici di Roma nella tarda antichità e nell'alto medioevo*, Archaeologica traiectina 10 (Groningen, 1975), 50. This consideration confirms Schmid's view ("Aachen und Jerusalem," 133) and rules out the alternative dating of Christmas 808 for the beginning of the conflict in the Holy Land one finds in some authorities, for example, V. Peri, "Leone III e il 'Filioque': echi del caso nell'agiografia greca," *Rivista di storia della Chiesa in Italia* 25 (1971): 3–58, at 26; and Bieberstein, "Der Gesandtenaustausch," 168.

50 For the Latin text of the Creed of Pope Leo III, preserved thanks to Abelard, and the Greek version that must have corresponded to that preserved in the Gelasian Sacramentary, see, for example, *Das Konzil von Aachen, 809*, 2:117–20.

51 "Interea revertentes praesentes fideles servientes vestri, Agamus videlicet et Roculfus...." *Epistolae selectae*, 8, 67.3–9. *Interea* probably means that the king's two faithful servants arrived separately from the person(s) who carried the letter. The "Agamus" who is named ahead of Roculf is hard to pin down. Presumably, the Roman spelling—possibly further distorted by careless transcription of the manuscript on which Baluze seems to have relied (see Delisle, "Notice," 249, concerning the errors which can still be detected in the Theodulf material)—conceals the Germanic root <hagan>, a name that is well attested among Carolingian aristocrats. Individuals with that name were associated with a church in Mainz and occur fairly often in the abundant transactions concerning Fulda and Lorsch. See, in general, M. Gockel, *Karolingische Königshöfe am Mittelrhein* (Göttingen, 1970), 295–98. Individuals with this name appear in the same document as men named with the local equivalents of Roculfus in the Middle Rhine Valley. See *Urkundenbuch des Klosters Fulda*, no. 263, 27 January 800, in a boundary clause, where Hroccholf is a witness; and, in Bavaria, *Die Traditionen des Hochstifts Freising*, no. 251, Föhring, 29 April 807.

all of his faithful (*fideles vestros*). Scholarly opinion generally denies that this Roculf is the same man we have observed in the emperor's entourage in 806 and 811.

The main argument against identifying Roculf with Charles's close collaborator in precisely those years is the notion that it would have been inappropriate for the patriarch to request that the pope commend to the emperor men who would presumably have been Charles's own envoys.[52] Furthermore, it has been reasoned, although Leo's phrasing "fideles servientes vestri" certainly means that Agamus and Roculf were Charlemagne's subjects—and perhaps more closely connected to the royal service—there is no other mention of such a mission in contemporary Carolingian records.[53]

These objections do not withstand close scrutiny. The expression "fideles servientes vestri" appears to me to be rare in papal correspondence in the last two or three decades of Charlemagne's rule. But in exactly the same period, Leo used an almost identical expression for one of Charlemagne's closest collaborators when he called Jesse, bishop of Amiens, "serviens vester" in another letter to the emperor.[54] Furthermore, the idea that a pope would not commend the king's own envoys to the ruler is groundless. For instance, Pope Hadrian I had written to Charles commending the king's envoys Bishop Possessor and Abbot Rabigaudus in not dissimilar terms.[55] That the pope urges the king to show mercy (*misericordia*) to his own envoys suggests that their mission involving the patriarch of Jerusalem had not met with unqualified success and that the pope felt they did not deserve punishment for the shortcomings.[56] Moreover, omission from contemporary court historiography is exactly what we should expect for difficulties involving the ruler. Thus, for instance, a decade or so earlier, the Royal Annals had consigned to silence another high-profile embassy that had yielded unsatisfactory results.[57]

52 S. Abel and B. von Simson, *Jahrbücher des Fränkischen Reiches unter Karl dem Grossen*, Jahrbücher der deutschen Geschichte (Berlin, 1883–88), 2:406 n. 3.

53 Borgolte (*Der Gesandtenaustausch*, 105–7) is cautious but accepts the reasoning by Abel and Simson about the inappropriateness of the patriarch's request for men who would have been Charles's envoys and adds the argument from silence. Brunner, *Oppositionelle Gruppen*, 83, simply identifies him with the count without further discussion.

54 Leo III, *Epistolae X* 2 (Jaffé, *Regesta*, 1: no. 2516; AD 808), 91.7.

55 *Codex carolinus* 52 (Jaffé, *Regesta*, 1: no. 2420; AD 775), 574.23–25: ". . . ipsi missi vestri, fideles in servitio fautoris vestri beati Petri . . . et nostri atque vestri repperimus; pro quo petimus, ut benignae eos suscipere iubeatis."

56 It is difficult to assess the nature of those shortcomings. They could have entailed anything from difficulties for the hostel or with local Arab officials to, quite plausibly, complications in diplomatic relations with the patriarch arising from the Filioque affair (see below, p. 176).

57 Charlemagne's dispatch to Constantinople of the chaplain Witbold and a certain John, about 786–88, in connection with the projected marriage of his daughter and Emperor Constantine VI, is known from the *Gesta patrum Fontanellensis coenobii* 12.1, 134.11–26. But the failed marriage agreement was passed over in silence when the Royal Annals were written up in the 790s. See McCormick, *Origins*, 882, nos. 210–11.

It follows, on the contrary, from the very fact that the pope requested mercy for the two men, as well as from the words with which he designates them, that Agamus and Roculf *were* on a mission for the king. And given that a man with the same, fairly distinctive, name was active on royal missions and closely associated with the court precisely from 806 to 811, it seems to me hard to deny that Charlemagne's *missus dominicus* of 806 is one and the same as his homonymous envoy some two years later. One further strand binds them together. We have already noted Adalhard's role in the governance of the empire in this period. The pattern of selection of Roculf as ambassador prefigures a similar appointment just a few years later. Then, Adalhard, in the course of his duties as *missus dominicus* in Italy, met Peter, abbot of Nonantola. He deepened his acquaintance with the man, and suggested that Peter accompany him back to Aachen to get the emperor's personal approval for a land transaction that Peter wanted. Peter did so and was promptly appointed Charlemagne's envoy to the emperor in Constantinople. Here too someone whom Adalhard encountered in the course of royal service was appointed ambassador soon thereafter.[58]

Although precise genealogies are hard to come by around 800, a convergence of anthroponymic, property, and circumstantial evidence makes clear that Roculf was a man to be reckoned with and may even point to his family connections. Formed by two roots in the fashion typical of Germanic names, "Roculf" and its variants are fairly well attested in the central lands of the Carolingian Empire: the name occurs in the written record over fifty times and designates an uncertain number of individuals.[59] Attestations cluster in the decades around 800, perhaps because the records do too.[60]

How many of these fifty-odd occurrences refer to the same persons is difficult to establish definitively. In addition to two unfree dependents, it is possible

58 For the details on Peter and Adalhard, see my forthcoming "Prosopography of Travelers"; in the meantime, see *I Placiti del 'Regnum Italiae'* 392–94, no. 106; compare Kasten, *Adalhard von Corbie*, 69; and *Codex diplomaticus Langobardiae* no. 188, 164–66.

59 The first, <hrōk>, seems to represent the convergence of different roots, prime among them an onomatopaeic word for making a loud noise (cf. English "croak"); the second is the same as our "wolf." For a critical discussion of the various attempts to distinguish different roots and senses, see H. Kaufmann, *Altdeutsche Personenamen: Ergänzungsband* (Munich, 1968), 199–201.

60 It is difficult to determine how far the name's chronological distribution reflects that of the records. This is clearly possible for the twenty-seven (of fifty-two) acts that involve Lorsch. Of the 3,596 transactions between AD 755 and 1000 inventoried by *Codex Laureshamensis*, 1:66–261, about 2,700 (75%) date from the reign of Charlemagne. At Fulda and Freising, this is not so clearly the case. In the 820s and 830s, the Fulda cartulary already comprised almost 2,000 acts (*Urkundenbuch des Klosters Fulda* 1: xviii). E. E. Stengel himself edited 529 acts for Fulda down to 802. Freising has preserved twenty-eight acts for the period 744–68 (an average of 1.16 per year), 285 from 769 to the death of Charlemagne for an average of 6.3 per year; the annual rate jumps to 13.5 for the shorter reign of Louis the Pious, from which 324 acts survive (*Die Traditionen des Hochstifts Freising*).

to distinguish at least three or four individuals—and possibly several more—over the two or three generations from 765 to 835, the period within which we may think that the ambassador and count was active.[61] The name can be seen among individuals from Pippin III's royal entourage and again in 791 and about 806 in Bavaria.[62] Other name bearers are a priest attested in a transaction at Lorsch in 777 and the Rocolfus who was dead by 802, when his paternal nephew Cunibert commemorated him along with his own brother, Diottolf. On the basis of property and association in transactions, this Rocolfus has been connected with the powerful Gerolding kinship network, itself married into the royal family.[63] Yet

61 Two unfree dependents are certainly not our man: at Bodenheim in 797 (*Urkundenbuch des Klosters Fulda*, no. 252), and at Strasburg in 774 (*Urkundenbuch der Stadt Strassburg* 1: no. 14).

62 Roolf (a phonetic variation on the roots <hrōk wulf>) was connected with court milieus through his father. At Lorsch, on 29 June 767, Roolf gave to the new abbey land at Ilvesheim to commemorate two (deceased) family members, his father Maurilo and brother Ado (*Codex Laureshamensis* no. 451, witnessed by a Hildibald, and written by the scribe Samuel). A year earlier, Maurilo had witnessed at Weinheim in the company, among others, of counts Warino and Cancur, relative of Chrodegang of Metz and the founder of Lorsch (*Codex Laureshamensis* no. 482, 8 March 766; cf. ibid., no. 417, 12 April 766). In 791 a Hrokwulf appears as a witness to the settlement of a Bavarian dispute arranged by Charlemagne's *missi dominici*—Arn, archbishop of Salzburg, Gerold (Charlemagne's brother-in-law and prefect of Bavaria, perhaps a relative of a middle Rhenish Roccolf), Meginfrid, surely the commander of some of the troops and Charlemagne's *camerarius* (cf. *Annales Einhardi* a. 791, 89), Wolfwolt and Rimicoz *iudex*, at Lorch on the Enns, where the king and his army had been staging the invasion of the Avars (*Die Traditionen des Hochstifts Freising* 1: no. 142, 20 September 791; cf. ibid. no. 143a). On the circumstances and identifications, see BM 314c; W. Störmer, *Früher Adel: Studien zur politischen Führungsschicht im fränkisch-deutschen Reich vom 8. bis 11. Jahrhundert*, Monographien zur Geschichte des Mittelalters 6 (Stuttgart, 1973), 1:220–21; and W. Brown, *Unjust Seizure: Conflict, Interest, and Authority in an Early Medieval Society* (Ithaca, 2001), 68–71. Around 806, in a meeting at Regensburg, attended by Arn of Salzburg, five other bishops, Count Audulf, and others, a Hrocholf was forced to renounce his claim to a church that he had unjustly usurped from the cathedral of Freising (*Die Traditionen des Hochstifts Freising* 1: no. 231). At Altötting on 15 December 806, in an assembly of Charlemagne's *missi dominici*, again including Arn, counts Audulf, Werinharius, and others, this or another Hroccolf and his relative Engilhard were forced to renounce the hereditary claim they had laid against a property of Wago, *capellanus*, and a well-known figure in the region who has been connected with the Alamannian ducal family. See W. Störmer, *Adelsgruppen im früh- und hochmittelalterlichen Bayern*, Studien zur bayerischen Verfassungs- und Sozialgeschichte 4 (Munich, 1972), 28, 69, 127, 167.

63 Roholf the priest witnessed the gift by Egisbert and Engilrad of a meadow at Wallstadt on 10 July 777 (*Codex Laureshamensis* no. 499). It is not entirely impossible that he is identical with the uncle Roccolfus, since it was this man's nephew, not his son, who organized the commemoration at Lorsch on 17 January 802, by a substantial land gift at Plankstadt (*Codex Laureshamensis* no. 783), although the absence of a mention of his priestly dignity might militate against the identification. The uncle is in any case likely identical with the Rocculfus who gave Lorsch substantial properties at Plankstadt on 14 June 778, witnessed by Tietolf (an obvious variant spelling of Diottolf, the Germanic roots being <theud> and <wulf>) (*Codex Laureshamensis* no. 778). See also Gockel (*Karolingische Königshöfe*, 281), who identifies the individuals in *Codex Laureshamensis* nos. 783 and 778. Gockel (*Karolingische Königshöfe*, 281–82 n. 594) further identifies this uncle Rocculfus, apparently dead in 802, with almost all the Roccolfs documented in transactions involving Lorsch and Fulda, and links this individual with the Geroldings, with the "Roccold" who witnessed gifts

another attestation concerns a Roccholf, son of Heimen and brother of Erlulf, whose mother Berahtswind and maternal uncle Wolfhart, at Mainz, made a gift to Fulda in 811.[64] Some individuals attested in the Rhenish materials have been identified with same-named people active in Bavaria, and it is not impossible that this may have been true of one or more of the various Roculfs.[65]

Though the Jerusalem envoy was certainly not the same man as the priest or the person who died by 802, no direct evidence allows us to rule the other Roculfs in or out. Indirect evidence seems more promising. Using his method of "leading names" (*Leitnamen*) and associations in property holding and transactions, Werner has argued from the presence of the (fairly uncommon) root <hrōk> (cf. English "croak") that the men named Hrokwulf belonged to the powerful kinship group of the Unruochings, whose main possessions lay in Flanders and northern France as well as Alemannia and whose name comprises the roots <un hrōk>.[66] The Unruoch for whom modern scholars have named this kinship group was a count in Charlemagne's entourage; he is plausibly believed to be the same man as the Unruoch who fathered Eberhard, margrave of Friuli and son-in-law of Louis the Pious.[67] Whether or not Count Unruoch and our Roculf were related, they served Charlemagne together as *missi dominici* in the spring of 806, and were both

---

of Amanold on behalf of his brother Hadabald to Fulda and Lorsch, at Dienheim and Bensheimer Hof, respectively, in or around 784 (*Urkundenbuch des Klosters Fulda* no. 168 and *Codex Lauresha-mensis* no. 266) as well as with the person mentioned in *Codex Laureshamensis* nos. 1574 (AD 766, property at Oppenheim), 1919 (765–78, property at Schwabenheim an der Selz or Pfaffenschwa-benheim), 1471 (at Flörsheim, 778–84, accepting the editor's emendation of "Rochold"), 1957 (776, Flörsheim and Enzheim), 2123 (782, Böchingen), 2202 (790, Menzingen), and in *Urkundenbuch des Klosters Fulda* nos. 54 (Bodenheim, 771), 169, 237, 261 (Dienheim, 784/85, 796, 799), 263 (Ülvers-heim, 800), 266 (Mainz, 800), 268 (Wonsheim, 800).

64 *Codex diplomaticus Fuldensis* no. 252, a vineyard at Dienheim, on 5 March 811. Roccholf was apparently not present. According to Gockel (*Karolingische Königshöfe*, 224 n. 54), Erlolf is the same man who gave land at Dienheim, in memory of Adeltrude (*Codex Laureshamensis* no. 1685, October 811–October 812).

65 See, for example, Störmer, *Adelsgruppen*, 42–45.

66 He reckons the count Hruoculf who held land at Tournai different from but related to the man who testified in 796 to a transaction involving Dienheim and men whom Werner identified as Unruochings, *Urkundenbuch des Klosters Fulda* no. 237 (see preceding note). K. F. Werner, "Bedeu-tende Adelsfamilien im Reich Karls des Grossen," in *Karl der Grosse, Lebenswerk und Nachleben*, ed. W. Braunfels, 5 vols. (Düsseldorf, 1965–68), 1:83–142, at 136.

67 See, for example, E. Hlawitschka, "Unruochinger," *LMA* 8 (1997): 1261; G. Tellenbach, "Der grossfränkische Adel und die Regierung Italians in der Blütezeit des Karolingerreiches," in *Stu-dien und Vorarbeiten zur Geschichte des grossfränkischen und frühdeutschen Adels*, ed. G. Tellen-bach, Forschungen zur oberrheinischen Landesgeschichte 4 (Freiburg im Breisgau, 1957), 40–70, here 57–58. Sedulius Scotus (*Carmen* 67.8, 109) identifies Eberhard as *Hunroci proles*, which word usually means "son of" in Sedulius's poetic diction: see, for example, *Carmen* 12.3–4, 28, and the other occurrences, easily examined in, for example, CLCLT-5, s.v.

The Documents

present to witness the aging emperor's will in 811.[68] If our Roculf is indeed connected with the occurrences of the name in the Middle Rhine Valley and Michael Gockel's deductions on the occurrences are well founded, he may have been related to the king by marriage through the family of Gerold, the father of Charlemagne's late wife Hildegard (d. 783). But whatever the genealogical details, his royal service proves what the patterns of name attestation may hint, that Roculf was a man to be reckoned with in the entourage of the aging Charlemagne.

Remarkable though the appearance of *clerici canonici* is in the royal *missi*'s document of 806, the use of the rare technical term there and in the roll may not necessarily go back to Roculf himself. We have also heard echoes of Italy, suggesting that someone with an Italian background (perhaps an associate of Adalhard) was involved in drafting the Holy Land documents. We do not know for sure that Roculf's mission was the one that prepared the documents preserved in the Basel roll. But the unusual technical term tightens the links between the human group around Charles the Great in 806 and the men who composed the documents preserved on the Basel roll. *How* these linguistic tics might have spread among such a group may become more precisely clear from advanced philological work with computerized databases. But we all are likely to know from our own experience how a specific social milieu tends to share jargon and turns of phrase. So it would come as little surprise that in the very small social world of Charlemagne's collaborators and advisors, men like Arn of Salzburg—who also witnessed Charles's will—and the writers associated with the court and its great men sometimes used the same distinctive expressions, especially for a phenomenon then of such consuming interest as the canonial institution.

One point of detail may strengthen the claim of Agamus and Roculf to the mission that compiled the records copied onto the Basel roll. When reporting on monasteries, the roll usually identifies the abbot by name and specifies the number of monks after naming the abbot.[69] However, no abbot at all is mentioned for the Frankish monastery on the Mount of Olives (line 23). Precisely during the embassy of Agamus and Roculf to the Holy Land, the abbot of this monastery was absent, for George/Eigilbald was visiting Charlemagne's court in 807. George returned to Jerusalem only during the sailing season of 808, when the Frankish ambassadors came back to Europe.[70] This is the situation reflected by the letter

---

68 Einhard, *Vita Karoli* 33, 41.9–11. Gockel, *Karolingische Königshöfe*, 253, seems to discount their kinship.

69 Certainly, for Mar Saba, St. Euthymius (line 30), and Choziba (line 31). See also my proposed readings for line 27 and the damaged part of line 30, if my restoration is accepted. No such details are offered for any convent.

70 McCormick, *Origins*, 893–94, R277.

the monks of the Frankish monastery sent to Pope Leo III that year, for Abbot George does not figure among the signatories.[71]

Against this embassy, one might invoke the two-year delay before Charlemagne acted on the information collected in the roll. However, the letters of Leo and the Frankish monastery on the Mount of Olives document the strains with the Holy Land church that erupted at the time of that embassy in 808. Their repercussions on papal-Carolingian relations could well explain such a delay and indeed the pope's pleas for Charles's mercy toward his envoys. This was also the period in which disorders and civil war swept over the caliphate after the death of Harun al Rashid in the spring of 809, when, as we have seen, the Holy Land was severely affected.[72] One does not have to subscribe to François-Louis Ganshof's belief that the Carolingian court was almost paralyzed in Charlemagne's last years to consider that the sudden crisis over the text of the Creed that had arisen in Jerusalem could have pushed other related business to the back burner.[73] The biography of the contemporary synkellos of the patriarch of Jerusalem records Eastern awareness of the pressure Leo felt from the Franks on this score.[74] The series of newly elucidated documents that prepared and emanated from the synod convoked at Aachen in November 809 to address this issue, and the failure, apparently, early in 810, of Charlemagne's ambassadors, Bernharius of Worms and—once again—Adalhard of Corbie, to extract Leo's acceptance of the Frankish version of the Creed's text with its wording *filioque* testify to the court's preoccupation with this issue.[75] Pope Leo III managed to win a victory of sorts by acknowledging the theological validity of the Franks' formulation, while at the same time refusing to change the text of the Creed as it was recited at Rome and which, as we have seen, he had had displayed at the tombs of the Apostles in 808. The fact that one of the disks raised at St. Peter's was inscribed in Greek can only have ensured its resonance with the large Greek-speaking monastic community of Rome, distinguished by its ancient

71 *Epistolae selectae pontificum Romanorum* 7, 66.21–23.

72 Above, chapter 8.1.

73 Ganshof, "La fin du règne," here 447–52.

74 *Vita Michael syncelli* 6, 54.30–56.16.

75 The documents are edited and discussed in detail in *Das Konzil von Aachen 809*. The *Annales regni Francorum* a. 809, 129, describe the synod and its date and mention the ambassadors' dispatch to Rome in one breath. This suggests that they were sent before the new year began on Christmas, according to the annalists' style. The date given by the summary of the discussions in Rome is "per indictionem secundam." Willjung has deduced that the summary was compiled by someone in the papal writing office: ibid., 109–10. If so, the date cannot be correct, for the second indiction at Rome had begun on 1 September 808 and ended on 31 August 809, before the Aachen synod took place. See Bresslau and Klewitz, *Handbuch der Urkundenlehre*, 1:414–15; compare 410, on the "Greek" indictions at Rome. However, a slip of one minim from the correct *ind. iii* would have been banal. Willjung's criticism (109 n. 96) of the observation by Abel and Simson, *Jahrbücher des Fränkischen Reiches unter Karl dem Grossen* 2:408 n. 3, of this error is incorrect, for it is based on a mathematical error in Willjung's calculation of the indiction number.

and enduring ties to the Holy Land.[76] Charlemagne might well have suspended a decision to dispatch large amounts of wealth to a church from which accusations of heresy emanated against the Franks, pending what his court clearly expected would be the pope's resounding validation of their Creed text. When that expectation was disappointed, the Frankish king nevertheless proceeded to plan the restoration of the churches of the Holy Land, as the topics raised at the meeting at Aachen in late 810 indicate. On the other hand, the fact that around this time a heavy new tribute of some sort was laid on the patriarchate and churches of Jerusalem forced the patriarch to seek financial help. The Byzantine biographer of the patriarch's synkellos claims he sought it from the pope, even as he offered to help Leo defend orthodoxy.[77] Since the Greek biographer is vociferous in his criticism of the "godless Franks," it would have been difficult for him to admit that the serious needs of the patriarchate in a time of great difficulty could well have inclined its officials to a less negative stance toward Charlemagne.[78] The patriarchs had until then enjoyed excellent relations with this famous Christian ruler, and they had every reason to expect help far beyond what the pope in Rome—himself largely tributary of the Frank's largess—might supply. Such a stance would not have been discouraged by the fact that the pope had given very public support to the hagiopolitan position that one should not tamper with the Creed.

In sum, the purpose of the roll is clear from its form, contents, and historical context. No less than for the inventorying that Charlemagne commanded across his empire, the aim was practical and administrative. The form is that of an administrative document. The records preserved on the Basel roll were compiled in the context of Charlemagne's embassies to Harun al Rashid and the Holy Land. The roll was certainly written within the period 801–14. It was most likely composed before the autumn of 810, and very possibly in 808 in connection with the embassy of Agamus and Roculf.

The roll and the planned intervention of which it was a part open a window on the operational style of Charlemagne's governance in his final years. We can observe with some precision how the king and his advisors tackled a particular problem of governance, in this case, a charitable intervention on behalf of a distant church. Probably in response to a request from overseas, the royal circle developed a plan and obtained diplomatic support and clearance from the caliph, as Einhard plainly states, in order to alleviate the indigence of the local Christians under Muslim rule. A team of royal envoys was sent to collect detailed statistics and

---

76 See above, chapter 2.2. On the Greek monasteries of Rome and their links to the Holy Land in this period, see McCormick, *Origins*, 219–24, with further references.

77 *Vita Michael syncelli* 6, 56.29–58.15; the date given there (at the beginning of Leo V's reign: 58.15–16, i.e., 813) is too late (ibid., 142–43 n. 56).

78 Ibid., 56.23, "τῶν ἀθέων Φράγγων."

measurements of the personnel, expenditures, and building needs of the orthodox Christian churches under the patriarch of Jerusalem. The result was laid out in at least three documents, copied on a roll to be presented to Charlemagne and his advisors for a decision in late 810. That decision presumably turned on whether to support the church beyond the gifts already transmitted in 802–3 and, if so, how much to send. In response to a request from a prestigious patriarch, the Carolingian ruler dispatched envoys, *missi*, at least one of whom came from his closer circle of leading men. They were to ask—and as the roll proves, they did proceed orally—specific questions. From the information on the roll, we can infer the questions the court must have scripted for the envoys. There is nothing surprising about this. The contemporary capitularies quoted at the outset of this chapter explicitly identify a set of questions the ruler expected his envoys to answer during those missions: "Let our *missi* investigate diligently and have written down, each in his own district, what each person has as a benefice and how many men have holdings in the benefice." The level of detail that the court was prepared to prescribe is obvious from both the existence of the meticulous recording preserved in the exemplary capitularies *De villis* and the *Brevium exempla* and the fact that they survive in a book produced in a remarkably long and slender codex format—reminiscent of nothing so much as a modern Michelin guide and perfectly suited to sliding into the saddle bags of men on a mission.[79] These models were meant to travel and serve as guidelines for inspecting envoys. Indeed, a chance survival has preserved a piece of another roll which shows us that Charles or his advisors scripted the very detail of words and gestures his envoys exchanged with the bishop of Rome: "Next you must give him the letter, saying in this fashion, 'Our Lord, your son, has sent the present letter to you, that is, asking of Your Holiness that Your Benignity receive it affectionately.' Then you must say, 'Our Lord, your son, has sent to you such gifts as he could prepare in Saxony and, when it pleases Your Holiness, we will show them [to you]. . . .'"[80] Some such set of questions and prescriptions must have accompanied the Frankish envoys traipsing about the Holy Land, as we can infer from the responses recorded on the Basel roll: how many churches are there in Palestine, what are their names or dedications, and how many Christian ecclesiastics serve them? How many of Charlemagne's subjects reside in those estab-

79 The manuscript Wolfenbüttel, Herzog-August-Bibliothek, Cod. Helmst. 254, measures 125 × 308 mm, an unusual format, as C. Brühl notes. *Capitulare de villis. Cod. guelf. 254 Helmst. der Herzog August Bibliothek Wolfenbüttel*, Dokumente zur deutschen Geschichte in Faksimiles. Reihe 1: Mittelalter, Bd. 1 (Stuttgart, 1971), 6. A similarly oblong format occurs in some of the earliest Christian codices (ca. 120–150 mm × 240–280 mm), a fact that may be connected with their use by travelers. See M. McCormick, "The Birth of the Codex and the Apostolic Life-Style," *Scriptorium* 39 (1985): 150–58, here 157.

80 Facsimile and diplomatic edition in *ChLA* 17: no. 655; also ed. Boretius, MGH Capit 1:225, no. 111. For a discussion of this type of document and further bibliography, see McCormick, "La lettre diplomatique," 141.

lishments? How many hermits lived outside Jerusalem, and where did they come from? What are the measurements of the roofs of the greatest shrines of Jerusalem and Bethlehem, including the ruined shrine raised by emperor Justinian? What are the annual expenditures of the patriarch? It is also probably no accident that a very similar set of questions seems to have guided Leidrad's compilation of his report on the state of his church of Lyons in the very same years.

These are not the questions of idle curiosity. Counting heads in Palestinian churches would allow the Frankish court to calculate the food or monetary requirements on the usual basis they applied so widely inside the Frankish Empire, whether it was Adalhard calculating the rations needed for his monastery's food supply or Louis the Pious's establishing the rations for traveling parties on official business.[81] Similarly, the effort to measure the roofs of the principal shrines of Palestine would allow the Franks to calculate the cost of repairing or replacing them. Finally, examining the actual yearly expenditures of the patriarch would allow a check on estimates the Frankish court might make for possible subsidies, and perhaps allow insight into unusual financial stresses on the patriarchate. Nor should we forget that the Frankish court actually organized the purchase of a dozen establishments around Jerusalem, not to mention, possibly, the revenue from a nearby market, to finance the operations of the Carolingian hostel on a permanent basis, a plan that seems to have worked until, in all probability, a later patriarch was forced to undermine it in an attempt to deal with his church's indebtedness. If all this seems too thorough, too detailed and well thought out for an early medieval intervention projected across the sea by a monarch whose powers were allegedly failing in these very years, then it is time for historians to reconsider some cherished assumptions. The historical evidence is more complicated.

Einhard's summary turns out to find detailed support and illustration from the Basel roll and its historical context: "where he had learned that Christians were living in poverty and he took pity on their indigence. This was the main reason he sought the friendship of overseas kings, so that a certain amount of relief and mitigation might reach the Christians who reside under their domination."[82] Even if this was as far as the royal entourage got in subvening the patriarchate of Jerusalem, it portrays a governing group that shows no sign of the "breakdown" of Ganshof's famous study. But was it as far as they got?

On every count on which their testimony allows verification, these documents show themselves to be authentic and as accurate as the manifestly competent and

---

81 On Adalhard's head count and estimated daily food requirements of his monastery see above, chapter 8.1, note 32. Louis's capitulary defined the number of loaves of bread and so forth required for traveling parties on official business and shows indirectly how the Carolingian court estimated expenses based on head counts. See MGH Capit 1:291.30–37, no. 141.29, discussed in McCormick, "Diplomacy," 26–27.

82 Einhard, *Vita Karoli* 27, 31.18–32.2.

scrupulous early ninth-century envoys of the great Charles could make them. They would have been the basis for calculating the alms to be sent to Jerusalem to repair the great Christian shrines there, as discussed at Aachen in late 810. Were the donations ever sent, and, if sent, were they received? If received, were they disbursed for the purposes of repair that Charlemagne had clearly envisaged? The archaeological investigation of the ruins of Nea Church and the still-standing but jealously partitioned and guarded Holy Sepulcher shrine may yet shed indisputable light on one of the last and most remarkable projects of the greatest Carolingian, should datable evidence of construction from this period emerge. In any event, as we saw at the very beginning of this study, Einhard says plainly Charlemagne *was accustomed* to send money ("pecuniam mittere solebat") to the Christians of Jerusalem as well as to those of Carthage and Alexandria. This should imply multiple dispatches of wealth. Two tenth-century sources that were impervious to Carolingian propaganda confirm this interpretation of the testimony of the Basel roll and Einhard. Although he attributes the financing to a fellow Egyptian, Eutychius (Sa'id ibn Batriq [877–940]), the Melkite patriarch of Alexandria, attests that, around 813, the dome of the church of the Anastasis threatened to collapse. He says that the patriarch Thomas—the same man who dispatched the 807 embassy to Charlemagne—rebuilt that very structure whose measurements appear in the Basel roll and, we may believe, were submitted to Charlemagne in 810.[83] That this was the same patriarch of Jerusalem who received the embassy of Agamus and Roculf and that Eutychius appears to situate the reconstruction, or more precisely the Muslim complaints about it, early in the reign of Caliph al Mamun (813–833) offer a first confirmation that the repairs implied by the roll and the summary record of Charlemagne's 810 meeting actually occurred.

The second independent confirmation of Charlemagne's building expenditures in the Holy Land comes from Constantinople, where contacts with the Palestinian church had intensified in the ninth century, in no small part thanks to immigrants such as Michael the Synkellos, whose biography we have often cited. When the Byzantine emperor Constantine VII (945–959) discussed the genealogy of the contemporary king of Italy, he notes in passing that the king's ances-

---

83 Eutychius, *Annales*, Latin translation, PG 111:907–1156, here 1130C–1132A, where he claims that an Egyptian named Bocam supplied the money for rebuilding. That over a century later an Egyptian author should highlight the generosity of a compatriot and perhaps was unaware of the distant Western king's role does not seem problematic in view of the other striking concordances. Eutychius's story about the Dome of the Anastasis is not one of the many interpolations that occur in this work, since the end of it figures after a lacuna in the Sinai manuscript, which appears to be the author's original, ed. and trans. Breydy, *Das Annalenwerk des Eutychios von Alexandrien*, cited here from the German translation, 127–28. On the author and work, see Sidney H. Griffith, *ODB* 2:760. I am grateful to Prof. Deborah Tor for kindly checking the translations of these Arabic texts for me and confirming my understanding of them.

tor Charlemagne was a Frankish ruler "who, sending much money and abundant wealth to Palestine, built a very large number of monasteries."[84]

3. Date and Purpose of the Basel Roll

But perhaps the best evidence that Charlemagne did realize his plan to subsidize the shrines of the Holy Land lies in the continuing efforts by later patriarchs of Jerusalem to obtain more funds from the Franks and other westerners. Thus, although they never got past Constantinople, Michael the Synkellos and the Graptoi brothers were sent west around 812 to raise funds.[85] Around 852, George, a monk of the same Mar Saba that supplied so many patriarchs in this period, after traveling to North Africa and Spain, mulled pursuing his quest for funds in Frankland.[86] Louis the German provided subsidies for Palestinian Christians, surely in response to an Eastern plea, as did Pope John VIII and King Alfred the Great of Wessex.[87] In 881 Elias, patriarch of Jerusalem, dictated a remarkable letter of introduction for his Western fund-raisers. It is surely no accident that he starts out by appealing to Charlemagne's descendants to send subsidies to the Holy Land to defray his extensive building repair debts.[88] Obviously, despite the upheavals that affected ninth-century Europe, from Jerusalem's perspective, the Western well had not gone dry.

Such continued fund-raising seems to me to explain the otherwise puzzling fact that the surviving text of the Basel roll dates a couple of decades or so after the compilation of the original text. It is true that Western readers were much interested by the Holy Land, and works on it were often copied in the ninth century. But the physical format of the Basel roll assures us that this copy was not made for reasons of edification or scholarly information. Had that been the case, we would expect the text to have been transcribed in codex format, like the pilgrim

---

84 *De administrando imperio* 26.8–10, 108: "ὅστις χρήματα ἱκανὰ καὶ πλοῦτον ἄφθονον ἐν Παλαιστίνῃ ἀποστείλας, ἐδείματο μοναστήρια πάμπολλα." The participle is used circumstantially to clarify the main verb, in the usage that predominates in early medieval Greek. Compare, for example, R. Browning, *Medieval and Modern Greek* (London, 1969), 68–69. In my experience, "to build" without further qualifiers (lacking, e.g., "ἐκ τῶν θεμελίων" [from the foundations]) in medieval Greek often means to "rebuild" or "restore."

85 The Life seems to be slightly misleading, in that it claims Michael was being sent to Rome at papal request to help the pope defeat the Frankish Filioque, and in order to obtain money for the churches to pay off the Arabs (*Vita Michael syncelli* 6, 56.29–58.7; on the date, ibid., 10–13). We may surmise that theological quarrels took a back seat when it came to approaching the chief bankroller of such subsidies, the Frankish emperor.

86 McCormick, *Origins*, 928, R508.

87 For Louis the German, see below, note 94. For John VIII and Alfred, see, respectively, McCormick, *Origins*, 953, R664, compare 951, R648; 958, R694.

88 Discussed above, chapter 4.3; compare McCormick, *Origins*, 956–57, R684.

accounts and other treatises on Holy Land topography copied so assiduously by Carolingian-era scribes.[89]

A particular historical context must explain why such a technical document would have been copied in Frankland between about 825 and 850. More specifically, the historical context needs to explain why it was copied not as a literary text, but as a purely administrative document. To what administrative purpose could this text have been applied once it had served Charlemagne's original act of generosity toward the Christian institutions of the Holy Land?

A very plausible context does occur in that later period. In 826 Charlemagne's son and successor, Louis the Pious, received at Ingelheim an embassy headed by Dominic, abbot of the monastery on the Mount of Olives; in 831 he received one from Caliph al Mamun.[90] At some point in his reign, and quite possibly in connection with one or both of these diplomatic contacts, Louis dispatched an embassy to Jerusalem on an unspecified mission. We can easily surmise that it responded to pleas for financial support emanating from the Holy Land such as those which had come surely to his father and which would come to his son, Louis the German.[91] Indeed, a later ninth-century observer states explicitly that the Christians of the Holy Land had sought financial help from Louis the Pious

89 For instance, Adomnan's account of the pilgrimage of Arculf, which survives in at least four ninth-century copies, Brussels, KBR, 2921–22, formerly at Stavelot; Paris, B.N.F., lat. 13048, from Corbie; Vienna, Ö.N.B., cod. 458, from Salzburg; Zurich, Zentralbibliothek, Rheinau 73, from St. Gall.

90 *Annales regni Francorum* a. 826, 169; compare McCormick, *Origins*, 912, R396. *Annales Bertiniani* a. 831, 4, and Astronomer, *Vita Hludowici imperatoris* 46, 466.11–16; compare McCormick, *Origins*, 915, R420.

91 We learn about the embassy incidentally, in connection with a participant, Raganarius, who was a monk of Fleury. Raganarius had been sent with others to Jerusalem by Louis the Pious, and was later sent by the monastery of Fleury to defend its land holding in Aquitaine. There he confronted Stephen, a local noble, in an attempt to recover a vineyard that his monastery claimed. The noble grasped his sword and, according to the words our informant attributes to him, threatened Raganarius, referring to his Jerusalem mission. The key phrases are "Mittitur ad id enitendum Raganarius monachus, magnae religionis vir, qui olim ab imperatore Ludovico cum aliis Hierusolimam missus fuerat. . . . Advocatus vero una cum Raganario monacho, ad locum sessionis terrae juxta morem legis adveniens, praedictam vineam ad jus ecclesiae sancti Benedicti sua auctoritate revocare nitebatur. Proinde Stephanus, impatientia levis animi commotus, Raganario monacho ita, ut sedebat in equo propinquans, furibunde locutus est: 'Tibi dico, Raganari monache, qui trans mare Jerusalem [*sic*] requisisti, per hunc testor ensem, quando tu et ego ab hoc recesserimus loco, S. Benedictus ex hac vinea nullam habebit potestatem." Adrevald, *Miracula Benedicti* (BHL 1124) 1.38, 81; compare McCormick, *Origins*, 903, R336. The use of *requirere* may provide a hint of the mission's purpose. Elsewhere in the miracles, Adrevald uses it in the common sense of "ask" (1.18, 45 and 1.26, 60), which does seem to not fit here. Another possible meaning in this context of conflict would be "lay claim to"; hence Stephen would be implying that, though Raganarius had gone as far as Jerusalem to lay claims, he was not going any farther with the present claim if Stephen's sword had anything to say about it. The implication would be that Stephen (or Adrevald) knew something more about the business of the embassy, and it too involved somehow defending church property.

as from Charlemagne.[92] Is it not possible that a new copy of our roll was prepared for the same administrative purpose that the original had once fulfilled—the calculation and assembly of a subsidy for the churches of the Holy Land—by the son and pious successor who is otherwise known to have discharged faithfully the testamentary obligations imposed on him by his father toward the various shrines of Europe?[93] These circumstances explain the riddle of a copy in roll format executed in the 820s or so and fit nicely Bischoff's original paleographical dating of the manuscript. If the dating to the second half of the ninth century printed in Bischoff's paleographical catalog should in the end prove correct, then Louis the German's decision to respond to an Eastern request to raise funds for the Holy Land Christians provides an equally apt historical context for the production of a new copy of the roll in administrative format for administrative purposes.[94]

92 See below, note 94.

93 Einhard, *Vita Karoli* 33, 41.12–15; compare Innes, "Charlemagne's Will," 838–41.

94 Louis the German raised funds to "redeem the Christians of the promised land" by taxing each household in the royal fisc one penny. Notker the Stammerer treats this as an obligation inherited from Charlemagne and Louis the Pious and seems to think their descendant, his addressee Charles III, was aware of it: "Ad huius rei testimonium totam ciebo Germaniam, quę temporibus gloriosissimi patris vestri Hludowici de singulis hobis regalium possessionum singulos denarios reddere compulsa est, qui darentur ad redemptionem christianorum terram promissionis incolentium, hoc pro antiqua dominatione atavi vestri Karoli avique vestri Hludowici ab eo miserabiliter implorantium" (*Gesta* 2.9, 65.5–12). See McCormick, *Origins*, 925, R488; compare Borgolte, *Der Gesandtenaustausch*, 136–37.

Chapter Nine

. . . .

FROM AACHEN
TO JERUSALEM

So this set of exceptional documents surely comes from an exceptional milieu, the entourage of Charles the Great, at the culminating and near final point of its historical development. They throw unusual light on the long-term development of the Christian church of Palestine and illuminate important facets of its history, from the dimensions and fate of individual buildings to comparative trends in religious sociology around the Mediterranean. They offer, moreover, one of the most striking illustrations of the relentless drive to count, inventory, and register that so palpably informed Charlemagne's circle in the last decades of his reign, as the great king and his advisors improvised their way toward a new style of governance in early medieval Europe. For once, we can sense the outlines of Carolingian administration in action. Only the fact that they concerned a place far from the shores of Europe can explain their relative neglect by early medievalists.

It seems pretty clear why Charlemagne and his advisors organized in the way that they did the mission and the financial support we have concluded they probably sent. The idea that in order to offer adequate financial support it was necessary to establish and calculate the amount of support that was actually needed, appears a priori sensible to twenty-first-century minds. In the light of the fascinating discussion of early medieval numeracy as well as patterns of rulership, it is healthy for us to observe that eighth-century minds seem to have been sensitive to similar considerations.[1] The documents preserved on the Basel roll give us a precise idea of the sorts of inventories that, until now, we have known almost exclusively from the prescriptive sources ordering that they be compiled or from models that served as guidelines for their compilation. Specialists of early medieval administration will want to compare them closely with those prescriptive sources, various

---

1   For the former, see A. Murray, *Reason and Society in the Middle Ages* (Oxford, 1985), 141–57; for the latter, J. R. Davis, "Patterns of Power: Charlemagne and the Invention of Medieval Rulership" (PhD diss., Harvard University, 2007).

ecclesiastical polyptychs, as well as, for instance, the fossils of the Imperial Polyptych preserved in a later record for the Rhaetian Alps.[2]

Roof measurements and the detailed numbers of religious men and women in a faraway land, along with the names of their prelates: here we see a face of Charlemagne's imperial ambition which is at once strangely familiar and unexpected. The great king's drive to measure, count, and precisely delimit the personnel, numbers, resources, and needs of an important church is not confined to this record, as we can sense from the care that his former envoy and associate Leidrad of Lyons invested in preparing an inventory of the state of his own church. But the observation that this same drive to count and subsidize was exercised thousands of kilometers across the sea in the heart of the Abbasid caliphate is arresting. There has long been a healthy skepticism about the external echo of Charlemagne's imperial pretensions, beyond the angry Byzantines. Yet the way in which Einhard's testimony about Charlemagne's intervention on behalf of Holy Land Christians finds confirmation in the Basel roll means we must take seriously Einhard's statement that Charlemagne acted similarly on behalf of the churches of Alexandria and Carthage.

It is worth recalling that in describing the shrines of Jerusalem, the authors of the documents on the Basel roll bothered to add only a small number of non-biblical details about the origins of the buildings whose state is described. One such detail concerns precisely the great ruinous church on which Charlemagne's long-ago mission casts new light: "St. Mary Nea, which Emperor Justinian built" (line 11). One is tempted to hear in this rare historical comment the echo of discussions in Aachen about an earlier imperial tradition. There is no need to rehearse the details of the act by which, on Christmas Day 800, Charlemagne seized control of the title of Roman emperor. But the awareness of and ambition to renew the traditions of the Roman emperors are patent in the monuments that survive from his court. The poet who composed the epic on "Charles the King and Leo the Pope" implicitly and repeatedly compared Charlemagne with Justinian's successor through his artful imitation of Corippus's panegyric on Justin II's coronation.[3] The newly minted emperor's own seal trumpeted the slogan "Renewal of the Roman Empire" ("RENOVATIO ROMAN[I] IMP[ERII]") and portrayed the Frankish ruler with a likeness apparently inspired by Constantine's.[4] In 806 the royal writing office produced a document that then appeared decisive for the future of the new empire—the plan for the division of the realm after Charlemagne's decease.

2   Imperial Polyptych ("Reichsurbar"). See above, chapter 7.3, note 59.
3   C. Ratkowitsch, *Karolus Magnus—alter Aeneas, alter Martinus, alter Iustinus. Zur Intention und Datierung des "Aachener Karlsepos,"* Wiener Studien, Beiheft 24 (Vienna, 1997), 17–59.
4   P. E. Schramm, "Drei Nachträge zu den Metallbullen der Karolingischen und Sächsischen Kaiser," *DA* 24 (1968): 1–15, here 5–10, with Tafel II.

There the ruler of most of western Europe assumed a title that clearly echoed the later Roman empire of Theodosius and Justinian: "Emperor Caesar Charles, most unvanquished king of the Franks and rector of the Roman Empire, Pious, Fortunate Victor and Triumphator ever Augustus."[5]

Why Charlemagne wished to offer such a gift to the Christian church in the Holy Land may seem obvious. The great king had long made handsome benefactions to the churches of his empire, as we know from the substantial series of his surviving diplomas on their behalf and the record of specific gifts, for instance, to St. Peter's basilica in Rome.[6] Occasionally details survive about some of his acts of largess, for instance, the fifteen carts of gold and silk plundered from the Avars, which he distributed to the church and poor of his empire.[7] Generosity to God's churches was constantly enjoined on the king as a prime virtue of the Christian ruler.[8] His body was not long cold before scathing comments circulated publicly about his sexual excesses and complicated domestic life, and it is clear that Charlemagne had more than a few sins on his conscience.[9] As he prepared to meet his maker and account for his life, one can well imagine the king was eager to pile up whatever advantage charitable donations could contribute to that fearsome final reckoning. But prestigious and holy though it might be, Jerusalem was a long way from Aachen, or so it might appear.

We began this investigation with the statement of Charlemagne's close advisor and client, Einhard, that the king's distribution of alms extended across the sea:

> He was very dedicated to maintaining the poor, and to the disinterested generosity that the Greeks call "alms" [*eleimosina*], as is natural for someone

5   "Imperator Caesar Karolus rex Francorum invictissimus et Romani rector imperii pius felix victor ac triumphator semper augustus": *Divisio regni*, ed. A. Boretius, MGH Capit 1:126, apparatus. On the context of this title, see M. McCormick, *Eternal Victory: Triumphal Rulership in Late Antiquity, Byzantium, and the Early Medieval West*, 2nd ed. (Cambridge, 1990), 381, with further references.

6   The exceptional preservation circumstances for documents from Saint-Denis give a good idea of the scope and frequency of gifts to the most favored shrines: *DD Kar* 1: nos. 55, 87–88, 92, 101, etc., as listed in ibid., 486–89. On the occasion of his imperial coronation, Charlemagne offered St. Peter's Basilica, among other things, a silver altar and various gold objects, including a votive crown, chalice, and paten weighing 143 pounds (*Liber pontificalis*, Duchesne, 2:7.30–8.11). If the Roman pounds in question were the late Roman-Byzantine ones of 319 grams, then this part alone of the many gifts given on that occasion weighed in at 46.57 kilograms, which corresponds to well over half of the reported annual expenditures of the Jerusalem patriarchate.

7   From the "First Set of Northern Annals," that is, *Annales Nordhumbrani* 155.22–27, which preserve independent evidence from lost Frankish annals of excellent quality. See, for example, M. Lapidge, "Byrhtferth of Ramsey and the Early Sections of the Historia Regum attributed to Symeon of Durham," *Anglo-Saxon England* 10 (1982): 97–122, here 115–22.

8   See, for example, Cathwulf's letter to Charlemagne after the conquest of Italy, 503.23–24.

9   Masterfully delineated by P. E. Dutton, *The Politics of Dreaming in the Carolingian Empire* (Lincoln, Neb., 1994), 50–80.

who was attentive to do so not only in his homeland and in his own kingdom, but also across the sea in Syria and Egypt and Africa, where he had
learned that Christians were living in poverty. He took pity on their indigence, and was accustomed to send money to Jerusalem, Alexandria,
and Carthage.[10]

Rhetorically speaking, Einhard structures the sentence as a sort of amplification,
insofar as the first places Einhard mentions—Syria, Egypt, and Africa—are the
broader regions in which the three sees of Jerusalem, Alexandria, and Carthage
are situated, and Einhard names those sees in the same order as the regions in
which they lie. That order does not reflect church precedence of the three sees, for
by those lights Alexandria should have come first.[11] That Jerusalem figures at the
top of the list may reflect the emotive power of the site, which had elicited intrepid
religious travel even in the difficult years of the seventh century and which continued to do so in the Carolingian period.[12] As the birthplace of the Christian religion and the locus of Jesus Christ's sacrifice and resurrection, not to mention its
all-pervasive stature in the biblical thought that so pervaded Carolingian culture,
the Holy City naturally held a unique prestige and importance for early medieval
Christians.[13]

Some signs hint that the Holy City may have meant even more to the Frankish elite around 800. In the same period that he explored supporting the Christian
church of the Holy Land, Charlemagne introduced a new coin, known traditionally as the "portrait" or the "temple" type of silver penny. The obverse featured
the famous classicizing portrait of Charlemagne with the legend KAROLVS
IMP(ERATOR) AVG(VSTVS) or its variants. The other side features a schematic
representation of a building that to many modern eyes evokes a classical temple:
the columned structure appears to have triangular roof pediment and stands on
two steps. Through the columns, one can see a cross; another cross marks the peak
of the roof (see fig. 6).

There seems to be no good reason behind the rather fanciful identification
of this structure as a temple except that the design of rather different temples on
Roman coins might have inspired the Carolingian engraver.[14] Among plausible
explanations, the colonnaded structure has been thought to represent St. Peter's

10 Einhard, *Vita Karoli* 27, 31.18–25.

11 A. Papadakis and A. Kazhdan, "Pentarchy," *ODB* 3:1599–1600.

12 McCormick, *Origins of the European Economy: Communications and Commerce, A.D. 300–900*
(Cambridge, 2001), 147–49.

13 J. Prawer, "Jerusalem in the Christian and Jewish Perspectives of the Early Middle Ages," in
Gli Ebrei nell'alto medioevo, 2 vols., Settimane 26 (1980), 2:739–95.

14 P. Grierson, "Money and Coinage under Charlemagne," in *Karl der Grosse*, ed. W. Braunfels
(Düsseldorf, 1965–68), 1:501–36, at 519.

Basilica in Rome and to refer to Charlemagne's imperial coronation.[15] More convincingly, the coin's legend, XPICTIANA RELIGIO, has been connected with a passage in Einhard, written at least a few years after the new issue. He explains that Charlemagne built his splendid new palace chapel at Aachen—in which project Einhard himself seems to have played an important role—because he was steeped in *religio Christiana*.[16] On this interpretation, the templelike structure would therefore represent the entrance to the atrium in front of the palace chapel, although we know nothing certain about its appearance.[17]

Victor Elbern offered an attractive new theory, based on the historical context at Charlemagne's court and some striking visual parallels. Elbern's analysis of the iconography of chalices led him to explore the deeply symbolic conflation in patristic and early medieval thought of chalice and eucharistic sacrifice, baptismal fount, the place of Christ's resurrection, and eschatology. As he shows, this constellation of ideas, objects, and associations was particularly alive at Charlemagne's court. Elbern detects it in the ivory chalice associated with Lebuin (d. 780), the Anglo-Saxon missionary among the Frisians. The chalice's design links with the bronze chancels of the palace chapel at Aachen have long been recognized. The connections seem clear also in the famous images of the "fount of life" in the court gospel books of Godescalc and St. Medard of Soissons, whose symbolic representation is presented in an architectural structure that encompasses a rotunda and a cupola surmounted by a Greek cross. Finally, Elbern identified late antique schematic representations of the monument of Christ's tomb in a stone relief preserved at Dumbarton Oaks (see fig. 7) and on lead pilgrims'

15 M. Prou, *Les monnaies carolingiennes* (Paris, 1896), xi; contra, see P. Grierson, "Symbolism in Early Medieval Charters and Coins," in *Simboli e simbologie nell'alto medioevo*, 2 vols., Settimane 23 (1976), 2:601–30, at 628, who thinks a reference to St. Peter's unlikely since the coin type was introduced some years after the imperial coronation. Nevertheless, the imperial title itself was only introduced on the coinage at that same later date, and it is unclear to me why the delay should militate against a reference to Rome.

16 Einhard, *Vita Karoli* 26, 30.23–26: "Religionem Christianam, qua ab infantia fuerat inbutus, sanctissime et cum summa pietate coluit, ac propter hoc plurimae pulchritudinis basilicam Aquisgrani exstruxit. . . ." The contemporary biography of Ansegisus, abbot of Fontenelle, says that Charlemagne made him "exactor operum regalium in Aquisgrani palatio regio sub Einhardo abbate," *Gesta sanctorum patrum Fontanellensis* 13, 150.50–52. This has usually been understood to mean that Einhard was deeply involved in the building and decoration of the palace, including the chapel. See, for example, V. H. Elbern, "Einhard und die karolingische Goldschmiedekunst," in *Einhard: Studien zu Leben und Werk*, ed. H. Schefers, Arbeiten der Hessischen Historischen Kommission n.F. 12 (Darmstadt, 1997), 155–78, at 156–57. Contemporaries will have recognized that Einhard was also alluding to his own achievements in this passage. Given his apparent role in the classicizing artistic innovation of that milieu, we should consider that Einhard may also have been involved in the striking new iconography of the imperial portrait coin.

17 Grierson, "Money and Coinage under Charlemagne," 519, as tacitly modified in idem, "Symbolism," 628–30. However, the expression "Christiana religio" is not so rare as Grierson there (629) supposed. See below, note 22.

ampullas from the Holy Land that resemble, rather strikingly, the flattened structure schematically represented on Charlemagne's last coinage. And so Elbern proposed identifying the enigmatic "temple" on that coinage with the Holy Sepulcher, the very rotunda whose roof measurements would have been presented to Charlemagne late in 810.[18]

The exact date of the new coin type is uncertain. It titles Charlemagne "Imperator Augustus" and therefore dates between 25 December 800 and 28 January 814. Philip Grierson originally favored locating this issue between 806 and 814 since a series of capitularies from Christmas 805 to 808 seems to reflect the sort of difficulties that previously had attended the introduction and acceptance of a new coin type.[19] Allowing specifically authorized exceptions, production of the coins at issue was explicitly restricted to the palace or, perhaps, royal fiscal centers (*ad curtem*), which restriction Grierson insightfully connected with the new type's high artistic standard of realistic portraiture, and the distinguished metalwork at

18   V. H. Elbern, "Der eucharistische Kelch im frühen Mittelalter," *Zeitschrift des deutschen Vereins für Kunstwissenschaft* 17 (1963): 1–76 and 117–88; idem, "Einhard." Grierson discussed this possibility with Elbern at Spoleto in 1975, as recorded in the "Discussione" of Grierson's paper (Grierson, "Symbolism," 632–34), but did not accept it in subsequent publications. R. Schumacher-Wolfgarten, "XPICTIANA RELIGIO: Zu einer Münzprägung Karls des Grossen," *Jahrbuch für Antike und Christentum* 37 (1994): 122–41, came to essentially the same conclusions as Elbern without making any reference to Elbern's more searching investigation. B. Kluge simply dismisses this identification as "improbable" in "Nomen imperatoris und Christiana religio. Das Kaisertum Karls des Grossen und Ludwigs des Frommen im Licht der numismatischen Quellen," in *799. Kunst und Kultur der Karolingerzeit: Karl der Grosse und Papst Leo III. in Paderborn; Beiträge zum Katalog der Ausstellung Paderborn, 1999*, ed. C. Stiegemann and M. Wemhoff (Mainz, 1999), 82–90, at 83. Unaware of Elbern's work, E. Robert, J. L. Desnier, and J. Belaubre used some of the same evidence to construe the coin image as the fountain of life in the sense of a baptistry: "La fontaine de vie et la propagation de la véritable religion chrétienne," *Revue belge de numismatique* 134 (1988): 89–106.

19   MGH Capit 1:116.27, no. 40.28 (AD 803), suggests problems with counterfeiters at that time, which perhaps encouraged the move to a new coin type. See also MGH Capit 1:125.19–22, no. 44.18 (Thionville, 805), which aims to thwart counterfeiters by restricting minting to "our palace" unless Charlemagne should authorize otherwise but which specifies that pennies that have been issued "now" ("illi tamen denarii qui modo monetati sunt"; this is the temporal meaning of the word *modo* in Charlemagne's capitularies, as I verified in the Brepols online concordance of the eMGH5) are still to remain legal tender. Restricted locales of minting and acceptance problems appear in 808. See MGH Capit 1:138.40, no. 51.6 (a list of headings only: *De moneta*) and a record of that same meeting (ibid., 140.10–11, no. 52.7): "De monetis, ut in nullo loco moneta percutiatur nisi ad curtem; et illi denarii palatini mercantur et per omnia discurrant," in a way that seems to indicate that the new palatine coins were already in circulation. Finally, a meeting at Aix in 809 specifies that Charlemagne's officials would lose their office if anyone in their jurisdiction rejects a penny that is pure and of good weight (ibid., 152.7–12, no. 63.7; compare the headings for this same meeting, 150.15, no. 62.7). This provision seems to echo the measures decreed at Frankfurt in 794, which were expressly intended to sanction the introduction and acceptance of new coins ("isti novi denarii," ibid., 74.31–38, no. 28.5) and which scholars generally connect with the introduction of the previous type of Charlemagne's coinage, Class 3 (Grierson, "Money and Coinage under Charlemagne," 509–11).

FIGURE 6
Charlemagne's XPICTIANA RELIGIO coin
issue: reverse showing "temple." Paris, Bibliothèque
Nationale de France, Cabinet des Médailles,
Prou no. 983 (photo courtesy of the Cabinet
des Médailles)

court in those years as well as with the relatively small numbers associated with palace issues in other reigns.[20]

The legend of the new coin type, "Xpictiana Religio," has struck some by its Greek lettering, but the use of Greek letters for the name of Christ is quite ordinary in contemporary Carolingian manuscripts.[21] It would be surprising if it had any special significance. Although it has been judged "rare" in pre-online scholarship, the expression "Christian religion" appears in Christian Latin right from the start, since Tertullian (fl. ca. 200) used it.[22] The *Cetedoc Library of Christian*

20 Grierson, "Money and Coinage under Charlemagne," 524–27. P. Grierson and M. Blackburn represent a change of opinion. See *Medieval European Coinage* (Cambridge, 1986), 1:208–9. Although they still allow that the new coins may have begun in 808, they assign them to 812–14 on the basis of their extreme rarity ("about thirty specimens have been recorded," ibid., 209) and a possible link with the recognition of Charlemagne's imperial status by the Byzantine emperor. Compare P. Grierson, "The Carolingian Empire in the Eyes of Byzantium," in *Nascita dell'Europa ed Europa carolingia: un'equazione da verificare*, 2 vols., Settimane 27 (1981): 2:885–916, at 911 n. 49. The latter consideration appears to me less than compelling, given Charlemagne's general lack of deference toward his Eastern rivals, palpable in the contemptuous outbursts of the *Opus Caroli regis*, his unhesitating absorption of their former territories in Italy and Istria, and the war he fought with them over Venice. J. Lafaurie offers a stronger argument by ingeniously calculating the average surviving coins per annum for the reign of Charlemagne and the first years of Louis the Pious. This, he argues, would indicate that the twenty-nine surviving coins of Charlemagne's final type were issued only for about 1.7 years, that is, after the Byzantine recognition. However, the apparent reference to the continuing circulation of the previous type in the capitulary of Thionville of 805 (above, previous note) indicates that the earlier coinage was not demonetized. If the old coins still circulated in the period when the portraiture pennies were issued, this would have lessened demand for the new coins at the same time that supply, in terms of the places where they could be made, would have been severely limited. In other words, the logic that one can deduce the duration of production of the portrait issue by the number of surviving specimens fails if the new coin type did not represent the totality of coins then in use: J. Lafaurie, "Les monnaies impériales de Charlemagne," *CRAI* (1978): 154–72.

21 W. M. Lindsay, *Notae Latinae: An Account of Abbreviation in Latin MSS. of the Early Minuscule Period (c. 700–850)* (Cambridge, 1915), 402–4.

22 See above, note 17. Tertullian, *Aduersus Marcionem*: "religionis Christianae sacramentum" (4.3.1, 548.14); "documenta Christianae religionis" (4.4.2, 550.8); *De ieiunio aduersus psychicos*: "si

FIGURE 7
Byzantine stone relief believed
to represent the shrine of the
Holy Sepulcher (photo cour-
tesy of Dumbarton Oaks, inv.
BZ.1938.56)

Latin Texts-5 shows that Augustine frequently wrote the term, particularly in Charlemagne's supposed favorite, the *City of God*. Bede used it too.[23] In Charlemagne's entourage, the term was favored by the *Opus Caroli regis*, authored chiefly by Theodulf of Orleans, with contributions from Alcuin.[24] The meaning is equivalent to the English "Christian religion." Generally speaking, it seems to lack the common monastic connotation that attaches to *religio* by itself in this period. The expression refers to proper belief and practice of the tenets of Christianity by the population and its rulers.

Wherever we situate the beginning of the new coinage between 806 and 812, the new design went into effect during the period when the imperial court was engaged in organizing an important subvention for the Holy Sepulcher, as indeed

---

magis ad religionem sapit Christianam" (10.8, 1268.25). Another early African father used the term four times: Arnobius, *Aduersus nationes* 1.2, 2.11–12; 1.3, 4.14; 3.1, 159.9, and 3.7, 165.7–8.

23 See Augustine, for example, *De ciuitate Dei* 2.6, 39.28; 10.32, 310.47; 17.4, 556.47, etc.; Bede, *Explanatio Apocalypsis* 2.8, PL 93:156B.

24 *Opus Caroli regis* 1:655, s.v. "religio." A few examples from Alcuin: *Ep.* 16, 141, 213, 280, respectively, 43.1, 223.20, 354.7, 438.1; compare his *Vita Richarii Centulensis* (BHL 7223) 1 and 12, 390.3 and 396.17.

for the entire church of the Holy Land. Christians had long focused on Jerusalem as a symbol of the most central mysteries of their faith, and as the physical place of memory of those mysteries. This fascination was alive in Carolingian culture also, as was the potential tension between the spiritualized understanding of Jerusalem as a state of mind and religious disposition and the magnetic power of the physical place of salvation history that we can see in Carolingian pilgrimage and religious settlement in the Holy Land.[25] It has indeed been thought that, even if the church of San Vitale in Ravenna may have suggested the architectural details of Charlemagne's palace chapel in Aachen, the symbolic model was the rotunda of the church of the Resurrection in Jerusalem.[26] This makes sense in historical terms. San Vitale is a beautiful structure, but it is not particularly significant from a theological point of view, whereas the church of the Resurrection might well be reckoned the preeminent shrine of the Christian religion. In a mental world that conflated the scenes of the Old and New Testament and relocated them to the shrine of the Resurrection, one can imagine the appeal of this model to a king whose courtiers hailed him as a new David and a new Solomon.[27] Indeed, if Alcuin knew his benefactor and royal master, he played exactly on this theme for the king's ears, for he called Aachen the Jerusalem in which Solomon was building a new temple.[28] In other words, the structure that symbolized Christian religion as Charlemagne was promoting it in his territories on his final issue of coins could well have reflected his palatine chapel at Aachen at the same time that it echoed its spiritual model, the Holy Sepulcher in Jerusalem. Charlemagne had just completed building the one, and was in the process of organizing needed repairs and subventions for the other at the time that the new coin was issued. But whatever

25 Prawer, "Jerusalem."

26 See the discussion and further references in H. K. Siebigs, "Neuere Untersuchungen der Pfalzkapelle zu Aachen," in *Einhard: Studien zu Leben und Werk*, ed. H. Schefers, Arbeiten der Hessischen Historischen Kommission, n.F., 12 (Darmstadt, 1997), 95–137, here 108–9. S. Schütte, "Der Aachener Thron," in *Krönungen: Könige in Aachen. Geschichte und Mythos*, ed. M. Kramp. 2 vols. (Mainz, 2000), 213–22, argues from details of the chapel's throne that it dates from Charlemagne's time, possessed a relic-like character, and may have incorporated materials from Jerusalem; he asserts that the dendrodating that connected the throne with Otto I must be abandoned on the basis of new dendrochronological and radiocarbon investigations whose results he will publish in a future study. I am grateful to Prof. Arnoud-Jan A. Bijsterveld for bringing this study to my attention.

27 For the conflation of the Old and New Testaments in the Holy Sepulcher church, see Prawer, "Jerusalem," 765–68. On Charlemagne and David, see H. H. Anton, *Fürstenspiegel und Herrscherethos in der Karolingerzeit*, Bonner historische Forschungen 32 (Bonn, 1968), 420–22.

28 Alcuin was politely demurring on Charlemagne's invitation to join him on campaign, emphasizing that he preferred to hear Solomon's wisdom in the city of peace, one of the traditional etymologies of the name of Jerusalem: ". . . et liceat mihi . . . in Hierusalem optatae patriae, ubi templum sapientissimi Salomonis arte Deo construitur, adsistere amabili conspectui vestro. . . ." (*Ep.* 145, 235.5–8). In this instance, the identification of Aachen and Jerusalem was prompted by a biblical allusion in the (lost) letter of Charlemagne to which Alcuin was responding (234.27–36).

the exact referent of the church on the coin, the Holy Land resonance of the sanctuary at the center of Charlemagne's exercise of power helps underscore the particular prestige that the distant shrine enjoyed at his court.

Beyond whatever pangs of conscience or fear may have gnawed at Charlemagne's ruminations about divine judgment at the end of his violent and egregiously sexual life, a last spiritual development may have helped turn Carolingian eyes toward the distant Holy Land. The Christians had adopted and adapted the Jewish eschatological beliefs that associated the Valley of Jehoshaphat and the Mount of Olives with the return of the Messiah and the Last Judgment. The expectation that Jerusalem would play a prominent role on the Last Day was deeply engrained in Christian thought.[29] One of the few non-hagiographical texts translated from Greek into Latin around 700 was an eschatological treatise attributed to Methodius. It prophesied how the last Roman emperor would go up to Jerusalem, take control once again of Golgotha—then located in the shrine of the Holy Sepulcher—place his crown on the True Cross, and hand his kingdom over to God before expiring and launching the end of the world.[30] Remarkably, four copies of this Latin translation survive from the eighth century alone and testify to the text's appeal in Carolingian religious circles.[31] An abbreviated version that seems tailored to northwestern Europe has even been connected with the preparations for Charlemagne's ill-fated invasion of Muslim Spain in 778.[32] The location of the Frankish monastery on the Mount of Olives presumably was not unrelated to the eschatological resonance of the site. Somebody at Charlemagne's court certainly was thinking about the Last Days. Seventeenth-century records of the mosaics of the Aachen chapel show that the iconography of the twenty-four Elders of the Apocalypse dominated the cupola before the nineteenth-century mosaics

29 Wilkinson, *Jerusalem Pilgrims before the Crusades*, 2nd ed. (Warminster, 2002), 312–13, 333; Prawer, "Jerusalem," 779–81 and 789–94.

30 Pseudo-Methodius, *Apocalypse* 14.2–6, 1:187–91. It is tempting to suspect that the unusually hurried mission of Zachary to Jerusalem early in 800, and his return with the keys of the Tomb and Calvary—the Latin term for Golgotha—in December 800 might have some connection with this cluster of beliefs (see *Annales regni Francorum* a. 800, 112), not to mention Einhard's claim that Harun al Rashid granted to Charlemagne that exactly the Holy Sepulcher might be "ascribed to his power" (ut illius potestati adscriberetur, concessit; *Vita Karoli* 16, 19.22). Compare Wilkinson, *Jerusalem Pilgrims*, 362–63, on the location of Golgotha within the shrine. The possible connection has also struck H. Möhring: see below, note 32.

31 In addition to which over two hundred manuscripts preserve the Latin text: Pseudo-Methodius, *Apocalypse* 1:19; for Paris, B.N.F., nouv. acq. lat. 1595, a fragmentary ninth-century manuscript which once belonged to Tours, see M. Laureys and D. Verhelst, "Pseudo-Methodius, Revelationes: Textgeschichte und kritische Edition. Ein Leuven-Groninger Forschungsprojekt," in *The Use and Abuse of Eschatology in the Middle Ages*, ed. W. Verbeke, D. Verhelst, and A. Welkenhuysen, Mediaevalia Lovanensia, ser. 1, Studia 14 (Louvain, 1988), 112–36, here 135, no. 190.

32 Möhring, "Karl der Grosse und die Endkaiser-Weissagung. Der Sieger über den Islam kommt aus dem Westen," 12 and 14.

that today's visitor sees.[33] Further eschatological tendencies have been detected in chronological calculations of the eighth century.[34]

Whether or not Alcuin wrote a surviving commentary on the Apocalypse, another witness to concern with the end of time in Charlemagne's entourage has garnered less attention than it deserves.[35] The king was well known for his ability to attract outstanding scholars; we get some inkling of the discussions that took place there from the scholars' written responses to subsequent queries that the king (or his secretary) addressed to them or that the court circulated more generally. Alcuin's correspondence offers well-known examples; other such consultations treated questions as diverse as the nature of shadows and nothingness as well as broader liturgical issues, for example, the correct forms of baptism.[36] Another set of questions and responses that survive from the royal entourage concerns Daniel, one of the Bible's important apocalyptic books. The court-linked manuscript that preserves it describes the little work as a "Book on diverse small questions with his responses, which Lord King Charles commanded be transcribed from the exemplar of Peter the Archdeacon."[37] Since the manuscript contains Peter of Pisa's grammatical treatise, apparently dedicated to the king, it is generally believed that Peter compiled the exegetical questions and answers, although his title of archdeacon has suggested that he composed the biblical treatise only after returning to Italy.[38] The work simply abridges and recasts in question-and-answer

33 See, for example, Kluge, "Nomen imperatoris," 157.

34 R. Landes, "Lest the Millennium Be Fulfilled: Apocalyptic Expectations and the Pattern of Western Chronography 100–800 C.E.," in *The Use and Abuse of Eschatology in the Middle Ages*, 137–211, here 168–201.

35 On the question of Alcuin's commentary on the Apocalypse see, with further references, Bullough, *Alcuin: Achievement and Reputation* (Leyden, 2004), 10.

36 Alcuin, for example, *Ep.* 136, 205–10; 149, 242–45. On *Ep.* 136, see Bullough, *Alcuin*, 46–47. The Carolingian debate on the nature of nothingness seems to have begun at court as well, and certainly involved court figures: M. L. Colish, "Carolingian Debates over *nihil* and *tenebrae*: A Study in Theological Method," *Speculum* 59 (1984): 757–95, here 759. On baptism, see Keefe, *Water and the Word*, 1:52–65.

37 "Incipit liber de diversis quaestiunculis cum responsionibus suis. Quem jussit domnus rex Carolus transcribere ex authentico Petri archidiaconi" (PL 96:1347B). See the discussion of these lines in P. Meyvaert, "Medieval Notions of Publication: The 'Unpublished' *Opus Caroli regis contra synodum* and the Council of Frankfurt (794)," *Journal of Medieval Latin* 12 (2002): 78–89, at 82–83. Elias A. Lowe (*Codices latini antiquiores*, 10: no. 1553) assigned the manuscript Brussels, KBR II 2572, to Charlemagne's command and very possibly the court. Bischoff doubted that it was the original prepared for the court library before 800 but allowed that it was certainly a copy of that original (which for our purposes comes down to the same thing) and probably from the broader court circle, made shortly after 800. See Bischoff, *Mittelalterliche Studien. Ausgewählte Aufsätze zur Schriftkunde und Literaturgeschichte* (Stuttgart, 1981), 3:154 n. 24, compare 158 n. 45; and Bischoff, *Katalog der festlandischen Handschriften des neunten Jahrhunderts (mit Ausnahme der wisigotischen)*, vol. 1, *Aachen-Lambach* (Wiesbaden, 1998), 164, no. 755.

38 M. Manitius, *Geschichte*, 1:452–53; compare M. Gorman, "Peter of Pisa and the Quaestiunculae Copied for Charlemagne in Brussels II 2572," *RBén* 110 (2000): 238–60.

format Jerome's Commentary on Daniel, following Jerome's words very closely indeed, if we may judge by the available edition. It starts out with the question of which were the four kingdoms that Nabochodonosor saw in his dream—a classic apocalyptic passage—and reproduces Jerome's judgment that, at the end of time, nothing is weaker than the Roman Empire.[39] Peter's compilation later returns to the idea that the end of the Roman Empire coincides with the end of the world, when ten kings will divide the empire and one will triumph over the others; he repeats Jerome's identification of the thrones that Daniel beheld (Daniel 7:9) with the twenty-four thrones of the Apocalypse (Apoc. 4–5).[40]

The title of this recycling of Jerome was copied in impressive capitals and explicitly links Charlemagne with the transcription; the questions suggest that biblical readings at court were sparking an interest in the possibility that the end of time was approaching, a suggestion not weakened by the decision to decorate the cupola of the spanking new chapel at Aachen with a scene from the Apocalypse. Indeed, one scholar who tracked eschatological thought in the eighth century went so far as to suggest that an effort to stave off the end of time motivated Charlemagne's imperial coronation.[41] In any case, it seems clear that the Holy City's association with the Last Days only strengthened royal interest in the place amid thoughts that the end of time was approaching in the opening decade of the ninth century.

If the spiritual attraction of Jerusalem seemed irresistible from many points of view, there were also good political reasons for the mighty king to be involved there. Not least was the competition with Byzantium. Charlemagne may have relished the opportunity to outdo the Eastern emperors in their own backyard. Certainly, his scorn for their pretension to care for churches within their kingdom seems palpable in the words of contempt about their roofless churches that we have already noted.[42] By taking the initiative of financing one of the most

---

39 Peter of Pisa, *Liber de diversis quaestiunculis* 1, PL 96:1347C, which abbreviates Jerome, *Commentarii in Danielem* 1.2, 794.399–795.406. Another work whose influence on the Carolingian court it might be interesting to investigate is Bede's *In Ezram et Neemiam prophetas allegorica expositio*, which sees in these biblical texts prophetic foreshadowings of the work of Christian kings in restoring Christian religion and its shrines, in anticipation of the Last Day, and even uses *Christiana religio* in the latter context: "Haec est namque maxima in hoc saeculo et in futuro laetitia iustorum perfectum esse opus ecclesiae conuersis etiam gentibus qui olim resistebant ad adiuuandum eius statum et confirmandam per orbem uniuersum pacem Christianae religionis" (2, 306.756–60). Compare, for example, "Haec ergo Artarxerses scribens Ezrae et amorem quem erga cultum religionis habebat litteris comprehendens patenter expressit quid futuris temporibus christiani reges deuotionis habituri quid erga fidem ueritatis essent acturi" (2, 318.1231–35).

40 *Liber de diversis quaestiunculis* 42, 1353D–1354A; compare Jerome, *Comm. in Danielem* 2.7, 844.592–607.

41 J. Gil, "Los terrores del año 800," in *Actas del simposio para el estudio de los códices del "Commentario al Apocalipsis" de Beato de Liébana* (Madrid, 1978), 215–47.

42 *Opus Caroli* cited above, chapter 7.3, note 52.

significant shrines of Christendom, a shrine that was still heavily staffed by Greek speakers and in close intellectual and personal contact with Constantinople, it is hard to avoid the impression that Charlemagne and his entourage were making a statement about how they viewed their own place in the world. The fact that the Frankish king's largess to the shrines of Palestine was still reckoned memorable in the imperial palace on the Bosporus more than a century later assures us that Charlemagne's intervention in the Holy Land did not go unnoticed there in his own time.[43] That the financial support for the Christian establishment necessitated good relations with the caliph in Baghdad was acknowledged by Einhard as the main reason Charlemagne sent legations to Mesopotamia seeking the good will of the Abbasid ruler.[44] But it cannot have hurt that during precisely these years, Charlemagne was at war with the two principal adversaries of Harun al Rashid, the Byzantine emperor and the Umayyad rulers of Spain, a continuing thorn in the side of the Abbasid dynasty, which had driven them from the Levant.

All the motivation in the world of course would have had little effect were it materially impossible for the king to be in communication with the Christian community of the Holy Land, much less organize the shipment of wealth there. In this respect too the constellation of Mediterranean shipping and communications had recently grown more favorable, for it was just in Charlemagne's lifetime that the rhythm of shipping between western Europe and the Islamic world had picked up. Around 800, Venetian ships seem to have been sailing to the Holy Land every year. The modeling of the first San Marco on the shrine of the Resurrection testifies to the same density of links in the early ninth century.[45] New archaeological evidence from Comacchio, Venice's early rival, might suggest a further set of links with the eastern Mediterranean.[46]

So the factors that allowed and encouraged the great king to intervene at the distant end of the Mediterranean were many and diverse. But the decision to investigate the situation in the Holy Land and bring succor to Christians there was Charles's. This was yet another way in which this most exceptional of early medieval kings set the pattern not only for his immediate offspring and successors but for all kings to come through the centuries of Europe's Middle Ages.

43   See above, chapter 8.2, note 84.
44   *Vita Karoli* 27, 31.25–32.2: "... ob hoc maxime transmarinorum regum amicitias expetens, ut Christianis sub eorum dominatu degentibus refrigerium aliquod ac relevatio proveniret."
45   On both these points, McCormick, *Origins*, 526–27 and 425, respectively.
46   S. Gelichi, "Tra Comacchio e Venezia. Economia, società e insediamenti nell'arco nord adriatico durante l'Alto Medioevo," in *Uomini, territorio e culto dall'Antichità all'Alto Medioevo. Genti nel Delta, da Spina a Comacchio. Catalogo della mostra. 16 dicembre–14 ottobre 2006* (Ferrara, 2007), 365–86, for example, 383.

Part Three

. . . .

TEXTS, TRANSLATION, AND TEXTUAL COMMENTARY

. . . .

Chapter Ten

THE BASEL ROLL:
CRITICAL EDITION AND TRANSLATION

T HIS IS A CRITICAL EDITION, that is to say that I have endeavored to produce a text that goes beyond the ink signs preserved on the parchment of
the Basel roll and offers clearly marked restorations and emendations to the damaged or erroneous elements of this very unusual text. Abbreviations are resolved
silently, the *ę* has been printed as ae, for it originally represented those letters in
ligature, and I have modernized the punctuation, capitalization, and marked para-
graphs.[1] Details of all restorations and other major editorial decisions are laid out
in the textual commentary (chapter 11).

The translation has hewed as closely to the Latin—in meaning, not in the
letter—as is commensurate with accurate rendering and good English. Given the
differences between Latin and English, the line indications in the latter sometimes can only be approximate. Jerusalem shrines whose general or precise locations are known can be located on map 1, as indicated in the footnotes. For those
outside of Jerusalem, see map 2, as noted.

Editorial Conventions

<abc>	restored text
**	lacuna (in this case, of approximately two letters or spaces)
[abc]	erasure
\a/	text added between the lines
abc	letters that are damaged but nevertheless identifiable with certainty
<u>abc</u>	letters that appear probable but not as unambiguous as they seem to have been in de Rossi's time

---

1   For details of the original, see above, chapter 6.2 and the roll itself, figures 1 and 2, and poster.

1 | *Breue* commemoratorii de illis casis Dei uel monasteriis qui sunt in sancta
2 ciuitate Hierusalem uel in circuitu e<i>us, | et de episcopis et presbiteris,
   diaconibus et monachis, uel cuncto clero per illa loca sancta Dei seruientibus,
3 seu monas | teria puellarum.

   Primum, in sancto sepulchro Domini: presbiteri viiii; diaconi xiiii;
4 subdiaconi vi; clerici cano | nici xxiii; custodes quos fragelites uocant xiii;
5 monachi xli; qui cum caereis antecedunt patr<i> | archam xii; ministri
   patriarchae xvii; praepositi ii; conputarii ii; notarii ii; custodes qui assidu<e>**
6 | praeuident sepulchrum Domini presbiteri ii; in sancto Caluario i, ad calicem
7 Domini ii, ad sanctam crucem et sudarium <·>i, | diaconus i; sincelo qui sub
8 patriarcha omnia corrigit i; cellerarii ii; thesaurarius i; qui fontes cus | todit i;
   portarii viiii. Sunt in summo cl, excepto ospitales iii.

9 | In sancta Sion: inter presbiteris et clericis xvii, excepto Deo sacratas et
10 inclusas ii. In sancto Petro, ubi ipse glorio | sus plorauit, inter presbiteris et clericis
   v. In Pretorio v.

DOCUMENT I

| An inventory memorandum[2] of God's houses and monasteries that are 1
in the holy city of Jerusalem and its environs, | and of the bishops, and the 2
priests, deacons and monks, and the entire clergy serving God in those holy
places, and the monas | teries of women.[3] 3

First, in the Holy Sepulcher of the Lord:[4] 9 priests; 14 deacons; 6 subdeacons;   1
| 23 canonical clerics; 13 guardians whom they call "whip-men" (*fragelites*); 41   4
monks; 12 [individuals] who precede the | patriarch with candles; 17 servants 5
of the patriarch; 2 provosts (*praepositi*);[5] 2 accountants; 2 notaries; guards who
continually | watch over the Lord's Tomb: 2 priests; at Holy Calvary: 1; at the 6
Lord's Chalice: 2; at the Holy Cross and the Face-Cloth: 1;[6] | 1 deacon; *synkellos* 7
who manages everything under the patriarch: 1; 2 cellarers; 1 treasurer; 1 who
takes care of the founts; | 9 porters. All told, there are 150, except for the 3 8
hostels.[7]

| In Holy Zion:[8] 17 priests and clerics, plus 2 recluse nuns. In St. Peter's, where 9   2, 3
that glorious | one wept:[9] 5 priests and clerics. In the Praetorium:[10] 5.   10   4

---

2   For this translation of *Breue commemoratorii*, see chapter 11, textual commentary.

3   For the expression *monasteria puellarum*, see chapter 11, textual commentary.

4   Map 1. For an overview of the history and archaeology of the complex surrounding the Tomb of the Lord, see J. Wilkinson, *Jerusalem Pilgrims before the Crusades*, 2nd ed. (Warminster, 2002), 361–68; K. Bieberstein and H. Bloedhorn, *Jerusalem: Grundzüge der Baugeschichte vom Chalkolithikum bis zur Frühzeit der osmanischen Herrschaft*, Beihefte zum Tübinger Atlas des Vorderen Orients, Reihe B, Geisteswissenschaften 100 (Wiesbaden, 1994), 2:183–217. For discussion of its staff and measurements at this time, see above, chapters 2.2 and 5.2, respectively.

5   In Carolingian parlance, the meaning of *praepositus* could range from the head of a religious community to the person overseeing the business affairs of a church. It is unclear what exactly the duties of the two *praepositi* of the Holy Sepulcher might have been, but their place in the list hints that it may have been more toward the latter than the former meaning.

6   The text implies that this was one priest.

7   Latin *hospitales*. See the discussion of this term and its meaning in this period in chapter 4.3.

8   Wilkinson, *Jerusalem Pilgrims*, 350–53; Bieberstein and Bloedhorn, *Jerusalem: Grundzüge der Baugeschichte*, 2:118–27; A. Külzer, *Peregrinatio graeca in Terram Sanctam: Studien zu Pilgerführern und Reisebeschreibungen über Syrien, Palästina und den Sinai aus byzantinischer und metabyzantinischer Zeit* (Frankfurt am Main, 1994), 186; Aist, *Christian Topography*, 139–48; as well as the references above, chapter 5.2, notes 33–35. For the dimensions of the shrine, see below, lines 56–57, and the discussion above, chapter 5.2. See also map 1.

9   Approximately located in the vicinity of the modern church of St. Peter in Gallicantu (see map 1). See Wilkinson, *Jerusalem Pilgrims*, 291, under "Caiaphas, House of"; Bieberstein and Bloedhorn, *Jerusalem: Grundzüge der Baugeschichte*, 3:414–15; and Külzer, *Peregrinatio graeca*, 216–17.

10   The location is controverted: Wilkinson, *Jerusalem Pilgrims*, 339; Bieberstein and Bloedhorn, *Jerusalem: Grundzüge der Baugeschichte*, 3:418–20. Among Greek pilgrims, Epiphanius alone locates the Praetorium close to Holy Zion, as could be the case here (Külzer, *Peregrinatio graeca*, 217).

11 | In sancta Maria Noua quod Iustinianus imperator extruxit, xii; in sancta
12   Tathelea i; in sancto Georgio ii; in sancta Maria, ubi nata | fuit, in Probatici
v, inclusas Deo sacratas xxv; in sancto Stephano, ubi sepultus fuit, clerici ii,
leprosi xv.

13 | In ualle Iosafath, in uilla quae dicitur Gethsemani, ubi sancta Maria sepulta
14   fuit, ubi sepulchrum eius est uenerabilis, | inter presbiteris et clericis xiii, monachi
15   vi, Deo sacratas inter inclusas et ibidem seruientes xv; in sancto Legontio |
presbiter i; in sancto Iacobo i; in sancto Quaranta iii; in sancto

In St. Mary Nea, which Emperor Justinian built, 12;[11] in St. Tathelea, 1;[12] in St. George, 2;[13] in St. Mary, where she was born, | at the Sheep Pool, 5;[14] 25 nun recluses; in St. Stephen, where he was buried, 2 clerics, 15 lepers.[15]

In the valley of Jehoshaphat, in the country place[16] that is called Gethsemane, where holy Mary was buried, where her venerable tomb is:[17] | 13 priests and clerics, 6 monks, 15 nuns including recluses and those who serve there; in St. Leontius:[18] | 1 priest; in St. James: 1;[19] | St. Forty:[20] 3; in St.

11 For the Nea Church of St. Mary, see map 1. See also Wilkinson, *Jerusalem Pilgrims*, 332, under "New St. Mary." The Basel roll offers the last mention of this shrine. Bieberstein and Bloedhorn (*Jerusalem: Grundzüge der Baugeschichte*, 2:292–97) assess its situation about 808 very optimistically. For the great shrine's dimensions as revealed by the Basel roll, see below, lines 50–52, and above, chapter 5.2.

12 Holy Land topographers universally correct saint "Tathelea" to "Thalelaeus," whose monastery Justinian "renewed" (Procopius, *Aedificia* 5.9.1, 4:169.9–10) and which a liturgical feast seems to locate on Zion. See Bieberstein and Bloedhorn, *Jerusalem: Grundzüge der Baugeschichte*, 3:422; compare Milik, "Notes d'épigraphie, IX," 360–61, no. 9. Wilkinson, *Jerusalem Pilgrims*, has no gazetteer entry for "Thaleleus" as he writes it, but see ibid., 353, under "Sion." This appears to be the last mention of this church.

13 Wilkinson, *Jerusalem Pilgrims*, 304, under "George, St. in Jerusalem"; J. T. Milik, "La topographie de Jérusalem vers la fin de l'époque byzantine," *Mélanges de l'Université Saint-Joseph* 37 (Beirut, 1960–61): 127–89, at 138–41; Milik, "Notes d'épigraphie, IX," 567–68. This seems to be the last mention of this church.

14 Map 1. See Wilkinson, *Jerusalem Pilgrims*, 346–48, "Sheep Pool"; Bieberstein and Bloedhorn, *Jerusalem: Grundzüge der Baugeschichte*, 3:167–68, where this is identified as the last mention of this shrine; compare Milik, "Notes d'épigraphie, IX," 363; and Külzer, *Peregrinatio graeca*, 218–19; see also Aist, *Christian Topography,* 150–54.

15 The shrine of St. Stephen's tomb lay a few hundred meters north of the city wall. See map 1 and Wilkinson, *Jerusalem Pilgrims*, 318; and Bieberstein and Bloedhorn, *Jerusalem: Grundzüge der Baugeschichte*, 2:227–37. This is the final mention of this shrine (ibid., 292).

16 Latin *villa*, from the Vulgate text of Matthew 26:36, which the Douay version translates as "country place." This is nevertheless probably an instance in which the Carolingian term *villa* is tantamount to "village."

17 Map 1. For the location, some 300 meters east of the Jericho Gate, see Wilkinson, *Jerusalem Pilgrims*, 305–6; Bieberstein and Bloedhorn, *Jerusalem: Grundzüge der Baugeschichte*, 3:251–56; Külzer, *Peregrinatio graeca*, 189–91; and Aist, *Christian Topography*, 174–78.

18 Bernard (*Itinerarium* 13, 316) also mentions this church and explicitly locates it in the Valley of Jehoshaphat or Kidron. See Wilkinson, *Jerusalem Pilgrims*, 306, s.n. "Gethsemane"; Bieberstein and Bloedhorn, *Jerusalem: Grundzüge der Baugeschichte*, 3:412–13; and Milik, "Notes d'épigraphie, IX," 560.

19 Map 1. See Wilkinson, *Jerusalem Pilgrims*, 312, under "Jehoshaphat, Valley of," identifying this shrine with the rock-cut tomb of Zechariah or Bene Hezir; see also Bieberstein and Bloedhorn, *Jerusalem: Grundüge der Baugeschichte*, 3:233–35; and Külzer, *Peregrinatio graeca*, 213.

20 No certain location; *Sancto Quaranto*, the scribe's misunderstanding of a Vulgar Latin expression for shrine "of the Holy Forty," that is, the Forty Martyrs of Sebasteia. See chapter 7.1; Wilkinson, *Jerusalem Pilgrims*, 320; Bieberstein and Bloedhorn, *Jerusalem: Grundzüge der Baugeschichte*, 3:416; and Milik, "Notes d'épigraphie, IX," 560 no. 30.

16   Christoforo i; in sancta Aquilena i; in sancto Quirico i; in sancto Stefa | no iii;
      in sancto Dometio i; in sancto Iohanne ubi natus fuit ii; in sancto Theodoro
17   ii; in sancto Sertio i; in sancto Cosme et Damiano ubi na | ti fuerunt iii, et
      ubi medicabant presbiter i; in sancto Monte Oliueti, ecclesiae iii: una Ascensa
18   Domini, inter presbiteris et cleri<cis> | iii;

Christopher:[21] 1; in St. Aquilena:[22] 1; St. Cirycus:[23] 1; in St. Stephen,[24] | 3; in St. Dometius:[25] 1; in St. John, where he was born:[26] 2; in St. Theodore:[27] 2; in St. Sergius:[28] 1; in Sts. Cosmas and Damian, where they were born:[29] | 3, and where they healed:[30] 1 priest. On the holy Mount of Olives, three churches: one, the Ascension of the Lord, priests and clerics:[31] | 3;

Line	Site
16	14, 15, 16, 17
	18, 19, 20
17	21, 22
	23
18	24

21   Uncertain location, although possibly in the Valley of Jehoshaphat (Kidron Valley). See Wilkinson, *Jerusalem Pilgrims*, 320; and Milik, "Notes d'épigraphie, IX," 560–61, no. 31. Bieberstein and Bloedhorn (*Jerusalem: Grundzüge der Baugeschichte*, 3:407) oppose their suggestion.

22   Wilkinson, *Jerusalem Pilgrims*, 319. Wilkinson (ibid., 313, under "Jehoshaphat, Valley of") follows Milik ("Notes d'épigraphie, IX," 560–61) in suspecting that the shrines of the Holy Forty, of St. Christopher, and of St. Aquilena all were located in the Kidron Valley. Bieberstein and Bloedhorn (*Jerusalem: Grundzüge der Baugeschichte*, 3:407 and 416) reject this.

23   St. Cirycus, also known as St. Quiricus. On possible locations for this church, see Wilkinson, *Jerusalem Pilgrims*, 318; Bieberstein and Bloedhorn, *Jerusalem: Grundzüge der Baugeschichte*, 3:408; and Milik, "La topographie de Jérusalem vers la fin de l'époque byzantine," 167–69. This appears to be the last mention.

24   Milik ("Notes d'épigraphie, IX," 558–59, no. 26) and Wilkinson (*Jerusalem Pilgrims*, 318), identify this church with a foundation of St. Melania the Younger on the Mount of Olives. Bieberstein and Bloedhorn (*Jerusalem: Grundzüge der Baugeschichte*, 3:421) think rather that this must be the church of St. Stephen's stoning next to the Zion church, on the east, mentioned by Bernard (*Itinerarium* 12, 315–16).

25   Location uncertain. See Wilkinson, *Jerusalem Pilgrims*, 320; compare Milik, "Notes d'épigraphie, IX," 573–74.

26   Milik ("Notes d'épigraphie, IX," 561–62) identifies it with the church of St. John, on the side of the Mount of Olives, mentioned by Bernard (*Itinerarium* 14, 316), which Milik further identifies with the shrine of the birthplace of St. John the Baptist in an anonymous Old Church Slavonic guide earlier than AD 1106–7 (see ibid., 357), which is accepted by Wilkinson (*Jerusalem Pilgrims*, 336, under "Olives, The Mount of").

27   Wilkinson, *Jerusalem Pilgrims*, 320, under "Sergius, Church of Saint": unlocated. Bieberstein and Bloedhorn (*Jerusalem: Grundzüge der Baugeschichte*, 3:417–18) note the possible association of a "building of John" and of Sts. Theodore and Sergius with an inscription mentioning a monastery of St. Sergius located in the lower Hinnom Valley. Milik ("Notes d'épigraphie, IX," 360–61, no. 6) suggests that a chapel of St. Sergius was joined to a church that was called both St. Theodore and St. Euphemia.

28   See previous note.

29   Wilkinson (*Jerusalem Pilgrims*, 316–17) locates it near the present-day "House of Veronica," at the sixth station on the present-day Via Dolorosa. See also Bieberstein and Bloedhorn, *Jerusalem: Grundzüge der Baugeschichte*, 3:408; and Milik, "La topographie de Jérusalem vers la fin de l'époque byzantine," 155–57, no. 7, with other good evidence for the location near the modern chapel of Veronica; compare Milik, "Notes d'épigraphie, IX," 363–64, no. 16. See also next note.

30   This church was probably in the Valley of Kidron (Jehoshaphat). See Bieberstein and Bloedhorn, *Jerusalem: Grundzüge der Baugeschichte*, 3:408; and esp. Milik, "Notes d'épigraphie, IX," 569–70, no. 51. Wilkinson's emendation of *medicabant* ("they were healing)" to *mendicabant* ("they were begging") is unwarranted (*Jerusalem Pilgrims*, 316–17).

31   Map 1 (now the Mosque of the Ascension). See Wilkinson, *Jerusalem Pilgrims*, 334–35; Bieberstein and Bloedhorn, *Jerusalem: Grundzüge der Baugeschichte*, 3:299–303; Külzer, *Peregrinatio graeca*, 195–96; Milik, "Notes d'épigraphie, IX," 557–58, no. 25; and, on Willibald's testimony on the churches on the Mount of Olives in his day, Aist, *Christian Topography*, 178–216.

alia, ubi docuit discipulos suos Christus, ubi sunt monachi iii, presbiter i; tertia in

19 honore sanctae Mariae, clerici i*i*<**>; | inclusi qui sedent per cellolas eorum: qui

20 Greca lingua psallent xi; Iorzani iiii; Syriani vi; Armeni ii; | Latini v; qui Saracina
lingua psallet i; iuxta illam scalam, quando subis in Montem sanctum: inclusi

21 ii, unus Grecus, | alter Syrus; ad summam scalam in Gethsaemani, inclusi iii,
Grecus et Syrus et Iorzanus; in ualle Iosaphat, inclusus i.

22 | Monasteria puellarum xxvi, de imperio domni Karoli quae ad sepulchrum

23 Domini seruiunt Deo sacratas xvii, inclusa | de Spania i; in monasterio sancti
Petri et sancti Pauli in Besanteo iuxta Montem Oliueti, monachi xxxv; ad

24 sanctum Lazarum in | Bethania, presbiter i; ad sanctum Iohannem quod tenent
Armeni, monachi vi.

Isti in Hierusalem sunt et in circuitu eius infra *milium* et supra.

a second, where Christ taught his disciples,[32] where there are 3 monks, 1 priest; a   **25**

third, in honor of St. Mary,[33] 2[34] clerics; | hermits (*inclusi*) who reside scattered   19 **26**

among their cells: 11 who sing the psalms in Greek; Georgians, 4; Syrians, 6;

Armenians, 2; | Latins, 5; one who sings the psalms in Arabic. Along the steps,   20

when you go up the holy mount:[35] 2 hermits (*inclusi*), one Greek | the other   21

Syrian. At the top of the steps in Gethsemane, 3 hermits (*inclusi*), a Greek, a

Syrian, and a Georgian; in the Valley of Jehoshaphat, 1 hermit (*inclusus*).

| A monastery[36] of 26 women[, of whom] 17 nuns who serve at the Holy   22 **27**

Sepulcher are from the empire of Lord Charles; 1 recluse | from Spain; in the   23

monastery of St. Peter and St. Paul at Besanteo,[37] alongside the Mount of Olives: **28**

35 monks; at St. Lazarus in | Bethany,[38] 1 priest; at St. John, which the Armenians   24 **29, 30**

hold,[39] 6 monks.

These are in Jerusalem and in its surroundings within upward of a mile.

---

32   Map 1. See Wilkinson, *Jerusalem Pilgrims*, 333–34; Bieberstein and Bloedhorn, *Jerusalem: Grundzüge der Baugeschichte*, 3:286–92; Külzer, *Peregrinatio graeca*, 194; and Milik, "Notes d'épigraphie, IX," 555–57, nos. 23–24.

33   Map 1. Bieberstein and Bloedhorn (*Jerusalem: Grundzüge der Baugeschichte*, 3:312–18) located the church on the grounds of the Islamic hospital; it was apparently the same as the Byzantine church recorded in A. Kloner, *Survey of Jerusalem: The Northeastern Sector*, Archaeological Survey of Israel (Jerusalem, 2001), 140*, no. 440.

34   Since the very end of the line is lost, space would allow, but not require, "ii<i>," that is, "3 clerics" (*clerici*). See chapter 11, textual commentary on this passage.

35   On the famous stepped streets of the Valley of Jehoshaphat (Kidron) going down from Jerusalem and up the side of the Mount of Olives, see below, lines 49–50, as well as Milik, "Notes d'épigraphie, IX," 367, no. 19; Wilkinson, *Jerusalem Pilgrims*, 313, under "Jehoshaphat, Valley of"; and Bieberstein and Bloedhorn, *Jerusalem: Grundzüge der Baugeschichte*, 3:224 and 262.

36   For this translation and construction of the Latin text, against Wilkinson (*Jerusalem Pilgrims*, 255), see chapter 11, textual commentary. This segment of the Breve treats two other establishments on the Mount of Olives, so that it is not impossible that this convent was located there also. However, textual proximity seems not always to reflect topographical proximity in the Breve (see above, chapter 7.4), and it is possible that, like other female establishments in the Holy Land, this convent was inside the city walls. This would seem especially likely if the nuns served daily at the Holy Sepulcher.

37   This is the Frankish monastery on the Mount of Olives. For what we know of it, and for *in Besanteo* as a phonetic rendering of an Aramaic place name *Bet Ṣanṭaya*, "the house of the locust trees," see above, chapter 4.2.

38   Wilkinson, *Jerusalem Pilgrims*, 285; Milik, "Notes d'épigraphie, IX," 566, no. 44; Külzer, *Peregrinatio graeca*, 144–45.

39   Map 1. For this establishment on the Mount of Olives, see Milik, "Notes d'épigraphie, IX," 562–63, no. 34. It lasted into the Fatimid period (Bieberstein and Bloedhorn, *Jerusalem: Grundzüge der Baugeschichte*, 3:327–36, cf. 412). The site is approximately 300 meters east of the Ascension mosque (cf. Kloner, *Survey of Jerusalem: The Northeastern Sector*, 138*, no. 429, with the color map, where 137*, no. 427, is the shrine of the Ascension, not the Assumption).

25 | Memoria de illis monasteriis quae sunt in extremis Hierusalem in terra promissionis.

26 In sancta Bethlem, ubi Dominus noster Iesus Christus | nasci dignatus est de sancta uirgine Maria, inter presbiteris et clericis et monachis xv; inclusi, qui in

27 columnis sedent in exemplo sancti | Symeonis ii. In monasterio sancti Theodosii, qu\o/d primum in illo erimo con*st*<ructum> *est* monachi lxx; Basilius *s*<uper

28 eos>.ᵃ | Succenderunt Sarraceni latrones ipsum monasterium et interfeceru*n*<t

29 multos i>*g*<ne crude>*le*, et al*ii* propter pa<ctum deiecerunt> | ad terramᵇ ecclesias ii ad ipsum monasterium aspicientes. In sancto Saba monachi c*l in

30 Pa*l*<eo monasterio> | quod sanctus Karitus construxit et ubi ipse sanctus ab uno miliario requiescit,

a   Another plausible restoration would be "s<epultus ibi>": see chapter 11, textual commentary on this line.
b   [ad <terram>] seems to have been written a second time, in the erasure; the erroneous, second copying was then carefully erased: see chapter 11, textual commentary on this line.

Texts, Translation, and Textual Commentary

DOCUMENT 2

| Memorial of the monasteries that are in the Promised Land outside   25
of Jerusalem[40]

In Holy Bethlehem,[41] where Our Lord Jesus Christ | deigned to be born from   26 **31**
the Holy Virgin Mary, including priests, clerics and monks: 15; hermits (*inclusi*)
who sit on top of columns on the example of St. | Symeon: 2. In the monastery   27
of St. Theodosius,[42] which was the first one built in that desert: 70 monks; Basil   **32**
<is over them>.[43] | Saracen bandits burned the monastery and killed <many   28
with cruel fire>,[44] and others, <on account of the ransom, demolished> | to the
ground[45] two churches dependent on that monastery. In St. Sabas,[46] 150[47] monks.   29 **33**
In the Ol<d Lavra>[48] | which St. Chariton built and where that saint rests, a mile   30 **34**

40 See map 2 for the sites mentioned in the Memorial.

41 For discussion of the Nativity Church, see above, chapter 5.2. See, in general, Wilkinson, *Jerusalem Pilgrims*, 286–88; Külzer, *Peregrinatio graeca*, 145–50; Y. Tsafrir, L. Di Segni, J. Green, et al., *Tabula Imperii Romani: Iudaea-Palaestina. Eretz Israel in the Hellenistic, Roman and Byzantine Periods; Maps and Gazetteer* (Jerusalem, 1994), 83. For the monument and an archaeological overview, beyond the bibliography cited above, see M. Avi-Yonah and V. Tzaferis, "Bethlehem," in *NEAEHL* 1:204–10.

42 The monastery in the Judaean desert northeast of Bethlehem, founded in 479 by St. Theodosius. For more details about it in this period, see above, chapter 2.2 and chapter 8.1, and, in general, Wilkinson, *Jerusalem Pilgrims*, 297, under "Deir Ibn Ubeid (Deir Dosi)"; Y. Hirschfeld, "List of the Byzantine Monasteries in the Judean Desert," in *Christian Archaeology in the Holy Land: New Discoveries*, ed. G. C. Bottini, L. Di Segni, and E. Alliata, Studium biblicum franciscanum, Collectio maior 36 (Jerusalem, 1990), 26–28; Külzer, *Peregrinatio graeca*, 173–74; Tsafrir, Di Segni, Green, et al., *Tabula Imperii Romani: Iudaea-Palaestina*, 110; and esp. Y. Hirschfeld, *The Judean Desert Monasteries in the Byzantine Period* (New Haven, 1992), 33–34, and passim.

43 Another plausible restoration would be "is buried there." See chapter 11, the textual commentary on this line.

44 For the violence inflicted on the Christian monasteries in the late eighth and early ninth century, see above, chapter 8.1. See chapter 11, textual commentary, for the restoration and more details.

45 The scribe has erased "to the <ground>," which was copied inadvertently a second time. See the textual commentary.

46 The Great Lavra, or Mar Saba, monastery in the Judaean desert five kilometers southeast of St. Theodosius, founded around 483 by St. Sabas. For more details about it in this period, see above, chapter 2.2 and chapter 8.1 and, in general, Wilkinson, *Jerusalem Pilgrims*, 342; Hirschfeld, "List of the Byzantine Monasteries," 31–32; Külzer, *Peregrinatio graeca*, 171–73; Tsafrir, Di Segni, Green, et al., *Tabula Imperii Romani: Iudaea-Palaestina*, 182–83, under "Megiste Laura"; and Hirschfeld, *Desert Monasteries*, 24–26, etc. For a detailed account of its archaeology, J. Patrich, *Sabas, Leader of Palestinian Monasticism: A Comparative Study in Eastern Monasticism, Fourth to Seventh Centuries* (Washington, D.C., 1995), 58–107.

47 For the number, see chapter 11, the textual commentary.

48 This is the monastery of Souka, or St. Chariton, founded in the fourth century, whose ruins have been identified at Khan Khureitūn, some seven kilometers southeast of Bethlehem. For justification of the restored name of this house, which reflects the common way around 800 of referring to it as *Palaia Lavra*, or the "Old Monastery," see chapter 11, the textual commentary. For

31 abba no<mine ****, mon>achi < **. In sancto Eutimio abba nomine *****, mo> |
    nachi xxx. In monasterio sanctae Mariae in Coziba a*bb*a *n*<omine Teofi>lactus,

32 *m*<onachi ***. In monasterio prope Iericho abba nomine> | Iohannes, monachi
    x. Construxit eum sanctus Gerasimus, ubi et ipse sanctus in corpo<re requiescit

33 ***********************>^c | et erexit in titulum, ad Iordanen, monasterium sancti
    Iohannis et ecclesia<m> alia<m> u<bi Dominus baptizatus est, abba *******, > |

34 monachi xxxv. Monasterium sancti Stephani prope Iericho: construxit e<um ****

35 monasterium in> | Monte Faran. In istis duobus, nescimus quanti sint.

c   For a plausible restoration of this lacuna as "in corpo<re requiescit. imp(erator) Anastasius
    exstruxit> et erexit in titulum, ad Iordanen, monasterium sancti Iohannis et ecclesia<m> una<m>
    u<bi ...," see chapter 11, textual commentary.

Texts, Translation, and Textual Commentary

away: the abbot, na<med ****; ** mo>nks<. In St. Euthymius,[49] the abbot,

named *****, | mo>nks: 30. In the monastery of St. Mary in Choziba,[50] the abbot, 31 35, 36

n<amed Theophy>lactus, m<onks ***. In the monastery near Jericho,[51] the abbot,

named> John, 10 monks. St. Gerasimus built it, where the saint's bo<dy rests. 32 37

************************[52]> | and erected as a monument, at the Jordan,[53] a 33

monastery of St. John and another church w<here the Lord was baptized, the 38

abbot *******>, | 35 monks. The monastery of St. Stephen,[54] near Jericho, it was 34 39

built by < ****. The monastery on> | Mount Pharan.[55] In these two, we do not 35 40

know how many they are.

more details, see Wilkinson, *Jerusalem Pilgrims*, 342; Hirschfeld, "List of the Byzantine Monasteries," 8–12; Külzer, *Peregrinatio graeca*, 163; and Tsafrir, Di Segni, Green, et al., *Tabula Imperii Romani: Iudaea-Palaestina*, 236, under "Suca." For the archaeology, see Hirschfeld, *Desert Monasteries*, 23–24, and Y. Hirschfeld, "Chariton," in *NEAEHL* 1:297–99.

49 Founded in 428, the monastery of St. Euthymius has been identified and excavated about ten kilometers east of Jerusalem at Khan el Aḥmar. For more details, see Wilkinson, *Jerusalem Pilgrims*, 342; Hirschfeld, "List of the Byzantine Monasteries," 15–18; Külzer, *Peregrinatio graeca*, 165; Tsafrir, Di Segni, Green, et al., *Tabula Imperii Romani: Iudaea-Palaestina*, 167, under "Khan el Aḥmar"; and Y. Hirschfeld, "Euthymius' Monastery," in *NEAEHL* 2:428–30.

50 The monastery, still active today, lies about three kilometers northwest of Jericho. It was founded around 480. See, in general, Wilkinson, *Jerusalem Pilgrims*, 294; Hirschfeld, "List of the Byzantine Monasteries," 29–31; Külzer, *Peregrinatio graeca*, 152; and Tsafrir, Di Segni, Green, et al., *Tabula Imperii Romani: Iudaea-Palaestina*, 104. On the remains, see Hirschfeld, *Desert Monasteries*, 35–37.

51 The monastery of St. Gerasimus was near the site of the modern monastery of Deir Ḥajla, about five kilometers southeast of Jericho. See Wilkinson, *Jerusalem Pilgrims*, 304; Hirschfeld, "List of the Byzantine Monasteries," 18–19; Tsafrir, Di Segni, Green, et al., *Tabula Imperii Romani: Iudaea-Palaestina*, 110; and esp. Hirschfeld, *Desert Monasteries*, 28–29 and 180–83. It was abandoned by the later twelfth century (Külzer, *Peregrinatio graeca*, 167).

52 The restorations offered by de Rossi and Tobler and Molinier are not fully satisfactory. I would propose accepting the obvious completion concerning the burial place of Gerasimus and beginning the new sentence, about the striking monuments raised by Anastasius on the bank of the Jordan, by conjecturing a text along the lines: "bo<dy rests. Emperor Anastasius built> and erected as a monument." See chapter 11, the textual commentary on this line, and the next note.

53 On the church that commemorated Jesus's baptism at the Jordan, and the nearby monastery of St. John the Baptist at Qaṣr el-Yahūd, see Wilkinson, *Jerusalem Pilgrims*, 321–22; Hirschfeld, "List of the Byzantine Monasteries," 35–36; Tsafrir, Di Segni, Green, et al., *Tabula Imperii Romani: Iudaea-Palaestina*, 152, under "Iohannis Baptistae ecclesiae"; and Külzer, *Peregrinatio graeca*, 168–69. Early medieval pilgrims were struck by the monuments here, to judge by the descriptions of Arculf and Hugeburc, as discussed in chapter 11, the textual commentary.

54 Wilkinson, *Jerusalem Pilgrims*, 313–14. This monastery, which seems not to be mentioned elsewhere, may perhaps be another name for the "monastery of the eunuchs," one of the two monasteries in the vicinity referred to in late antiquity as monasteries of Elias. They have been located at Khan Mugheifir, about two kilometers southeast of Jericho (Hirschfeld, "List of the Byzantine Monasteries," 22–23). Another hermitage dated by the excavator to the ninth century, and preserving a Syriac inscription, has been located four kilometers east of Jericho (R. Cohen, "Monasteries," in *NEAEHL* 3:1063–70, here 1068).

55 That is Pharan, founded in the fourth century and identified in the vicinity of Ein Fara, about eight kilometers northeast of Jerusalem. See Wilkinson, *Jerusalem Pilgrims*, 337, under "Paran";

In Galilea in ciuit<ate sancta Nazareth, ubi Dominus ****** ecclesia *** monachi>

36 | xii. Uno miliario a Nazareth, ubi Christum Dominum Iudaei praecipitare

37 uol*u*<erunt, monasterium in> | honore sanctae Mariae, monachi viii. In Chanan

38 Galileae, ubi Dominus de aqua *u*<inum fecit ecclesia monachi   . Iuxta ma> | re
Tiberiadis, monasterium quod uocatur Eptapegon, ubi Dominus satiauit populi

39 *su*<i quinque panibus et duobus> | piscibus quinque milia: ibi sunt monachi x.
Item iuxta mare, ecclesia quam uocant *Duodec*<i>*m* <Thronorum, ubi Dominus

40 ********* cum disci | pulis suis; ibi est mensa ubi cum illis sedit. Ibi sunt presbiter
i, clerici ii. In Tiberia ciuit*ate*, Teo*p*<hilus episcopus

In Galilee, in the <holy> cit<y of Nazareth,[56] where the Lord . . . a church
. . . monks:> | twelve. At the first milestone from Nazareth, where the Jews
wan<ted> to throw Christ the Lord down headlong,[57] <a monastery in> | honor
of St. Mary, 8 monks.[58] In Cana of Galilee, where the Lord made from water
w<ine . . . a church . . . monks. . . .[59] By the Sea> | of Tiberias, the monastery
which is called Heptapegon,[60] where the Lord satisfied five thousand of <his >
people <with five loaves of bread and two>[61] | fishes; there are 10 monks there.
Similarly, by the sea, the church that they call "The Twelve <Thrones," where the
Lord ate with> his | disciples; there is the table where he sat with them;[62] there
are 1 priest and 2 clerics there. In the city of Tiberias,[63] Theop<hilus bishop;

Hirschfeld, "List of the Byzantine Monasteries," 6–7; Tsafrir, Di Segni, Green, et al., *Tabula Imperii Romani: Iudaea-Palaestina*, 202, under "Pharan II, Ain"; and Hirschfeld, *Desert Monasteries*, 21–23.

56   On Nazareth, see Wilkinson, *Jerusalem Pilgrims*, 330–31; and Tsafrir, Di Segni, Green, et al., *Tabula Imperii Romani: Iudaea-Palaestina*, 194. On the archaeology, see V. Tzaferis and B. Bagatti, "Nazareth," in *NEAEHL* 3:1103–06.

57   Luke 4:29.

58   The monastery of the Virgin in line 37 may well continue the entry about the shrine of the "Saltus Domini," the Mount of the Lord's Leap, located at Jebel el-Qafse, two kilometers south of Nazareth. A cave chapel has been identified on the site. See Ovadiah and de Silva, "Supplementum," 220–21; see also Abel, *Géographie*, 2:395.

59   Located at either Khan Qana or Kafr Kanna. See Wilkinson, *Jerusalem Pilgrims*, 291–92; Tsafrir, Di Segni, Green, et al., *Tabula Imperii Romani: Iudaea-Palaestina*, 96–97; Ovadiah, *Corpus*, 99–100, and Ovadiah and de Silva, "Supplementum (2)," 143–44; and B. Bagatti, *Ancient Christian Villages of Galilee* (Jerusalem, 2001), 41–45.

60   The monastery of the Seven Springs (Greek *Heptapegon*, corrupted into Arabic as *Ain et-Tabgha*) is well known. See Wilkinson, *Jerusalem Pilgrims*, 345–46, under "Seven Springs"; Külzer, *Peregrinatio graeca*, 175; Tsafrir, Di Segni, Green, et al., *Tabula Imperii Romani: Iudaea-Palaestina*, 142; Ovadiah, *Corpus*, 56–60, and Ovadiah and de Silva, "Supplementum (2)," 130; and M. Avi-Yonah and A. Negev, "Heptapegon," in *NEAEHL* 2:614–16. If Arculf is indeed talking about the same spot (Adomnan, *De locis sanctis* 2.24.2, 218.6–10), this foundation had been restored within the last twelve decades. According to Avraham Negev in Avi-Yonah and Negev ("Heptapegon"), the 1968 excavations by Bagatti and Loffreda produced evidence for a seventh- or eighth-century church here. It is unclear whether he is referring to the possible building at the "Twelve Thrones–Primacy of Peter" shrine mentioned in the 1970 publication (see below, note 65). I have been unable to consult S. Loffreda, *The Sanctuaries of Tabgha*, 2nd ed. (Jerusalem, 1978).

61   See chapter 11, the textual commentary.

62   For the site of the Twelve Thrones, see Wilkinson, *Jerusalem Pilgrims*, 346, and chapter 11, the textual commentary. For the excavation of the lakeside church, known today as "The Primacy of Peter," in which a rock ledge was found which seems to have been identified as the Table, and outside of which a series of 6 column drums seems to be the remains of what were called the "Twelve Thrones," as well as the possibility of some rebuilding here in the early Arab period, see S. Loffreda, *Scavi di et-Tabgha: relazione finale della campagna di scavi 25 marzo–20 giugno 1969* (Jerusalem, 1970), 48–105, esp. 97–98.

63   The lakeside town and administrative center seem to have been doing well in the eighth and ninth centuries. See Walmsley, *Early Islamic Syria*, 77–79; compare Gil, *History of Palestine*, 174–85. See, in general, Wilkinson, *Jerusalem Pilgrims*, 360; Külzer, *Peregrinatio graeca*, 271–72; and Y. Hirschfeld, G. Foerster, and F. Vitto, "Tiberias," in *NEAEHL* 4:1464–73.

41   inter presbiteris> | et monachis et canonicis xxx, ecclesias v, monasterium

42   puellarum i. In monte sancto Tabor, episcopus Teophan*iu*<s, ecclesiae> | iiii: una
       in honore sancti Saluatoris ubi locutus cum Moysi et Elia fuit, secunda sancti

43   Moysi, tertia sancti Eliae, quarta <******>; | monachi uero xviii. In Sabastia,
       ubi corpus sancti Iohannis requiescit, ecclesia magna fuit; modo est in terra

44   diffusa. | Tantum ubi illud sepulchrum ipsius gloriosi Baptistae positum est ex

45   parte non cecidit, et ecclesia ubi ille carce*r f*<uit> | ubi decollatus est; Basilius
       episcopus; inter presbiteris, monachis, et clericis xxv. In Samaria quam Naboli

46   uocant ecc<le>*si*<a> | magna, ubi illa sancta mulier Samaritana requiescit, et

47   aliae ecclesiae; episcopus et clerici et inclusus super colum<na.> | In sancto monte
       Syna, ecclesiae iiii: una ubi Dominus locutus est cum Moysi in uertice montis;

48   alia sancti Eliae; t*e*<r>*t*ia sanct<***;> | quarta monasterium sanctae Mariae; abba

49   Elias, monachi xxx. Gradicula ad subiendum uel desce<nd>endum xii*i* | milia
       dcc. Quando descendis de Hierusalem

including priests> | and monks and canons: 30; five churches, and one convent.   41   **46, 47**

On the Holy Mount Tabor, bishop Theophanius, four <churches>:[64] | one in   42   **48**

honor of the Holy Savior, where he spoke with Moses and Elias, a second of St.

Moses, a third of St. Elias, a fourth <******>, | and 18 monks.   43

In Sabastia,[65] where the body of St. John rests, there was a big church; now it   **49**

has fallen down to the ground. | Only where the tomb of the glorious Baptist is   44

placed has it partially not fallen, and there is a church where the prison <was>

| where he was beheaded. The bishop Basil, 25 priests, monks, and clerics. In   45

Samaria, which they call Nablus, a big church, | where the holy Samaritan   46   **50**

woman rests, and other churches;[66] a bishop and clerics and a hermit (*inclusus*) on

a column. | On the Holy Mountain of Sinai, four churches:[67] one where the Lord   47   **51**

spoke with Moses at the top of the mountain; a second of St. Elias; a third of St.

<***>; | the fourth, the monastery of St. Mary; an abbot named Elias, 30 monks.   48

There are 13,700 | steps to go up or down.[68] When you go down from Jerusalem   49

---

64   On the site, see Wilkinson, *Jerusalem Pilgrims*, 356, under "Tabor, Mount"; Külzer, *Peregrinatio graeca*, 269–70; Tsafrir, Di Segni, Green, et al., *Tabula Imperii Romani: Iudaea-Palaestina*, 246–47; Ovadiah, *Corpus*, 71–72, and Ovadiah and de Silva, "Supplementum (2)," 132; and M. Avram, "Galilee: The Hellenistic to Byzantine Periods," in *NEAEHL* 2:453–58, here 456–57, for a later Roman church with, perhaps, a monastery. The fourth church must be a new one: an Armenian pilgrim writing around 630 says there were three: the Lord's church and two smaller ones dedicated to Saints Moses and Elias. See R. W. Thomson, "A Seventh-Century Armenian Pilgrim on Mount Tabor," *Journal of Theological Studies*, n.s., 18 (1967): 27–33, here, 32; compare 30, and, for the date, 29. This is therefore a case of new church-building in the seventh or eighth century. Wilkinson and Külzer speculate that the new church honored Melchizedek.

65   That is, Sebastia. For the significance of this document's use of the Arabic form of the name, see above, chapter 7.2. An overview of the site may be found in Wilkinson, *Jerusalem Pilgrims*, 344–45; Külzer, *Peregrinatio graeca*, 255–56; Tsafrir, Di Segni, Green, et al., *Tabula Imperii Romani: Iudaea-Palaestina*, 220–21, under "Samaria, Sebaste"; and N. Avigad, "Samaria," in *NEAEHL* 2:1300–10, here 1309–10.

66   Wilkinson, *Jerusalem Pilgrims*, 331; Külzer, *Peregrinatio graeca*, 259; Tsafrir, Di Segni, Green, et al., *Tabula Imperii Romani: Iudaea-Palaestina*, 194–95; I. Magen, "Shechem: Neapolis," in *NEAEHL* 4:1354–59.

67   On the shrines of Mount Sinai in general, see Wilkinson, *Jerusalem Pilgrims*, 350; Külzer, *Peregrinatio graeca*, 260–66. For the modern dedications of the "later chapels" on Mount Sinai (Jebel Musa), see I. Finkelstein, "Byzantine Monastic Remains in the Southern Sinai," *DOP* 39 (1985): 39–79, here 42 n. 14.

68   The evidence external to the roll supposedly supporting the former reading of "7,700" steps (see chapter 11, textual commentary) has vanished with a critical edition of Epiphanius and its clear reference to "seven βασμίδια" on the climb to the top of Jebel Musa (*Descriptio Palaestinae* 7.15, 75). For a photo of the "Path of the Steps" from St. Catherine's to Jebel Musa, see Finkelstein, "Byzantine Monastic Remains in the Southern Sinai," fig. 15 (cf. fig. D, no. 29); for one of the considerably longer ones, the "Path of the Cisterns (Sikket Shahareij)," also distinguished by stone steps, see fig. 16 (and fig. D, no. 34; see also the discussion on 56–57). The climb up required an ascent of about 700 meters (from about 1,550 meters above sea level) to 2,250 meters. On architectural interest in

50 in uallem Iosaphat, ubi est sepulchrum sanctae Mariae, habet <gradi> | cula
cxcv; ad subire in montem Oliueti, dxxxvii. Ipsa ecclesia sanctae *M*ar<i>ae q*uo*d

51 ill*e* terrae motus f<regit> | et in terram demersit, habet mensuram de ambobus

52 lateribus in longe de*xteros xx*<x>*iiii, in uno fronte xxx<v>; | per medium in
aduerso, xxxii; in longo per medium l. Ecclesia in Bethlem: in longo, dexteros

53 xxxviii; | in fronte superiore, in illa cruce, xxiii; in alio fronte, xvii; colunas lxviiii.

54 Illa ecclesia de sepulch*r*o | Domini: in giro, dexteros cvii; illa alcuba, liii; a sancto

55 Sepulchro usque ad sanctum Caluarium, dexteros xxvii; | a sancto Caluario
usque ubi sancta Crux inuenta fuit, dexteros xviiii; inter sanctum Sepulchrum et

56 sanctum Caluarium et sanctum Con | stantinum: illorum tectum in integrum

57 habet in longo dexteros xcvi, in aduerso xxx. Ecclesia sancta Sion in longo | habet
dexteros xxxviiii, in transuerso xxvi.

DOCUMENT 3

58 | **Dispensa patriarchae inter presbiteris, diaconibus, monachis, clericis, et**

59 **omne congregatione eccle<siae per unum> | annum:**
solidos dcc *et p*<atria>*rch*a solidos dl; in fabricaturam ecclesiarum solidos ccc;
in c*a*<**************>

60 | *in******m sol*idos x*xx* **********o; in* <S>a̲r̲r̲<a>c̲e̲<nis> *sol*idos lxxx; in
ministris Sarraceno*r*<um>

[Damaged end of the present state of the roll]

Texts, Translation, and Textual Commentary

into the Valley of Jehoshaphat, where the tomb of St. Mary is, there are 195 steps;
| to go up on the Mount of Olives, 537.[69]   50

The church of St. Mary,[70] which the earthquake ruined | and sank into the   51
earth, measures on both sides 34[71] dexters in length, on one extremity 3<5>[72];
| through the middle, across, 32; in length, through the middle, 50. The church 52
in Bethlehem:[73] in length, 38 dexters; | on the upper[74] extremity, at the transept, 53
23; on the other extremity, 17; 69 columns. The church of the Sepulcher | of   54
the Lord:[75] around, 107 dexters; the dome, 53; from the Holy Sepulcher up to
Holy Calvary, 27 dexters; | from Holy Calvary to where the Holy Cross was   55
discovered,[76] 19 dexters; including the Holy Sepulcher and Holy Calvary and
Holy | Constantine: their roof altogether is 96 dexters in length, 30 across. The 56
church of Holy Zion[77] is | 39 dexters in length; 26 across.   57

DOCUMENT 3

| **Expenditures of the patriarch, including for priests, deacons, monks, clerics,** 58
and the entire congregation of the church <for one> | year:[78]   59

700 solidi, and the patriarch, 550 solidi. For the church fabric, 300 solidi; for
ca************** | *in*****m 30 solidi; for the Saracens, 80 solidi; for the servants of 60
the Saracens . . .

[Damaged end of the present state of the roll.]

---

the steps in late antiquity, see also I. Ševčenko, "The Early Period of the Sinai Monastery in the
Light of Its Inscriptions," *DOP* 20 (1966): 255–64, here 257, with 263, no. 11.

69 The stepped streets of the Kidron Valley and Mount of Olives. See Wilkinson, *Jerusalem
Pilgrims*, 313, under "Jehoshaphat, Valley of"; and esp. Bieberstein and Bloedhorn, *Jerusalem:
Grundzüge der Baugeschichte*, 3:224 and 262.

70 The great Nea Church built by Justinian and rediscovered in 1970. See above, chapter 5.2, for
this building and the significance of the roll's evidence about this and the following buildings.

71 Latin "de*xteros xx*<x>iiii."

72 See chapter 11, the textual commentary for the reading.

73 That is, the Nativity church, already mentioned above. See lines 25–26, and the discussion of
this passage, above, chapter 5.2.

74 "Upper" here is used in the familiar Latin sense of "eastern," which derived from the fashion in
which the ancients imagined, and usually depicted, space: the surest direction, before the invention
of the compass, the one in which the sun rose, was depicted at the top of the map

75 See above, lines 3–8, and discussion of this evidence, above, chapter 5.2.

76 That is, the apse of the Constantinian basilica. See above, chapter 5.2, with note 72.

77 See above, line 9, and discussion of this evidence, above, chapter 5.2.

78 See above, chapter 1.1, for discussion of this unique information on the expenditures of an early
medieval patriarchate.

Chapter Eleven

■ ■ ■ ■ ■ ■ ■ ■ ■ ■ ■ ■ ■ ■

TEXTUAL COMMENTARY

THE DAMAGED STATE OF THE MANUSCRIPT means that some readings of the text are not obvious; in a number of lines the text must be restored by comparison and conjecture or the reasons behind my reading adduced. Passages for which the reading is debatable and the numerous differences between this edition and its predecessors require some justification. To facilitate the detailed discussion of the actual and potential readings, the lemmata here represent diplomatic transcriptions of the text of the manuscript, rather than the critically edited text as given in the previous chapter. The conventions for restored text, lacunae (which, for larger gaps, are only estimates), erasure, etc. are the same as for the critical edition. Resolved abbreviations appear in (). I have not wasted ink by cataloging Molinier's constant, silent, and usually unfounded alterations to the text.

Line   Text
Commentary

---

1   *Breue commemoratorii*
My translation as "An inventory memorandum" reflects the way both words were used separately in administrative contexts at and around Charlemagne's court and especially the very close parallel of the Werden inventory. There the words appear together and are immediately followed by the Proto-Romance *de* ("of") for the genitive and the definite article: "breue commemoratorio de illa," just as here. The original document from which the Basel roll was copied may well have had "breue commemoratorio" and undergone correction by the copyist. See further above, chapter 6.3 and chapter 7.1. If, on the other hand, we assume that the reading *Breue commemoratorii* was the authentic one and wished for a more literal rendering of these words, then one could find no more elegant solution than "Summary of a report," as proposed by my learned friend Paul E. Dutton.

---

2   pr(es)b(iter)is

The manuscript abbreviates most occurrences of this word. On line 10 it is spelled out *presbiteris*, and we have restored that spelling throughout.

2–3   monas | teria puellarum

Monasterium puellarum is a common early medieval expression for monasteries of women, especially but not exclusively in Gaul. On the plural here, see below, on lines 21–23 (specifically 22).

6   sudarium <·>i

The parchment has deteriorated; there is space for one point before the roman numeral and no sign of another numeral there. The scribe's usual practice places a raised point before and after numbers: see above chapter 6.3, with note 12.

8   sunt in summo ·c·l· excepto ospitales ··iii·

In this case, the scribe has not corrected the faulty aspiration of *hospitales* (see chapter 7.1). The rest of line 8 is blank, marking the end of a section.

As noted elsewhere, the correct mathematical total of the enumerated personnel is 162, not 150. Joel Kalvesmaki has suggested that the enumerated personnel in the patriarchal establishment would indeed total 150 if the 12 candle bearers of lines 4–5 were left out. Now introducing a new group with "qui" is exactly paralleled in line 7, so that the twelve candle bearers are not likely a subgroup of the 41 monks, nor is there any other case of such double-counting in the documents. The intrusion of a merely ceremonial note—that a subset of the monks carry candles—would be hard to explain: it seems irrelevant to the purpose at hand, the enumeration of how many people served the patriarch (and therefore needed to be sustained by patriarchal revenues). So these twelve candle bearers were indeed a group separate from and additional to the monks. However, the suggested construction may offer a valuable insight into the numerical error. If the scribe did not simply drop the "xii" that should have figured after "cl", it is possible that, during the transcription of the original text onto the Basel roll, as the copyist extensively corrected the original's popular Latin in order to bring it into line with the norms of the 820s or 830s, he or she misconstrued the line in question and took the 12 as a subgroup of the 41 monks, and so corrected the original and correct sum of 162 to 150.

10   inpr&orio·v·

The rest of line 10 is blank, marking the end of a section.

12   leprosi ·xv·

The rest of line 12 is blank, marking the end of another section.

18   The end of the line is lost with the edge of the sheet. There could have been room for two more signs, that is, a total of "i*i*<i·>," i.e., "three" if we allow that one of the spaces was occupied by the usual punctuation.

21–23   alter syrus ad su(m)ma(m) scalamin g&hsæmani inclusi ··iii· grecus&syrus & iorzanus· inualleiosaphat inclusus ·i· | monasteria puellarum xxvi· deimperio domni karoli quae adsepulchrum d(omi)ni seruiunt d(e)o sacratas xvii· inclusa | despania··i·

After *inclusus i* the rest of line 21 is blank, signaling the end of the segment. In effect, the significant space at the end of a line marks the strongest punctuation in the roll. Wilkinson was unaware of this and misconstrued "monasteria puellarum xxvi" as part of the description of the hermits scattered in the Kidron Valley. To make sense of *monasteria* (see below), he mistranslates it as "cells for 26 women."[1] The layout of the roll and the Latin itself make quite clear, on the contrary, that the new line starting with *monasteria puellarum* begins a new sense unit, and that the 17 nuns from the empire of Lord Charles who serve the Holy Sepulcher are a subset of that convent's population. See also above, chapter 4.1.

The roll elsewhere treats *monasterium* as neuter (lines 2–3 [in the plural], "monasteria puellarum"; line 38, "monasterium quod uocatur"; line 41, "monasterium puellarum") or masculine (lines 31–32, "In monasterio . . . . construxit eum . . ."; cf. line 34, "Monasterium sancti Stephani . . . construxit e<um> . . ."; although of course the demonstrative pronoun *id* was probably long dead by this time.[2] Conceivably in this one instance *monasteria* could be a feminine singular, although it has no parallel in the roll and few outside it. In any case this cannot be the neuter plural: there certainly were not twenty-six convents in Jerusalem. It is mostly likely a simple slip of the pen for *monasterium*. Although it did happen that neuter plurals became feminine, *monasteria* as a feminine is exceedingly rare.[3] Rather, it was more common for *monasterium* to become masculine (cf. Old French *moustier*).[4]

---

1   J. Wilkinson, *Jerusalem Pilgrims before the Crusades*, 2nd ed. (Warminster, 2002), 255.

2   V. Väänänen, *Introduction au latin vulgaire*, 3rd ed. (Paris, 1981), 120.

3   See *ThLL* 8:1402.70–71. The example in Cyprian, *Vita Caesarii Arelatensis* (BHL 1508) 1.58, is relegated to variants in the best edition, *Sancti Caesarii Arelatensis opera omnia*, ed. G. Morin, 2 (Maredsous, 1942): 320.19.

4   See, for example, M. A. Pei, *The Language of the Eight*[sic]*-Century Texts in Northern France* (New York, 1932), 163. Forms such as *monasteriae* are simply alternate spellings of *monasterii*,

---

24   ad s(an)c(tu)m iohannem quodtenent armeni monachi ·vi·

A large space follows the number "vi·" The scribe seems to have wanted clearly to demarcate the end of this first text. "ISTI IN HIERUSALEM SUNT et in circuitu . . ." is an *explicit* whose first four words are in rustic capitals and follow the large space. The scribe so wanted the next document, starting with its title "Memoria de illis monasteriis . . .", to begin the next new line, that he shrank his letter size drastically, and copied the last two words of the explicit below the end of the line. The line placed below those two words is in a different, lighter ink from that of the main text.

27   inmonasterio s(an)c(t)i theodosii· qu\o/dprimu(m) inillo erimo con*st*\<ructum\> est monachi lxx· basilius *s*\<uper eos\>

de Rossi thought that Basil must be the name of the abbot. He suggests the next word should be something like *superior* but recognized that this particular word would be anachronistic.

Tobler and Molinier offer *sepultus ibi*. Their reading would be a tight fit, but it is possible spacewise.

In the twelfth century, pilgrims were shown the cave of Basil, the disciple of St. Theodosius, adjacent to the cave and tomb of St. Theodosius, under the monastery church.[5] Basil is supposed to have "inaugurated" his mentor's tomb and died a miraculous death. It is conceivable that the text alludes to this tradition, which turns up in the life of Theodosius attributed to Theodore, bishop of Petra.[6] Nevertheless, evidence for a cult of this Basil is scant, which makes it less plausible that the Western envoys spent ink on so obscure a figure.[7] On the other hand, entries for monasteries certainly or arguably give the abbot's name four more times. If the Basil mentioned here was not the saint's disciple, then de Rossi's hypothesis will be strengthened. *Super eos* fits the space and seeming sense well; the main argument against it would be that this is the only case where the name of the abbot follows the number of monks; but this very anomaly would clarify the presence of the additional, explanatory words.

---

reflecting the homophony of *i*, *e*, and *ae* in early Medieval Latin. Compare J. Vielliard, *Le latin des diplômes royaux et chartes privées de l'époque mérovingienne*, Bibliothèque de l'École des hautes études 251 (Paris, 1927), 30–31.

5   John Phocas, *Descriptio brevis . . . locorum sanctorum* 17, p. 18.

6   Theodore of Petra, *Vita Theodosii* (BHG 1776) 21.23–24.20; compare the Metaphrastic *Vita Theodosii Coenobiarchae* (BHG 1778) 15–18, PG 114:469–553, here 481D–485C.

7   For example, *Le calendrier palestino-géorgien* reveals no liturgical commemoration of such a Basil in the local Palestinian liturgy of our period.

28   **Succenderunt sarraceni latrones ipsu(m) monasteriu(m) &
interfecerun<t multos i>g<ne crude>*le***

de Rossi saw space for seventeen letters, including *t*; he attempted no restoration.

Tobler and Molinier restored the missing text as "interfecerunt <ibi multos monachos>".

While the general sense seems appropriate, the words suggested by Tobler and Molinier make a rather tight fit, especially with the two *m*'s; they take no account of the descender, which is almost certainly the remainder of a *g*, and of the two final, uncertain letters. The final letter has a horizontal stroke which suggests *e* or *t*, while the penultimate letter includes an ascender, the position of which indicates it was probably a *d* or an *l*.

One can imagine a number of possible restorations, involving numbers or numerical adjectives of monks killed; the context suggests they may have been killed *igne*. The last word may have been an adjective in the ablative (*crudele*)[8] or perhaps an adverb.

28–29   **&al*ii*propter pa<ctu(m) deiecerunt> | ad terram [*ad******]*p.c.**
ecclesias ·ii· ad ipsu(m) monasterium aspicientes·

de Rossi: "propter pa<vorem fugerunt>; ad terram <dejecerunt> ecclesias ii ad ipsum monasterium aspicientes."

Tobler and Molinier: "propter pa<ganos fugerunt>; ad terram <prostra-uerunt> ecclesias ij ad ipsum monasterium aspicientes."

de Rossi believed that the word written in the erasure on line 29 was *dejece-runt*. Both editions presume a change in subject, since they take *alii* to refer to *multos*, the hypothetical object of *interfecerunt* (see preceding comment). They also suppose a second change of subject for the verb describing the destruction of the churches. The main problem with both reconstructions is that actually there is no textual lacuna after *terram* in line 29. The letters that follow it have been carefully erased, presumably by the scribe himself. The text must therefore have made sense without those letters. Furthermore, under ultraviolet light, the first two letters appear to be *ad*: the ascender of the *d* is clear. The space of the erasure is identical to that occupied by the words *ad terram*. It therefore appears that the scribe simply copied the same words twice by mistake, caught the error afterward and erased it. This means in turn that the verb that puts the churches "on the ground"

---

8   On the exceedingly common Late Latin substitution of -*e* for classical -*i* in the ablative singular, as in my restoration, see, for example, M. Bonnet, *Le latin de Grégoire de Tours* (Paris, 1890), 359.

must have figured in the lacuna at the end of line 28. This in its turn casts doubt on the objects of *propter* advanced by de Rossi, Tobler, and Molinier.

The solution of the word that begins with *pa-* is inspired by the fact that the difficulties described here are part of the disturbances that marked Palestine and Syria in the later years of the reign of Harun al Rashid.[9] *Pactum* is appealing because it can mean a tribute or political ransom in Italian Latin and Byzantine Greek. The Greek use of *pakton* (πάκτον) is well attested in this period.[10] In Italian texts, in addition to Anastasius Bibliothecarius's rendering of Theophanes' Byzantine Greek, the word was used in this way at Monte Cassino, precisely in connection with monks attempting to buy off a Muslim raider.[11] In fact, Hugeburc records in the eighth century that the Christians were repeatedly forced to pay ransom to the Arabs to prevent the pulling down of the shrine of the Annunciation in Nazareth.[12] The sense of the damaged section of the roll would then be, "and other (Arabs) demolished two churches belonging to the monastery because of the ransom [which was not paid]."

29   ins(an)c(t)o saba monachi ·c*l·

de Rossi and Tobler and Molinier: "cl." Because of a tear in the parchment, it is difficult out make out the mark in the third position of the signs indicating the number of monks of Mar Saba. The reading of de Rossi and Tobler and Molinier does not indicate any space between the *c* and the *l*, suggesting that for them the reading "cl" was unproblematic, an interpretation which appears confirmed by Tobler's earlier (and generally high quality) diplomatic transcription "·cl·". From what is visible under ultraviolet light, it is just conceivable that the scribe did not follow his usual practice and wrote ·ccl·. Nonetheless, the surest bet is that the expert scribe did follow his custom and wrote a raised point to separate

---

9   For example, the attacks of 797. See Stephen of Mar Saba, *Martyrium XX monachorum saba-itarum*, for example, 2, 2.28–3.7; and Theophanes, *Chronographia* AM 6301 (= AD 809), 1:484.5–19, describing a five-year period after the death of Harun and mentioning specifically St. Theodosius's and disarray with respect to "τά τε δημόσια πράγματα" (line 12), which can mean "taxes" as well as "affairs of state."

10   For example, Theophanes AM 6288, 470.11 and 13; AM 6169, 359.17 and 20. It occurs in Constantine VII's *De administrando imperio*, passim, index, 326, s.v.

11   Theophanes in Anastasius Bibliothecarius's translation, 2:224.11 and 187.34, respectively; the ninth-century chronicle from Monte Cassino: *Chronica Sancti Benedicti Casinensis* 477.29, on which work, see W. Wattenbach, W. Levison, and H. Löwe, *Deutschlands Geschichtsquellen im Mittelalter: Vorzeit und Karolinger* (Weimar, 1963), 4:436.

12   *Vita Willibaldi* 95.23–24: "Illam aecclesiam christiani homines sepe conparabat ad paganis Sarracinis, qui illi volebat eam destruere."

the hundreds' place from the tens' place, and the roll read ·c·l·, exactly as in line 8; compare line 50: c·xcv·.

**29–30   in pa*l*<eo monasterio> | quod s(an)c(tu)s karitus construxit &
· ubi ipse s(an)c(tu)s abunomiliario requiescit**

de Rossi attempted no restoration; Tobler and Molinier conjectured "in pa<rvo monasterio>". Their restoration confuses the historical picture. In any case, the palaeographical evidence of the manuscript, though partial, is clear: the top of a letter's long ascender is unmistakable at the beginning of the lacuna; its position relative to the *a* means that the letter can be only a *b* or an *l*.

Scholars have usually recognized that this entry refers to the great monastery of Souka, or St. Chariton, whose ruins have been identified at Khan Khureitūn. The problem is how to reconcile this with "Small Monastery," the restoration proposed by Tobler and Molinier.[13] This is certainly not the "Mikron" monastery, since St. Sabas founded that one in the sixth century, and our text makes clear that this house went back to the fourth-century St. Chariton.[14] By 818 Chariton's body had indeed been moved from its original burial place at Pharan to the "Souka," or "Old Lavra," for a letter of Theodore Stoudite to the unnamed abbot and monks of St. Chariton's tells us so.[15] Hirschfeld also grasped the problem and proposed, implicitly, that here the Breve refers not to St. Chariton but to another small monastery near it, which he has associated with Byzantine ruins in 'Ein es-Sakhari.[16] The problem would then become why the Memorial skips over a major monastery, for there is insufficient space for another monastery to have figured in the lacuna.

This new reading resolves the quandary. St. Chariton's was called in Greek "ἡ Παλαιὰ Λαύρα" (i.e., "hē Palaia Laura," The Old Lavra).[17] The Memorial simply

13   See, for one attempt, Wilkinson, *Jerusalem Pilgrims*, 293, under "Chariton."

14   For Sabas's μικρὸν κοινόβιον, see Cyril of Scythopolis, *Vita Sabae* 28, 113.6; and J. Patrich, *Sabas, Leader of Palestinian Monasticism: A Comparative Study in Eastern Monasticism, Fourth to Seventh Centuries* (Washington, D.C., 1995), 145–46.

15   Theodore Stoudite, *Ep.* 278, 2.415–18, here 416.32 (AD 818); compare S. Vailhé, "Répertoire alphabétique des monastères de Palestine [1]," *ROC* 4 (1899): 525. Note that Theodore refers to St. Chariton's as "τῆς μεγίστης λαύρας," that is, "the greatest (or "biggest") lavra," 415.3. An epithet meaning "great" appears to be traditional in this period (see above, chapter 2.2, note 23) and, in any case, makes some sort of conflation with the putative *mikron* of Tobler and Molinier even less plausible.

16   Y. Hirschfeld, "List of the Byzantine Monasteries in the Judean Desert," in *Christian Archaeology in the Holy Land: New Discoveries*, eds. G. C. Bottini, L. Di Segni, and E. Alliata, Studium biblicum franciscanum, Collectio maior 36 (Jerusalem, 1990), 62–63.

17   See Anonymous, "Les premiers monastères de la Palestine," *Bessarione* 3 (1897–98): 39–58, here 50–58, esp. 50, and Vailhé, "Répertoire alphabétique [1]," 524–25. See also Hirschfeld, "List of the

transliterated the descriptive Greek name of the monastery, "the Old Monastery" as the *Paleum* (or *Palea*?) *monasterium*. The ninth-century *Parvum monasterium* of Tobler and Molinier is therefore a ghost abbey, which can be removed from the religious topography of the Holy Land.

30   abbano<(m)i(n)e*****mon>achi·

de Rossi: "abba no********monachi"; Tobler and Molinier: "abba no<mine....> monachi".

de Rossi estimated that some eight letters were missing before *monachi*. Today some twenty-six millimeters separate the beginning of the *o* of *no<mine>* and the location of the missing *o* in *<mon>achi*. Although there is some crumpling of the parchment at this point, that measurement approximates the actual extent of the lacuna. The extreme regularity of the hand again allows us to surmise possible parameters for what is missing. Judging from the average size of the appropriate letters and space between them in these and surrounding lines, if the last five letters of *nomine* were written out, they would occupy about fifteen millimeters; the first letter and usual spacing of *<mon>achi* would require another five or six millimeters, which would imply an extremely and, probably, impossibly short name, occupying only the remaining five or six millimeters. Proper names are generally written out in full.[18] Even "Elias" requires some twelve millimeters (line 47). *Nomine* was therefore abbreviated, presumably in the usual fashion "noie": the three missing letters (including the partially visible *o*) would have occupied about seven millimeters; with the first letter and spaces required by *monachi*, that leaves some thirteen millimeters for the missing name. *Iohannis*, the form of "Johannes" preserved on the roll, takes twenty-one millimeters; *Basilius* takes eighteen millimeters (lines 27 and 45); and *Stefano* takes twenty-one and seventeen millimeters (lines 12 and 15–16). Thus the missing abbot's name will have been shorter than these names. Elias, Thomas (especially if spelled Tomas), and other similarly short names count among the candidates. The hypothesis of Thomas would place the Breve before the elevation of the hegoumenos of that name to the patriarchal see, which occurred no later than 807.[19]

Byzantine Monasteries," 8–12. For additional Greek attestations of this name from precisely our period, see Stephen of Mar Saba, *Martyrium XX Sabaitarum*, where Palaia Lavra is the most common way of referring to this house (5, 4.26 and 31; 14, 13.7–8; 15, 14.7–8; 16, 14.14); its monks were called Παλαιολαυρῖται: ibid., 19, 15.33.

18   See, for example, *Iohannes* in lines 16, 24, 32, 33, 43.

19   See, on this stage of Thomas's career, Stephen of Mar Saba, *Martyrium XX Sabaitarum* 14, 13.6–8.

30–31   mon>achi ·<***in s(an)c(t)o eutimio abba no(m)i(n)e **** mo> |
nachi ·xxx··

Based on his erroneous reconstruction of the sheet, de Rossi believed that several lines were lost; he offers no text but presumes the monastery of St. Euthymius figured here. Tobler and Molinier reconstitute "<. . . .In sancto Euthymio mo>."

All concur that the important house of St. Euthymius, whose ruins have been identified at Khan el Aḥmar, must have figured here. It would certainly fit in terms of geography (the list is now moving eastward from Jerusalem toward Jericho and then toward the Jordan) and what is known of Palestinian monasticism in the period: Theophanes mentions this monastery, and construction work between the eighth and twelfth centuries is archaeologically documented at the site.[20]

Space considerations mean that the wording proposed by Tobler and Molinier, which echoes the formulation of the reference to Mar Saba rather than that used, for example, for Choziba, is probably right since "inmonasterio scieutimii" would have no chance of fitting in the space available, whether or not an abbot's name was given.

There is no room for an additional entry beyond that for St. Euthymius. The evidence is insufficient to warrant conjectural restorations of the missing name of the abbot.

31   in monasterio s(an)c(t)ae mariæ incoziba a*b*ba *n*<o(m)i(n)e
teofi>lactus

de Rossi: "in monaster<io*****************************>laetus."

Tobler and Molinier: "In monasterio Sancte Marie in Coziba abba <nomine> Letus."

de Rossi's erroneous reconstruction of the roll caused him not to see the connection between his reading "***laetus" and the monastery at Choziba. He thought thirty-one letters were missing between *monasterio* and *laetus*. He read the damaged first letter of *n*<*oie*> as an *i* and scrupulously conceded that the copy he had made from the manuscript bore *alba* so that he was no longer sure whether he had erred in transcribing or faithfully rendered the manuscript. One could indeed construe the last stroke visible before the lacuna as an *i* or the beginning of

---

20 Theophanes, *Chronographia* AM 6301, 1:484.17–18; compare Hirschfeld, "List of the Byzantine Monasteries," 15–18; Vailhé, "Répertoire alphabétique [1]," 533–34; A. Ovadiah, *Corpus of the Byzantine Churches in the Holy Land* (Bonn, 1970), 97–103; compare Wilkinson, *Jerusalem Pilgrims*, 302, s.v. "Euthymius."

an *n* and the second letter of *abba* as an *l*, but in both cases, the usual usage of the document urges us to read *abba n<oie>*. Tobler and Molinier made the connection with Choziba and invented the perplexing situation of a Greek abbot bearing the unusual Latin name of Laetus. Tobler and Molinier filled the lacuna with the word *nomine*.

The *c* of *lactus* is clear and I am sure of the reading of the end of the abbot's name. The oddity of a Latin-named abbot of Choziba disappears from Palestinian history of the ninth century. With the new reading, it is easy to restore *teofi>lactus*, which fits the space well if we presume the scribe used the common abbreviation *no(m)i(n)e*. Thus we recover for Byzantine prosopography the name of a ninth-century abbot of this important monastery (see chapter 5.1).

31–32   *m*<onachi * in monasterio prope iericho abba no(m)i(n)e> |
iohannes monachi ·x· construxit eu(m) s(an)c(tu)s gerasimus ubi &
ipses(an)c(tu)s incorpo<re**

de Rossi, though still a victim of his false reconstruction, correctly proposed to restore the word *monachi*: "******<monachi>*****<in monasterio>******<abba> /Johannes." Tobler and Molinier restored ". . . . . In monasterio, ubi baptizabat> Iohannes,"

My restoration accepts de Rossi's basic understanding of the line; the monastery built by St. Gerasimus is that usually identified by the saint's name; the ruins have been identified some five kilometers southeast of Jericho, several kilometers from the present course of the Jordan.[21] It is unlikely that the founding saint's name would have been repeated twice in the same entry. I have therefore proposed that, in the lacuna, the monastery was identified by its proximity to Jericho, on the model of St. Stephen's in line 34.

Tobler and Molinier seemed to have no evidence for linking this monastery with the place where John the Baptist was believed to have baptized Christ, a biblical event normally associated with the next monastery listed. As de Rossi clearly saw, it is preferable to take *Iohannes*, one of the most common Byzantine names,[22] to be the name of the abbot.

With respect to the overall statistical portrait of the Holy Land, there is room for only one monastery in the lacuna, and that is the house whose description continues on line 32.

---

21   See above, chapter 10, note 51.
22   See A. Kazhdan and A.-M. Talbot, "John," *ODB* 1:1042–43.

32–33   **iohannes monachi ·x· construxit eu(m) s(an)c(tu)s gerasimus
ubi & ipses(an)c(tu)s incorpo<re requiescit *********************>** |
**& erexit intitulu(m)· ad iordanen monasteriu(m) s(an)c(t)i iohannis
& ecclesia<m> alia<m>**

de Rossi restores "corpo<re requiescit. ibi et ecclesiam quam ipse construxit>."

Tobler and Molinier restore "in corpo<re requiescit; ibi & ecclesiam ipse construxit> & erexit in titulum."

Even allowing for the usual abbreviation of the final letter of *ecclesiam*, according to the scribe's usual spacing of letters and words, the restoration proposed by previous editors adds up to too much text to fit.

de Rossi felt that *ecclesiam* was needed in the lacuna because of the reference to "ecclesia alia" in the next line. But this reasoning fails on two grounds. As the previous editors have construed these lines, they contain two separate entries concerning two separate complexes, so it is unclear why the second entry would distinguish "another" church with respect to the preceding entry. Moreover, in its other enumerations of complexes containing multiple churches, the Memorial implicitly or explicitly counts the monastery church as one of a series. In line 42, one of the "five churches" is clearly the monastery's own church since there is no room in the lacuna for a fifth church (cf. too the textual notes on this passage); at Sinai, the "fourth" church is explicitly identified as the monastery itself (line 48).

de Rossi wrestled with *titulus*, taking it to mean "parish church," in the Roman sense. Here he thought it could mean a church where the hermits gathered for their Sunday service. The word does occur frequently in the analogous sense of a local, parish church within a diocesan organization in Carolingian administrative parlance, and it is conceivable that this is the sense here. However, the Memorial nowhere else descends to this level of internal functional detail; rather, its comments typically concern the founder's identity, physical state, recent events, tombs, or biblical associations. *Titulus* could also mean a "tomb" or a "monument." Nevertheless the phrase "erigere (in) titulum" usually means "erect (as) a monument" and is so used in the Vulgate (e.g., Genesis 28:18; 31:45, 35:20; 2 Samuel 18:18, etc.), which should guide our interpretation.

It may be that a new syntactical unit began in the lacuna. Although one would be tempted to think the name of the monastery of Kalamon may have figured here, it would seem difficult to fit the "monasterium in honore sanctae Mariae, monachi *."[23] "Monasterium Calamon, monachi *" seems more plausible in

23   For the dedication to the Virgin, see Vailhé, "Les laures de Saint Gérasime et de Calamon," *Échos de l'Orient* 2 (1898–99): 116.

topographical terms, but does not solve the problem, for syntactically what has been lost must include the subject of the verb "erexit" on line 33. It is more likely that in addition to "monasterium sancti Iohannis," "et alia<m> ecclesia<m>" is also the direct object of "erexit" and whatever verb occurred in the lacuna. The sense would then be that monastery of St. John the Baptist and the apparently structurally remarkable nearby riverside church were "erected as monuments" to Christ's baptism, as indeed the church, mounted on vaults to avoid flooding, certainly was by Anastasius I.[24] The lacuna would then have read something like <imp anastasius exstruxit>, which would just fit; the record of imperial largess would parallel the Breve's mention of Justinian in line 11. In late antiquity, the site had been marked by a marble column and an iron cross; late seventh- and early eighth-century travelers still described a cross in the Jordan, hence the reference to a monument.[25]

Against this construction, one might observe that there is a raised point after *titulum*. However, elsewhere on the roll this punctuation mark does not constitute a strong break (cf. line 30, "et·"), and it may simply set off the prepositional phrase describing the "monument." Also, the scribe failed to correct *ecclesia* to the classical accusative form, but this would not be the first failure to correct a morphological vulgarism (cf. the nominative plural *sacratas* in line 12). Rightly or wrongly, the scribe may have thought the *ad* marked the beginning of a new entry, since the *a* is slightly though not unambiguously large. A prepositional phrase specifying location usually does open an entry, but there are two certain exceptions (line 21, "ad summam scalam"; line 34, "prope Iericho").

In any event, none of the proposed constructions suggest there was room for another, lost entry of a monastic community in the lacuna. There are insufficient grounds for deducing anything about the abbot's name.

33–34   u<bi d(omi)n(u)s baptizatus est. abba *****> | monachi ·xxx v·**

de Rossi proposed "ubi dominus baptizatus est"; Tobler and Molinier suggested "u<bi peregrini descendunt ad fluvium>."

de Rossi's restoration seems satisfactory in sense. It is, however, a little short, since *dominus* is always abbreviated on the roll with the *nomen sacrum* form *dns*.

24 Theodosius, *De situ Terrae Sanctae* 20, 121.22–28; Vailhé, "Répertoire alphabétique des monastères de Palestine [2 and 3]," *ROC* 5 (1900): 19.

25 See Adomnan, *De locis sanctis* 2.16, 213.6–18; Hugeburc, *Vita Willibaldi* 4, 96.15–20; and Bernard, *Itinerarium* 18, 318. According to Adomnan, the cross was then made of wood. Bernard mentions the monastery and no cross, but his account is so succinct at this point as to exclude deductions from silence. See for further references, above, chapter 10, note 53.

That offered by Tobler and Molinier fits the spacing better, but it seems a trivial statement that in any case does not conform to the pattern of the roll.

The first word in the lacuna is almost certainly *ubi*, judging from the roll's usage elsewhere. An explanation of the biblical or historical association of the site would make sense here. In fact *ubi* occurs twenty-nine times on the roll. Only once does it refer to a contemporary circumstance other than a tomb location (line 18, "ubi sunt monachi . . ."); otherwise it identifies a tomb (six times) or, in the vast majority of cases, it specifies the biblical event associated with a place. This is very likely true as well of the shrine associated with Christ's baptism.

The remaining space presumably followed the usual pattern and gave the name of the abbot. In any case, any form of biblical association means insufficient room for an additional monastery here, so the thirty-five monks must be at the monastery of St. John the Baptist. This is quite interesting from a historical perspective, since we know that around 725, this monastery had only about twenty monks (see above, chapter 2.2, note 74)

34–35: "monachi ·xxx v· monasteriu(m) s(an)c(t)i stephani propeiericho construxit e<um **** monasteriu(m) in> | montefaran inistis duob(us) nescimus quantisint·,"

de Rossi: "construxit e<um ********* Monasterium**** in>."

Tobler and Molinier: "construxit E<. . . . . Monasterium Sancti Theoctisti> in."

Tobler and Molinier are victims of their own inaccuracy, since they have elsewhere silently corrected the manuscript's *eum* (modifying *monasterium*, i.e., of St. Stephen, near Jericho) to classical *id*, and so failed to recognize the pattern in the roll's usage (e.g., line 32). Little if anything is known of this monastery; compare above, chapter 10, note 54. The Memoria's compilers apparently recorded the name of its founder in the lacuna.

The *monasterium* seems an unavoidable restoration, according to the general pattern of the entries. This, plus the proper name of the person who built the monastery of St. Stephen—a minimum of four letters (*Elias*? see above, chapter 10, note 54) and possibly more—leaves insufficient room for a hypothetical third house in the lacuna. This fits moreover with the report of line 35 "in these two . . . ."

35–36   montefaran inistis duob(us) nescimus quantisint·, in galilea inciuit<ate s(an)c(t)a nazar&h ubi d(omi)n(u)s . . . ecclesia . . . monachi> | xii

de Rossi: "civit<ate Nazareth***************** monachi>"

Tobler and Molinier: "civit<ate sancta Nazareth, monachi>"

Neither earlier restoration accounts for the entire space, but there seems to be insufficient room for more than one institution, especially if the roll followed its usual pattern of mentioning the shrine at Nazareth and identifying its biblical significance. The assumption that Nazareth was treated in the lacuna is generally accepted by those who have studied the document. It appears justified, given that Nazareth was the key New Testament site in Galilee and that the entry continues by situating the next house by its distance from Nazareth. The religious at Nazareth will presumably have been monks.

36–37   unomiliario anazar&h ubi xp(istu)m d(omi)n(u)m iudæi praecipitare uolu<erunt monasterium in> | honores(an)c(t)ę mariae monachi ˙viii˙,

de Rossi: "uolu<erunt ********monasterium in>."

Tobler and Molinier: "uol<uerunt, constructum monasterium & ecclesia in>."

Anything beyond de Rossi's restoration is pure hypothesis; the proposal of Tobler and Molinier lacks convincing parallels in the text. I could see most of the second *u* of *uoluerunt* on the manuscript itself.

The monastery of the Virgin in line 37 may well continue the entry about the shrine of the "Saltus Domini" located at Jebel el-Qafse, two kilometers south of Nazareth. See chapter 10, n. 58. The ending of uolu<erunt> and the necessary words *monasterium in* limit the maximum missing text to about twenty letters. It is not completely impossible that the shrine of the Lord's Leap was different from the monastery that begins on line 37, but that has appeared to earlier commentators to be unlikely, and I share that opinion.

37–38   in chanan galileę ubi d(omi)n(u)s de aqua *u*<inum fecit ecclesia monachi . iuxta ma> | re

de Rossi: "uin<um fecit *********Juxta ma>."

Tobler and Molinier: "uin<um fecit, monachi. . . . Supra ma>re".

Today the first letter after *aqua* is uncertain, but it could well be a *u*. There now is not enough parchment left for the three letters the other editors have read at this point, but there is no reason to doubt de Rossi's otherwise scrupulous reporting. Toward the end of the lacuna, I prefer to follow de Rossi and the Memorial's own usage and restore *iuxta* rather than *supra*: compare "item iuxta mare" in line 39.

Room is sufficient for details about the staff of the church in Cana; it was big according to Hugeburc's description of Willibald's visit.[26] We must presume then

26 Hugeburc, *Vita Willibaldi* 4, 95.26.

some missing statistical information for Cana. Whether the personnel were *clerici* or *monachi* makes no difference from the point of view of the size of the lacuna. Because Epiphanius Hagiopolites' account of the Holy Land, variously dated between the seventh and the ninth century, mentions a monastery at the site of the miracle, it is legitimate to keep the conjecture of Tobler and Molinier that *monachi* figured here, recognizing of course its hypothetical character.[27] There is little likelihood that mention of another house has been lost in this lacuna.

38–39   monasteriu(m) quoduocatur eptapegon ubid(omi)n(u)s satiauit populi*su*<i quinque panibus & duobus> | piscib(us) quinq(ue) milia· ibisuntmonachi ··x·

de Rossi and Tobler and Molinier restore "populi su<i quinque panibus et duobus>", where Tobler and Molinier use the ampersand.

The lacuna supplied details of the miracle of the loaves and fishes (Matthew 14:15–21, etc.); there is room for a little more text than what previous editors have proposed, and more still if the roll abbreviated the ablative endings or used numerical forms. In any case, the conclusion of the biblical reference on line 39 assures us that no statistical material is missing.

39–40   ite(m) iuxtamare ecclesia qua(m) uocant *d*uodec<i>*m* <thronoru(m) ubi d(omi)n(u)s prandidit cum disci> | pulissuis ibiest mensa ubi cumillis sedit ibi sunt pr(es)b(iter) ·i· clerici ·ii·

de Rossi: "duodecim <apostolorum *******disci>pulis."

Tobler and Molinier: "duodec<im thronorum, & ibi fuit Dominus cum disci>pulis."

The restoration of Tobler and Molinier would fit the roll's usual abbreviations and spacing pattern. The site of Christ's meal with his disciples after the Resurrection was in fact known as the "Twelve Thrones" (Dodekathronon; see chapter 10, note 62). The usual pattern of biblical associations suggests the easy restoration: *ubi d(omi)n(u)s* . . . for *dominus* certainly figured in the lacuna as the missing subject of *sedit*. The missing verb may have been *comedit*, *manducavit* (perhaps more appropriate to the author's Latinity) or, most likely of all, *prandidit*, echoing the wording of the passage associated with this place in John 21:12 ("Dicit eis Iesus: venite prandete . . .") and John 21:15: "cum ergo prandissent. . . ."

27 Epiphanius, *Descriptio Palaestinae* 12, 80.15. On the range of dates assigned to Epiphanius, see above, chapter 2.1, note 16. On the hypothetical monastery see chapter 2.2, note 22.

40–41   intiberia ciuit*ate* teo*p*<hilus e(pisco)p(u)s inter pr(es)b(ite)ris> |
& monachis &canonicisxxx· ecclesias·v· monasteriu(m) puellaru(m)··i·

de Rossi: "Teo<******* episcopus>."

Tobler and Molinier: "Theo<dorus episcopus, inter presbyteros>."

The last three words of my restoration are assured by the episcopal status of the church in Tiberias, which must have included priests in its staff, and by the regular formula of the roll, "inter pr(es)b(ite)ris monachis . . ." and its variants (nearly identical: line 45; cf. lines 9, 10, 14, 17, 26, 45, 59). On the expression, above, chapter 7.1.

Although it is not apparent on the photograph, visual inspection under ultraviolet light showed that the fourth letter of the bishop's name had a long descender, which is very probably a *p*. This rules out the reconstruction of the bishop's name suggested by Tobler and Molinier.

The possibilities for his name are three: Theophylactus, Theophanius (for the ending cf. line 41) and Theophilus. The available space makes the third option almost certain.

There are no statistics or houses missing from this entry.

41   . . . in montes(an)c(t)o tabor e(pisco)p(u)s teophan*iu*<s ecclesię>

de Rossi: "Theophani<us, ecclesiae"

Tobler and Molinier: "Theophan<es, ecclesie>"

The spacing is such in this line that there is very little room left after the bishop's name, whence the probable reading of an *e-caudata*.

42   quarta <******>

de Rossi and Tobler and Molinier offer the same reading; de Rossi thought there were six letters missing, whereas Tobler and Molinier apparently thought there were five lacking. The saint's name that certainly figured in the lacuna must have been very short, especially if the abbreviation *sci* or *sc(a)e* preceded it.

44   & ecclesia ubi ille carce*r f*<uit>

de Rossi: "carcer fuit."

Tobler and Molinier: "carce<r> fu<it, &>."

de Rossi's edition indicates the final letters were still visible when he saw the manuscript; I could barely distinguish the presence of the last letter of *carcer* when I examined the original; I was able to see only the top of the vertical stroke of the *f*.

There is no room for Tobler and Molinier's *&*, which is not required for the text.

Line   Text
Commentary

45   insamaria qua(m) naboliuocant ecc<le>*si*<a>

de Rossi could see the entire last word. Part of the *s* and part of the *i* are visible on the photograph, but I could not see them when I inspected the manuscript firsthand.

47   ins(an)c(t)o monte syna ecclesiae ·iiii· una ubid(omi)n(u)s locutusest cu(m)moysi inuertice montis· alia s(an)c(t)i eliæ· te<r>*t*ia s(an)c<(t)i***

de Rossi saw room for four letters at the end of the line; Tobler and Molinier: "sancti <Elisei>".

I saw what looked like the vestiges of three or four letters; the last two may be traces of ascenders, which might support the hypothesis of Tobler and Molinier, but the saint's name must be very short: <ioh(annes)> is also a possibility.

48–49   gradicula adsubiendum ueldesce<nd>endu(m) xii*i* | milia ·dcc·

de Rossi: "vii | milia DCC."

Tobler and Molinier: "vij millia dcc."

"vii" might appear correct from the photograph alone. Under ultraviolet light, the letters *xiii* were clear: the only slight hesitation was for the last minim of the number *xiii*.

50   ipsa ecclesia s(an)c(t)ae *m*ar<i>ae q*uo*d ille terrae motus f<regit>

de Rossi did not detect the *f* and so suggested *quassauit* or a similar verb; Tobler and Molinier proposed "<euertit>".

The first letter was clear to me and excludes both suggestions. *Frango* seems the best choice (cf. *ThLL* 6.1:1242.3–6).

51–52   inlonge de*xteros xx*<x·>iiii· inuno fronte xxx<v> | permedium inaduerso ·xxx·ii· inlongo permedium ··l·,

The third digit of the first measurement and, particularly, the fourth digit of the second measurement are nearly invisible today, but they were clear to de Rossi. A raised point can be hypothesized in the space before "iiii".

52   ecclesia in*b*&hlem inlongo dexteros xxxviii<·>

de Rossi and Tobler and Molinier read "xxxviii." de Rossi misread "b&hlem" as "<sca> Hierusalem."

There is definitely writing after the third *i*; it appears to me to be the raised point; the comparison of this measurement with modern ones of this building (above chapter 5.2) indicates that this is right.

Texts, Translation, and Textual Commentary

57   hab& dexteros xxxviiii· intransuerso ·xxvi·

The last two-thirds of line 57 are left blank, signaling the beginning of a new document on line 58.

58–60   contain the beginning of the last document, "Annual expenditures of the patriarch." It is virtually unique for the entire early Middle Ages, Byzantine or Latin, and the severe damage it has undergone is all the more to be regretted. It is uncertain how far, if at all, it may have continued after line 60. Given the detail and precision which mark the other data on the roll, we may suspect that it did continue beyond line 60, although perhaps not by much (see above, chapter 1.1). My readings differ substantially from those of my predecessors. Most of the improvement over de Rossi is due to the use of ultraviolet light in Basel and the opportunity to use transparencies to actually superimpose various potential restorations in the expertly regular script of the roll onto a magnificent life-size photograph prepared by the Basel library. An additional advantage was the electronic library of the Latin series of the Corpus christianorum (CLCLT-5) and the other electronic text databases, which allowed exhaustive searches for words that fit the parameters imposed by space and whatever letters were visible.

58   dispensa patriarchae interpr(es)b(ite)ris diaconib(us) monachis·
clericis & omne congregatione eccle<siae perunum>

de Rossi: "eccle<siae per unum>."

Tobler and Molinier: "eccle<sie per>".

de Rossi's restitution accounts for the space better, particularly if we assume the usual spacing of the preposition right against the word it modifies. In any case, it is unlikely that anything that changes the meaning of the line appeared here.

59   annum solidos dcc & p<atria>rcha sol(i)d(os)· d l infabricatura(m)
ecclesiarum sol(i)d(os) ·ccc· in ca<**************>

de Rossi: "annum solidos dcxxxv; ****** solidos dl; in fabricaturam ecclesiarum solidos CCC, in ec<**********>".

Tobler and Molinier: "annum solidos dcxxx, <servientibus> solidos dxl, in fabricaturam ecclesiarum solidos ccc, in ec<clesias in civitate>."

Under ultraviolet light, the second *c* of *dcc* looks quite probable; I saw no evidence of an *x* at this point. One of the *x*'s read by previous editors is certainly the ampersand (*et*): although the entire ligature is not visible, enough of the spear and the upper bow appear above the two-line space, within which are confined letters like *o*, *e*, *u*, and so forth, to rule out an *x*, since *x* always respects the two-line space in this hand. There is insufficient space between the second *c* and the ampersand for another digit: it was either blank or contained a raised point.

The ampersand meant that a second, and presumably closely related, expenditure to that for the total clergy (of the patriarchal establishment, we must presume) followed. The last in this group of letters looks like an *a*; the penultimate is a *b* or, more likely, *h*. The attack stroke of the first letter is visible: it might be a short *i-longa*, an *n*, a *p*, and so forth. In view of the way in which late antique managers categorized church revenues[28] and the exceedingly few Latin words that end in *-ha*, the stroke is almost certainly that of the *p*. The word that figured here must therefore have been "patriarcha," which would fit perfectly the sense, the space, and the traces of the last four letters of the word.

In the entry that follows building maintenance, the first letter after the preposition *in* is certainly a *c*, not the *e* previous editors have given. The second letter is probably *a*, *e*, or *o*. The possibilities seem too numerous to reward speculation.

60   *in****m sol(i)*d(os) ·xxx <*****>o in*a****< > *sol(i)*d(os) lxxx in
ministris sarracenor<*um*>

de Rossi: "******* solidos xxx; ******* ad Sarrace<nos> solidos lxxx; in ministris Sarracenor<um>. . . ."

Tobler and Molinier: "solidos cxl, ad Sarrac<enos> solidos dlxxx, in ministris Sarracenor<um solidos. . . . .>"

There is no number missing before the first *x* of *xxx* in line 60.

In the middle of line 60, "*in*s<u>a</u>rr<u>r</u><a>c<u>e</u><nis> *sol*(i)d(os) lxxx," for the first word, *in* looks most likely; *ad* today appears less likely, but not impossible. For the second word, part of what looks like it could be the initial *s*, the very tops of the *r*'s and, probably, the *c* can just be made out; the first *a* seems fairly clear. All of this reinforces de Rossi's usual reliability and authorizes the reading *Sarrac<*. Unlike de Rossi, Tobler and Molinier misread here the *d* of the abbreviation *sold* (which occurs thrice in lines 59–60) as the first digit of the number that follows, thereby erroneously increasing the payment from *lxxx* to *dlxxx*, that is, by 500 solidi.

Comparison with line 56 shows that the end of line 58 counted about eleven more letters or spaces than have survived; 59 had about fifteen more letters. Since *sold.* and a number—a minimum of one space plus a space to either side—almost certainly figured in the lacuna at the end of line 59, the eight remaining available

---

28 See above, chapter 1.1.

---

spaces strongly suggest that the end of the line completed the budgetary entry that began with *in ca****. The implication of this is that we have gotten down fairly swiftly to much smaller sums and that, as far as the size of individual items in the budget is concerned, most of the major item headings are probably represented on what survives of this document.

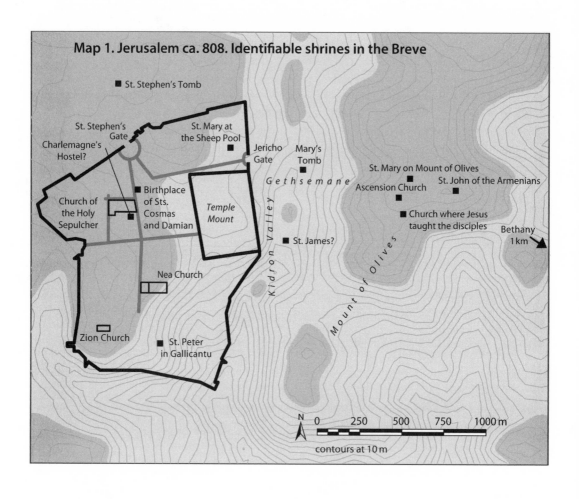

Map 1. Jerusalem ca. 808. Identifiable shrines in the Breve

St. Stephen's Tomb

St. Stephen's Gate

Charlemagne's Hostel?

St. Mary at the Sheep Pool

Jericho Gate

Mary's Tomb

St. Mary on Mount of Olives

Ascension Church

St. John of the Armenians

Gethsemane

Church of the Holy Sepulcher

Birthplace of Sts. Cosmas and Damian

Temple Mount

Church where Jesus taught the disciples

Bethany 1 km

St. James?

Nea Church

Kidron Valley

Mount of Olives

Zion Church

St. Peter in Gallicantu

N

0   250   500   750   1000 m

contours at 10 m

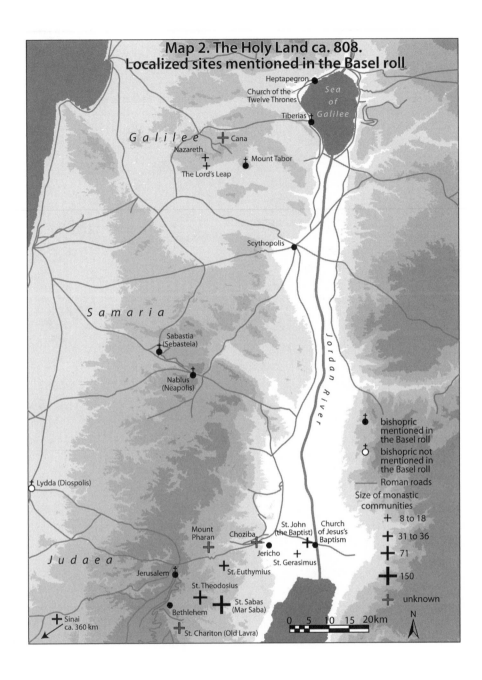

Map 2. The Holy Land ca. 808.
Localized sites mentioned in the Basel roll

Heptapegon

Church of the
Twelve Thrones

Sea
of
Galilee

Tiberias

Galilee

Cana

Nazareth

Mount Tabor

The Lord's Leap

Samaria

Scythopolis

Jordan River

Sabastia
(Sebasteia)

Nablus
(Neapolis)

Lydda (Diospolis)

bishopric
mentioned in
the Basel roll

bishopric not
mentioned in
the Basel roll

Roman roads

Size of monastic
communities

8 to 18

31 to 36

71

150

unknown

Mount
Pharan

Choziba

St. John
(the Baptist)

Church
of Jesus's
Baptism

Jericho

St. Gerasimus

Judaea

Jerusalem

St. Euthymius

St. Theodosius

St. Sabas
(Mar Saba)

Bethlehem

Sinai
ca. 360 km

St. Chariton (Old Lavra)

0   5   10   15   20km

N

239

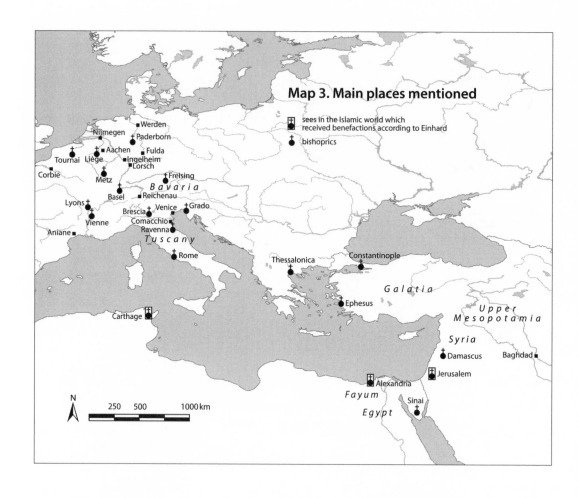

Map 3. Main places mentioned

sees in the Islamic world which received benefactions according to Einhard

bishoprics

Werden
Nijmegen
Paderborn
Aachen
Fulda
Tournai
Liège
Ingelheim
Lorsch
Corbie
Metz
Freising
Bavaria
Basel
Reichenau
Lyons
Brescia
Venice
Grado
Vienne
Comacchio
Aniane
Ravenna
Tuscany
Rome

Thessalonica
Constantinople
Galatia
Ephesus
Upper
Mesopotamia
Syria
Damascus
Baghdad
Carthage
Jerusalem
Alexandria
Fayum
Sinai
Egypt

N

250   500   1000 km

ABBREVIATIONS

AASS	*Acta sanctorum*, 3rd ed., 71 vols. (Paris, 1863–1940)
AB	*Analecta Bollandiana* (Brussels, 1882–)
AJA	*American Journal of Archaeology* (New York, 1886–)
BACr	*Bullettino di archeologia cristiana* (Rome, 1863–)
BASOR	*Bulletin of the American Schools of Oriental Research* (Ann Arbor, etc., 1919–)
BHG	*Bibliotheca hagiographica graeca*, 3rd ed., *Auctarium*, ed. F. Halkin, SubsHag 8a and 47; 3 vols. (Brussels, 1957–69)
BHL	*Bibliotheca hagiographica latina antiquae et mediae aetatis*, ed. Socii Bollandiani, SubsHag 6 and 12, 2 vols. (Brussels, 1898–1901 [1949]); *Novum supplementum*, ed. H. Fros, SubsHag 70 (Brussels, 1986)
BM	J. F. Böhmer, E. Mühlbacher, et al., *Die Regesten des Kaiserreichs unter den Karolingern*, Regesta Imperii 1; 3rd ed. (Hildesheim, 1966)
ByzF	*Byzantinische Forschungen* (Amsterdam, 1966–)
BZ	*Byzantinische Zeitschrift* (Stuttgart, 1892–)
CCCM	Corpus christianorum, Continuatio mediaevalis (Turnhout, 1971–)
CCSG	Corpus christianorum, Series graeca (Turnhout, 1977–)
CCSL	Corpus christianorum, Series latina (Turnhout, 1953–)
ChLA	*Chartae latinae antiquiores*, ed. A. Bruckner et al. (Olten, 1954–)
CLCLT-5	*Library of Latin Texts (CLCLT-5)* [CD-ROMs], ed. P. Tombeur (Turnhout, 2002)

CRAI	*Comptes rendus des séances de l'année de l'Académie des inscriptions et belles-lettres* (Paris, 1857–)
CSCO	Corpus scriptorum christianorum orientalium (Paris, etc., 1900–)
CSEL	Corpus scriptorum ecclesiasticorum latinorum (Vienna, 1866–)
DA	*Deutsches Archiv für Erforschung des Mittelalters* (Marburg, etc., 1950–)
DOP	*Dumbarton Oaks Papers* (Cambridge, MA, etc., 1941–)
EHB	*The Economic History of Byzantium*, ed. A. E. Laiou, 3 vols. (Washington, D.C., 2002)
EHR	*English Historical Review* (Harlow, etc., 1886–)
*EI*²	*Encyclopaedia of Islam,* 2nd ed., ed. P. Bearman et al., 13 vols. (Leyden, 1960–2009)
*EI*² *Online*	*Encyclopaedia of Islam,* 2nd ed., ed. P. Bearman et al., Brill Online (Leyden, 2010) [http://www.brillonline.nl/]
eMGH5	Monumenta Germaniae Historica [CD-ROM] (Turnhout, 2005)
FM	*Fontes minores* [part of Forschungen zur byzantinischen Rechtsgeschichte] (Frankfurt am Main, 1976–)
IEJ	*Israel Exploration Journal* (Jerusalem, 1950–)
LMA	*Lexikon des Mittelalters*, 8 vols. (Munich, 1977–95)
MGH	Monumenta Germaniae Historica
Briefe	Die Briefe der deutschen Kaiserzeit (Weimar, 1949–)
Capit	Capitularia regum Francorum, ed. A. Boretius and V. Krause (Hanover, 1883–97)
Conc	Concilia, ed. A. Werminghoff et al. (Hanover, 1893–)
DD Kar	Diplomata Karolinorum, ed. E. Mühlbacher et al. (Hanover, etc. 1906–)
DD Mer	Die Urkunden der Merowinger, ed. T. Kölzer et al. (Hanover, 2001)
Ep	Epistolae, ed. L. M. Hartmann, E. Dümmler et al. (Berlin, 1891–)
EpSel	Epistolae selectae (Berlin, 1955–78)

MGH (*continued*)

FontIur	Fontes iuris Germanici antiqui in usum scholarum ex Monumentis Germaniae historicis separatim editi (Hanover, 1869–)
Formulae	Formulae Merowingici et Karolini aevi, ed. K. Zeumer (Hanover, 1886)
GestPontRom	Gesta pontificum Romanorum, ed. T. Mommsen (Berlin, 1898)
LLNat	Leges nationum Germanicarum (Hanover, 1902–)
Poetae	Poetae latini medii aevi, ed. E. Dümmler, L. Traube et al. (Berlin, 1881–)
ScriptRerGerm	Scriptores rerum Germanicarum in usum scholarum (Hanover, etc., 1839–)
ScriptRerLangob	Scriptores rerum Langobardicarum et Italicarum saec. VI–IX (Hanover, 1878)
ScriptRerMerov	Scriptores rerum Merovingicarum (Hanover, 1884–1951)

NEAEHL	*The New Encyclopedia of Archaeological Excavations in the Holy Land*, ed. E. Stern, A. Lewinson-Gilboa, and J. Aviram (Jerusalem, 1993)
ODB	*The Oxford Dictionary of Byzantium*, ed. A. Kazhdan et al., 3 vols. (Oxford, 1991)
PG	Patrologiae cursus completus, Series graeca, ed. J.-P. Migne, 161 vols. in 166 pts. (Paris, 1857–66)
PL	Patrologiae cursus completus, Series latina, ed. J.-P. Migne, 221 vols. in 222 pts. (Paris, 1844–80)
RBén	*Revue bénédictine* (Maredsous, 1884–)
RevBibl	*Revue biblique* (Paris, 1915–)
ROC	*Revue de l'Orient chrétien* (Paris, 1896–1946)
Settimane	Settimane di studio del Centro italiano di studi sull'alto medioevo (Spoleto, 1953–)
SubsHag	Subsidia hagiographica (Brussels, 1886–)
ThLL	*Thesaurus Linguae Latinae* (Leipzig, 1900–)
ZDPV	*Zeitschrift des Deutschen Palästina-Vereins* (Leipzig, etc., 1878–)

BIBLIOGRAPHY

Primary Sources

Adalhard of Corbie. *Statuta seu brevia*. Edited by J. Semmler. In *Corpus consuetudinum monasticarum* 1, ed. K. Hallinger. Siegburg, 1963.

Ado of Vienne. *Chronicon*. PL 123.

Adomnan. *De locis sanctis*. Edited by L. Bieler. CCSL 175. 1965.

Adrevald. *Miracula Benedicti* [BHL 1124]. Edited by E. de Certain. In *Les miracles de saint Benoît*. Paris, 1858.

Agnellus. *Liber pontificalis ecclesiae Ravennatis*. Edited by O. Holder-Egger. MGH ScriptRerLangob. 1878.

Alcuin. *Epistolae*. Edited by E. Dümmler. MGH Ep 4. 1895.

———. *Vita Richarii Centulensis* [BHL 7223]. Edited by B. Krusch. MGH ScriptRerMerov 4. 1902.

Amalarius of Metz. *Epistolae*. Edited by J. M. Hanssens. In *Amalarii episcopi opera liturgica omnia*, Studi e Testi 138–40. Vatican City, 1948–50.

Anastasius Bibliothecarius. *Chronographia tripertita*. See Theophanes.

Angilramn of Metz. Statute on Payments. Edited by M. Andrieu. "Règlement d'Angilramne de Metz (768–791) fixant les honoraires de quelques fonctions liturgiques." *Revue des sciences religieuses* 10 (1930): 349–69.

Annales Bertiniani. Edited by F. Grat, J. Vielliard, S. Clémencet, and L. Levillain. *Annales de Saint-Bertin*. Paris, 1964.

Annales Einhardi. Edited by F. Kurze. MGH ScriptRerGerm. 1895.

Annales Nordhumbrani. Edited by R. Pauli. MGH Scriptores 13. 1881.

Annales regni Francorum. Edited by F. Kurze. MGH ScriptRerGerm. 1895.

Ansegisus. *Collectio capitularium*. Edited by G. Schmitz. MGH Capit, n.s., 1. 1996.

Arbeo of Freising. *Vitae sanctorum Haimhrammi et Corbiniani* [BHL 2538]. Edited by B. Krusch. MGH ScriptRerGerm 13. 1920.

Ardo. *Vita Benedicti Anianensis* [BHL 1096]. Edited by G. Waitz. MGH Scriptores 15.1. 1887.

The Armenian [Pilgrim] Guide. Translated by [H. Nahabedian] in J. Wilkinson. In *Jerusalem Pilgrims before the Crusades*. 2nd ed. Warminster, 2002.

Arn of Salzburg. *Instructio pastoralis*. Edited by A. Werminghoff. MGH Conc 2.1. 1906.

Arnobius. *Aduersus nationes libri VII*. Edited by C. Marchesi. 2nd ed. Turin, 1953.

The Astronomer. *Vita Hludowici imperatoris*. Edited by E. Tremp. *Thegan, Die Taten Kaiser Ludwigs. Astronomus, Das Leben Kaiser Ludwigs*. MGH ScriptRerGerm 64. 1995.

Augustine. *De ciuitate Dei*. Edited by B. Dombart and A. Kalb. CCSL 47–48. 1955.

Bede. *De locis sanctis*. Edited by J. Fraipont. CCSL 175. 1965.

———. *De templo*. Edited by D. Hurst. CCSL 119A. 1969.

———. *Explanatio Apocalypsis.* PL 93.

———. *Homiliarum euangelii libri ii.* Edited by D. Hurst. CCSL 122. 1955.

———. *In Ezram et Neemiam prophetas allegorica expositio.* Edited by D. Hurst. CCSL 119A. 1969.

———. *In Marci euangelium expositio.* Edited by D. Hurst. CCSL 120. 1960.

Benedict of Nursia. *Regula.* Edited by R. Hanslik. 2nd ed. CSEL 75. 1977.

———. *St. Benedict's Rule for Monasteries.* Translated by Leonard J. Doyle. 1948. Reprint, Collegeville, MN, n.d..

Bernard the Monk. *Itinerarium.* Edited by T. Tobler and A. Molinier. In *Itinera hierosolymitana et descriptiones Terrae Sanctae*, 1.2:309–20. Geneva, 1880.

———. J. Mabillon, *Acta sanctorum ordinis s[ancti] Benedicti* 2 (Venice, 1734): 472–75.

Boniface of Fulda. *Epistolae. Die Briefe des heiligen Bonifatius und Lullus.* Edited by M. Tangl. MGH EpSel 1. 1955.

Breve commemoratorii de casis Dei vel monasteriis. Edited by G. B. de Rossi. "Un documento inedito sui luoghi santi di Gerusalemme e della Palestina." *BACr* 3 (1865): 81–88.

———. Edited by T. Tobler. In *Descriptiones Terrae Sanctae ex saeculo VIII, IX, XII et XV*, 77–84, 364–68. Leipzig, 1874.

———. Edited by T. Tobler and A. Molinier. In *Itinera hierosolymitana et descriptiones Terrae Sanctae bellis sacris anteriora et latina lingua exarata*, 1.2:301–5. Geneva, 1877–85.

Brevium exempla. Edited by A. Boretius. MGH Capit 1. 1883.

———. Edited by C. Brühl. *Capitulare de villis. Cod. guelf. 254 Helmst. der Herzog August Bibliothek Wolfenbüttel.* Stuttgart, 1971.

Breviarius de Hierosolyma. Edited by R. Weber. CCSL 175. 1965.

Le calendrier palestino-géorgien du Sinaiticus 34 (Xe siècle). Edited by G. Garitte. SubsHag 30. Brussels, 1958.

Capitulare de villis. Edited by A. Boretius. MGH Capit 1. 1883.

———. Edited by C. Brühl, *Capitulare de villis: Cod. guelf. 254 Helmst. der Herzog August Bibliothek Wolfenbüttel.* Stuttgart, 1971.

Cartae Senonicae. Edited by K. Zeumer. MGH Formulae.

Cartulaire de l'abbaye de Saint-Père de Chartres. Edited by [B.] Guérard. In Collection des cartulaires de France 1, vol. 1. Paris, 1840.

Cartulaire de l'abbaye de Saint-Victor de Marseille. Edited by [B.] Guérard. In Collection des cartulaires de France 8, vol. 1. Paris, 1857.

Cathwulf. *Epistola ad Carolum.* Edited by E. Dümmler. MGH Ep 4. 1895.

Christian of Stavelot. *Expositio super Librum generationis.* Edited by R. B. C. Huygens. CCCM 224. 2008.

Chronica Sancti Benedicti Casinensis. Edited by G. Waitz. MGH ScriptRerLang 1878.

The Chronicle of Zuqnīn, Parts III and IV, A.D. 488–775. Translated by A. Harrak. Toronto, 1999.

Cicero. *De re publica, de legibus, Cato maior de senectute, Laelius de amicitia.* Edited by J. G. F. Powell. Oxford, 2006.

Codex Carolinus. Edited by W. Gundlach, MGH Ep 3. 1892.

Codex diplomaticus Cavensis. Edited by M. Morcaldi, M. Schiani, and S. de Stephano. Vol. 1. Naples, 1873.

Codex diplomaticus Fuldensis. Edited by E. F. J. Dronke. Kassel, 1850.

Codex diplomaticus langobardiae. Historiae patriae monumenta 13. Turin, 1873.

Codex Laureshamensis. Edited by K. Glöckner. 3 vols. Darmstadt, 1929–36.

Codice diplomatico longobardo. Edited by Luigi Schiaparelli, C. Brühl, and H. Zielinski. 5 vols. Fonti per la storia d'Italia 62–66. Rome, 1929–2003.

Collectio Flaviniacensis. Edited by K. Zeumer. MGH Formulae.

Columban of Bobbio. *Epistolae.* Edited by G. S. M. Walker. *S. Columbani opera.* Scriptores latini Hiberniae 2. Dublin, 1957.

Commentarium in Lucam. Edited by J. F. Kelly. CCSL 108C. 1974.

Constantine VII Porphyrogenitus. *De administrando imperio.* Edited by G. Moravcsik. Translated by R. J. H. Jenkins. 2nd ed. Corpus fontium historiae byzantinae 1. Washington, D.C., 1967.

Cyprian, Firminus, and Viventius. *Vita Caesarii Arelatensis* [BHL 1508]. Edited by G. Morin. In *Sancti Caesarii Arelatensis opera omnia,* vol. 2. Maredsous, 1942.

Cyril of Scythopolis. *Vita Sabae* [BHG 1608]. Edited by E. Schwartz. In *Kyrillos von Skythopolis.* Texte und Untersuchungen 49.2. Leipzig, 1939.

Documenti relativi alla storia di Venezia anteriori al mille. Edited by R. Cessi. Padua, 1940.

Einhard. *Vita Karoli magni.* Edited by O. Holder-Egger and G. Waitz. 6th ed. MGH ScriptRer-Germ 1911.

Elias III of Jerusalem. *Epistola.* Edited by L. d'Achery. In *Spicilegium sive collectio veterum aliquot scriptorum* 3, 363–64. Paris, 1723.

Epiphanius Hagiopolites. *Descriptio Palaestinae.* Edited by H. Donner. "Die Palästinabeschreibung des Epiphanius Monachus Hagiopolita." *ZDPV* 87 (1971): 42–91.

Epistolae selectae pontificum Romanorum. Edited by K. Hampe. MGH Ep 5. 1898–99.

———. Edited by Stephanus [Étienne] Baluzius. *Miscellanea* [= *Miscellaneorum liber septimus*] 7:14–17. Paris, 1715.

Epistolae variorum. Edited by E. Dümmler. MGH Ep 6. 1902–25.

Ermoldus Nigellus. *In honorem Hludowici Pii.* Edited by E. Faral. *Ermold le Noir, Poème sur Louis le Pieux et Épîtres au roi Pépin.* Paris, 1932.

Eugippius. *Epistola ad Paschasium.* Edited by P. Régerat. *Eugippe. Vie de Saint Séverin.* SC 374. Paris, 1991.

———. *Vita Severini.* Edited by T. Mommsen. MGH ScriptRerGerm 1898.

Eutychius of Alexandria. *Annales* [Latin translation]. PG 111:907–1156.

———. *Annales* [autograph]. Edited by M. Breydy. *Das Annalenwerk des Eutychios von Alexandrien.* CSCO, Scriptores Arabici, 44–45. 1985.

———. *Annales.* Edited by L. Cheikho, B. Carra de Vaux, and H. Zayyat. *Eutychii patriarchae Alexandrini Annales.* CSCO, Scriptores Arabici, 6–7. 1906–9.

Expugnationis Hierosolymae A.D. 614 recensiones Arabicae. Edited and translated by Gérard Garitte. CSCO, Scriptores Arabici, 26–29. 1973–74.

———. *La prise de Jérusalem par les Perses en 614.* Edited and translated by Gérard Garitte. CSCO, Scriptores Iberici, 11–12. Louvain, 1960.

Formulae Andecavenses. Edited by K. Zeumer. MGH Formulae.

Formulae salicae Lindenbrogianae. Edited by K. Zeumer. MGH Formulae.

Formulae Salzburgenses. Edited by K. Zeumer. MGH Formulae.

———. Edited by B. Bischoff. *Salzburger Formelbücher und Briefe aus Tassilonischer und Karolingischer Zeit.* Sitzungsberichte der Bayerischen Akademie der Wissenschaften, Philos.-hist. Kl., no. 4. Munich, 1973.

Formulae Turonenses. Edited by K. Zeumer. MGH Formulae.

George of Cyprus. *Descriptio orbis Romani.* Edited by H. Gelzer. Leipzig, 1890.

George. *Vita Theodori Syceotae* [BHG 1748]. Edited by A. J. Festugière. *Vie de Théodore de Sykéon.* SubsHag 48.1. Brussels, 1970.

Gerbert of Rheims. *Epistolae.* Edited by F. Weigle. *Die Briefsammlung Gerberts von Reims.* MGH Briefe 2. Weimar, 1966.

Die Gesetze der Langobarden. Edited by F. Beyerle. Weimar, 1947.

Gesta Dagoberti. Edited by B. Krusch. MGH ScriptRerMerov 2. 1888.

Gesta sanctorum patrum Fontanellensis coenobii. Edited by P. Pradié. *Chronique des abbés de Fontenelle (Saint-Wandrille).* Paris, 1999.

Gregory I. *Registrum.* Edited by D. Norberg. CCSL 140–140A. 1982.

Gregory of Tours. *Liber in gloria martyrum.* Edited by B. Krusch and W. Levison. MGH ScriptRerMerov 1.2. 1969.

Grohmann, A. *From the World of Arabic Papyri.* Cairo, 1952.

Hariulf. *Chronique de l'abbaye de Saint-Riquier.* Edited by F. Lot. Paris, 1894.

Heraclius. *Novellae*. Edited by J. Konidaris. "Die Novellen des Kaisers Herakleios." *FM* (= Forschungen zur byzantinischen Rechtsgeschichte 8) 5 (1982): 33–106.

Hincmar of Rheims. Capitularies. Edited by R. Pokorny, M. Stratmann, and W. D. Runge. MGH Capitula episcoporum 2. 1995.

———. *De ordine palatii*. Edited by T. Gross and R. Schieffer. MGH FontIur 3. 1980.

Hugeburc. *Vita Willibaldi* [BHL 8931]. Edited by O. Holder-Egger. MGH Scriptores 15.1. 1887.

Hyacinth. *Descriptio Terrae Sanctae*. Edited by J. Campos. "Otro texto de latín medieval hispano. El presbitero Iachintus." *Helmantica* 8 (1957): 77–89.

Imperial Polyptych ("Reichsurbar"). Edited by E. Meyer-Marthaler and F. Perret. *Bündner Urkundenbuch*, 1:375–96. Chur, 1955.

In diebus Georgii. Edited by W. A. Neumann. *Theologische Quartalschrift* 56 (1874): 528–29.

———. Edited by Priebsch, *Diu vrône Botschaft*, 68.11–69.15.

———. Edited by P. Jaffé and G. [W.] Wattenbach, *Ecclesiae metropolitanae Coloniensis codices manuscripti*, 110. Berlin, 1874.

Inventory of Bergkirchen bei Jesenwang. Edited by B. Bischoff in Bischoff et al., *Mittelalterliche Schatzverzeichnisse*, no. 12.

Irmino. Polyptych of Saint Germain des Prés. Edited by K. Elmshäuser, A. Hedwig, and D. Hägermann. *Das Polyptychon von Saint-Germain-des-Prés*. Cologne, 1993.

———. Edited by [B]. Guérard. *Polyptyque de l'abbé Irminon*. 2 vols. Paris, 1844.

Jerome. *Commentarii in Danielem*. Edited by F. Glorie. CCSL 75A. 1964.

John Hymmonides. *Vita Gregorii Magni* [BHL 3641]. PL 75.

John Moschus. *Pratum spirituale*. PG 87.3.

John of Ephesus. *Historiae ecclesiasticae fragmenta*. Translated by W. J. Van Douwen and J. P. N. Land. "Joannis episcopi Ephesi Syri monophysitae . . . fragmenta." *Verhandelingen der koninklijke Akademie der wetenschappen, Afdeeling Letterkunde* 18.2. 1889.

John Phocas. *Descriptio brevis . . . locorum sanctorum*. Edited by I. Troitsij. "Ioanni Phoki skazanie vkrattse o gorodach stranach ot Antiochii do Ierusalima." *Pravoslavnnyi palestinskij sbornik* 8.2. St. Petersburg, 1889.

Justinian. *Novellae*. Edited by R. Schoell and W. Kroll. In *Corpus iuris civilis*, vol. 3. Berlin, 1912.

Justinian, Doge of Venice. Will. Edited by L. Lanfranchi and B. Strina, *Ss. Ilario e Benedetto e S. Gregorio*. Fonti per la storia di Venezia, 2, Archivi ecclesiastici, Diocesi Castellana. Venice, 1965.

Das Konzil von Aachen, 809. Edited by H. Willjung. MGH Conc 2, Supplementum 2. Hanover, 1998.

Lactantius. *Diuinae institutiones*. Edited by S. Brandt. CSEL 19. Vienna, 1890.

Leidrad. Letter to Charlemagne and Brief. Edited by A. Coville. In *Recherches sur l'histoire de Lyon du Vme siècle au IXme siècle (450–800)*, 285–88. Paris, 1928.

Leo III. *Epistolae X*. Edited by K. Hampe. MGH Ep 5. 1898–99.

Leontius. *Vita Stephani Thaumaturgi* [BHG 1670]. AASS Iul. 3. 1867.

———. *The Life of Stephen of Mar Sabas* [Arabic trans.]. Edited and translated by J. C. Lamoreaux. CSCO, Scriptores Arabici, 50–51. 1999.

Liber historiae Francorum. Edited by B. Krusch. MGH ScriptRerMerov 2. 1888.

Liber pontificalis. Edited by L. Duchesne and C. Vogel. 2nd ed. 3 vols. Paris, 1955.

———. Edited by T. Mommsen. *Libri Pontificalis pars prior*. MGH GestPontRom.

Marculfi formulae. Edited by K. Zeumer. MGH Formulae.

Martène, E., and U. Durand. *Veterum scriptorum et monumentorum historicorum, dogmaticorum, moralium, amplissima collectio*, 1. Paris, 1724.

———. *Thesaurus novus anecdotorum*. Paris, 1717.

Pseudo-Methodius. *Apocalypse*. Edited by W. J. Aerts and G. A. A. S. Kortekaas. *Die Apokalypse des Pseudo-Methodius. Die ältesten griechischen und lateinischen Übersetzungen*. CSCO, Subsidia, 97–98. 1998.

Murbach Statutes. Edited by J. Semmler. In *Corpus consuetudinum monasticarum* 1, ed. K. Hallinger. Siegburg, 1963.

Nilos Doxapatres. *Taxis ton patriarchikon thronon armenisch und griechisch*. Edited by F. N. Finck. Vagharshabad [Echmiadzin], 1902.

———. Edited by H. Gelzer. "Ungedruckte und wenig bekannte Bistümerverzeichnisse der orientalischen Kirche." *BZ* 1 (1892): 245–82.

Notker the Stammerer. *Gesta Karoli magni imperatoris*. Edited by H. F. Haefele. MGH ScriptRerGerm, n.s., 12, 2nd ed. 1980.

Opus Caroli regis contra synodum (Libri Carolini). Edited by A. Freeman and P. Meyvaert. MGH Conc 2, Supplementum 1. Hanover, 1998.

Optatus of Milevis. *Contra Parmenianum Donatistam*. Edited by C. Ziwsa. CSEL 26. 1893.

Pactus legis Salicae. Edited by K. A. Eckhardt. MGH LLNat 4.1. 2002.

Paschasius Radbertus. *Expositio in Mathaeo*. Edited by B. Paulus. CCCM 56. 1984.

Passio Agapes, Chioniae et Irenes [BHL 118]. AASS Aprilis 1:248–50.

Passio Anastasiae [BHL 401]. Edited by H. Delehaye. *Étude sur le légendier romain. Les saints de novembre et décembre*. SubsHag 23. Brussels, 1936.

Passio Felicis, Regulae et sociorum [BHL 2887]. Edited by I. Müller. "Die frühkarolingische Passio der Zürcher Heiligen." *Zeitschrift für schweizerische Kirchengeschichte* 65 (1971): 132–87.

Peter of Pisa. *Liber de diversis quaestiunculis*. PL 96.

I Placiti del "Regnum Italiae," 1. Edited by C. Manaresi. Fonti per la storia d'Italia 92. 1955.

Procopius. *De aedificiis*. Edited by J. Haury and G. Wirth. *Opera omnia*, vol. 4. Leipzig, 1964.

Recueil des actes d'Eudes, roi de France (888–898). Edited by R. H. Bautier. Paris, 1967.

Recueil des chartes de l'abbaye de Stavelot-Malmédy. Edited by J. Halkin and C. G. Roland, vol. 1. Brussels, 1909.

Reichenau Memorial Book. Edited by J. Autenrieth, D. Geuenich, and K. Schmid. MGH Libri memoriales et necrologia, n.s., 1. Hanover, 1979.

Rimbert. *Vita Anskarii*. Edited by G. Waitz. MGH ScriptRerGerm 1884.

Rule of the Master. Edited by A. de Vogüé. *La règle du maître*. SC 105–7. Paris, 1964–65.

Sabas, Rule. Edited by A. Dmitrievskij. "Kinovial'nijya pravila prep. Cavvij Osvyaščennago, vručennijya im pred končinoju preemniku svoemu igumenu Melitu" [The cenobitic rule of St. Sabbas, transmitted on his decease to his successor higoumen Melitos]. *Trudij Kievskoj Dukhovnoj Akademii* 31.1 (1890): 170–92.

———. Edited by E. Kurtz. In *BZ* 3 (1894): 167–70.

Les sceaux byzantins de la collection Henri Seyrig. Edited by J. C. Cheynet, C. Morrisson, and W. Seibt. Paris, 1991.

Sedulius Scotus. *Carmina*. Edited by I. Meyers. CCCM 117. 1991.

Stephen of Mar Saba. *Martyrium XX Sabaitarum* [BHG 1200]. Edited by A. Papadopoulos-Kerameus. "Sbornik palestinskoj i sirijskoj agiologii." *Pravoslavnyj palestinskij sbornik* 19.3 (1907): 1–41.

Synaxarium Constantinopolis. AASS Nov. Propylaeum. 1902.

Al Tabari. *The Early ʿAbbāsī Empire*. Translated by John A. Williams. 2 vols. Cambridge, 1988–89.

Tertullian. *Aduersus Marcionem*. Edited by AE. [= E.] Kroymann. CCSL 1. 1954.

———. *De ieiunio aduersus psychicos*. Edited by A. Reifferscheid and G. Wissowa. CCSL 2. 1954.

Thegan. *Gesta Hludowici imperatoris*. Edited by E. Tremp. *Thegan, Die Taten Kaiser Ludwigs. Astronomus, Das Leben Kaiser Ludwigs*. MGH ScriptRerGerm 64. 1995.

Theodore of Petra. *Vita Theodosii coenobiarchae* [BHG 1776]. Edited by H. Usener. In *Der heilige Theodosios: Schriften des Theodoros und Kyrillos*. Leipzig, 1890.

Theodore Stoudite. *Epistulae*. Edited by G. Fatouros. Corpus fontium historiae byzantinae 31. Berlin, 1992.

Theodosius. *De situ Terrae Sanctae*. Edited by P. Geyer. CCSL 175. 1965.

Theodulf of Orleans. *Carmina*. Edited by E. Dümmler. MGH Poetae 1. 1881.

Theophanes. *Chronographia* [and Latin translation of Anastasius Bibliothecarius]. Edited by C. De Boor. 2 vols. Leipzig, 1883–85.

——. *The Chronicle of Theophanes the Confessor: Byzantine and Near Eastern History, AD 284–813*, Translated by C. Mango, R. Scott, and G. Greatrex. Oxford, 1997.

Die Traditionen des Hochstifts Freising. Edited by T. Bitterauf. 2 vols. Quellen und Erörterungen zur bayerischen Geschichte, n.F., 4–5. Munich, 1905.

Die Traditionen des Hochstifts Passau. Edited by M. Heuwieser. Quellen und Erörterungen zur bayerischen Geschichte, n.F., 6. Munich, 1930.

Die Urbare der Abtei Werden a.d. Ruhr. A. Die Urbare vom 9.–13. Jahrhundert. Edited by R. Kötzschke. Rheinische Urbare 2. Publikationen der Gesellschaft für Rheinische Geschichtsforschung 20. Bonn, 1906 [Düsseldorf, 1978].

Urkunden- und Quellenbuch zur Geschichte der altluxemburgischen Territorien bis zur burgundischen Zeit. Edited by C. Wampach, vol. 1. Luxemburg, 1935.

Urkundenbuch der Stadt Strassburg, vol. 1. Edited by W. Wiegand. Strasburg, 1879.

Urkundenbuch des Klosters Fulda. Edited by E. E. Stengel. Veröffentlichungen der Historischen Kommission für Hessen und Waldeck 10. Marburg, 1913–58.

Vita Antonii Ruwah arabica. Edited and translated by I. Dick. "La passion arabe de S. Antoine Ruwaḥ, néo-martyr de Damas (†25 déc. 799)." *Le Muséon* 74 (1961): 109–33.

Vita Gregorii Agrigenti [BHG 707]. Edited by A. Berger. *Leontios Presbyteros von Rom. Das Leben des heiligen Gregorios von Agrigent*. Berliner byzantinische Arbeiten 60. Berlin, 1995.

Vita Johannis Eleemosynarii [BHG 887v]. Edited by H. Delehaye. "Une vie inédite de saint Jean l'Aumonier." *AB* 45 (1927): 5–73.

Vita Johannis Eleemosynarii [BHG 887w]. Edited by E. Lappa-Zizicas. "Un épitomé inédit de la Vie de S. Jean l'Aumonier par Jean et Sophronios." *AB* 88 (1970): 265–78.

Vita Mathildis [BHL 5683]. Edited by B. Schütte. *Die Lebensbeschreibungen der Königin Mathilde*. MGH ScriptRerGerm, n.s., 66. 1994.

Vita Michael syncelli [BHG 1296]. Edited by M. B. Cunningham. *The Life of Michael the Synkellos*. Belfast Byzantine Texts and Translations 1. Belfast, 1991.

Vita Theodorae imperatricis [BHG 1731]. Edited by A. Markopoulos. "Βίος τῆς αὐτοκράτειρας Θεοδώρας." *Symmeikta* 5 (1983): 249–85.

Vita Theodosii Coenobiarchae [BHG 1778]. PG 114.

Wala. *Breue memorationis*. Edited by Josef Semmler. In *Corpus consuetudinum monasticarum* 1, ed. K. Hallinger. Siegburg, 1963.

Das Wiener Fragment der Lorscher Annalen. Edited by F. Unterkircher. Codices selecti 15. Graz, 1967.

William of Tyre. *Chronicon*. Edited by R. B. C. Huygens, H. E. Mayer, and G. Rösch. CCCM 63–63A. 1986.

Secondary Sources

Abel, F. M. *Géographie de la Palestine*. 2 vols. Paris, 1933.

Abel, S., and B. von Simson. *Jahrbücher des Fränkischen Reiches unter Karl dem Grossen*. Jahrbücher der deutschen Geschichte. Berlin, 1883–88.

Abrahamse, D. de F. "Women's Monasticism in the Middle Byzantine Period: Problems and Prospects." *ByzF* 9 (1985): 35–58.

Aist, R. *The Christian Topography of Early Islamic Jerusalem: The Evidence of Willibald of Eichstätt (700–787 CE)*. Turnhout, 2009.

Allgemeine Deutsche Biographie. 56 vols. 1875–1912. Reprint, Berlin, 1967–71.

Andrieu, M. "Règlement d'Angilramne de Metz (768–791) fixant les honoraires de quelques fonctions liturgiques." *Recherches de sciences religieuses* 10 (1930): 349–69.

Anonymous. "Les premiers monastères de la Palestine." *Bessarione* 3 (1897–98): 39–58.

Anton, H. H. *Fürstenspiegel und Herrscherethos in der Karolingerzeit*. Bonner historische Forschungen 32. Bonn, 1968.

Ashtor, E. "The Diet of Salaried Classes in the Medieval Near East." *Journal of Asian History* 4 (1970): 1–24.

—————. *Histoire des prix et des salaires dans l'Orient médiéval.* Monnaie, prix, conjoncture 8. Paris, 1969.

—————. *A Social and Economic History of the Near East in the Middle Ages.* Berkeley, 1976.

Auzépy, M.-F. "De la Palestine à Constantinople (VIIIe–IXe siècles): Étienne le Sabaïte et Jean Damascène." *Travaux et mémoires* 12 (1994): 183–218.

Avi-Yonah, M., and H. Geva. "Jerusalem: The Byzantine Period." In *NEAEHL* 2:768–85.

Avi-Yonah, M., and A. Negev. "Heptapegon." In *NEAEHL* 2:614–16.

Avi-Yonah, M., and V. Tzaferis. "Bethlehem." In *NEAEHL* 1:204–10.

Avigad, N. "A Building Inscription of the Emperor Justinian and the Nea in Jerusalem (Preliminary Note)." *IEJ* 27 (1977): 145–51.

—————. *Discovering Jerusalem.* Oxford, 1984.

—————. "Excavations in the Jewish Quarter of the Old City of Jerusalem, 1970." *IEJ* 20 (1970): 135–40.

—————. "Samaria." In *NEAEHL* 2:1300–10.

Avigad, N. and H. Geva. "The Nea Church." *IEJ* 32 (1982): 159.

Avni, G. "The Urban Limits of Roman and Byzantine Jerusalem: A View from the Necropoleis." *Journal of Roman Archaeology* 18 (2005): 373–96.

Avram, M. "Galilee: The Hellenistic to Byzantine Periods." In *NEAEHL* 2:453–58.

Bagatti, B. *Ancient Christian Villages of Galilee.* Jerusalem, 2001.

Bahat, D., M. Ben-Dov, H. Geva, et al. "Jerusalem: Early Arab to Ayyubid Periods." In *NEAEHL* 2:786–804.

Baldovin, J. F. *The Urban Character of Christian Worship: The Origins, Development, and Meaning of Stational Liturgy.* Orientalia Christiana analecta 228. Rome, 1987.

Battaglia, S., and G. Bàrberi Squarotti. *Grande dizionario della lingua italiana.* 21 vols. [Turin], 1961–84.

Baumgarten, P. M. *Giovanni Battista de Rossi, der Begründer der christlich-archäologischen Wissenschaft. Eine biographische Skizze.* Cologne, 1892.

—————. *Giovanni Battista de Rossi, fondatore della scienza di archeologia sacra. Cenni biografici.* Translated by G. Bonavenia. Rome, 1892.

Beck, H. G. *Kirche und theologische Literatur im byzantinischen Reich.* Handbuch der Altertumswissenschaft 12.2.1. Munich, 1959.

Bergh, Å. *Études d'anthroponymie provençale: I. Les noms de personne du Polyptyque de Wadalde (a. 814).* Göteborg, 1941.

Berlière, U. "Le nombre des moines dans les anciens monastères." *RBén* 41 (1929): 231–61; 42 (1930): 19–42.

Beyssac, J. *Abbayes et prieurés de l'ancienne France.* Vol. 10, *Province ecclésiastique de Lyon.* Archives de la France monastique 37. Ligugé, 1933.

Biddle, M. "The Tomb of Christ: Sources, Methods and a New Approach." In *"Churches Built in Ancient Times": Recent Studies in Early Christian Archaeology,* ed. K. Painter, Occasional Papers from the Society of Antiquaries of London 16, 73–147. London, 1994.

Bieberstein, K. "Der Gesandtenaustausch zwischen Karl dem Grossen und Hārūn ar-Rašīd und seine Bedeutung für die Kirchen Jerusalems." *ZDPV* 109 (1993): 152–73.

Bieberstein, K., and H. Bloedhorn. *Jerusalem: Grundzüge der Baugeschichte vom Chalkolithikum bis zur Frühzeit der osmanischen Herrschaft.* 3 vols. Beihefte zum Tübinger Atlas des Vorderen Orients. Reihe B, Geisteswissenschaften 100. Wiesbaden, 1994.

Binns, J. *Ascetics and Ambassadors of Christ: The Monasteries of Palestine, 314–631.* Oxford, 1994.

Bischoff, B. *Katalog der festlandischen Handschriften des neunten Jahrhunderts (mit Ausnahme der wisigotischen).* Vol. 1, *Aachen-Lambach.* Wiesbaden, 1998.

—————. *Mittelalterliche Studien. Ausgewählte Aufsätze zur Schriftkunde und Literaturgeschichte.* 3 vols. Stuttgart, 1966–81.

—————. *Die südostdeutschen Schreibschulen und Bibliotheken in der Karolingerzeit.* 2 vols. Wiesbaden, 1960–80.

Bischoff, B., and M. Lapidge. *Biblical Commentaries from the Canterbury School of Theodore and Hadrian.* Cambridge Studies in Anglo-Saxon England 10. Cambridge, 1994.

Bischoff, B., et al. *Mittelalterliche Schatzverzeichnisse.* Veröffentlichungen des Zentralinstituts für Kunstgeschichte 4. Munich, 1967.

Blatt, F., ed. *Novum glossarium mediae Latinitatis ab anno DCCC usque ad annum MCC: M–N.* Copenhagen, 1959–69.

Bonnet, M. *Le latin de Grégoire de Tours.* Paris, 1890.

Borgolte, M. *Der Gesandtenaustausch der Karolinger mit den Abbasiden und mit den Patriarchen von Jerusalem.* Münchner Beiträge zur Mediävistik und Renaissance-Forschung 25. Munich, 1976.

de Boüard, A. *Manuel de diplomatique française et pontificale.* Paris, 1929–52.

Braudel, F. *The Structures of Everyday Life: The Limits of the Possible.* New York, 1981.

Bresslau, H., and H. W. Klewitz. *Handbuch der Urkundenlehre für Deutschland und Italien.* 3rd ed. Berlin, 1958.

Briand-Ponsart, C., and C. Hugoniot. *L'Afrique romaine de l'Atlantique à la Tripolitaine, 146 av. J.-C.–533 ap. J.C.* Paris, 2006.

Brown, W. *Unjust Seizure: Conflict, Interest, and Authority in an Early Medieval Society.* Ithaca, 2001.

Browning, R. *Medieval and Modern Greek.* London, 1969.

Brubaker, L., J. F. Haldon, and R. G. Ousterhout. *Byzantium in the Iconoclast Era (ca. 680–850): The Sources, an Annotated Survey.* Birmingham Byzantine and Ottoman monographs 7. Aldershot, 2001.

Bruckner, A. *Scriptoria Medii Aevi Helvetica. Denkmäler Schweizerischer Schreibkunst des Mittelalters.* 14 vols. Geneva, 1935–78.

Brühl, C. *Capitulare de villis: Cod. guelf. 254 Helmst. der Herzog August Bibliothek Wolfenbüttel.* Dokumente zur deutschen Geschichte in Faksimiles, Reihe 1, Mittelalter, 1. Stuttgart, 1971.

Brunner, H. *Zur Rechtsgeschichte der römischen und germanischen Urkunde.* Berlin, 1880.

Brunner, K. *Oppositionelle Gruppen im Karolingerreich.* Veröffentlichungen des Instituts für Österreichische Geschichtsforschung 25. Vienna, 1979.

Bühler, A. "Studien zur Entstehung und Überlieferung der Kapitularien Karls des Grossen und Ludwigs des Frommen." *Archiv für Diplomatik* 32 (1986): 305–501.

Bulliet, R. W. "Conversion Stories in Early Islam." In Gervers and Bikhazi, *Conversion and Continuity,* 123–33.

———. *Conversion to Islam in the Medieval Period: An Essay in Quantitative History.* Cambridge, 1979.

———. "Process and Status in Conversion and Continuity." In Gervers and Bikhazi, *Conversion and Continuity,* 1–12.

Bullough, D. *Alcuin: Achievement and Reputation.* Leyden, 2004.

———. "*Aula renovata*: The Carolingian Court before the Aachen Palace." *Proceedings of the British Academy* 71 (1985): 267–301.

Cahen, C. "Djizya," in *EI²* online. Leyden, 2007.

Calamai, A. *Ugo di Toscana. Realtà e leggenda di un diplomatico alla fine del primo millennio.* Florence, 2001.

Callahan, D. F. "The Problem of the 'Filioque' and the Letter from the Pilgrim Monks of the Mount of Olives to Pope Leo III and Charlemagne: Is the Letter another Forgery of Adémar of Chabannes?" *RBén* 102 (1992): 75–134.

Campos, J. "Otro texto de latín medieval hispano. El presbitero Iachintus." *Helmantica* 8 (1957): 77–89.

Charanis, P. "The Monk as an Element of Byzantine Society." *DOP* 25 (1971): 61–84.

Cholij, R. *Theodore the Stoudite: The Ordering of Holiness.* Oxford, 2002.

de Clercq, C. *La législation religieuse franque de Clovis à Charlemagne. Étude sur les actes de conciles et les capitulaires, les statuts diocésains et les règles monastiques (507–814).* Université de Louvain, Recueil de travaux, 2nd ser., 38. Louvain, 1936.

Cohen, R. "Monasteries." In *NEAEHL* 3:1063–70.

Colish, M. L. "Carolingian Debates over *nihil* and *tenebrae*: A Study in Theological Method." *Speculum* 59 (1984): 757–95.

Corbo, V. C. *Il Santo Sepolcro di Gerusalemme. Aspetti archeologici dalle origini al periodo crociato.* 3 vols. Jerusalem, 1981–82.

Coüasnon, C. *The Church of the Holy Sepulchre in Jerusalem.* London, 1974.

Coville, A. *Recherches sur l'histoire de Lyon du Vme siècle au IXme siècle (450–800).* Paris, 1928.

Dagron, G. "The Urban Economy, Seventh–Twelfth Centuries." In *EHB* 2:393–461.

Darrouzès, J. *Recherches sur les ὀφφίκια de l'Église byzantine.* Archives de l'Orient chrétien 11. Paris, 1970.

Dauphin, C. *La Palestine byzantine. Peuplement et populations.* BAR International Series 726. Oxford, 1998.

Davis, J. R. "Patterns of Power: Charlemagne and the Invention of Medieval Rulership." PhD diss., Harvard, 2007.

Delehaye, H. "Une vie inédite de saint Jean l'Aumonier." *AB* 45 (1927): 5–73.

Delisle, L. "Notice sur les manuscrits originaux d'Adémar de Chabannes." *Notices et extraits des manuscrits de la Bibliothèque Nationale et autres bibliothèques* 25, no. 1 (1896): 241–358.

Delogu, P. "Oro e argento in Roma tra il VII ed il IX secolo." In *Cultura et società nell'Italia medievale. Studi per Paolo Brezzi*, 273–93. Rome, 1988.

Deshusses, J., and B. Darragon. *Concordances et tableaux pour l'étude des grands sacramentaires.* Fribourg, 1982.

Di Segni, L. "Christian Epigraphy in the Holy Land: New Discoveries." *ARAM Periodical* 15 (2003): 247–67.

Dick, I. "La passion arabe de S. Antoine Ruwaḥ, néo-martyr de Damas (†25 déc. 799)." *Le Muséon* 74 (1961): 109–33.

Durliat, J. *De la ville antique à la ville byzantine. Le problème des subsistances.* Collection de l'École française de Rome 136. Rome, 1990.

Eckhardt, W. A. *Die Kapitulariensammlung Bischof Ghaerbalds von Lüttich.* Göttingen, 1955.

Eddé, A.-M., F. Micheau, and C. Picard. *Communautés chrétiennes en pays d'Islam du début du VIIe siècle au milieu du XIe siècle.* Condé-sur-Noireau, 1997.

Ehrenkreutz, A. H. "Money." In *Wirtschaftsgeschichte des vorderen Orients in Islamischer Zeit.* Handbuch der Orientalistik 1.6.6.1, 84–97. Leyden, 1977.

Elbern, V. H. "Einhard und die karolingische Goldschmiedekunst." In *Einhard: Studien zu Leben und Werk*, ed. H. Schefers, Arbeiten der Hessischen Historischen Kommission, n.F., 12, 155–78. Darmstadt, 1997.

———. "Der eucharistische Kelch im frühen Mittelalter." *Zeitschrift des deutschen Vereins für Kunstwissenschaft* 17 (1963): 1–76, 117–88.

Falce, A. *Il marchese Ugo di Tuscia.* Florence, 1921.

Fedalto, G. *Hierarchia ecclesiastica orientalis. Series episcoporum ecclesiarum christianarum orientalium.* Padua, 1988.

Février, P.-A., J.-C. Picard, C. Pietri, and J. F. Reynaud. "Lyon." In *Province ecclésiastique de Lyon (Lugdunensis Prima)*, ed. B. Beaujard, P.-A. Février, J.-C. Picard, et al., 15–35. Vol. 4 of *Topographie chrétienne des cités de la Gaule, des origines au milieu du VIIIe siècle.* Paris, 1986–2007.

Fiaccadori, G. "Proleitourgia." *La parola del passato* 44 (1989): 39–40.

Fichtenau, H. *The Carolingian Empire.* Translated by P. Munz. Oxford, 1963.

Finkelstein, I. "Byzantine Monastic Remains in the Southern Sinai." *DOP* 39 (1985): 39–79.

Fleckenstein, J. *Die Hofkapelle der deutschen Könige.* 2 vols. Schriften der Monumenta Germaniae historica 16. Stuttgart, 1959–66.

———. "Die Struktur des Hofes Karls des Grossen im Spiegel von Hinkmars 'De ordine palatii.'" *Zeitschrift des Aachener Geschichtsvereins* 83 (1976): 72–79.

Flobert, P. *Les verbes déponents latins des origines à Charlemagne.* Paris, 1975.

Foss, C. "Archaeology and the 'Twenty Cities' of Byzantine Asia." *AJA* 81 (1977): 469–86.

———. "The Persians in Asia Minor and the End of Antiquity." *EHR* 90 (1975): 721–47.

Francovich Onesti, N. *Vestigia longobarde in Italia (568–774). Lessico e antroponimia.* Rome, 1999.

Ganshof, F. L. *The Carolingians and the Frankish Monarchy: Studies in Carolingian History.* Translated by J. Sondheimer. Ithaca, 1971.

———. "L'Échec de Charlemagne." *CRAI* (1947): 248–54.

———. "La fin du règne de Charlemagne. Une décomposition." *Zeitschrift für Schweizerische Geschichte* 28 (1948): 433–52.

———. "Observations sur la date de deux documents administratifs émanant de Charlemagne." *Mitteilungen des Instituts für österreichische Geschichtsforschung* 62 (1954): 83–91.

———. *Was waren die Kapitularien?* Translated by W. A. Eckhardt and B. W. Franz. Darmstadt, 1961.

Garitte, G. *Le calendrier palestino-géorgien du Sinaiticus 34 (Xe siècle).* SubsHag 30. Brussels, 1958.

Geertman, H. *More veterum. Il Liber Pontificalis e gli edifici ecclesiastici di Roma nella tarda antichità e nell'alto medioevo.* Archaeologica traiectina 10. Groningen, 1975.

Gelichi, S. "Tra Comacchio e Venezia. Economia, società e insediamenti nell'arco nord adriatico durante l'Alto Medioevo." In *Uomini, territorio e culto dall'Antichità all'Alto Medioevo. Genti nel Delta, da Spina a Comacchio. Catalogo della mostra, 16 dicembre–14 ottobre 2006,* 365–86. Ferrara, 2007.

Gelzer, H. "Ungedruckte und wenig bekannte Bistümerverzeichnisse der orientalischen Kirche." *BZ* 1 (1892): 245–82.

Gervers, M., and R. J. Bikhazi, eds. *Conversion and Continuity: Indigenous Christian Communities in Islamic Lands, Eighth to Eighteenth Centuries.* Papers in Mediaeval Studies 9. Toronto, 1990.

Gil, J. "Los terrores del año 800." In *Actas del simposio para el estudio de los códices del "Commentario al Apocalipsis" de Beato de Liébana,* 215–47. Madrid, 1978.

Gil, M. "Dhimmī Donations and Foundations for Jerusalem (638–1099)." *Journal of the Economic and Social History of the Orient* 27 (1984): 156–74.

———. *A History of Palestine, 634–1099.* Translated by E. Broido. 2nd ed. Cambridge, 1997.

Gockel, M. *Karolingische Königshöfe am Mittelrhein.* Göttingen, 1970.

Goitein, S. D. *A Mediterranean Society: The Jewish Communities of the Arab World as Portrayed in the Documents of the Cairo Geniza.* 6 vols. Berkeley, 1967–93.

Goldfus, H. "Urban Monasticism and Monasteries of Early Byzantine Palestine: Preliminary Observations." *ARAM Periodical* 15 (2003): 71–79.

Gorman, M. "Peter of Pisa and the Quaestiunculae Copied for Charlemagne in Brussels II 2572." *RBén* 110 (2000): 238–60.

Grierson, P. "The Carolingian Empire in the Eyes of Byzantium." In *Nascita dell'Europa ed Europa carolingia: un'equazione da verificare,* 2:885–916. Settimane 27. 1981.

———. "Money and Coinage under Charlemagne." In *Karl der Grosse: Lebenswerk und Nachleben,* ed. W. Braunfels, vol. 1, 501–36. Düsseldorf, 1965.

———. "Symbolism in Early Medieval Charters and Coins." In *Simboli e simbologie nell'alto medioevo,* 2:601–30. Settimane 23. 1976.

Grierson P., and M. Blackburn. *Medieval European Coinage.* Vol. 1. Cambridge, 1986.

Griffith, S. H. "The Arabic Account of 'Abd al-Masīḥ an-Naǧrānī al-Ghassānī." *Le Muséon* 98 (1985): 331–74.

———. "From Aramaic to Arabic: The Languages of the Monasteries of Palestine in the Byzantine and Early Islamic Periods." *DOP* 51 (1997): 11–31.

———. "Greek into Arabic: Life and Letters in the Monasteries of Palestine in the Ninth Century." In *Arabic Christianity in the Monasteries of Ninth-Century Palestine,* VIII, 117–38. Aldershot, 1992.

Grohmann, A. *Einführung und Chrestomathie zur arabischen Papyruskunde.* Prague, 1955.

———. *From the World of Arabic Papyri.* Cairo, 1952.

Grumel, V. *La chronologie.* Traité d'études byzantines. Vol. 1. Paris, 1958.

Guillemain, B. "Chiffres et statistiques pour l'histoire ecclésiastique du moyen âge." *Le moyen âge* 59 (1953): 341–65.

Hage, W. *Die syrisch-jacobitische Kirche in frühislamischer Zeit nach orientalischen Quellen*. Wiesbaden, 1966.

Halphen, L. *Charlemagne et l'empire carolingien*. Paris, 1947.

Hartmann, W. *Die Synoden der Karolingerzeit im Frankenreich und in Italien*. Paderborn, 1989.

Harvey, W. *Structural Survey of the Church of the Nativity, Bethlehem*. London, 1935.

Hatlie, P. *The Monks and Monasteries of Constantinople, ca. 350–850*. Cambridge, 2007.

Hélin, M. "Dexter et dextri." *Bulletin du Cange. Archivum latinitatis medii aevi* 28 (1958): 161–64.

Heusler, A. *Geschichte der Öffentlichen Bibliothek der Universität Basel*. Basel, 1896.

Hiestand, R. "Die Anfänge der Johanniter." In *Die Geistlichen Ritterorden Europas*, ed. J. Fleckenstein and M. Hellmann, Vorträge und Forschungen 26, 31–80. Sigmaringen, 1980.

Hirschfeld, Y. "Chariton." In *NEAEHL* 1:297–99.

———. "Euthymius' Monastery." In *NEAEHL* 2:428–30.

———. *The Judean Desert Monasteries in the Byzantine Period*. New Haven, 1992.

———. "List of the Byzantine Monasteries in the Judean Desert." In *Christian Archaeology in the Holy Land: New Discoveries*, ed. G. C. Bottini, L. Di Segni, and E. Alliata, Studium biblicum franciscanum, Collectio maior 36, 1–90. Jerusalem, 1990.

Hirschfeld, Y., G. Foerster, and F. Vitto. "Tiberias." In *NEAEHL* 4:1464–73.

His, E. *Basler Gelehrte des 19. Jahrhunderts*. Basel, 1941.

Holtzmann, W. "Papst-, Kaiser- und Normannenurkunden aus Unteritalien." *Quellen und Forschungen aus italienischen Archiven und Bibliotheken* 35 (1955): 46–85.

Horden, P., and N. Purcell. *The Corrupting Sea: A Study of Mediterranean History*. Oxford, 2000.

Innes, M. "Charlemagne's Will: Piety, Politics and the Imperial Succession." *EHR* 112 (1997): 833–55.

Jaffé, P. *Regesta pontificum Romanorum ab condita ecclesia ad annum post Christum natum MCXCVIII*. 2nd ed. Ed. S. Löwenfeld, F. Kaltenbrunner, and P. Ewald. Leipzig, 1885–88.

Jaffé, P., and G. [W.] Wattenbach. *Ecclesiae metropolitanae Coloniensis codices manuscripti*. Berlin, 1874.

Jones, A. H. M. *The Later Roman Empire, 284–602: A Social, Economic, and Administrative Survey*. Oxford, 1964.

Jones, A. H. M., J. R. Martindale, and J. Morris. *The Prosopography of the Later Roman Empire*. Cambridge, 1971–92.

Kallner-Amiran, D. H. "A Revised Earthquake Catalogue of Palestine." *IEJ* 1 (1950–51): 223–46.

Karagiannopoulos, I. E., and G. Weiss. *Quellenkunde zur Geschichte von Byzanz (324–1453)*. 2 vols. Schriften zur Geistesgeschichte des östlichen Europa 14. Wiesbaden, 1982.

Kasten, B. *Adalhard von Corbie. Die Biographie eines karolingischen Politikers und Klostervorstehers*. Düsseldorf, 1985 [1986].

Kaufmann, H. *Altdeutsche Personennamen: Ergänzungsband*. Munich, 1968.

Kazhdan, A. P. *Armiyane v sostave gospodstvujuščego klassa Vizantijskoj Imperii v xi–xii vv*. Erevan, 1975.

———. "Vizantijskie goroda v VII–IX vv." *Sovetskaja arkheologija* 21 (1954): 164–88.

Kazhdan, A., L. F. Sherry, and C. Angelidi. *A History of Byzantine Literature (650–850)*. Athens, 1999.

Keefe, S. A. *Water and the Word: Baptism and the Education of the Clergy in the Carolingian Empire*. Notre Dame, 2002.

Kennedy, H. "From *polis* to *madina*: Urban Change in Late Antique and Early Islamic Syria." *Past and Present* 106 (1985): 3–27.

———. "The Last Century of Byzantine Syria: A Reinterpretation." *ByzF* 10 (1985): 141–83.

Kleinclausz, A. "La légende du protectorat de Charlemagne sur la Terre Sainte." *Syria: Revue d'art oriental et d'archéologie* 7 (1926): 211–33.

Kloner, A. *Survey of Jerusalem: The Northeastern Sector.* Archaeological Survey of Israel. Jerusalem, 2001.

Kluge, B. "Nomen imperatoris und Christiana religio. Das Kaisertum Karls des Grossen und Ludwigs des Frommen im Licht der numismatischen Quellen." In *799, Kunst und Kultur der Karolingerzeit: Karl der Grosse und Papst Leo III. in Paderborn; Beiträge zum Katalog der Ausstellung Paderborn, 1999,* ed. C. Stiegemann and M. Wemhoff, 82–90. Mainz, 1999.

Knowles, D. *The Monastic Order in England: A History of Its Development from the Times of St. Dunstan to the Fourth Lateran Council, 940–1216.* 2nd ed. Cambridge, 1963.

———. *The Religious Orders in England.* Cambridge, 1957.

Knowles, D., and R. N. Hadcock. *Medieval Religious Houses, England and Wales.* 2nd ed. [London], 1971.

Kölzer, T. *Merowingerstudien.* 2 vols. MGH, Studien und Texte 21, 26. Hanover, 1998.

Konidaris, J. "Die Novellen des Kaisers Herakleios." *FM* (= Forschungen zur byzantinischen Rechtsgeschichte 8), 5 (1982): 33–106.

Körting, G. *Lateinisch-romanisches Wörterbuch. Etymologisches Wörterbuch der romanischen Hauptsprachen.* 3rd ed. New York, 1923.

Kosto, A. "Hostages in the Carolingian World (714–840)." *Early Medieval Europe* 11 (2002): 123–47.

Krautheimer, R. *Corpus basilicarum christianarum Romae: The Early Christian Basilicas of Rome (IV–IX cent.).* 5 vols. Vatican City, 1937–77.

Krusch, B. *Die Lex Bajuvariorum: Textgeschichte, Handschriftenkritik und Entstehung mit zwei Anhängen, Lex Alamannorum und Lex Ribuaria.* Berlin, 1924.

Külzer, A. *Peregrinatio graeca in Terram Sanctam: Studien zu Pilgerführern und Reisebeschreibungen über Syrien, Palästina und den Sinai aus byzantinischer und metabyzantinischer Zeit.* Frankfurt am Main, 1994.

Kurze, W. *Monasteri e nobiltà nel Senese e nella Toscana medievale. Studi diplomatici, archeologici, genealogici, giuridici, e sociali.* [Siena], 1989.

Lafaurie, J. "Les monnaies impériales de Charlemagne," *CRAI* (1978): 154–72.

Laiou, A. E. "The Byzantine Economy: An Overview." In *EHB* 3:1145–64.

Lampe, G. W. H. *A Patristic Greek Lexicon.* Oxford, 1961.

Landes, R. "Lest the Millennium Be Fulfilled: Apocalyptic Expectations and the Pattern of Western Chronography 100–800 C.E." In *The Use and Abuse of Eschatology in the Middle Ages,* ed. W. Verbeke, D. Verhelst, and A. Welkenhuysen, Mediaevalia Lovanensia, Series 1, Studia 15, 137–211. Louvain, 1988.

Lapidge, M. "Byrhtferth of Ramsey and the Early Sections of the Historia Regum Attributed to Symeon of Durham." *Anglo-Saxon England* 10 (1982): 97–122.

Lappa-Zizicas, E. "Un épitomé inédit de la Vie de S. Jean l'Aumonier par Jean et Sophronios." *AB* 88 (1970): 265–78.

Laurent, V., ed. *Le corpus des sceaux de l'Empire byzantin.* 2 vols. Paris, 1963–81.

Laureys, M., and D. Verhelst. "Pseudo-Methodius, Revelationes: Textgeschichte und kritische Edition. Ein Leuven-Groninger Forschungsprojekt." In *The Use and Abuse of Eschatology in the Middle Ages,* ed. W. Verbeke, D. Verhelst, and A. Welkenhuysen, Mediaevalia Lovanensia, Series 1, Studia 14, 112–36. Louvain, 1988.

Levtzion, N. "Conversion to Islam in Syria and Palestine and the Survival of Christian Communities." In Gervers and Bikhazi, *Conversion and Continuity,* 289–311.

Levy-Rubin, M. "The Reorganisation of the Patriarchate of Jerusalem during the Early Muslim Period." *ARAM Periodical* 15 (2003): 197–226.

Lindsay, W. M. *Notae Latinae: an Account of Abbreviation in Latin MSS. of the Early Minuscule Period (c. 700–850).* Cambridge, 1915.

Little, L. K., ed. *Plague and the End of Antiquity: the Pandemic of 541–750.* Cambridge, 2007.

Loffreda, S. *The Sanctuaries of Tabgha.* 2nd ed. Jerusalem, 1978.

―――. *Scavi di et-Tabgha: relazione finale della campagna di scavi 25 marzo–20 giugno 1969*. Jerusalem, 1970.

Löfstedt, E. *Il latino tardo: aspetti e problemi*. Translated by C. Cima Giorgetti. Brescia, 1980.

Lowe, E. A. *Codices latini antiquiores: A Palaeographical Guide to Latin Manuscripts Prior to the Ninth Century*. 12 vols. Oxford, 1934–72.

Lundström, S. *Lexicon errorum interpretum Latinorum*. Acta Universitatis Upsaliensis, Studia Latina Upsaliensia 16. Uppsala, 1983.

Luttrell, A. "The Earliest Hospitallers." In *Montjoie: Studies in Crusade History in Honour of Hans Eberhard Mayer*, ed. B. Z. Kedar, J. Riley-Smith, and R. Hiestand, 37–54. Aldershot, 1997.

Magen, I. "Shechem: Neapolis." In *NEAEHL* 4:1354–59.

Magness, J. *The Archaeology of the Early Islamic Settlement in Palestine*. Winona Lake, 2003.

―――. Review of *Die Ausgrabungen unter der Erlöserkirche im Muristan, Jerusalem (1970–1974)*, by K. J. H. Vriezen, I. Carradice, and E. Tchernov. *BASOR* 298 (1995): 87–89.

Manitius, M. *Geschichte der lateinischen Literatur des Mittelalters*. 3 vols. Handbuch der klassischen Altertumswissenschaft 9.2. Munich, 1911–31.

Martindale, J. R., ed. *Prosopography of the Byzantine Empire 1 (641–867)*. CD-ROM. Aldershot, 2001.

McCormick, M. "Bateaux de vie, bateaux de mort: maladie, commerce, transports annonaires et le passage économique du Bas-Empire au moyen âge." In *Morfologie sociali e culturali in Europa fra tarda antichità e alto medioevo*, 1:35–122. Settimane 45. 1998.

―――. "The Birth of the Codex and the Apostolic Life-style." *Scriptorium* 39 (1985): 150–58.

―――. "Byzantium and the West A.D. 700–900." In *New Cambridge Medieval History*, ed. R. McKitterick, vol. 2, 349–80. Cambridge, 1995.

―――. "Charlemagne and the Mediterranean World." In *Am Vorabend der Kaiserkrönung. Das Epos "Karolus Magnus et Leo Papa" und der Papstbesuch in Paderborn 799*, ed. P. Godman, J. Jarnut, and P. Johanek, 193–218. Berlin, 2002.

―――. "Diplomacy and the Carolingian Encounter with Byzantium Down to the Accession of Charles the Bald." In *Eriugena: East and West. Papers of the Eighth International Colloquium of the Society for the Promotion of Eriugenian Studies*, ed. B. McGinn and W. Otten, 15–48. Notre Dame, 1994.

―――. *Eternal Victory: Triumphal Rulership in Late Antiquity, Byzantium, and the Early Medieval West*. 2nd ed. Cambridge, 1990.

―――. "The Imperial Edge: Italo-Byzantine Identity, Movement and Integration, A.D. 650–950." In *Studies on the Internal Diaspora of the Byzantine Empire*, ed. H. Ahrweiler and A. E. Laiou, 17–52. Washington, D.C., 1998.

―――. "La lettre diplomatique byzantine du premier millénaire vue de l'Occident et l'énigme du papyrus de Paris." In *Byzance et le monde extérieur*, Byzantina Sorbonensia 21, 135–49. Paris, 2005.

―――. *Origins of the European Economy: Communications and Commerce, A.D. 300–900*. Cambridge, 2001.

―――. "Textes, images et iconoclasme dans le cadre des relations entre Byzance et l'Occident carolingien." In *Testo e immagine nell'alto medioevo*. 1:95–162. Settimane 41. 1994.

―――. "Les pèlerins occidentaux à Jérusalem, VIIIe–IXe siècles." In *Voyages et voyageurs à Byzance et en Occident du VIe au XIe siècle*, ed. A. Dierkens, J.-M. Sansterre, and J.-L. Kupper, 289–306. Geneva, 2000.

―――. "Prosopography of Travelers in the Early Medieval Mediterranean." In preparation.

McCormick, M., P. E. Dutton, P. A. Mayewski, and N. Patterson. "Volcanoes and the Climate Forcing of Carolingian Europe, A.D. 750–950." *Speculum* 82 (2007): 865–95.

McKitterick, R. *The Carolingians and the Written Word*. Cambridge, 1989.

Metz, W. *Zur Erforschung des karolingischen Reichsgutes*. Erträge der Forschung 4. Darmstadt, 1971.

———. "Zur Geschichte und Kritik der frühmittelalterlichen Güterverzeichnisse Deutschlands." *Archiv für Diplomatik* 4 (1958): 183–206.

Meyer-Lübke, W. *Grammaire des langues romanes*. Translated by E. Rabiet. 4 vols. New York, 1923.

Meyer, G., and M. Burckhardt. *Die mittelalterlichen Handschriften der Universitätsbibliothek Basel, Abteilung B: Theologische Pergamenthandschriften*. Vol. 1. Basel, 1960.

de Meyier, K. A., and P. F. J. Obbema. *Codices Vossiani Latini*. Vol. 2, *Codices in Quarto*. Codices manuscripti 14. Leyden, 1975.

Meyvaert, P. "Medieval Notions of Publication: the 'Unpublished' *Opus Caroli regis contra synodum* and the Council of Frankfurt (794)." *Journal of Medieval Latin* 12 (2002): 78–89.

Milik, J. T. "Notes d'épigraphie et de topographie palestiniennes," *RevBibl* 66 (1959): 550–75.

———. "Notes d'épigraphie et de topographie palestiniennes: IX. Sanctuaires chrétiens de Jérusalem à l'époque arabe (VIIe–IXe s.)." *RevBibl* 67 (1960): 354–67, 550–91.

———. "La topographie de Jérusalem vers la fin de l'époque byzantine." *Mélanges de l'Université Saint-Joseph* 37 (Beirut, 1960–61): 127–89.

Möhring, H. "Karl der Grosse und die Endkaiser-Weissagung: der Sieger über den Islam kommt aus dem Westen." In *Montjoie: Studies in Crusade History in Honour of Hans Eberhard Mayer*, ed. B. Z. Kedar, J. Riley-Smith, and R. Hiestand, 1–19. Aldershot, 1997.

Mordek, H. *Bibliotheca capitularium regum Francorum manuscripta*. MGH Hilfsmittel 15. Munich, 1995.

———. "Karolingische Kapitularien." In *Überlieferung und Geltung normativer Texte des frühen und hohen Mittelalters: vier Vorträge gehalten auf dem 35. Deutschen Historikertag 1984 in Berlin*, ed. H. Mordek, Quellen und Forschungen zum Recht im Mittelalter 4, 25–50. Sigmaringen, 1986.

———. *Kirchenrecht und Reform im Frankenreich. Die collectio vetus Gallica, die älteste systematische Kanonessammlung des fränkischen Gallien; Studien und Edition*. Beiträge zur Geschichte und Quellenkunde des Mittelalters 1. Berlin, 1975.

Morony, M. G. "The Age of Conversions: A Reassessment." In Gervers and Bikhazi, *Conversion and Continuity*, 135–50.

Morrisson, C., and J.-C. Cheynet. "Prices and Wages in the Byzantine World." In *EHB* 2:815–78.

Murray, A. *Reason and Society in the Middle Ages*. Oxford, 1985.

Nelson, J. L. "Literacy in Carolingian Government." In *The Uses of Literacy in Early Mediaeval Europe*, ed. R. McKitterick, 258–96. Cambridge, 1992.

———. "The Voice of Charlemagne." In *Belief and Culture in the Middle Ages: Studies Presented to Henry Mayr-Harting*, ed. R. Gameson and H. Leyser, 76–88. Oxford, 2001.

Neumann, W. A. Review of Titus Tobler, *Descriptiones Terrae Sanctae* (Leipzig, 1874). *Theologische Quartalschrift* 56 (1875): 521–31.

Niermeyer, J. F., C. van de Kieft, and G. S. M. M. Lake-Schoonebeek, *Mediae Latinitatis lexicon minus*. Leyden, 1993.

Oberdorfer, B. *Filioque: Geschichte und Theologie eines ökumenischen Problems*. Forschungen zur systematischen und ökumenischen Theologie 96. Göttingen, 2001.

Oexle, O. G. *Forschungen zu monastischen und geistlichen Gemeinschaften im westfränkischen Bereich*. Münstersche Mittelalter-Schriften 31. Munich, 1978.

Oikonomides, N. "Quelques boutiques de Constantinople au Xe s.: Prix, loyers, imposition (*Cod. Patmiacus* 171)." *DOP* 26 (1972): 345–56.

Ostrogorsky, G. "Löhne und Preise in Byzanz." *BZ* 32 (1932): 293–333.

Ovadiah, A. *Corpus of the Byzantine Churches in the Holy Land*. Bonn, 1970.

Ovadiah, A., and C. G. de Silva. "Supplementum to the Corpus of the Byzantine Churches in the Holy Land." *Levant* 13 (1981): 200–61.

———. "Supplementum to the Corpus of the Byzantine Churches in the Holy Land (Part II)." *Levant* 14 (1982): 122–70.

Parisse, M., and J. Leuridan, eds. *Atlas de la France de l'an mil. État de nos connaissances*. Paris, 1994.

Patlagean, E. *Pauvreté économique et pauvreté sociale à Byzance, 4e–7e siècles*. Paris, 1977.

Patrich, J. *Sabas, Leader of Palestinian Monasticism: A Comparative Study in Eastern Monasticism, Fourth to Seventh Centuries*. Washington, D.C., 1995.

Peeters, P. *Recherches d'histoire et de philologie orientales*. SubsHag 27. Brussels, 1951.

———. "S. Antoine le Néo-martyr." *AB* 31 (1912): 410–50.

Pei, M. A. *The Language of the Eight*[sic]*-Century Texts in Northern France*. New York, 1932.

Peri, V. "Leone III e il 'Filioque.' Echi del caso nell'agiografia greca." *Rivista di storia della Chiesa in Italia* 25 (1971): 3–58.

Philippart, G., and M. Trigalet. "Latin Hagiography before the Ninth Century: A Synoptic View." In *The Long Morning of Medieval Europe: New Directions in Early Medieval Studies*, ed. J. R. Davis and M. McCormick, 111–29. Aldershot, 2008.

Pixner, B. "Church of the Apostles Found on Mt. Zion." *Biblical Archaeology Review* 16, no. 3 (1990): 16–35, 60.

Ponsich, P. "Saint-Michel de Cuxa au siècle de l'an mil (950–1050)." *Les cahiers de Saint-Michel de Cuxa* 19 (1988): 7–32.

Prawer, J. "Jerusalem in the Christian and Jewish Perspectives of the Early Middle Ages." In *Gli Ebrei nell'alto medioevo*, 2:739–95. Settimane 26. 1980.

Priebsch, R. *Diu vrône Botschaft ze der Christenheit: Untersuchungen und Text*. Grazer Studien zur deutschen Philologie 2. Graz, 1895.

Prinz, O., and J. Schneider. *Mittellateinisches Wörterbuch bis zum ausgehenden 13. Jahrhundert*. Munich, 1967–.

Prou, M. *Les monnaies carolingiennes*. Paris, 1896.

Ratkowitsch, C. *Karolus Magnus—alter Aeneas, alter Martinus, alter Iustinus. Zur Intention und Datierung des "Aachener Karlsepos."* Wiener Studien, Beiheft 24. Vienna, 1997.

Redlich, O. *Die Privaturkunden des Mittelalters*. Munich, 1911.

Reeg, G., and F. Hüttenmeister. *Tübinger Atlas des Vorderen Orients*: Map B VI 16, "Israel nach der rabbinischen Literatur." Wiesbaden, 1984.

Renard, H. "Die Marienkirche auf dem Berge Sion in ihrem Zusammenhang mit dem Abendmahlssaale." *Das heilige Land* 44 (1900): 3–23.

Reynaud, J.-F. *Lugdunum Christianum: Lyon du IVe au VIIIe s. Topographie, nécropoles et édifices religieux*. Documents d'archéologie française 69. Paris, 1998.

Riant, P. "La donation de Hugues marquis de Toscane, au Saint-Sépulcre et les établissements latins de Jérusalem au Xe siècle." *Mémoires de l'Académie des inscriptions* 31 (1884): 151–95.

Richard, J. "Les relations de pèlerinage au moyen âge et les motivations de leurs auteurs." In *Wallfahrt kennt keine Grenzen: Themen zu einer Ausstellung des Bayerischen Nationalmuseums und des Adalbert Stifter Vereins, München*, ed. L. Kriss-Rettenbeck and G. Möhler, 143–54. Munich, 1984.

Riché, P. *Daily Life in the World of Charlemagne*. Translated by J. A. McNamera. 2nd ed. N.p., 1988.

Rose, V. *Verzeichniss der lateinischen Handschriften der Königlichen Bibliothek zu Berlin*. Vol. 1. Die Handschriften-Verzeichnisse der Königlichen Bibliothek zu Berlin 12. Berlin, 1893.

de Rossi, G. B. "Basilea. Testamento inciso in marmo sopra un sepolcro." *BACr* 1 (1863): 94–95.

———. "Un documento inedito sui luoghi santi di Gerusalemme e della Palestina." *BACr* 3 (1865): 81–88.

Rouche, M. "La faim à l'époque carolingienne. Essai sur quelques types de rations alimentaires." *Revue historique* 250 (1973): 295–320.

Runciman, S. "Charlemagne and Palestine." *EHR* 50 (1935): 606–19.

Russell, J. "Anemourion." In *EHB* 1:221–28.

———. "The Palaeography of the Madaba Map in the Light of Recent Discoveries: A Preliminary Analysis." In *The Madaba Map Centenary 1897–1997*, ed. M. Piccirillo and E. Alliata, 125–33. Jerusalem, 1999.

Russell, K. W. "The Earthquake Chronology of Palestine and Northwest Arabia from the 2nd through the Mid-8th Century A.D." *BASOR* 260 (1985): 37–59.

Saint-Roch, P. *Correspondance de Giovanni Battista de Rossi et de Louis Duchesne: 1873–1894.* Collection de l'École française de Rome 205. [Rome], 1995.

Salamon, M., A. Coppa, M. McCormick, M. Rubini, R. Vargiu, and N. Tuross. "The Consilience of Historical and Isotopic Approaches in Reconstructing the Medieval Mediterranean Diet." *Journal of Archaeological Science* 35 (2008): 1667–72.

Sansterre, J.-M. *Les moines grecs et orientaux à Rome aux époques byzantine et carolingienne.* 2 vols. Académie royale de Belgique, Mémoires de la classe des lettres, Collection in 8°, 2nd ser., 66. Brussels, 1983.

Sarah, G., M. Bompaire, M. McCormick, A. Rovelli, and C. Guerrot, "Analyses élémentaires de monnaies de Charlemagne et Louis le Pieux du Cabinet des Médailles: l'Italie carolingienne et Venise." *Revue numismatique* 164 (2008): 355–406.

Schick, R. *The Christian Communities of Palestine from Byzantine to Islamic Rule: A Historical and Archaeological Study.* Studies in Late Antiquity and Early Islam 2. Princeton, N.J., 1995.

Schmid, K. "Aachen und Jerusalem. Ein Beitrag zur historischen Personenforschung der Karolingerzeit." In *Das Einhardkreuz. Vorträge und Studien der Münsteraner Diskussion zum arcus Einhardi,* ed. K. Hauck, Abhandlungen der Akademie der Wissenschaften in Göttingen, Philologisch-historische Klasse, 3rd ser., 87, 122–42. Göttingen, 1974.

———. *Gebetsgedenken und adliges Selbstverständnis im Mittelalter. Ausgewählte Beiträge.* Sigmaringen, 1983.

———. "Mönchslisten und Klosterkonvent von Fulda zur Zeit der Karolinger." In *Die Klostergemeinschaft von Fulda im früheren Mittelalter,* Münstersche Mittelalter-Schriften 8.2.2, 571–639. Munich, 1978.

———. ed. *Die Klostergemeinschaft von Fulda im früheren Mittelalter,* 5 vols. Münstersche Mittelalter-Schriften 8. Munich, 1978.

Schmid, K., and O. G. Oexle. "Voraussetzungen und Wirkung des Gebetsbundes von Attigny." *Francia* 2 (1974): 71–122.

Schmitt, G., J. Wagner, and R. Rademacher. *Tübinger Atlas des Vorderen Orients*: Map B V 17.2: "Die römischen Provinzen Palaestina und Arabia (70–305 n.Chr.)." Wiesbaden, 1988.

Schramm, P. E. "Drei Nachträge zu den Metallbullen der Karolingischen und Sächsischen Kaiser." *DA* 24 (1968): 1–15.

Schumacher-Wolfgarten, R. "XPICTIANA RELIGIO: Zu einer Münzprägung Karls des Grossen." *Jahrbuch für Antike und Christentum* 37 (1994): 122–41.

Schütte, S. "Der Aachener Thron." In *Krönungen: Könige in Aachen. Geschichte und Mythos,* ed. M. Kramp, 213–22. 2 vols. Mainz, 2000.

Semmler, J. "Zu den bayrisch-westfränkischen Beziehungen in karolingischer Zeit." *Zeitschrift für bayerische Landesgeschichte* 29 (1966): 344–424.

Ševčenko, I. "The Early Period of the Sinai Monastery in the Light of Its Inscriptions." *DOP* 20 (1966): 255–64.

Siebigs, H. K. "Neuere Untersuchungen der Pfalzkapelle zu Aachen." In *Einhard: Studien zu Leben und Werk,* ed. H. Schefers, Arbeiten der Hessischen Historischen Kommission, n.F., 12, 95–137. Darmstadt, 1997.

Sonntag, R. *Studien zur Bewertung von Zahlenangaben in der Geschichtsschreibung des früheren Mittelalters. Die Decem Libri Historiarum Gregors von Tours und die Chronica Reginos von Prüm.* Münchener historische Studien, Abteilung mittelalterliche Geschichte 4. Kallmünz, 1987.

Spufford, P. *Money and Its Use in Medieval Europe.* Cambridge, 1988.

Staehelin, A. *Geschichte der Universität Basel, 1818–1835.* Studien zur Geschichte der Wissenschaften in Basel 7. Basel, 1959.

Störmer, W. *Adelsgruppen im früh- und hochmittelalterlichen Bayern.* Studien zur bayerischen Verfassungs- und Sozialgeschichte 4. Munich, 1972.

———. *Früher Adel: Studien zur politischen Führungsschicht im fränkisch-deutschen Reich vom 8. bis 11. Jahrhundert.* 2 vols. Monographien zur Geschichte des Mittelalters 6. Stuttgart, 1973.

Stotz, P. *Handbuch zur lateinischen Sprache des Mittelalters*. Handbuch der Altertumswissenschaft 2.5. Munich, 1996.

Stüwer, W. *Das Erzbistum Köln. Die Reichsabtei Werden an der Ruhr*. Germania sacra, n.F., 12.3. Berlin, 1980.

Tafel, S. "The Lyons Scriptorium." *Palaeographia latina* 2 (1923): 66–73; 4 (1925): 40–70.

Talbot, A.-M. M. "A Comparison of the Monastic Experience of Byzantine Men and Women." *Greek Orthodox Theological Review* 30 (1985): 1–20.

Tellenbach, G. "Der grossfränkische Adel und die Regierung Italians in der Blütezeit des Karolingerreiches." In *Studien und Vorarbeiten zur Geschichte des grossfränkischen und frühdeutschen Adels*, ed. G. Tellenbach, Forschungen zur oberrheinischen Landesgeschichte 4, 40–70. Freiburg im Breisgau, 1957.

Thesaurus linguae Graecae: A Digital Library of Greek Literature. http://www.tlg.uci.edu/.

Thomas, J. P., A. C. Hero, and G. Constable, eds. *Byzantine Monastic Foundation Documents: A Complete Translation of the Surviving Founders' Typika and Testaments*. 5 vols. Washington, D.C., 2000.

Thomson, R. W. "A Seventh-Century Armenian Pilgrim on Mount Tabor." *Journal of Theological Studies*, n.s., 18 (1967): 27–33.

Tobler, T. *Descriptiones Terrae Sanctae ex saeculo VIII, IX, XII et XV*. Leipzig, 1874.

Tobler, T., and A. Molinier, eds. *Itinera hierosolymitana et descriptiones Terrae Sanctae bellis sacris anteriora et latina lingua exarata*. 2 vols. Geneva, 1877–85.

Trapp, E., W. Hörandner, J. M. Diethart, M. Cassiotou-Panayotopoulos, S. Schönhauer, E. Schiffer, M. Hammer, J. Declerck, M. Hinterberger, R. Volk, G. Fatouros et al., eds. *Lexikon zur byzantinischen Gräzität besonders des 9.–12. Jahrhunderts*. Vienna, 1993–.

Tsafrir, Y. "Procopius and the Nea Church in Jerusalem." *Antiquité tardive* 8 (2000): 149–64.

Tsafrir, Y., L. Di Segni, J. Green, I. Roll, and T. Tsuk. *Tabula Imperii Romani: Iudaea-Palaestina. Eretz Israel in the Hellenistic, Roman and Byzantine Periods; Maps and Gazetteer*. Jerusalem, 1994.

Tsafrir, Y., and G. Foerster. "The Dating of the 'Earthquake of the Sabbatical Year' of 749 C. E. in Palestine." *Bulletin of the School of Oriental and African Studies* 55 (1992): 231–35.

———. "Urbanism at Scythopolis-Bet Shean in the Fourth to Seventh Centuries." *DOP* 51 (1997): 85–146.

Tzaferis, V., and B. Bagatti. "Nazareth." In *NEAEHL* 3:1103–6.

Uddholm, A. *Formulae Marculfi. Études sur la langue et le style*. Uppsala, 1953.

Väänänen, V. *Introduction au latin vulgaire*. 3rd ed. Paris, 1981.

Vailhé, S. "Les laures de Saint Gérasime et de Calamon." *Échos de l'Orient* 2 (1898–99): 106–19.

———. "Répertoire alphabétique des monastères de Palestine [1]." *ROC* 4 (1899): 512–42.

———. "Répertoire alphabétique des monastères de Palestine [2 and 3]." *ROC* 5 (1900): 19–48, 272–92.

Van Nice, R. L. *Saint Sophia in Istanbul: An Architectural Survey*. Washington, D.C., 1965–86.

Varinlioğlu, G. "Urban Monasteries in Constantinople and Thessaloniki: Distribution Patterns in Time and Urban Topography." In *Archaeology in Architecture: Studies in Honor of Cecil L. Striker*, ed. J. J. Emerick and D. M. Deliyannis, 187–98. Mainz, 2005.

de Vaux, R. "Une mosaïque byzantine à Ma'in." *RevBibl* 47 (1938): 227–58.

Venarde, B. L. *Women's Monasticism and Medieval Society: Nunneries in France and England, 890–1215*. Ithaca, 1997.

Verhein, K. "Studien zu den Quellen zum Reichsgut der Karolingerzeit [1]," *DA* 10 (1954): 313–94.

———. "Studien zu den Quellen zum Reichsgut der Karolingerzeit [2]," *DA* 11 (1955): 333–92.

Verhulst, A. E. "Karolingische Agrarpolitik. Das Capitulare de Villis und die Hungersnöte von 792/93 und 805/06." *Zeitschrift für Agrargeschichte und Agrarsoziologie* 13 (1965): 175–89.

Veronese, A. "Monasteri femminili in Italia settentrionale nell'alto medioevo. Confronto con i monasteri maschili atraverso un tentativo di analisi 'statistica.'" *Benedictina* 34 (1987): 355–416.

Vielliard, J. *Le latin des diplômes royaux et chartes privées de l'époque mérovingienne*. Bibliothèque de l'École des hautes études 251. Paris, 1927.

Vincent, H., and F. M. Abel. *Jérusalem. Recherches de topographie, d'archéologie et d'histoire.* Paris, 1912–26.

Vogel, M., and V. Gardthausen. *Die griechischen Schreiber des Mittelalters und der Renaissance.* Beihefte zum Zentralblatt für Bibliothekswesen 33. Leipzig, 1909.

Walmsley, A. *Early Islamic Syria: An Archaeological Assessment.* London, 2007.

von Wartburg, W. *Französisches etymologisches Wörterbuch. Eine Darstellung des galloromanisches Sprachschatzes.* Bonn, 1922–2003.

Watson, A. M. *Agricultural Innovation in the Early Islamic World: The Diffusion of Crops and Farming Techniques, 700–1100.* Cambridge, 1983.

Wattenbach, W., W. Levison, and H. Löwe. *Deutschlands Geschichtsquellen im Mittelalter: Vorzeit und Karolinger.* 6 fasc. Weimar, 1952–73.

Werner, K. F. "Bedeutende Adelsfamilien im Reich Karls des Grossen." In *Karl der Grosse: Lebenswerk und Nachleben,* ed. W. Braunfels, vol. 1, 83–142. Düsseldorf, 1965.

Wickham, C. *Framing the Early Middle Ages: Europe and the Mediterranean 400–800.* Oxford, 2005.

Wilkinson, J. *Jerusalem Pilgrims before the Crusades.* 2nd ed. Warminster, 2002.

Winkelmann, F., and R.-J. Lilie, eds. *Prosopographie der mittelbyzantinischen Zeit.* 6 vols. Berlin, 1998.

Zettler, A. "Zu den Mönchslisten und zur Geschichte des Konvents." In *Die Reichenauer Mönchsgemeinschaft und ihr Totengedenken im frühen Mittelalter,* ed. R. Rappmann and A. Zettler, 233–78. Sigmaringen, 1998.

INDEX VERBORUM

of the documents on the Basel Roll

Term: Numbers refer to lines in the Basel manuscript, indicated in the edition in parentheses.

Conjectured occurrences in the restored lacunae are given in angle brackets.

Discussed: Numbers refer to pages where the term is discussed.

Term	Discussed	Term	Discussed

GENERAL INDEX

The General Index reports Greek terms under their place in the English alphabet. For words that occur in the texts of the Basel roll, see the Index Verborum. All other Latin words are indexed here.

coins, used in Basel roll, 8; *see also* dinar, *mancosus,* metalwork, penny, solidus

Columban of Bobbio, 140 note 25

Commachio, 196

Commemoratorium sancti Severini, Eugippius, 131 note 29

commonita, 163 note 30

commonitorium, 130 note 27
 for Charlemagne's ambassadors to pope, 158–59

Constantine I
 Holy Sepulcher, 97, 99
 basilica, Holy Sepulcher complex, in *Memoria de illis monasteriis,* 216.55–56, 217

Constantine V, 45

Constantine VI, 171 note 57

Constantine VII Porphyrogennitus, on Charlemagne and the Holy Land, 79, 180–81

Constantinople, 94, 106, 168, 181
 Blachernae, 25–26
 Carolingian ambassadors in, 166 note 38, 171 note 57
  and church roofs, 147–48
 Charlemagne's largess in Palestine, remembered, 196
 decline of monasteries, 38–39
 Hagia Sophia, 16, 103
  narthexes, 106
  personnel, 24, 25
 monasteries, monks, 61
  numbers, 8th–9th centuries, 45–46
  Stoudios, monks, numbers, 60
  women's, proportion, 63
 and Palestine, 44, 52, 75, 180
 patriarch, 16

construction, cost, 22

convents, *see* monasteries, women's; nuns

conversion
 Christians, to Islam, 44, 48
 local ruler, Jerusalem, to Christianity, 87

Corbie monastery, 83 note 31, 144, 182 note 89
 monks, numbers, 62

Coreb or Chorib, *see* Khorembe

Corippus, 185

Cornelimünster, monastery, monks, numbers, 62

Corteolona, 132

Cotehrammus, count, 131 note 30

councils (813), 146, 155–56; *see also the name of place where council held*

counterfeiters, 189 note 19

counts, royal, in Freising documents, 131
 lawbook, 132

court, royal Frankish, 14, 17
 under Charlemagne, 83
 and eschatology, 193–94

intellectual activities, 194
 lingo and ideas in Basel documents, 154
 minting, metalwork, 189–90
 people associated with, 131

Cousance, 74

Cozroh, 131 note 30

Creed 169, 176–77
 Latin, Greek texts, 170 note 50

Cross, True, 31, 193
 in *Breue commemoratorii,* 200.6, 201
 discovery site, Holy Sepulcher complex, 97
 in *Memoria de illis monasteriis,* 216.55, 217

crown, votive, 186 note 6

Crusades, Crusaders, 82, 142

Cunibert, 173

curtis, ad curtem, minting, 189–90

custodians, shrines and relics, Holy Sepulcher, 31

Cuxa, 89 note 52

Dagobert I, 145 note 41

Daniel, Book of, 194–95

David, 192

De Karolo rege et Leone papa, 185

deaconesses, 24, 25

deacons, Holy Sepulcher, 31
 numbers, 24, 25, 42

deir, 38 note 34

Deir Dosi, St. Theodosius, monastery (q.v.), 39

Deir Ḥajla, ʿEin Ḥajla, St. Gerasimus, monastery (q.v.), 39, 211 note 51

Deir Mar Jiryis, Choziba, monastery (q.v.), 39

Deir Mar Saba, St. Sabas, monastery, Judaea (q.v.), 39

demography, Palestine, no decline? 42–43 note 57

Descriptio mancipiorum ecclesie Massiliensis, 128

deuotio, 81 note 22

dextans, 100

dexter, 99–101

Dienheim, 174 note 63, 174 note 64

διέπων, ὁ, 140 note 27

diet, 21

dinars, 10
 manqush, 8
 weight, 12

Dionysius, monk of Stoudios, in Holy Land, 44 note 63

Diospolis (Lydda, Lod), 34, 79
 bishop, bishopric, 28, 35, 52 note 11
  missing from Basel roll, 27–28
 cathedral clergy, 37, 50
 Saint Cyriacus, monastery, 28 note 11
 Saint George, shrine, 27

Diottolf, 173

Dispensa patriarchae, 6, 8, 128
 English translation, 217

Latin text, 216
textual state, 235
Divisio regni, 185–86
Djūrzān, al, 141
Dodekathronon, 233; *see also* Thrones, Twelve
Dome of the Rock, 143
Dominic, abbot, Frankish monastery, Mount of
Olives, 79, 88 note 47, 182
Droant, count, 131 note 29
Dumbarton Oaks, bas relief, 188
Dutton, Paul E., 219

earthquake (749), 35 note 29, 98
and decline of Palestinian church, 43, 161
ruined Nea church, 159–60
and Nea Church in *Memoria de illis monasteriis*,
216.50–52, 217
Eberhard of Friuli, 174
Eckhardt, Wilhelm, 146
economy, trend, 5
Palestine, 8th century, 46 note 73
Egilbald, *see* George-Egilbald
Egisbert, 173 note 63
Egypt, 36, 37, 115
Christians, 187
and Charlemagne, xiii
wheat prices, 12, 20, 21
ʿEin es-Sakhari, 224
ʿEin Fara, 39, *see also* Pharan, Mount
Einhard
role in art production, coin design? 188, 188 note 16
Vita Karoli
and Basel roll, 179
on Arab rulers, Christians, overseas, xiii, 7–8,
177, 185
on Charlemagne's gifts to Christians in Arab
world, 186–87, 188
uses "inter . . . et," 137 note 12
Elbern, Victor, 188
Elders, 24 of the Apocalypse, 193–95
Eleona, *see* Mount of Olives
Elias, hegoumenos, Mount Sinai, 94
in *Memoria de illis monasteriis* 214.48, 215
Elias, hegoumenos? Saint Chariton, 95 note 9
Elias, monastery, near Jericho, 211 note 54
Elias, possible name, builder, monastery of St.
Stephen, Judaea, 230
Elias, prophet, church, Mount Sinai, in *Memoria de
illis monasteriis*, 214.47, 215
Elias, prophet, church, Mount Tabor, 215 note 64
in *Memoria de illis monasteriis*, 214.42, 215
Elias, prophet, in *Memoria de illis monasteriis*,
214.42, 215
Elias II, patriarch, Jerusalem, 52 note 11, 160 note 18

Elias III, patriarch, Jerusalem, 87, 181
endowments, religious, 86
Engilhard, 173 note 62
Engilrad, 173 note 63
England, 8
women's monasticism, 65
ἐπευθύνειν, 140 note 27
Ephesus, 16, 77 note 6
Epiphanius, *Descriptio Palaestinae*, 201 note 10, 215
note 64, 232
Eptapegon, *see* Heptapegon
Erkanfrida, 131 note 29
Erlolf, Erlulf, 174, 174 note 64
Ermoldus Nigellus, 44 note 41
eschatology, 189, 193–95
Ettenheimmünster, monastery, population, 62
eucharist, 189
Eugippius, 131 note 29
Eunuchs, monastery of the, 211 note 54
Eustathius, *see* Eustratius of Diospolis
Eustratius, 40 note 43
Eustratius, *basilikarios*, 141, 142 note 32
Eustratius, monk, official, Holy Sepulcher,
bishop of Lydda, 28 note 12, 51 note 8,
52 note 11
Eutychius (Saʿid ibn Batriq), patriarch, Alexandria,
180
Expenditures of the Patriarch, translation, 217; *see
also Dispensa patriarchae*
Expugnatio Hierosolymae, 40 note 43

fabric, church, 8
of Jerusalem churches, in *Memoria de illis
monasteriis*, 216.59, 217
Face-Cloth, Jesus, 31
in *Breue commemoratorii*, 200.6, 201
Fayyum, wheat prices, 20
Felix, bishop of Urgel, 67
Felix, monk, Frankish monastery, Mount of Olives,
79, 166
fidelis seruiens uester, meaning, 171
Filioque, 155, 181 note 85
origins, 59, 168
Charlemagne, Leo III, Jerusalem, 176–77
finances, church, 7–22, 67–68
fisc, royal, minting, 189–90
flagellum, 138
Flanders, 174
Fleury, 182 note 91
Flörsheim, 174 note 63
Fontenelle, 188 note 16
food, earning power, 18–22, 164
foot, Byzantine, vs. Roman, 101
format, *see* codex

Judaea, desert monasteries and monks, 28–30, 50, 51
  Arabic toponymy, 38, 39
  in *Memoria de illis monasteriis*, 208.27–210.35,
    209–11
  Persian conquest, 43
  populations, 31–32, 34, 39–40
Judith ("Julitta"), of Tuscany, 89
Judith, wife of Droant, 131 note 29
Jumièges, monastery, population, 62
Justin II, 185
Justinian, 186
  bishops, election fees, 14–15
  and Charlemagne, 185
  Hagia Sophia, personnel, 24
  hospital, Jerusalem, 15
  Nativity church, 99
  Nea church, 103
    in *Breue commemoratorii*, 202.11, 203
  Saint Thalelaea (Tathelea), monastery, 203 note 12
Justinian, doge of Venice, 17

Kafr Kanna, 213 note 59
Kalamon, monastery, 28–29, 228–29
Kastellion, monastery, 29–30
Khan el Aḥmar, 39, 211 note 49, 226; *see also* Saint
    Euthymius
Khan Khureitūn, 39, 224; *see also* Saint Chariton,
    monastery
Khan Mugheifir, 211 note 54
Khan Qana, 213 note 59
Khorembe, 29 note 18
Khoura, monastery, 29
Kidron Valley, *see* Jehoshaphat, Valley of
Kinneret, Lake, 152; *see also* Tiberias, Lake of
ḳubba, al, 140
Kyriakos, St., 162; *see also* Saint Chariton, monastery

Lactantius, 7
Laetus, spurious name, 94, 226–27
Last Supper, shrine, *see under* Jerusalem
Latin, Latinity
  aspiration, 219
  Basel roll documents
    deponents, 135
    diminutive for positive, 137
    interpretation, 153
    lexical features, 137
    morphology, 136
    spelling, 135
  Carolingian administrative records, 134
  in Holy Land church, 56, 57, 58
  late popular, 135, 219
    passé composé, 147 note 51
  phonology, 141

psalmody, hermits, in *Breue commemoratorii*,
    206.20, 207
  semi-vowel, 141 note 31
  see also tics, linguistic
Latins, monasteries of the, *see* Saint Mary of the
    Latins
Lavra, Great, *see* Saint Sabas, Judaea
Lavra, Old or Palaia, *see* Saint Chariton
Le Mans, 145
lead, roof, Grado, 148
Lebuin, 188
lectors, 24, 25
Legontio, 136
Leidrad, archbishop of Lyons, 184–85
  canonicus clericus, 146
  on hostels, 84 note 32
  report to Charlemagne, 66–72, 163–64, 179
  roofs, 148
Leitnamen, 174
Leo III pope, 17
  letter to Charlemagne, Filioque, 166–71 passim
  pressure from Charlemagne, Jerusalem, 176–77
  letter from monks of Mount of Olives, 78
Leontius of Mar Saba, 28–29, 161
lepers, 33, 42, 203 note 15
  in *Breue commemoratorii*, 202.12, 203
  numbers rounded, 129
Liber pontificalis, 148
liberalitas, gratuita, 7
Liège, 131 note 28, 146, 167
lighting, church, 8
litterae elongatae, 126 note 17
liturgical vessels, pawned, 87
liturgy, Jerusalem, anniversaries, 77
  processions, 103
liturgy, Lyons, cathedral, hours, 70–71
Liudger, bishop of Münster, 131, 132
Liutprand, king of the Lombards, 130 note 26
Loaves and Fishes, miracle in *Memoria de illis
    monasteriis*, 212.38–39, 213
Loaves and Fishes, shrine, *see* Heptapegon
Lobbes, monastery, population, 62
Lod, 27; *see also* Diospolis
logothetai, 140
Lombard? Campio, 72 note 63
Lombards, women's monasticism, 64–66
Lorch on the Enns, 173 note 62
Lord's Leap, shrine, near Nazareth, 30 note 21, 213
    note 58, 231
  monastery of St. Mary, in *Memoria de illis
    monasteriis*, 212.36–37, 213
  population, 36, 37, 129 note 124
Lorsch, 137 note 12, 170 note 51, 172 note 60
Lot, *see* Diospolis

abbots' names, 79
building descriptions, character, 95
churches, lost, 92
English translation, 209–17
geographical organization, 226
Latin text, 208.25–216.57
numbers, rounded, 129
precedence, disregards, 152
statistics, problems, 30
Memorial of the Monasteries that are in the
    Promised Land, English translation, 209–17
Menzingen, 174 note 63
Mesopotamia, 12, 20, 21
Messiah, 193
metalwork, minting, Charlemagne's court, 189 note
    19, 189–90
Ps.-Methodius, Apocalypse, Carolingian court, 193
    Christian apostasy, 44
Metz, 145
    Arab coins, 10
    and Lyons, 69
Michael the Synkellos, Jerusalem, 51 note 8, 99, 177
    Filioque, 176
    sent west, 181
Michael, patriarch, Alexandria, 81 note 22
Mikron, monastery, 224
Milan, 138 note 19
missaticum, 146, 166
missi dominici, 172, 173 note 62, 174–75
    capitulary (806), 147–48, 175
    Leidrad, 67
    visit Liège, Aachen (806), 146–47
    see also ambassadors
Moechian affair, 94
Molinier, Auguste, 122–23
Molosme, monastery, population, 62
monasteries, monasticism
    Carolingian Empire, bigger, 59, 61–62
        vs. canonial movement, Lyons, 72
    double, 60, 64 note 45
    England, 59
    Jerusalem, 12
        in *Breue commemoratorii*, 200.4, 201, 202.13–
            14, 203, 206.18, 23, 24, 207
        and Constantinople, 38
        dominant, 51
        Frankish, *see* Mount of Olives, Holy Sepulcher
        western, envoys of patriarch, 87
        staff Charlemagne's hostel, 88
    Palestine
        compared to Byzantine, 60–61
        compared to Carolingian, 74–75
        Constantine VII on Charlemagne's
            constructions, 180–81

desert vs. urban, 53–54
outside Jerusalem, in *Memoria de illis
    monasteriis*, 208.25–214.46, 209–15
total number, 55
size, average, 31–32
size, desert vs. urban, 53
size, spatial distribution, male vs. female, 41,
    49, 52
religio? 191
women's monasteries
    in *Breue commemoratorii*, 200.2–3, 201, 206.22,
        207
    Byzantine Empire, 63
    Constantinople, 65
    England, 63–64
    France, 63–64, 65
    Frankish, episcopal control tightens? 72
    Italy, 64–65
    Lyons, 68 note 58, 70, 71
    Jerusalem, include westerners, 151
    Persian conquest, 40
    Palestine, no abbesses named in Basel roll, 175
        note 69
    proportion vs. male, 64–65
    terminology, 219
    urban, 53–54
    urban vs. rural, 53–54, 63, 65–66
    see also nuns
    see also Constantinople, England, Jerusalem,
        Lombards, Lyons, Mount of Olives, Rome,
        Tiberias
monasteria, 220
monasterium, 136
monasterium puellarum, 219
money, 8, 10
    purchasing power, 47
Monte Cassino, 223
monument, Jesus's baptism, in *Memoria de illis
    monasteriis*, 210.32–33, 211
mosaic, Aachen, 193–95
Moses, 152
    church, Mount Tabor, 215 note 64
        in *Memoria de illis monasteriis*, 214.41–42, 215
    church, Mount Sinai, in *Memoria de illis
        monasteriis*, 214.47, 215
moustier, 220
Münster in Gregoriental, monastery, population, 62
Murbach roll, *see* Manuscripts cited, Colmar

Nablus, *see* Neapolis
Nabochodonosor, 195
Naboli, 141; *see also* Neapolis
Nahal Qidron, 77 note 6
Nantua, 69

Nativity church, Bethelehem, 92, 99
  columns, 98
  ecclesiastics, numbers, 36, 37
    in *Memoria de illis monasteriis*, 208.25–26, 209
  Frankish monks barred from, 169
  measurements, 97, 101–2, 114
    in *Memoria de illis monasteriis*, 216.52–53, 217
  roof, 148
Nazareth, 129 note 124, 213 note 58, 231
  Annunciation church, 223
  monastery of Saint Mary, Lord's Leap, 30 note 21, 53, 54 note 20, 60
    in *Memoria de illis monasteriis*, 212.35–37, 213
    personnel, 36, 37, 55
  place in *Memoria de illis monasteriis*, 152–53
Nea church, of the Virgin, Jerusalem, 35, 84 note 34, 85, 92, 185
  archaeology, 126, 180
    in *Breue commemoratorii*, 202.11, 203
  earthquake, 98–99, 105, 159–61
  entrance structures, 107, 109
  Frankish envoys, itinerary, 150 note 66
  measurements, 103–11, 114
    in *Memoria de illis monasteriis*, 216.50–52, 217
  narthex, 106
  personnel, 33
Neapolis (Naboli, Nablus), 31, 54, 151–52
  bishop, 95
  ecclesiastics, 30, 34, 36, 37, 50
    in *Memoria de illis monasteriis*, 214.45–46, 215
    sequence, 152–53
  name form, 140
  stylites, 34
Neilos Doxopatres, 152
Nestorian Hermitage, 27 note 9
Neuweiler, monastery, population, 62
Nicaea II, Ecumenical Council, 147–48
Niederaltaich, monastery, population, 62
Nijmegen, 144, 146
Noe, bishop of Tiberias, 95 note 12
Nonantola, 172
notaries, 32
notitia, 130 note 26
Notker the Stammerer, 183 note 94
Notre-Dame-de-la-Bruyère, 74
numeracy, innumeracy, 6 note 2, 11, 184, 219
  and the Basel roll, 99
numerals, 219
nuns, women monastics
  counting, 26–27
  Jerusalem
    in *Breue commemoratorii*, 200.9, 201, 202.12, 203, 202.14, 204
    from Carolingian Empire, 76–77, 79

    in *Breue commemoratorii*, 206.22, 207
    decline since late antiquity, 40–41
  Holy Zion, monastery, 99
  Lyons, 68 note 58, 70
  numbers, 36, 37
    compared to male monks, Byzantine empire, 63
  Tiberias, 30
    in *Memoria de illis monasteriis*, 214.41, 215
  see also monasticism, women's

oikonomos, Saint Sabas, Judaea, 143
Old Church Slavonic Guide, 205 note 26
Old Lavra, *see* Saint Chariton
olive groves, pawned, 87
Olives, Mount of, 85, 150, 151
  churches, in *Breue commemoratorii*, 204.16–206.23, 205
  Eleona site, 151
  eschatology, 193
  Frankish monastery, 78 note 10, 166, 182
    abbot not mentioned, 175
    books from Charlemagne, 79
    in *Breue commemoratorii*, 206.23, 207, 207 note 36
    dedication, *see* Sts. Peter and Paul "in Bisanteo" (q.v.), 175
    end, 80
    envoys to Charlemagne, 78 note 10
    eschatology, 193
    gloss, 78
    letter to Leo III, 78, 79, 168
    location, 151
    new, 47
    property to Charlemagne's hostel? 85
    silence in Bernard and Christian of Stavelot, 88
    size, relative, 59
    topography, 150 note 62
  hermits, 54, 141
    (*inclusi, inclusa*) in *Breue commemoratorii*, 206.19–21, 23 and 207
  steps
    in *Breue commemoratorii*, 206.20, 207
    in *Memoria de illis monasteriis*, 216.50, 217
  Teaching of the Disciples, shrine, 151
    in *Memoria de illis monasteriis*, 206.18, 207
    monks, 55
    personnel, 33
  Willibald of Eichstätt, 205 note 31
  women, monastery of, late antique, 40
    early medieval, location? 76–77
Olympos, 65
Oppenheim, 174 note 63
Optatus, bishop of Milevis, 127 note 20
Opus Caroli regis (Libri Carolini), 191

orality, writing and Basel documents, 149, 153–54
orguia, 101
ostiarii, numbers, 24, 25
Otker, 131 note 30
Otto I, 192 note 36

Paderborn, 10
πάκτον, 223
Palaestina I, II, 152
Παλαιὰ Λαύρα, Palaia Lavra, 51, 139, 224; *see also*
    Saint Chariton, monastery
Παλαιολαυρῖται, 139, 225
Palestine
    Arab conquest, 43–44
    bishoprics, 45, 47
    Christians, and western rulers, 181, 182–83, 183
        note 94
    church, churches
        and Charlemagne, 79, 196
        compared to Carolingian, 75
        construction, Muslim strictures, 35
        decline, 34, 42–45, 46, 47–48
        differing views on state of, 3, 7
        Einhard, 7, 179, 180
        Greek to Arabic, 138–40
        monastic dominance, 51
        personnel, 23
        recruitment geography, 44
        religious, decline in numbers, 34–48
        religious, spatial distribution, 50
        repairs, 46 note 73
        village, 46
    disorders, 162, 176, 223
    economy, 46 note 73
    emigration, and church decline, 43, 45
    Italy, 43
    monasteries
        decline, 47
        and non-Greeks, 58;
        outside Jerusalem, 208.25–214.46, 209–15
        numbers of monasteries, 35–38
        see also monasticism, monasteries
    Persian conquest, 43
    topography
        and precedence of churches, 151–53
        treatises on, Carolingian copies, 181–82
    towns, order in Basel roll, 151–52
Paleum Monasterium (Palaia Lavra), 139; *see* Saint
    Chariton
pallium, 79
Pantelleria, 115
papyrus, 126
parchment, 219
Paschasius Radbertus, 112 note 169

Passau, 131 note 29
paten, 186 note 6
paths, footpaths, Holy Land, 152
patriarchs, patriarchate, Jerusalem, xiii, 11, 14–15, 128
    Alcuin, 67 note 54
    annual expenditures, 22–32, 165
        in *Dispensa patriarchae*, 216.58–60, 217
        inflated? 6
    Arab tribute, 177
    Aramaic and Greek, 143
    archdeacon, 169
    building debts, 181
    candle bearers, 219
    Charlemagne, 166, 176; *see also* Jerusalem
    finances, 7–14, 19–22, 181, 235–37
    intruder, 95
    personnel, 31–32, 219
    and Saint Sabas monastery, 51
    servants, 32
    seeks support from pope, 177
        western Europe, 181
    and Theodore Stoudite, 38, 44 note 63
    wealth, 11–22
    see also In diebus Georgii; Jerusalem
patrimonium, 15 note 35
Paul, St., dedication, 78 note 9
Paulinus, patriarch of Aquileia, 169
Pavia, 132
penny, 183 note 94
    Charlemagne, portrait or temple type, 187
        date, 189–90, 190 note 20
        depicts Holy Sepulcher/Aachen? 191–92
        Einhard's role? 188 note 16
    Frankish, 8 note 8
    Venice, 17 note f
Pentecost, 102
perfume, 79
Peter, abbot of Nonantola, 172
Peter, Primacy of, church, 213 note 60
Peter IV Candiano, 90
Peter of Pisa, 194–95
Petra, 40, 221
Pfaffenschwabenheim, 174 note 63
Pharan, Mount, monastery, 30, 51 note 6, 211 note 55
    Arabic toponym, 38
    Chariton, St., tomb, 224
    in *Memoria de illis monasteriis*, 210.34–35, 211
    population, 36, 37, 55
φραγελλιταί (*fragelites*), 32, 138–39
pilgrims, pilgrimage, Holy Land, 28, 56, 84, 221
    Arab conquest, 43 note 57
    narratives, 92
        measurements, 96–97
    Carolingian, 47, 79–91, 192

Saints Cosmas and Damian, Jerusalem, shrines, topography, 150
Saints Peter and Paul "at Besanteo," Mount of Olives, Frankish monastery
history, 77–81
personnel, 33, 55
see also Mount of Olives, Frankish monastery
Saints Zosimas and Anthimos, monastery, Judaea, 28 note 16
Salic Law, 83
Saltus Domini see Lord's Leap
Salzburg, 67 note 54, 182 note 89
Samaria, 36, 37, 140
Christian religious, 50
see also Neapolis
Samaritan Woman, tomb, in *Memoria de illis monasteriis*, 214.45–46, 215
Samuel, scribe, 173 note 62
Saône, 71
Saracen, Saracens, in *Dispensa patriarchae*, 216.60 (twice), 217
bandits burn monastery, in *Memoria de illis monasteriis*, 208.28, 209
patriarchal payment to, 13
servants, 9
Savigny, 69
Savior, Holy, church, Mount Tabor, in *Memoria de illis monasteriis*, 214.42, 215
Saxon hostages, 126 note 16
Saxony, 10, 178
Schmid, Karl, 122–23
Schriftprovinz, upper Rhine, Alemannia, 135
scribe, Basel roll, 135–36
script, for diplomatic dialogue, 178
Scythopolis (Beth Shean), 35 note 29, 160
seal, seals, Charlemagne's, 185
lead, Hadrian, monastery of the Latins, 88
Palestinian churches, 35
Sebaste, Sebastia, Sabastia, 151–52
bishop, 95
church personnel, 36, 37
in *Memoria de illis monasteriis*, 214.43, 215
monastery, 53
monks, 54 note 20
numbers, 55
name, classical form, 140
Saint John the Baptist, 35
sequence in *Memoria de illis monasteriis*, 152, 153
see also Sabastia
Sebasteia, martyrs, 203 note 20
Sedulius Scotus, 174 note 67
Senones, monastery, population, 62
Sens, 100 note 25
Septuagesima Sunday, 168 note 44

Sepulcher, Holy, church complex, 31, 93
Arabic term, dome, 141
bas relief, 188, 191
in *Breue commemoratorii*, 200.3–8, 201
Calvary, 113
on cardo, 103
Charlemagne and, 188–96
donations (806), 137 note 12
on Charlemagne's "temple" coins, 188–89
Constantinian basilica, 113
Cross's discovery, 113
dome, 140, 180
measurements, 96, 97
gloss, Carolingian, 78
Hugh of Tuscany, gifts, 89
investigation of Frankish orthodoxy, 169
itinerary of Frankish envoys? 150
keys, 193 note 30
measurements, 96, 97, 111–13, 114
in *Memoria de illis monasteriis*, 216.53–56, 217
monks, numbers, 55
personnel 13, 24–26, 31, 32, 33, 74
arithmetical error, 99
quality of numbers, 129
phragellitai, 138–39
structure, present vs. original, 99
repairs needed, 98, 99
roof, 96, 113
rotunda, 111, 112
Tomb of Jesus, 97
western nuns, 76, 77 note 6
in *Breue commemoratorii*, 206.22, 207
Sergius I, patriarch, Constantinople, 25
Sergius I, pope, 111 note 169
Sermon on the Mount, shrine, 152
Seven Springs *see* Heptapegon
Sexagesima Sunday, 168 note 44
sexton, 141
Sheep Pool, Jerusalem, 151
in *Breue commemoratorii*, 202.11–12, 203
see also Saint Mary at the Sheep Pool
Shroud of Jesus, 97
Sicily, Palestinian immigration, 43 note 58
Sieber, Ludwig, 122–23
silk, 79, 186
Sinai, Mount
monastery, monks, shrines, 54 note 20, 128, 142, 143, 152
in *Memoria de illis monasteriis*, 214.47–49, 215
population, 34, 36, 37, 55
Gregory I, pope, letters to, 82 note 25
hegoumenos, 94
steps, 96, 128
in *Memoria de illis monasteriis*, 214.48–49, 215

Thomas, possible hegoumenos's name, Saint
    Chariton, 95 note 9
thrones, Apocalypse, 195
Thrones, Twelve, shrine, 213 note 60, 213 note 61, 233
    in *Memoria de illis monasteriis*, 212.39–40, 213
    personnel, 36, 37
Tiberias, 152, 153
    bishop, bishopric, 35 note 29, 95, 233
    in *Memoria de illis monasteriis*, 212.40–214.41,
        213–15
    cathedral, personnel, 36, 37
    monastery, men, 53, 54 note 20
        numbers, 55
    monastery, women, 30, 31, 34, 50, 52, 64
        numbers, 55
Tiberias, Lake of (Kinneret, Sea of Galilee), 152
    in *Memoria de illis monasteriis*, 212.37–38, 212.39,
        213
tics, linguistic, 154, 175
Tietolf, 173 note 63
tin, 148
Tobler, Titus, 122–23
Tomb, of the Lord, 193 note 30
    in *Breue commemoratorii*, 200.6, 201
    see also Holy Sepulcher
Tournai, 167, 174 note 65
Tours, 148 note 54, 193 note 31
Transfiguration, *see* Tabor, Mount
treasurer, 32
Twelve Thrones, *see* Thrones, Twelve

Ulversheim, 174 note 63
Umayyads, 43, 46, 196
Unroch, Unruoch, Unruochings, 166, 174
Urgel, 67
Uspenskij Psalter, *see* St. Petersburg, National
    Library of Russia

Venice, xiii, 190 note 20
    doge, 17, 90 note 52
    Old St. Mark's and Holy Sepulcher, 196
Veronica, chapel, Jerusalem, 205 note 29
Via Dolorosa, Jerusalem, 205 note 29
Vienne, 69
villa, 87
villa, "village," 203 note 16
Vincent, Hugues, 102–103
vineyards, 87

Virgil, bishop of Salzburg, 67 note 54
Visigoths, 72 note 63

Wackernagel, Wilhelm, 121
Wago, *capellanus*, 173 note 62
Wala, half-brother of Adalhard of Corbie, 133
Wallstadt, 173 note 63
Warino, count, 173 note 62
water clock, 79
Wearmouth-Jarrow, 81 note 22
Weinheim, 173 note 62
Werden, 131, 132, 219
Werinharius, count, 173 note 62
Werner, Karl-Ferdinand, 174
Wessex, 181
wheat, prices, 12, 18–21
whip-men, in *Breue commemoratorii*, 200.4, 201
William, archbishop of Tyre, 90 note 54
Willibald, bishop of Eichstätt, 27, 166 note 36, 205
    note 31
    on monastery of St. John the Baptist, 47
Witbold, envoy to Constantinople, 171 note 57
Wolfhart, 174
Wolfwolt, 173 note 62
women, attestation rate, vs. men in medieval sources,
    63 note 39, 63–64
    monasteries, urban vs. rural, 74, 75
    proportion to male houses, ecclesiastics, 72, 73, 75
    religious, Jerusalem, 40, 76–77
    see also monasticism, women's; nuns
Wonsheim, 174 note 63
writing, in Carolingian administration, 153–54
writing offices, 144, 176 note 75

xenodochium, 83
XPICTIANA RELIGIO, coin legend, 188, 190; *see
    also Christiana religio*

Zachary, envoy to Jerusalem, 193 note 30
Zechariah, 203 note 19
Zion, Holy, church, Jerusalem, 76 note 2, 92, 98, 128,
    150, 205 note 24
    in *Breue commemoratorii*, 200.9, 201
    measurements, 97, 102–3, 114, 203 note 12
        in *Memoria de illis monasteriis*, 216.57, 217
    monastery, women, 52, 99
    personnel, 33, 55
Zurich, 100 note 25